T0366731

RIPE FOR REVOLUTION

RIPE FOR REVOLUTION

Building Socialism in the Third World

JEREMY FRIEDMAN

HARVARD UNIVERSITY PRESS

Cambridge, Massachusetts
London, England

2021

Copyright © 2021 by the President and Fellows of Harvard College

ALL RIGHTS RESERVED

Printed in the United States of America

First printing

Library of Congress Cataloging-in-Publication Data

Names: Friedman, Jeremy Scott, 1982- author.
Title: Ripe for revolution : building socialism in the Third World / Jeremy Friedman.
Description: Cambridge, Massachusetts : Harvard University Press, 2021. |
Includes bibliographical references and index.
Identifiers: LCCN 2021022706 | ISBN 9780674244313 (hardcover)
Subjects: LCSH: Socialism—Developing countries. | Socialism—Southern Hemisphere. |
Globalization—Developing countries. | Globalization—Southern Hemisphere. |
Developing countries—Politics and government. | Southern Hemisphere—
Politics and government.
Classification: LCC HX517.8 .F74 2021 | DDC 335.009172/4—dc23
LC record available at https://lccn.loc.gov/2021022706

CONTENTS

RIPE FOR REVOLUTION

INTRODUCTION

Socialist Revolution as a Global Process

On February 3, 1964, standing in front of a large crowd in Mogadishu, Somalia, at the end of a groundbreaking tour of ten newly independent African states, Chinese premier Zhou Enlai declared, "Revolutionary prospects are excellent throughout the African continent." Sixteen months later, before twenty thousand at the National Stadium in Dar es Salaam, Tanzania, Zhou proclaimed, "An exceedingly favorable situation for revolution prevails today not only in Africa, but also in Asia and Latin America." Zhou's remarks, condensed by some in the Western press into a declaration that Africa, Asia, and Latin America were "ripe for revolution," sent shockwaves around the world: dedicated Cold Warriors feared that Red China was attempting to subvert the fragile new states of the developing world.[1]

The furor reached such a high pitch that Tanzania's exasperated president, Julius Nyerere, told visiting senator Robert Kennedy that "Africa is very much ripe for revolution and I can assure you Chou En Lai is not responsible."[2] Nyerere was undoubtedly right that revolutionary energies did not need to be artificially implanted by nefarious outsiders. As the imperialist system crumbled, fledgling postcolonial governments faced millennial hopes for prosperity in the face of desperate poverty and political instability throughout the Third World.[3] Revolutionary transformation was on the agenda of many in Africa, Asia, and Latin America, but what sort of revolution? There was no proletariat to seize the means of production, and not much means of production to seize. Marxist models of revolution, whether in Maoist, Stalinist, Titoist, or other variants, had taken form in very different political and economic contexts—and with much blood spilled. Development through capitalism was seen as a long,

1

difficult slog—not to mention that it was one of the driving forces of the imperialism that had oppressed these regions. Socialism was another possible way forward. But how could it be adapted to Third World conditions?

There were as many answers as there were countries and leaders willing to try some version of socialism. In the first decades after World War II, as Asian and then African countries gained their independence, no one—whether in Beijing, Cairo, Jakarta, Moscow, New Delhi, or elsewhere—knew exactly how to build socialism in the newly independent states. There were precedents: neither China nor Russia had been highly industrialized countries at the time of their revolutions, and the Soviets in particular saw the experience of their Central Asian republics as relevant to the postcolonial world.[4] As Fred Halliday has pointed out, while Marxism had envisioned socialist revolution as taking place in the most advanced capitalist economies, Marxism-Leninism became instead a method for "catching up" with them.[5] But China and Russia were also enormous countries with large internal markets and vast natural resources, at least some industry, and, perhaps most important, powerful communist regimes that had established themselves militarily in the crucible of civil war. Most African and Asian states were predominantly peasant countries with little industry and tiny working classes, where it was less a matter of socializing the means of production than creating them. But political systems—and, in some cases, a coherent national identity—also needed to be constructed. All of this had to happen in societies riven by ethnic divisions in which the liberation struggle had often been centered on identities other than class, and where religious institutions were pervasive and politically influential. Additionally, while some of the leaders of the newly independent states were sympathetic to Marxism, most were not, and very few were anxious either to copy the Chinese or Soviet models or to allow another outside power to infringe upon their hard-won sovereignty.

The result was an extended, international process of trial and error in pursuit of a model of socialist development for the Third World. During the Comintern era (1919–1943), debate had not really advanced much beyond the question of how to make a revolution and take power. Communist parties in the colonial world, where they existed, were still small enough that it was mostly a matter of allying with larger bourgeois parties in the hope of one day transitioning to socialism.[6] In the wake of the Soviet victory in World War II and decolonization, both opportunity (in terms of new states looking for development aid and expanded Soviet capabilities) and necessity (in terms of the imperative to compete with the West in an apparently zero-sum conflict) appeared sooner than anticipated. The result was a scramble to construct a viable model of socialist development for the postcolonial world. Theories were developed, policies were adopted, and lessons were learned regarding a host of questions: Which should take priority in development—industry or agriculture? How much should the state do versus the private sector? Would democracy or authoritarianism better serve the interests of making socialism popular? Which should come first, building a communist party or a working class? Should religious interests be accommodated or combatted? Should ethnic feelings be suppressed or co-opted? Academics and policy makers in existing socialist states produced a plethora of answers under the rubrics of new and Comintern-era labels: "noncapitalist path of development," "state of national democracy," and "revolutionary democracy."[7] While these frameworks played a role in guiding policy, the search for a viable model of socialism took the form of a process of trial and error in which policies were improvised with regard to local conditions. At the same time, these local experiments shaped evolving conceptions of building socialism elsewhere. As one policy solution was adopted in a given country, other nations looked on in an effort to determine its success and whether it was worthy of emulation.

The Second World Meets the Third

First and foremost, this process of learning and adaptation took place within the Soviet bureaucracy, through waves of foreign involvement, information gathering, and policy feedback loops that included academic institutes, the International Department of the Central Committee, institutions responsible for foreign aid such as the Gosudarstvennyi komitet po vneshnim ekonomicheskim sviaziam (GKES, the State Committee for Foreign Economic Ties created in 1957), supposedly nongovernmental organizations including the Soviet Solidarity and Peace Committees, and up to the Komitet gosudarstvennoy bezopasnosti (KGB; Committee for State Security), the Foreign Ministry, and the politburo. Certain key figures in the Soviet Union held their positions throughout most of this period, allowing for both institutional continuity and the accumulation of knowledge and experience. Boris Ponomarev fought in the Russian Civil War (1918–1920) and served for seven years on the Comintern

Executive (1937–1943) before heading the Soviet Central Committee's International Department, the Comintern's true successor, throughout most of its existence (1955–1986). His longtime deputy, Rostislav Ul'ianovskii, had headed the section on the Far East and the Colonies in the Comintern's International Agrarian Institute in the early 1930s before being purged as a Trotskyite, but was then rehabilitated and joined the International Department in 1961.[8] The GKES, the primary vehicle for coordinating economic aid to the developing world, was headed by Semyon Skachkov, a former tractor engineer, from 1958 to 1983. Throughout the Cold War, the Soviet Union was by far the dominant player in this international conversation due to the resources it deployed, its international superpower status, and the dedication of its leadership to the cause of world revolution.

The Soviets were not the only players. Bulgaria, China, Cuba, Czechoslovakia, East Germany, Romania, Yugoslavia, and even North Korea involved themselves in the process of building socialism in the Third World. They did this partly in order to expand their influence, partly because their self-conceptions as communists who adhered to "proletarian internationalism" depended on it, and partly because their aid, advice, and presence were solicited by developing countries themselves.[9] Though this was an unbalanced relationship, it was not completely one-sided. Third World actors had their own conceptions of socialism and Marxism, and while outsiders often tried to impose their own views, their leverage was often limited—and, in some cases, policy makers in Beijing, Moscow, or elsewhere were willing to consider the viability of approaches developed in places like Cairo, Dar es Salaam, Jakarta, or Santiago.

"World revolution" became more than a mobilizing slogan or an eschatological conviction. It became an institutional reality. Many of the actors involved in this story, even those who did not identify as Marxists or Marxist-Leninists, saw their own process of domestic development as tied to a broader international transformation that encompassed decolonization, modernization, and the construction of socialism resulting in a new world order. The central claim of the Third Worldist movement that reached its climax in the mid-1970s was that change could only come via international transformations, without which domestic governments could do little to build prosperity at home. International connections between the existing communist states and developing countries became concrete through the provision of aid and expertise, exchange of knowledge, experience, education, and culture, and at times foreign policy coordination, in particular toward the advancement of what were labeled national liberation movements. While the power in these connections often followed the provision of aid and expertise from the existing communist states to their clients, the experimental nature of the project and the international commitment to world revolution meant that Third World actors had room to maneuver rather than being dictated to by Beijing and Moscow. Furthermore, there were times when the Chinese or Soviets would take their cues from local actors who had knowledge of conditions on the ground.

The Limits of Bipolarity

During the Cold War, the nature of this international process of constructing socialism was obscured to a degree by the bipolar structure of geopolitics. As the quest for allies and political support became a zero-sum game in Moscow and Washington, DC, it became easier to view states as falling on one side or the other of the Cold War divide based on alliances, United Nations votes, or foreign policy positions. This geopolitical bipolarity was translated to the realm of domestic politics—particularly in the West, where many on the Left sought to distance themselves from the so-called free world's Cold War adversaries, especially as anticommunists sought to use communist ties, real or imagined, to tar and discredit their political opponents. The result was a sort of siloization of the Left. Communists were separated from other types of Marxists, as well as democratic socialists, social democrats, New Leftists, and others. This contemporary siloization, however, has been reified by many scholars writing about the Left even after the end of the Cold War.[10] A large part of this can be explained by the difficulties involved in accessing archival resources in communist and former communist countries, as well as by the scale of the project and the languages involved in re-creating an integrated history of socialism in this period. Yet while it was certainly the case that geopolitical divisions had important effects on domestic politics in both developed and developing countries, the bipolarity of the Cold War should not prevent us from seeing socialism as a fluid and evolving project, where the doctrinal debates between various types of communist, Marxist, and non-Marxist socialists did not always impede practical collaboration.

As the Cold War itself recedes farther into the past, there has been a growing effort to put the struggle between economic systems in broader and more varied contexts. Odd Arne Westad's magisterial volume *The*

Cold War begins the story in the 1890s with what he calls "the first global capitalist crisis," which affected the Left by slowing its progress toward democratic power and "produced a revitalized extreme Left."[11] As the rise of industrial capitalism, aided by new technologies of transportation and communication in the late nineteenth century, abetted the advent of high imperialism, so did the collapse of that imperial system create new demands and sites of contestation for systems of sovereignty and property. Adom Getachew has written about "anticolonial worldmaking," attempts to reshape international politics in the wake of decolonization in order to transform economic relations as well as political ones. Her narrative begins with the Third International, better known as the Comintern.[12] It was precisely this form of "anticolonial worldmaking" that frightened the neoliberal "globalists," who, according to Quinn Slobodian, sought instead to create international institutions that would prevent new holders of sovereignty from interfering with existing forms of property.[13] Caught in between were the developmental economists (discussed by David Engerman, Sara Lorenzini, and others) who mostly attempted to achieve economic growth in postcolonial states within the confines of the existing midtwentieth-century international political and economic structures.[14]

These frameworks have enabled historians to examine previously overlooked international relationships. James Mark, Artemy Kalinovsky, and Steffi Marung have drawn attention to what they term "alternative globalizations"—namely, programs of globalization and international exchange that are not centered on the West or the expansion of capitalism.[15] Some scholars have focused on the foreign policies and international agendas of smaller Second World actors like Cuba, Czechoslovakia, and Vietnam.[16] Others have centered on states in the Third World, making them protagonists in the broader Cold War story and emphasizing the ways in which domestic politics shaped the roles played by international actors.[17] Even scholars studying the former Soviet Union itself have looked for channels of influence and exchange whose impacts have endured beyond the bipolar competition.[18] Despite these burgeoning fields of scholarship, however, it is unclear how our overall picture of the twentieth and early twenty-first centuries has actually changed to accommodate these attempts at "alternative globalizations" and "anticolonial worldmaking." Are these merely vanished worlds that historians are recovering, a catalog of detours, lost causes, and foregone opportunities? Engerman has written with regard to India that, with all the outside attempts to influence India's development strategy, their "net effect was zero."[19] Fredrik Logevall and Daniel Bessner have argued unambiguously that "after 1945, the United States was the most powerful nation in the world; when it wanted to, it shaped global affairs."[20] What, therefore, is the import of all this searching for the paths through the twentieth century that do not chart the rise of American power and the victory of neoliberalism, that do not lead to the "end of history" and the Washington Consensus?

The answer is that while the Soviet Union collapsed, the world of the early twentieth century is as much a creation of the losing side in the Cold War as of the winning side. Socialism did not die with the USSR. As Slobodian notes, "neoliberal globalism remains one argument among many."[21] Understanding the legacies of the Cold War for the post–Cold War world therefore requires not only that we analyze the political and economic competition among countries espousing different ideologies but that we examine what that competition did to those ideologies themselves. It requires breaking down the barriers between political and intellectual history and treating policy makers as producers and employers of ideas as well as policies. This has already begun on the capitalist side of the conflict. Scholars such as Daniel Ekbladh, Daniel Immerwahr, and Amy Offner have examined how Western—and particularly American—notions of capitalist development evolved over time through the practice of economic engagement and developmental aid in the Third World.[22] Ideas and policies that originated in the West were transplanted to developing world contexts, and often transformed; and in some cases, lessons learned found their way back to Western capitals, or at least changed the way Western countries imagined the road of capitalist development for others.

Socialism was subject to similar processes, and countries that proclaimed themselves to be socialist (and were committed to the concept of a socialist world revolution) were similarly experimental, learning and adapting as circumstances dictated. That did not mean an abandonment of their ideological commitments any more than it did for the Western countries that sought to promote capitalist development by experimenting with state planning. At the margins, the adaptive approaches of both socialists and capitalists mixed the roles of the state and the private sector such that it was not always clear whether an economy was fundamentally socialist or capitalist. Tanzanian *ujamaa* was a case in point.[23] While the Canadian high commissioner in Dar es Salaam saw it as "an immunization against Maoism or Stalinism," his British colleague in London saw it as "a very nasty weed indeed and one which will permit no other plants to thrive alongside it."[24] By recapturing this process of trial and error in the socialist world, we can examine how socialist models of revolution and development, like capitalist ones, were transformed by the postcolonial encounter. Sebastian Berg, writing about the Left in the United Kingdom and the United States after the fall of the Berlin Wall, remarks on how even those who thought they had distanced themselves from Soviet communism found their world shaken to its core.[25] In reality, Berg writes, even the New Left had not completely repudiated the Soviet Union, and imagining the future of socialism necessitated reckoning with its demise. With socialism now having gained renewed support and vigor since the financial crisis of 2008, it behooves historians to trace the evolution of socialism as both ideology and practice through the attempts to implement it in varied circumstances across the world during the Cold War. This book aims to understand the history of socialism as a transnational project.

How to Make a Revolution

The fundamental question of revolution and development was twofold: how to take power, and what to do with it once you had it. Traditionally, as exemplified by the Leninist classics *What Is to be Done?* and *State and Revolution*, communists had seen this as a two-step process: first the party of the working class takes power, and then it imposes a dictatorship of the proletariat that begins the transformation to a socialist, and eventually communist, system. But without a working class or a communist party in most cases, this question got a lot more complicated, and stages seemed to merge or overlap. Without a Bolshevik party or a seizure of the Winter Palace, how was one to know exactly when power had been taken? With power in the hands of a radical nationalist figure like Sukarno in Indonesia, or a committed non-Marxist socialist like Julius Nyerere in Tanzania, had the revolution already taken power, or did it have still to be taken from those in power? Certainly those currently in power would be wary of an "ally" who saw them as a roadblock to revolution. Democracy presented a particularly tricky version of this question. When Salvador Allende won the 1970 presidential election in Chile, the Left took control of the executive. But it still did not control the legislature and, as would soon become clear, nor did it control the media or the military. So had the revolution taken power in Chile? In a two-stage process, once power has been taken, the full attention of the regime can then turn to the transformation of the economy and society. But if power is still to be taken, or has somehow only been partially taken, the question of what policies to implement becomes much more difficult. What if there is only enough political support for reformist half measures, but not enough for a fundamental transformation? And if one implements such half measures, does that risk delaying the revolution indefinitely by entrenching the current noncommunist regime and possibly sapping revolutionary momentum? If one pushes for radical measures prematurely, however, that risks a backlash that could marginalize the truly revolutionary forces. Instead of policy becoming a tool of transformation *after* taking power, it becomes yet another tool *for* taking power. In the case of Chile, the focus of Allende, the Chilean Communist Party, and the Soviets was on winning control of the National Congress of Chile and then winning the next presidential election (in 1976), and their economic policies were therefore geared toward that rather than the fundamental economic transformation they sought. The Chilean Socialist Party did not agree with this approach, and sought to gain power by sparking an immediate revolutionary upheaval. In Iran, the Tudeh Party supported the Islamists' progressive economic measures, firm in the belief that the Islamists could not manage an economy and thus their regime would inevitably collapse. More than forty years later, it still had not. In the end, the question of taking power exposed a basic cleavage between communists and their noncommunist socialist or leftist allies: while the communists were willing to consider many possible roads to socialism, they were never in doubt about the endpoint, which did not envision those allies in power.

Besides the question of power, there were other problems that the postcolonial developing world presented for the construction of socialism. Foremost among these was how to effect socialist economic development in agrarian economies with minimal industrial development. Communism, as Vladimir Lenin famously remarked, equaled soviets plus electrification.[26] In other words, it meant industrialization, which was crucial economically, militarily, and politically, since without industry there was no proletariat. In the 1930s the Soviet Union accomplished the industrialization of a largely peasant economy, but it did so through a violent collectivization program that not only killed millions but ultimately turned what was once the world's largest grain exporter into a perennial grain importer. China under Mao Zedong first tried to find a less confrontational way of socializing agriculture to procure resources for industrialization before tragically attempting its own Great Leap Forward.[27] Other communist states tried to find ways to socialize agriculture that would be more productive and less disruptive, though generally with little success.

9

The failure of Fidel Castro's 1968 plan to harvest ten million tons of sugar in Cuba is one example.[28] By the time they were trying to develop socialism in the postcolonial world, even the Soviets had recognized the failures of the Stalinist model of agriculture and were trying to reform it.[29] There were more than enough reasons why the experience of existing socialist states in transforming agricultural economies into industrial ones was seen as largely inapplicable, but on top of these was the fact that these new, fragile states did not dispose of the political authority to even contemplate such violently disruptive initiatives.

The task then was to find a way that would be both politically and economically feasible under postcolonial conditions for transforming agrarian economies into budding industrial ones. Could they simply build industry with aid from socialist countries? That would prevent the growth of local capitalism, but it would put a tremendous burden on socialist states and create suspicion of their true motives. What about bootstrapping their way via voluntary collectivization and the production of an agricultural surplus? Tanzania's experience would provide the test case for that. Without resources to make collective farms more productive, this too would come to seem like a dead end. What about encouraging small-scale farming and seeking foreign investment to stimulate industry? That is what Angola would attempt, but, as it turned out, that path ultimately led away from socialism. A key issue was that, in unstable political circumstances, it was not simply a matter of finding the most productive agricultural policy but also the most popular one. This put land reform at the top of the agenda. While traditional Marxism-Leninism sought to collectivize farming both for greater efficiency and to prevent the rise of a small proprietor class in the countryside, people in the developing world associated freedom and independence above all with the right to own the land that they worked. Yet land reform itself turned out to be tricky politically. In Indonesia and Iran it faced opposition from Islamic organizations that had the power to mobilize enough people to topple regimes. Perhaps the clearest example of the political stakes of land reform was evident in Chile; land reform was at the top of the Left's agenda, but the socialists and communists had very different notions of what it was meant to accomplish. The communists wanted confiscation of holdings over eighty hectares so as not to alienate the middle farmers that they hoped to bring into the coalition. The socialists wanted to confiscate all holdings over forty hectares to mobilize the landless peasantry for the upcoming civil war. Land reform was thus as much a tool of political consolidation as of economic development, and the two would often turn out to be contradictory imperatives.

As the Chilean case demonstrates, socialist development was complicated further by the question of democracy. While the existing socialist states quickly established one-party regimes, it was not immediately clear that that was the best path for developing countries. The question of "bourgeois democracy" and the attitude that socialist and/or communist parties were to take toward it had long divided the Marxist Left. (It would continue to do so through the end of the Cold War and beyond, as evidenced by the Eurocommunist debate in the 1970s and 1980s.)[30] For the most part, Marxist parties in the developed world supported democracy as long as they were seeking to avoid repression and needed time to grow, but rejected it once they achieved a dominant position. Yet the question looked quite different in a postcolonial and/or developing world context. Given the positions of these states vis-à-vis their recent colonial history or neocolonial political and economic relationships, nearly all political forces saw themselves as anti-imperialist, with some degree of legitimacy, and so it was not as easy to identify true "reactionaries." Seeking to suppress democracy, especially by a party already seen as tied to an outside power—as the Partai Komunis Indonesia (PKI; Indonesian Communist Party) or the Tudeh Party were in Indonesia and Iran, respectively—ran the risk of giving the impression that a new colonial power was seeking dominance. On the other hand, if democracy could be portrayed as a Western import and a tool for continuing Western interference in local politics, then perhaps democracy could be successfully undermined—and often with the support of local leaders, to boot. The question was whether democracy would ultimately help or hurt the political power of those seeking socialist development. Though each country's situation was different, there was also a significant degree of learning, attempting to derive lessons from the experience of political parties elsewhere. Following the Iranian Revolution of 1979, the Tudeh Party would make reference to the experience of Allende's government in deciding to support the Islamist repression of liberal democracy, for example. As the Angolan and Iranian cases demonstrate, by the end of the Cold War, multiparty electoral democracy was often seen to contain more dangers than opportunities for the advancement of socialism.

The question of democracy was intertwined with the question of national cohesion, particularly in the case of newly independent states. In the struggle for independence, the key divide between the oppressors and the oppressed had seemed to many to be racial or ethnic rather than based on economics or class. After independence, once the uniting factor of the struggle itself was gone, these new states were faced with the task of creating a cohesive national identity out of peoples delineated by often arbitrary borders with their own ethnic, racial, and religious cleavages. In many cases, political and economic power within newly independent states was often closely associated with certain groups that were seen as more favored by the colonial power, creating ready-made tensions. Complicating matters for socialists was that, since Marxist ideology was often the province of those who were more urban, educated, and therefore privileged, those promoting socialism and a class-based view of society were precisely those perceived as ethnically or racially privileged. The Movimento Popular de Libertação de Angola (MPLA; Popular Movement for the Liberation of Angola) faced just such a situation, composed as it was largely of *mestiços* (mixed-race people) and Kimbundu, the tribe that lived near the capital of Luanda. The MPLA had a perennial problem in that its advocacy of a racially neutral class-based view of oppression was seen by others as a self-serving attempt to preserve its own privilege. In Indonesia, the PKI was identified both with the predominance of Java over the outer-lying islands and a Chinese immigrant community seen as economically advantaged by the Dutch. Communists therefore faced a difficult choice. While Marxist tradition declared that workers had no nationality, Lenin had cleverly distinguished between the nationalism of oppressed and oppressor nations, arguing that the former could be revolutionary, since they were anti-imperialist.[31] Embracing narratives of racial, ethnic, or national identity and their associated hierarchies of victimhood could prove politically profitable. It could also be risky—not least for the Soviets themselves, who were perpetually in danger of being presented as a white imperialist power.

While questions of race, ethnicity, and nationality were tricky for socialists in the developing world, the experience of existing socialist states at least provided some useful examples of accommodation. Religion was another matter. The association of Marxism with atheism was strong, and reinforced by the violent and repressive policies toward religion in the People's Republic of China (PRC), the USSR, and elsewhere. In countries where religious institutions were politically, socially, and economically powerful and religious observance was widespread, socialists had few greater liabilities than their association with atheism. In places like Indonesia and Iran they were attacked as being anti-Islamic, especially since, as has been noted, their advocacy of land reform often conflicted with the interests of Islamic institutions. Trying to present themselves as being loyally Marxist without being anti-Islamic proved a difficult political tight-rope, and failure to walk it ultimately contributed to the tragedy that befell the communists in Indonesia. Socialists and communists elsewhere, led by the Soviets, who learned from the Indonesian experience, began to distinguish between oppressed and oppressor religions, with Buddhism and Islam counted among the former, as a way of allowing themselves to take a more cooperative approach to dealing with the role of religious forces in politics. As they reevaluated the role of religion and religious actors in the process of world revolution, even some elements of Chris-tianity, led by practitioners of liberation theology, came to be seen as po-tential revolutionary allies. This transformation ultimately facilitated the alliance of the oddest of bedfellows in Iran, with the support of the Tudeh Party for Ayatollah Khomeini helping to produce one of the strangest out-comes of the Cold War: an anti-imperialist, anticapitalist, modernizing theocracy in the Islamic Republic of Iran.

The present volume attempts to trace this process of socialist experimen-tation in the countries of the Third World over the chronological and geo-graphical space of the Cold War. With a topic so vast, it cannot claim to be exhaustive. Many countries could have been chosen for examination—Algeria, Egypt, Ethiopia, Ghana, Guatemala, India, Nicaragua, and the Republic of Congo, just to name a few—and that is the point: this is a story of global significance that touched nearly every country in the de-veloping world in some way. I have chosen five countries that not only span the space and time of the Cold War but were each perceived as para-digmatic cases that attracted global attention because they were held up as models for both their regions and as ways to solve broader questions of socialist development. Since this book is about experimentation with socialism along the political and ideological spectrum, I have not chosen countries such as Cuba and Vietnam, where communist parties were able to claim a monopoly on political power. The five countries I have chosen—Indonesia, Chile, Tanzania, Angola, and Iran—became crucial Cold War battlegrounds that resisted formal adherence to the Soviet Bloc and ex-perimented with forms of socialism not under the domination of a com-munist party. These five countries are not so much cases as episodes of a larger engagement between socialist powers and developing states. They are not meant to be parallel but rather sequential, illustrating a process of evolution in the socialist project over the course of the Cold War.

Chapter 1 begins with Indonesia, which in many ways serves as a kind of microcosm of the Cold War in the Third World. The fifth largest country in the world by population, Indonesia in the early 1960s had the world's largest nonruling communist party, which became the most powerful political organization in the country and seemed perpetually on the verge of taking power. The PKI wavered between armed struggle and peaceful competition, caught between democracy and dictatorship at home and between Chinese and Soviet influence from abroad. Both the PKI and the Soviets eventually chose to abandon democracy and support Indonesian president Sukarno's dictatorship as the quickest path to socialism. When Sukarno ultimately eschewed economic development in favor of anti-imperialist saber-rattling, the PKI and the Soviets parted ways. The PKI increasingly allied itself with the Chinese, who together with Sukarno sought to focus on an international anti-imperialist struggle and the creation of an Asian Axis rather than economic development at home. The destruction of the PKI in 1965, arguably the pivotal event in the Cold War in Asia, would be mined for lessons for other socialists and communists around the world. In particular, the Soviets came to see the abandonment of multiparty parliamentary democracy and the embracing of Sukarno's dictatorship as a mistake. Moscow also drew lessons from the PKI's handling of religion, which had the effect of antagonizing much of the Muslim peasantry. This would spark a reevaluation of the role of Islam in the national liberation movement, where it would increasingly be seen as a potential ally and mobilizing tool rather than as an obstructionist, reactionary element.

Chapter 2 continues with the theme of the relationship between socialism and democracy in the case of the Unidad Popular (UP; Popular Unity) government led by Salvador Allende in Chile, which came to power in 1970. The PKI had been one of the chief promoters of the "peaceful path"—a policy choice that Moscow encouraged—and the Soviets attributed its tragic destruction to a Chinese-influenced "adventurist" attempt to seize power militarily. When Chile elected a Marxist president, Leonid Brezhnev, the Soviet leader, saw the Via Chilena (Chilean Path) as a potential example for both Latin America and Latin Europe, including France and Italy, where other communist parties could come to power through elections at the head of coalitions. The Chinese, on the other hand, never saw Allende as a true socialist revolutionary, despite the sympathy of both Allende and the Chilean Socialist Party for the PRC, which Allende and other socialist leaders had visited multiple times. The UP government itself was fractured by this question of the peaceful path to power, and elements of the coalition began to work at cross-purposes. The demise of Allende's regime, famously attributed to the machinations of the administration of President Richard M. Nixon, was therefore as much a product of its internal divisions, which mirrored those on the global Left, as it was a product of its enemies' activities. The violent overthrow of the Allende government, the persecution and murder of thousands of leftist politicians, and the advent of a right-leaning military dictatorship under General Augusto Pinochet had the effect of largely ending the search for a peaceful path, at least in Latin America, where guerrilla struggles, especially in Central America and the Andes, would dominate the rest of the 1970s and 1980s. Even the Soviets would come to the conclusion that "a revolution must be able to defend itself."[32]

Chapter 3 examines Tanzanian *ujamaa*, the most coherent attempt to establish a uniquely African version of socialism. African Socialism typically meant invoking precolonial communitarian traditions and rejecting the necessity of class struggle as an artifact of European industrialization. Before the Tanzanian experiment, many Marxists rejected African Socialism as unscientific, and the Soviet approach to building socialism in Africa had revolved around aid-based industrialization. This ended in disaster as political leaders became wary of Soviet interference. Tanzania provided the possibility of a new path. With the Arusha Declaration of 1967, President Julius Nyerere proclaimed a program of building socialism on the basis of self-reliance and agricultural development. Despite Nyerere's close diplomatic relations with Beijing and his open rejection of Marxism, the Soviets were intrigued by his experiment, wondering if he could succeed in blazing a path to socialism in Africa where they had already failed. Nyerere's experiment ended in disaster when an attempt to force peasants into villages resulted in famine and economic collapse. When Angola's new leaders turned to Moscow upon gaining independence a few years after the failure of Tanzanian *ujamaa*, the Soviets made sure that the creation of a class-based vanguard party came first before an economic development plan could be put in place. That development plan would once again prioritize industrial development and foreign capital, but now much of that capital would come from Western investment.

Deriving lessons from the failures in Tanzania, the idea was that the proper political structure could ensure the ideological survival of the regime through a period of economic experimentation.

Chapter 4 takes up the story of Angola from the beginning of the liberation struggle in the early 1960s to the establishment of a Marxist-Leninist state in the late 1970s. The liberation of Africa had been seen by many on the continent as primarily a question of race rather than class. Independence was about replacing white people with black people in positions of power, not necessarily about an economic restructuring of society. This created a problem for the propagation of Marxism in Africa—especially for the Soviets, who represented what was seen as a white, European, industrialized, former imperialist power. In Angola, the attempt of the Portuguese to hold their colony produced a lengthy armed insurrection conducted by three different liberation movements: the Frente Nacional de Libertação de Angola (FNLA; National Front for the Liberation of Angola), the MPLA, and the União Nacional para a Independência Total de Angola (UNITA; National Union for the Total Independence of Angola), each of which operated in different parts of the country with different tribal identities and different foreign supporters. The Soviets supported the MPLA, led by a mixed-race group of Portuguese-educated Marxists. Once Angola attained independence, the MPLA leadership found itself facing challenges both internal to the movement in the form of black nationalism, and external in the form of the FNLA and UNITA, both of which were supported by foreign powers. As a result, the MPLA leadership also relied heavily on external support from Cuba, East Germany, the USSR, Yugoslavia, and others who helped it build a "vanguard" party with a powerful military and police apparatus. This was a strategy of revolution from above, based on political control, rather than revolution from below, and the result was the imposition of a party-state that remained in power some forty-five years later.

Chapter 5 looks at the Iranian Revolution and how Islamism came to replace socialism as the anti-imperialist ideology par excellence in the Middle East. I argue that it was a result of two key factors: first, the failure of socialism in the developing world to establish itself as a viable method for producing economic development, justice, and national dignity; and second, the growth of Islamism in response to the midcentury popularity of socialism as an alternative, and potentially superior, anticapitalist and anti-imperialist ideology. In short, Islamism in Iran claimed to be able to succeed where socialism had failed. The Iranian communists of the Tudeh

Party, advised by East Berlin and Moscow, did not believe that theocracy could serve as a viable model of governance in the modern age. Consequently, they chose to actively support Ayatollah Khomeini's consolidation of clerical rule. This was because they were applying the lessons of previous episodes in Third World socialist revolutions—in particular, the overthrow of Allende in Chile. They saw bourgeois democracy as a threat, and liberals and moderates as potential allies for the US Central Intelligence Agency in a counterrevolutionary conspiracy; as such, they identified Khomeini as the Allende figure—namely, the charismatic leader who could keep the revolution alive by uniting the people against the Americans and the remnants of the old regime. After the suppression of the Tudeh Party, rather than turn against the regime in Tehran the way that they had turned against that of Pinochet in Chile, the Soviets continued to seek a working relationship with Iran, acknowledging the revolutionary nature of the regime. Meanwhile, a struggle took place inside the Islamist camp between those revolutionary leaders who sought to transform the Iranian economy along socialist lines and more traditional clerics who sought to preserve private property and limit the role of the state. The result was a mixed regime that is still trying to determine the nature of its own revolution in both its economic structure and its international position. In many ways, the Islamic Republic of Iran is both the strangest and most logical product of the Third World revolution.

The book's conclusion looks at the ways in which the project of building socialism in the Third World changed during the course of the Cold War. The end result of this process of trial and error was an apparent reversal of the Marxist notion that material conditions are primary and determine political conditions. By the end of the Cold War few socialists still sought to collectivize agriculture or socialize the means of production immediately upon taking power, yet their regimes took the form of Leninist party-states. These parties needed sources of ideological legitimacy, but these shifted from socialist economic egalitarianism and modernization to various forms of national, ethnic, and religious self-assertion that converged on a common anti-imperialist theme. Though the model of the Soviet-style centrally planned economy might have died with the Cold War, socialism—even Marxist socialism—has survived in forms iterated through experimentation in the latter half of the twentieth century. While this book traces some of that trajectory, its chief purpose is to prepare the way for a broader examination of the spectrum of global socialist development in the twentieth and twenty-first centuries.

1

ASIAN AXIS

The Indonesian Communist Party and the Struggle for Power in Sukarno's Indonesia

I am a friend of the nationalists, but of the revolutionary nationalists.

I am a friend of the religious group, but of the revolutionary religious group.

I am a friend of the Communists, because the Communists are a revolutionary people.

—Sukarno, 1964

Therefore, to announce the construction of communism, as the Soviet comrades are doing, at a time when an enormous part of humanity is suffering in penury and experiencing hunger and deprivation, cannot be correct from a political point of view.

—Dipa Nusantara Aidit, 1963

As Indonesia celebrated the seventeenth anniversary of its independence in 1962, President Sukarno declared, "I know that on this present 17 August you are all looking to me . . . 'What does Bung Karno want to say?' 'What is the President going to enjoin upon us?' 'What will the Great Leader counsel?'"[1] Sukarno, Indonesia's first president from 1945 to 1967, was not known for his modesty but instead for his love of public speaking: he would go on at length even during torrential rainstorms, so much so that the British ambassador to Indonesia, Leslie Fry, once begged for a "special hardship allowance" because "strong men wilt and are carried away to bed on their return from these ordeals; indeed, the last Soviet Ambassador was flown back to Moscow to die."[2] Sukarno was also well known for his prodigious sexual appetites and devotion to what one American diplomat called "less uplifting American film exports."[3] Born in 1901 to a member of the Javanese *priyayi,* a class composed of aristocratic bureaucrats, Sukarno had been the charismatic leader of the independence struggle since the late 1920s. Though his actual program for postindependence Indonesia was rather nebulous, he was well read on political ideologies and developed his own views of the world situation and Indonesia's place within it. Until 1956, however, Sukarno's actual political power was limited, while Indonesia's political scene was a chaotic brew of political parties, economic interests, and regional and religious movements. In response, he built what he called Guided Democracy to bring order to the chaos. By the time he spoke those words on the seventeenth anniversary of Indonesian independence, the fate of the country did indeed hang on what Bung (brother or comrade) Karno had to say.

The problem was that no one quite knew what to make of Sukarno's unpredictable, rambling, and often indecipherable pronouncements. While the Americans hoped until late 1964 that Sukarno might still prove to be a barrier to communist expansion in Asia, the British disagreed. London's ambassador wrote in 1963 that "his [Sukarno's] concepts and slogans amount to little more than a muddle-headed form of totalitarian socialism. . . . President Sukarno is therefore an ideal tool for Communism."[4] Indonesia at the time was home to the world's largest nonruling communist party, the Partai Komunis Indonesia (PKI; Indonesian Communist Party). It was also the oldest communist party in East Asia, and had played a prominent role in Indonesia's struggle for independence since the early 1920s, attempting to seize power twice, in 1926 and 1948, but was crushingly repressed both times. Still, by the mid-1960s the PKI and its affiliated organizations claimed as members 20 to 25 percent of Indonesia's population of roughly one hundred million. As a prominent, powerful communist party in one of the earliest states to achieve independence after World War II, the PKI in Indonesia provided an important test case for the possibility of socialist revolution in the developing world.

Building socialism in Indonesia, whether through Sukarno, the PKI, or some combination of the two, would be no simple task. A sprawling archipelago that had never before formed a single state, Indonesia was one of the most unwieldy creations of European imperialism. Its overlapping

diversities—ethnic, linguistic, religious, economic, social, and historical—created political and economic fissures that were not easily resolved. Though the bulk of the population lived on Java, particularly in the island's densely populated central and eastern regions, the wealthiest and most commercial parts of the country were on the outer islands, particularly Sumatra. The separation of political and economic power exacerbated ethnic and religious tensions, as Sulawesians, Sumatrans, and others feared being subject to a "Javanese empire." Islam in Central Java and East Java incorporated and accommodated local customs and pre-Islamic traditions, known as *adat*.[5] Elsewhere, particularly in West Java and Sumatra, modernizing Islamic currents from the Middle East were transforming doctrines and practices and fomenting political pressures for a more Islamic state. The fact that these *santri* (a term used to describe Muslims of this ilk) tended to be wealthier, more commercially oriented urban dwellers who spoke languages other than Javanese created a ready

MAP 1.1 Indonesia in 1965.

constituency for opposition to a centralizing socialist state power in Java. Indonesian political parties either had to form coalitions with parties representing constituencies with fundamentally different interests and visions of the country, or—if they aspired to be truly national, as the PKI did—to find ways to appeal to others outside their base regions.

Indonesia's geographic, ethnic, and economic diversity exemplified the difficulties that communists in newly independent states in Africa and Asia would have. The necessity of building national cohesion in the archipelago would test their ability to embrace a nationalist narrative while maintaining their class identity and international commitments. The role of Islam, and the tensions within the Islamic community between different religious and political tendencies, would test the appeal of communism in a deeply religious society. All of this was taking place initially within a multiparty democratic system in which coalition governments fell apart on a nearly annual basis. The PKI would have to decide how to adapt to this environment and make it serve the ends of socialist revolution. Indonesia also provided an archetype of what would prove to be a troublesome figure throughout the postcolonial world: the left-leaning radical nationalist demagogue who often paid more attention to geopolitics than economics, paid only lip service to socialism, and regarded communist parties with something between suspicion and outright hostility. President Sukarno turned out to be the greatest riddle of all for the PKI.

The PKI's strategic choices in this environment set both positive and negative precedents for communists throughout the developing world. Despite its presence in a region where many other communist parties chose guerrilla insurgency, and its own legacy of armed uprisings, the PKI would embark on a peaceful path to power focused on parliamentary politics in 1951, one of the first communist parties in the postcolonial world to do so. This decision would engender tension within the PKI and would lead to recriminations with every setback. Despite the PKI's success in the 1955 parliamentary elections and its increasing power in electoral politics due to an exponentially expanding membership, the party leadership ultimately chose to embrace Sukarno's turn toward Guided Democracy in 1957, believing that Sukarno's promises to include communists in the government were a surer route to power than coalition politics. The choice to embrace authoritarianism rather than defend democracy also entailed a shift from a focus on economics to a decided emphasis on Sukarno's anti-imperialist politics, and with it a redefinition of the role of communism in the postcolonial world. While this policy seemed to bring the PKI closer to power, the party's top leadership nevertheless opted to depart from the peaceful path in 1965, with tragic consequences. The reasoning behind this decision, as we will see, was examined intensely by both the Indonesian communists and their comrades abroad.

Indonesia's geographic, demographic, and strategic importance, as well as the size and prominence of its communist party, attracted a great deal of attention from the Cold War powers. The nation was a focal point of American foreign policy during the Sukarno era, leading to a wealth of scholarly interest funded in part by the US government and largely centered at Cornell University's Southeast Asia Program.[6] The United States saw Indonesia as a bulwark against communist expansion in Asia, and Washington sought to use aid to buy the loyalty of Jakarta and to bolster the PKI's domestic competition. At times American policy produced the opposite result: pushing Indonesian public opinion toward sympathy for the communist side. Nevertheless, American hopes that Sukarno, despite

FIGURE 1.1 President Sukarno on the cover of *Newsweek* magazine, the same week that US president Lyndon Johnson approved Operation Rolling Thunder, a plan for the sustained bombing of North Vietnam. *(Used with permission of Newsweek. All rights reserved.)*

his prickly nature and bombastic rhetoric, was still the best option for controlling the PKI and limiting the supposed expansionist ambitions of the People's Republic of China (PRC) persisted well into 1964. Once Washington determined that Sukarno had definitively sided with Beijing and the PKI, however, the United States sought to ensure his removal and transfer power to the Indonesian military. In the wake of the September 30, 1965, coup attempt, the United States seized its chance to ensure the destruction of the PKI, setting the stage for over three decades of Suharto's dictatorship.

For the Soviets, who had had a close relationship with the Indonesian communists since the early days of the Comintern, Indonesia was crucial on several fronts. The possibility of communists coming to power in such a large and strategic Asian country offered perhaps the greatest demonstration of communism's ascendance in the Cold War competition, especially since it seemed it could happen peacefully. At the same time, Sukarno's willingness to challenge the West and pursue an anti-imperialist foreign policy meant that Moscow stood to benefit from the existing Indonesian regime. This necessitated some awkward calculations: How could the Soviet Union support both Sukarno and the PKI's path to power at the same time? Could Sukarno and the PKI maintain their alliance? If so, on what terms? As the Soviets discovered, the PKI leaders were making similar calculations, but their alliance with Sukarno neglected the economic agenda the Soviets saw as key to building socialism in Indonesia. In this the Soviet agenda shared a good deal with the American agenda in Indonesia: both hoped to get Jakarta to focus on domestic economic development rather than the geopolitical crusade they saw as serving the interests of the third major competitor for influence in Indonesia, the PRC.

Beijing's ascendant influence in Indonesia came later than that of Moscow or Washington but, for a brief period, from late 1963 until the coup in 1965, it likely eclipsed that of its superpower rivals. The delay was in part a product of the tension produced by the status of some two million ethnic Chinese in Indonesia, who constituted a large portion of the commercial and lending classes.[7] Animosity toward the ethnic Chinese, whose citizenship status and loyalty was a sore point, was perpetually on the verge of boiling over, handicapping both the PRC and the PKI (the latter seen as an ally of Beijing). Nevertheless, by mid-1963 the willingness and, indeed, eagerness of Beijing to support Sukarno's anti-imperialist agenda, coupled with the perceived high-handedness of the Soviet Union and the United States (particularly in the conditions they attached to aid), led to China's rise as Indonesia's ally of choice, culminating in Sukarno's speech of August 17, 1965, when he declared a Jakarta–Phnom Penh–Hanoi–Beijing–Pyongyang axis.[8] Within months, however, the budding Sino-Indonesian relationship would be in shambles. Though both the Soviet Union and the United States retained good relations with Suharto's military regime, the Chinese became the primary foreign targets of the new regime's wrath.

The spectacular rise and fall of Indonesian communism had repercussions far beyond its national borders. For policy makers in Washington, the likelihood of Indonesia turning communist increased the importance of holding the line against communism in South Vietnam, because they saw Indonesia as the largest domino in the "Domino Theory."[9] Had the coup happened in 1963, it is conceivable that the United States would never have sent ground troops into South Vietnam.[10] Meanwhile, the collapse of the budding Sino-Indonesian alliance, which removed Beijing's most important ally and signaled the failure of its early 1960s foreign policy offensive in Africa and Asia, helped set the stage for the Cultural Revolution in 1966. Beyond geopolitics, however, the lessons of the PKI loomed large for communists throughout the developing world. As the largest nonruling communist party—and one that seemed, in a kind of Zeno's paradox of politics, perpetually on the verge of gaining power without ever reaching it—the PKI's strategic decisions doubled as answers to basic questions of the communist cause in the developing world: How were communists supposed to take power? What was the purpose of their taking power? And what was the role of an individual country—particularly in the Third World—in the global communist revolution? The PRC, the USSR, and communists around the world would seek to learn from Indonesia about issues such as the approach to land reform, the mobilization of workers and peasants, Islam, dealing with the armed forces, parliamentary democracy, and the role of leaders like Sukarno. The experience of the PKI was also revealing of the dynamics within the so-called international communist movement itself. At the same time that the PKI sought to establish itself as an independent party, its leaders sought Soviet guidance on questions of their own domestic strategy. Yet, despite the increasing Soviet dissatisfaction with the Indonesians, Moscow ultimately chose not to support alternatives to the PKI. The relations between communist parties, though not necessarily equal, nevertheless seemed to impose obligations and constraints in both directions. The PKI experience demonstrates that parties in the developing world were not mere clients of Beijing or Moscow, but neither were they fully independent of them. Following the PKI's destruction, voices on different sides of the increasingly fractured international communist movement would also seek to use the painful experience of the PKI to push their own theories and agendas about communists' role in the world.

Indonesian Communism before Formal Independence, 1914–1949

Having the first communist party in Asia (founded four months before the Chinese Communist Party, or CCP), Indonesia, along with Vietnam, experienced a deeper communist involvement than other countries in their independence struggles. This meant that the PKI would not only be subject to the twists and turns of Comintern policy as it sought to find a successful strategy in the colonial world, but also that the nation's experience would be instructive for communists elsewhere. Many of the tensions and choices that would define the later trajectory of the PKI were evident as early as the 1920s. The early relationship of communists to Islam was a difficult problem: Comintern instructions ultimately hurt the PKI in ways that some leading Indonesian communists recognized and protested. This set the stage for enduring suspicions of a PKI anti-Islamic agenda that would recur with violent consequences in the 1960s. Similarly, the PKI's ambiguous relationship with nationalist organizations, again often dictated by the whims of the Comintern, would help create a situation in which other political parties would have difficulty allying with the PKI or welcoming it into governing coalitions. Part of the problem was that twice, first in 1926 and then again in 1948, a policy of cooperation suddenly turned into one of violent confrontation instigated by the PKI—the first time without the support of Moscow and the second time possibly with it. While the future PKI leadership would learn important lessons from this period on the key issues of how to relate to Islam, nationalist organizations, and the relative merits of peaceful and armed paths to power, this period also established legacies that the party's opponents would not soon forget.

Marxism in various forms became prominent very early on in Indonesia's long struggle for independence. As early as 1914 Indonesia saw the creation of the Indische Sociaal-Democratische Vereeniging (ISDV; Indies Social Democratic Association), nearly all of whose initial members were from the Netherlands, led by a young Dutch labor organizer, Hendricus Josephus Franciscus Marie Sneevliet. By itself, the tiny ISDV had little influence, but it soon found its way to participating in the activities of the first mass nationalist organization in Indonesia, Sarekat Islam (SI; Islamic Association), which had been founded at the end of 1911. Initially organized by Javanese merchants to protect their interests against Chinese traders, SI quickly came to appeal to a much broader social base and represent a wider nationalist impulse. By 1919, SI claimed a membership of two and a half million, though that might have been a significant exaggeration.[11] Given that it was common at the time for active Indonesians to belong to more than one such organization, the ISDV began to attract prominent members within the SI, as well as encourage its own members to play a role within the larger group. By the end of the World War I, the result was that the ISDV had a significant amount of influence in the affairs of SI.

In the wake of the First Comintern Congress, held in Moscow in March 1919, the ISDV constituted itself as the PKI, on May 23, 1920. It was then under the leadership of Semaun, a railroad employee and member of the lesser Javanese nobility.[12] At the Second Comintern Congress a few months later, where Sneevliet, under the pseudonym Maring, would represent the PKI, Bolshevik party leader Vladimir Lenin's line defeated that of the Indian communist Manabendra Nath Roy, and communists in the colonial world would be directed to cooperate with the "national revolutionary movement," even where it was led by bourgeois liberation movements, since it was premature to expect parties to act on their own with only the proletariat to rely on.[13] This seemed to validate the PKI's cooperation with SI, just as it would form the basis of the cooperation of the CCP, founded the following year, with the Guomindang. The problem for the Indonesian communists, however, was that Lenin also directed party members in the colonial world to "combat Pan-Islamism and similar trends, which strive to combine the liberation movement against European and American imperialism with an attempt to strengthen the position of the khans, landowners, mullahs, etc."[14] In a country where Islam was central to the nationalist struggle, these two Comintern directives would prove to be mutually exclusive.

The Comintern directive against Pan-Islamism, loyally supported by the PKI, provided grounds for those within SI who were dissatisfied with the increasing influence of the Left within the organization to voice their discontent.[15] By October 1921, battles within the central organization of SI had resulted in the expulsion of the PKI from the leadership, though not from the local affiliates.[16] In the meantime, Semaun was replaced as PKI leader by Tan Malaka, who proved to be less willing to follow Comintern orders. Malaka—the son of a village head from West Sumatra who studied in the Netherlands from 1913 to 1919 before moving to Java and joining the PKI in 1921—was described by one scholar as "a romantic figure with mass appeal," and he would be one of the few politicians who could rival Sukarno as a symbol of Indonesian nationalism.[17] In 1922 Malaka outlined the PKI's predicament at the Fourth Comintern Congress:

> In 1921 a split occurred as a result of clumsy criticism of the leadership of Sarekat Islam. The government through its agents in Sarekat Islam exploited this split, and it also exploited the decision of the Second Congress of the Communist International: Struggle against Pan-Islamism! What did they say to the simple peasants? They said: See, the Communists not only want to split, they want to destroy your religion! That was too much for a simple Muslim peasant. The peasant thought to himself: I have lost everything in this world, must I lose my heaven as well? That won't do!

Instead he argued that Pan-Islamism should be embraced for the same reasons as bourgeois nationalism:

> Today, Pan-Islamism signifies the national liberation struggle, because for the Muslims Islam is everything: not only religion, but also the state, the economy, food, and everything else. And so Pan-Islamism now means the brotherhood of all Muslim peoples, and the liberation struggle not only of the Arab but also of the Indian, the Javanese and all the oppressed Muslim peoples. This brotherhood means the practical liberation struggle not only against Dutch but also against English, French and Italian capitalism, therefore against world capitalism as a whole. That is what Pan-Islamism now means in Indonesia among the oppressed colonial peoples, according to their secret propaganda—the liberation struggle against the different imperialist powers of the world.

Despite his pleas, the congress reiterated its opposition to Pan-Islamism.[18] As the splits within SI deepened, the PKI tried to consolidate its hold over certain former SI sections to build its organizational infrastructure. The new, more isolated, and more combative PKI began to focus its efforts toward militant revolutionary action rather than the peaceful mass struggle that had earlier characterized SI activity. With the PKI now essentially in breach of the Comintern directive to cooperate with the nationalists, Soviet general secretary Joseph Stalin directly accused the PKI of a "left deviation" at a speech at the Communist University of the Toilers of the East on May 8, 1925.[19] Nevertheless, the PKI leadership, against the opposition of the exiled Tan Malaka, opted for a revolutionary uprising, which took place between November 1926 and January 1927. The uprising was poorly planned, however, and was for the most part crushed within weeks, leading to some thirteen thousand arrests.[20] PKI leaders Alimin and Musso, the former who would become a member of the Communist Party of the Soviet Union (CPSU) in 1927, had traveled to Moscow to ask the Comintern for help in the planned uprising, but with little success, and the odds against it were obvious in an exchange during a July 1926 meeting held by the Comintern Executive Committee's Undersecretariat for Indonesia:

> [Head of Comintern Information Department John] Pepper: And the Dutch army has cannon, machine guns, etc. modern equipment?
> [PKI secretary] Alimin: Yes, they have all modern equipment.
> Pepper: You have no arms at all?
> Alimin: We have about 5[00] or 600 revolvers.[21]

While the Sixth Comintern Congress in 1928 would hail the Indonesian uprising as evidence of "the general crisis of the world capitalist system," the PKI was banned, and its top leaders were either in prison or exile.[22]

Though Musso would briefly sneak back into Indonesia in 1935 to set up an illegal communist underground, the party would only openly emerge again with Indonesia's declaration of independence and proclamation of a republic on August 17, 1945. But the new PKI was initially under the influence of the now determinedly anti-Stalinist Malaka, who saw President Sukarno and Vice President Mohammad Hatta as Japanese collaborators who could not be trusted. It was not until later in 1946, with the return of veteran party leaders in good standing with Moscow, Alimin and Sardjono, that the PKI would revive its ties with the underground and adopt a new policy of cooperation with the republican leadership in exchange for promises of democratic freedoms and social measures. The PKI established a "united front from above," together with the Socialist and Labor Parties, that called itself the Sajap Kiri (Left Wing) within the Komite Nasional Indonesia Pusat (KNIP; Central Indonesian National Committee) that functioned as the parliament, a tactic endorsed by Moscow at the time. Under the Socialist Party prime minister Sutan Sjahrir, the PKI supported the republican government's attempts to come to a negotiated agreement with the Netherlands, while the Soviets counted Indonesia and Vietnam as the two examples of a "true war of national liberation" and were optimistic about the influence wielded by the PKI.[23] On July 3, 1947, a new cabinet was formed under Amir Sjarifuddin, who would later reveal himself to be an undercover communist, with another crypto-communist, Setiadjit, as vice premier, and two known PKI members as ministers. It seemed as if the PKI would play a decisive role in the politics of the nascent republic.

A 1947 report from Leonid Baranov, the head of the Foreign Affairs Department of the Soviet Central Committee, to Stalin's chief ideologist, Andrei Zhdanov, shows just how bullish Moscow was on the Indonesian Republic in this period. Even President Sukarno was described as "holding leftist convictions, cooperates with the communists. Fights for the preservation of the sovereignty of the republic. Is a partisan of the shaping of the state structure on the basis of the principles of socialism, advocates for the nationalization of the main types of industry and the establishment of councils [soviets] of worker-peasant deputies. Is well-acquainted with the classical works of Marxism-Leninism and in his speeches often cites the works of Lenin. Openly expresses deep sympathy for the Soviet Union." With the support of the Sajap Kiri and Sukarno, the PKI published a ten-year plan that envisioned the nationalization of large enterprises (with paid compensation), agrarian reform and the mechanization of agriculture, and state control of the processes of production and distribution.[24] Since the governing coalition was dominated by the Sajap Kiri, the report even saw Masjumi (a Muslim party formed in 1943 under Japanese occupation that largely represented the wealthier commercial classes of the outer islands) as being forced to bow to the popular nationalist mood and therefore worthy of inclusion in the coalition. The Soviet report criticized the PKI for not including Masjumi in the government, a measure of just how robust Moscow thought the PKI's position really was. The prospects for communist success in Indonesia seemed bright indeed.

Then, on September 22, 1947, in the Polish town of Szklarska Poręba on the Polish-Czechoslovak border, Zhdanov announced a new two-camp doctrine at the opening conference of the Cominform that would replace the "united front" view characteristic of the wartime years.[25] Derived from the perceived mistakes of the French and Italian communists in the postwar years, this new doctrine meant that Moscow was now taking the possibility of cooperation with so-called bourgeois parties off the table. A new Soviet report on Indonesia, entitled "The Political Situation in Indonesia after the Gathering of the Representatives of the Nine Communist Parties," was now far more critical of the PKI, seeing the party's position in favor of negotiations with The Hague as evidence of weakness in the face of American pressure, which it attributed to "the incorrect tactical line of the Communist Party on the question of relations with other [bourgeois Indonesian] parties." Contradicting the verdict of the earlier report, this new one noted that the Soviet line "calls into doubt the tactic of the Indonesian Communist Party and its relations with the other parties that entered into the socialist bloc."[26] The report pushed a harder line for the PKI and signaled the end of the united front policy in Indonesia. E. M. Zhukov, writing in the main CPSU journal *Bol'shevik* two months later, now said that the PKI should see as its enemies not only foreign imperialists but also their "internal social backers."[27] When followed in Indonesia, this created a great deal of tension between the PKI and its partners in Sjarifuddin's coalition government. On January 23, 1948, Sjarifuddin's government fell, opening the door for a more radical posture to be adopted by the PKI and its supporters against the new Hatta cabinet and the policy of negotiation with the Netherlands. The Sajap Kiri was now reorganized as the Front Demokrasi Rakjat (FDR; People's Democratic Front), which opposed the Hatta government through its strong positions in the labor movement and the Indonesian Army. While Hatta sought to increase his control over the army by demobilizing troops and "rationalizing" its administration, the FDR organized strikes, and the situation became tenser. By mid-July, as the FDR leaders began to lose hope that the confrontation could be resolved politically, they started to make plans to use their remaining strength in the military for an armed confrontation if necessary.[28]

On August 3, 1948, Musso, having now spent more than a decade living in the USSR, unexpectedly returned to Indonesia. By itself this signaled Moscow's interest in Indonesian events, and the impression that Musso had arrived with instructions from the Kremlin was confirmed by his declaration of what he called the Gottwald Plan, named for the communist leader of Czechoslovakia who had just seized power via coup. Musso was quickly instated as the leader of the PKI and, at his insistence, the party adopted a new program called the New Road for the Indonesian Republic. Adopting a Zhdanovite two-camp view, the program criticized the previous PKI policy of remaining in the background and called for the Socialist and Workers Parties that had been created as PKI fronts to be merged with the PKI, which would now lead an uncompromising struggle against the imperialists.[29] The hope was that this larger united PKI could pressure Hatta into resigning, and the FDR would form a new cabinet in which the communists would occupy key posts.[30] As Musso and other PKI leaders toured the country to garner greater support for the new program, officers loyal to the PKI and worried about Hatta's rationalization program struck back preemptively, sparking another uprising, this one centered on the East Javanese city of Madiun. Caught by surprise, Musso and his fellow PKI leaders jumped to support the insurrection, which was once again crushed, this time by the forces of the Indonesian Republic, after Sukarno went on the radio and demanded that people choose between him and Musso. Musso was killed in battle on November 1, and the PKI, while not officially banned, was almost totally destroyed; its reputation was now damaged, as it was seen to have attacked the Indonesian Republic during its independence struggle.

Though the uprising took Musso by surprise, it does seem that armed action was at least potentially in his plans for the PKI and, unlike in 1926, this time Moscow might have approved. There has been a lot of speculation among scholars that orders were given at a February 1948 conference in Kolkata sponsored by the World Federation of Democratic Youth and the International Union of Students for Communists in Asia to launch armed uprisings.[31] While the fact that uprisings were launched soon after the conference in Burma, Malaya, and Indonesia gave credence to the theory, no hard evidence of such orders has yet materialized. The possibility remains, however, that the Soviets had at least signed off on plans that included an eventual military option. Musso's New Road program first took form as a draft resolution following a meeting in Prague with Paul De Groot, the head of the Dutch Communist Party, in early June 1948. At that meeting De Groot and Musso discussed the possibility of obtaining arms through either Czechoslovakia or Sweden; at the time it was not clear if the arms were meant to be used against the Netherlands or the Indonesian Republic.[32] Both parties knew that the contents of the discussion would be passed back to Moscow, though in this case the information did not reach the Central Committee of the CPSU until August, a delay that perhaps indicated the planned time frame. In any event, the Soviets seemed to be caught off guard by the September 1948 uprising (which came to be known as the Madiun Affair), and Soviet press coverage largely relied on Western sources in the country. Internally, information reaching the Soviet Foreign Ministry from Telegrafnoye agentstvo Sovetskogo Soyuza (TASS; Telegraph Agency of the Soviet Union) correspondents and others initially reflected an optimistic view of events. According to a report dated October 1, 1948, "If one takes into account that the government of Hatta has already been attacking the Communist region for ten days and is not able to achieve success, this undoubtedly shows that that Communists control significant territory, and that a significant portion of the Republican army has gone over to the Communist side." The tide soon turned, and two weeks later Mikhail Suslov, a member of the CPSU Secretariat, met with Dutch Communist Party leaders before the final defeat of the uprising to tell them that the PKI should be fighting the imperialists, not the Indonesian Republic.[33] Publicly, however, the Soviets would adopt the line that the later PKI would promote regarding the Madiun events: It was a provocation by Hatta's government for the purpose of destroying the PKI. Both the PKI and the Soviets would deny any responsibility for the Madiun Affair.

From Armed Rebellion to Peaceful Path: The PKI and Indonesia's Experiment with Democracy, 1949–1957

In the early years of Indonesian independence, the PKI would resurrect itself from the ashes of Madiun, a remarkable recovery that would see it become possibly the strongest political party in Indonesia by 1957. This recovery was enabled by a new, younger leadership cohort that would adopt the strategy of a peaceful path to power, growing the party's base while seeking allies in the parliament. At a time when communists were fighting in Korea, Malaya, and Vietnam, the peaceful strategy of the PKI offered an alternative path to power in the postcolonial world and one that seemed to be succeeding. The PKI's rejuvenation as a political force in Indonesia would reach its crowning moment with the 1955 parliamentary elections, but those elections failed to break the impasse that had led to political paralysis and continuous confrontation in Indonesian politics; in the search for alternatives, Sukarno would reemerge with his plan for Guided Democracy. Despite the PKI's successes during this period of parliamentary democracy, its leadership would ultimately choose to back Sukarno's suppression of the parliament and vast expansion of presidential powers. The Soviets would endorse this choice, but it would ultimately have fateful consequences for the PKI.

In the months after the Madiun Affair, the Netherlands launched another police action against the nascent Indonesian Republic. The shock of this bloody assault spurred the new United Nations (UN) Security Council into action and, now that the government of Sukarno and Hatta had proven itself to Washington as a reliable fighter against communism, the United States put pressure on the Netherlands to grant formal independence to Indonesia, which it formally granted on December 27, 1949.[34] In its early years, the Indonesian government was headed first by Hatta and then by a series of cabinets led by the relatively conservative Masjumi. In this initial period Indonesia leaned strongly toward the United States, and its leaders focused on both attracting foreign investment and nurturing local private enterprise, with the commanding heights of the economy still largely in the hands of Dutch business interests.

In this hostile political environment, the PKI tried to recover from the Madiun disaster. The remaining politburo members were not able to re-establish contact until August 1949, and they held a conference in September to chart a path forward. While the party officially reaffirmed Musso's New Road program of August 1948, Tan Ling Jie, an ethnic Chinese who now became a leading figure in the party, argued that under these conditions it made sense to delay merging the other PKI-dominated parties into the PKI in order to give the party an outlet for legal political activity.[35] More militant members rejected this line and advocated for armed struggle. The whole discussion had something of an air of unreality, as the party's organization in the countryside had been destroyed, its control of the trade unions had been lost, and its leaders could not even agree on an agricultural policy, let alone a way to deal with the question of national and ethnic division, to which it had never devoted much attention in the past.[36] It took new leadership to forge a political machine out of the quarreling remnants of the PKI.

This new leadership comprised four individuals, all of whom were a generation younger than the previous leaders and had come of age in the years of Japanese occupation and the independence struggle rather than during the earlier period of nationalist awakening and Dutch repression. Dipa Nusantara Aidit, who became general secretary of the PKI, was an ethnic Malay from the North Sumatran city of Medan. Born in 1923, Aidit was involved in politics from an early age, joining the left-wing organization Barisan Pemuda Gerindo in 1939; his father became a member of parliament from the Masjumi party in 1951.[37] While Aidit joined the illegal PKI in 1943, like other future leaders of his generation he also belonged to several Japanese-sponsored youth organizations in which he gained experience in political mobilization.[38] It was these organizations, paradoxically, that provided Indonesian youth with the military training

34

FIGURE 1.2 The general secretary of the PKI, Dipa Nusantara Aidit, speaking at a Communist Party rally on the eve of Indonesia's parliamentary elections, September 1, 1955. The elections would create a four-way division of power in the Indonesian parliament, setting the stage for Sukarno's Guided Democracy plan. *(Howard Sochurek / Getty Images)*

that enabled them to fight for independence in the postwar years. Aidit's two deputies, Mohammad Hatta Lukman and Njoto, were born in 1920 and 1925, respectively, and were both Javanese whose fathers had both been involved with the PKI at an early stage. Sudisman, who would take over as the PKI's general secretary after Aidit's death in 1965, was born in the East Javanese city of Surabaya in 1920 and followed a political trajectory that was similar to Aidit's. All four were promoted to the politburo in September 1948 by Musso, but Aidit and Lukman managed to escape Indonesia in the immediate aftermath of the Madiun Affair, reportedly fighting with the Viet Minh in Vietnam before ending up in China.[39] After eighteen months abroad, they returned in 1950, ready to take the reins of party leadership. These four remained in control of the party until the coup of 1965 and defined the new path that the party would take to reconstruct its political fortunes.

On January 7, 1951, the PKI Central Committee announced a new politburo consisting of these four, plus the aging and infirm Alimin. Though Tan Ling Jie and others had sought to hold on to some influence, they lost a power struggle in the fall of 1950, and both they and their policies were discredited. In their place the Aidit leadership would outline a new party strategy, though it owed something to Musso's New Road program, which the new leadership continued to affirm. The new program was formally enshrined at the Fifth PKI Congress in March 1954. It began with the premise that Indonesia was a still a semifeudal and semicolonial country, evidenced by the dominant role of foreign—particularly, Dutch—capital and the heavy rents paid by peasants to landowners. As a consequence, Indonesia was still at the stage of national anti-imperialist rather than socialist revolution, and it behooved the party to follow a modified united front policy. This meant that "the working class, the peasants, the petty bourgeoisie, and the national bourgeoisie must unite in one national front," with the working class in the lead, allied with the peasantry.[40] While the enemies of the party were said to include domestic landlords and comprador bourgeoisie, as well as the foreign imperialists, the battle against imperialism was to take priority for the time being, and cooperation with domestic elites against foreign imperialists was permissible. In practice this meant that the PKI looked to form political coalitions with nearly any party willing to work with it, which in the first years of independence meant especially the Partai Nasional Indonesia (PNI; Indonesian Nationalist Party), of which Sukarno himself had once been a leader. The PKI sought to support friendly coalition governments and even join cabinets when possible, though this would prove to be too much for its bourgeois partners. In the meantime, the party was to focus on building its organizational capacity and expanding its membership to increase its political weight in the country. In particular, in recognition of its continuing weakness in the countryside, the PKI attempted to pay more attention to the interests of the peasantry and repudiated its previous advocacy of nationalization of all land, though this would be mostly empty rhetoric until the late 1950s.[41]

Throughout the period of Aidit's leadership the PKI asserted that the program of the Fifth Congress was its own intellectual product, specifically devised to fit the conditions of Indonesia. Given the PKI's previous history of close ties with the Comintern and conflict with the republican government during the independence struggle, the claim that it was following its own Indonesian path was central to its popular resurrection and legitimacy, allowing the rest of the Indonesian political scene to accept the PKI as a legitimate player and (it hoped) coalition partner. The program, especially as elucidated publicly, seemed to reflect moderation and was used to differentiate the PKI from communist parties elsewhere whose activities might be perceived as alarming. Given the party's subsequent advocacy of each communist party's right to choose its own path, this story seemed both believable and necessary, and the scholarship on the PKI has mostly accepted the substance of this claim.[42]

Archival materials now available in Moscow tell a different story, however. In October 1950, Liu Shaoqi, secretary of the Central Committee of the CCP, forwarded to Stalin a series of proposals for the future strategy of the PKI.[43] The proposals had been worked out by Chinese and Indonesian communist leaders, though the latter were not named specifically. (As has been noted, Aidit and Lukman had spent much of late 1949 and early 1950 in China.) Perhaps unsurprisingly given the recent success of the Chinese communists, the proposals envisioned a Chinese-type guerrilla campaign based on a national united front that would concentrate on the rural areas in order to surround the cities, where legal struggle among the workers would continue. The militancy of these proposals rings true in light of Aidit's analysis of the Indonesian situation at the January 1951 plenum that elevated him to the leadership. In that report, which was not officially published but is now available in the Russian archives, Aidit argued that the fact that Sukarno and Hatta were now in power signaled the defeat of the 1945 revolution, since power had not shifted between classes, and that the American role in Indonesia was growing, aided by the comprador bourgeoisie and feudalists. Accordingly, he said the party's preparation for armed struggle was already underway. The PKI had reportedly organized "secret armed ranks" and had armed groups operating in North Sulawesi and West Java.[44] Meanwhile, the party's task was to isolate the "national bourgeoisie" from the masses and work out a new party statute that would create a "real Bolshevik party."[45] This approach seemed far from the one that the party would ultimately adopt at the Fifth PKI Congress.

Stalin responded to the proposals in February 1951, writing that the PKI should focus for the time being on "liquidating feudal landholdings" to distribute land to the peasants as private property. This would help build the party's base and make possible a political alliance with the bourgeoisie. Stalin told the PKI leaders that their current struggle was against the Netherlands and that it was premature to name the Americans as the main enemy. He argued strongly against adopting a Chinese-style guerrilla strategy; not only did the party lack the necessary forces, but the insular nature of Indonesia made it impossible to retreat (as the CCP had done on the Long March) or be resupplied by land, as the Chinese communists were by the Soviet Union. Stalin accused the PKI of adopting "leftist phraseology" in seeking to defeat all imperialists and jumping straight to socialism all at once.[46]

It took a while for the PKI to respond to Stalin's letter; the party had suffered a new wave of repression in August 1951, and its top leaders had either been arrested or gone into hiding. Finally, in March 1952, a PKI reply reached Moscow courtesy of the Chinese. The letter began with a history lesson, in which the PKI educated the Soviet leadership on landownership in Indonesia. In 1870 the colonial government had taken over the ownership of the land from the feudal landlords and mostly rented it out to foreigners, though it did give land to some Indonesians in a few areas. As a consequence, Indonesia did not have a class of feudal landlords "as existed in old China or contemporary India." Therefore, Indonesia's struggle against feudalism was a struggle against "feudal customs and habits," while the struggle of the peasants for land was rather a struggle against imperialist forces—"that is, against the government."[47] As a result, the party maintained its differences on agrarian policy, which envisioned nationalization of foreign landholdings and was unclear on how land would be distributed to the peasants. The PKI did, however, agree with the Soviets on the need to focus on political rather than armed struggle. As for the accusation that they had been using "leftist phraseology" and seeking to solve all problems at once, the PKI wrote that while that criticism was true of the party in the past, when its cadres were insufficiently educated due to the lack of Marxist literature in Indonesia, now that they were "starting to study Marxist-Leninist literature and the works of Mao Zedong more or less systematically" it was no longer accurate.[48]

In the wake of this response, the Soviets chose not to respond positively to a PKI proposal for a trilateral meeting of Chinese, Indonesian, and Soviet communists.[49] The next stage was then a letter to Stalin from the representative of the PKI in Beijing, Iskandar Subekti, and a member of the PKI Central Committee, Asmu, who came to Moscow in October 1952 to represent the PKI at the Nineteenth CPSU Congress. In the letter Asmu and Subekti asked why the struggle against Dutch imperialism must be the primary task and why they should only create an "anti-feudal front" for the time being.[50] Clearly, despite their protests to the contrary, the Indonesian communists still had not accepted the Soviet critique. In another letter, Asmu and Subekti proposed to have Aidit and Njoto meet with Stalin, as they would be traveling to Moscow in December following visits to Czechoslovakia and the Netherlands. In preparation, the Soviets prepared a list of issues with the documents thus far presented to them by the PKI for internal use. The running theme of these issues was that the Indonesians were still too radical for Moscow's tastes. For example, it was deemed problematic that "the Indonesian comrades sometimes characterize all of the national bourgeoisie as an agent of imperialism." Similarly, the Indonesian demand for the nationalization of important economic enterprises was premature. The biggest mistake was that "the Indonesian comrades claim that in their country there are no feudal landlords, the land belongs to the government which is under imperialist influence, and therefore the primary task of the Indonesian people is the struggle against imperialism, not against feudalism." Finally, the Indonesians "prematurely call out American imperialism, increasing the number of their enemies and depriving themselves of tactical options in the struggle."[51] Two years after receiving the original proposals, Moscow was still unhappy with the Indonesian response and the number of disagreements seemed to have increased.

Aidit and Stalin finally met face-to-face in January 1953. Though no record of the meeting itself is available, Aidit's letter to Stalin following the meeting is. In essence, Aidit finally accepted Stalin's positions. He wrote that the PKI's 1951 program on agrarian policy had been composed before receipt of Stalin's letter, but that his party now understood how much its lack of support among the peasantry had hurt it, and the PKI was grateful for the Soviet advice. The party would now be for distributing land to the peasants as private property rather than any form of nationalization. In response, Stalin also proposed that the PKI try to place its people in leading positions in the armed forces and arm the populace for self-defense. These ideas would reappear, in part through the suggestion of Zhou Enlai, in the early 1960s.[52]

It seems then that the impetus for the moderation that characterized the policy formally adopted by the PKI at its Fifth Congress came not from the new Indonesian leadership but rather from Stalin himself. That is not to say that much of the evolution in PKI policy between 1951 and 1954 was not a product of the Aidit leadership dealing with changing political circumstances at home, but it does seem that much of the "groping," as described by one scholar, was actually the product of a give-and-take with Moscow. In any case, the national united front approach focused on building parliamentary coalitions and seeking to build a membership base in the countryside was certainly not a program that Aidit, Lukman, Njoto, and Sudisman had ready to go when they assumed leadership of the PKI in January 1951. Instead it reflected the hard-earned lessons, and also possibly the foreign policy priorities, of the man that Aidit still referred to as the "great teacher and leader of humanity": Josef Stalin.[53]

The new approach that would define the tenure of Aidit's leadership was formally codified at a party plenum in October 1953 and then adopted as the new PKI platform at the Fifth PKI Congress in March 1954. Notably, the US embassy in Jakarta, years before the open break between the PRC and USSR, devoted much of its analysis of the congress to whether the leadership changes and the new party program reflected the ascendance of a "pro-Moscow, anti-Peking" wing of the PKI. More insightfully, the American diplomats picked up on the crucial tensions within the new PKI approach that would lead to some difficult choices down the road, noting,

> Aidit claimed that the Madiun uprising was a failure because the PKI lacked the rural base and that it would have to get such a base in order to achieve final victory. This goal will inevitably lead to difficulties for the PKI because it can easily conflict with the principal aim of the party, which is to form a national united front. Because of the greater importance attached by Aidit to a national

front, one can conclude that the PKI will, if necessary, deny itself the luxury of a mass base in the countryside, with all the meaning that has for an indigenous Communist revolution in a predominantly agricultural country. Some PKI members will doubtlessly recognize this and come to the conclusion that the present leadership is serving firstly in the foreign policy interests of Moscow.[54]

The US embassy report following Aidit's speech at a November 1954 plenum put the matter even more starkly, and could not resist the opportunity to play communist strategist: "If the PKI were to champion the interests of the peasants and workers more aggressively than they have done in the recent past, the party would develop mass support more rapidly. But in this case the tolerance of the PKI by the government might abruptly come to an end. Whether or not current PKI policy is correct from the standpoint of establishing communist power in Indonesia is questionable. A coup d'etat or the peaceful formation of a middle of the road government, including parties now in opposition, would place the PKI in isolation again."[55]

As these reports indicate, and as the very fact that the PKI was allowed to hold a legal congress in Jakarta in 1954 attests, the PKI had made remarkable strides in its political reemergence between 1951 and 1954. A party that had been nearly destroyed after launching an armed insurrection against the government, with membership reduced to less than ten thousand after the Madiun incident, now boasted a membership of 165,206; by October 1954, Aidit claimed that the PKI had reached five hundred thousand members. *Harian Rakjat,* the main PKI newspaper, increased its circulation from two thousand in July 1951 to fifteen thousand by February 1954, and then to fifty-five thousand by January 1956.[56] The success of the PKI was not limited to its own membership, however. It increasingly became part of the Indonesian political mainstream.

The growing weight of the PKI combined with national political shifts to make it a much more influential party and therefore a more desirable coalition partner. (As of 1951, the PKI held thirteen of the 232 seats in the provisional parliament, known as the Dewan Perwakilan Rakyat [DPR; People's Representative Council], that remained in place until the elections of 1955.)[57] The early governments had been dominated by the conservative Masjumi, and the PKI therefore existed in a state of only semi-legality in 1951–1952. These governments had followed a pro-Western path in foreign policy, and none other than Adolf Hitler's economist,

Hjalmar Schacht, was sought out by the government as an economic adviser in 1951. Schacht told the Indonesians to open the country to foreign investment, avoid nationalization, and create a strong military and police force.[58] Unsurprisingly, especially given Sukarno and Hatta's history of collaboration with the Japanese in this period, the Soviets considered Indonesia's government to be fascist, and the PKI's view was only marginally more positive. But the Masjumi-dominated Sukiman cabinet fell when the foreign minister agreed to accept American aid under the terms of the Mutual Security Act of 1951.[59] This required economic aid recipients to cooperate with the United States in the security field. The resulting scandal not only toppled the government but also stoked anti-American and anti-imperialist feeling in Indonesia. Now, for the first time, a member of the PNI, Wilopo, would become prime minister. This time the PKI, though not represented in the cabinet, would support the government on the grounds that it was a bourgeois democratic government and thus preferable to "fascist bourgeois" governments, though the Wilopo government would repeatedly disappoint the PKI.[60]

It was under the premiership of Wilopo's successor, Ali Sastroamidjojo, that the PKI would truly join the political mainstream. Ali represented the left wing of the PNI, and his cabinet, announced on July 31, 1953, was the first not to include any Masjumi representation; it would therefore likely rely on PKI votes in the DPR. The Ali cabinet departed from the economic policies of its predecessors, strongly promoting "Indonesianization" of the economy, which largely entailed favorable government policies toward Indonesian firms, whose number consequently exploded between 1953 and 1955.[61] In foreign policy, the Ali cabinet similarly charted a new course, increasing the level of anti-Netherlands rhetoric, especially around the issue of the continued Dutch occupation of West Irian (Western New Guinea); finally allowing the opening of a Soviet embassy in Jakarta (delayed since 1950) and the exchange of ambassadors; and convening the first conference of the heads of state of Africa and Asia in the West Javanese mountain town of Bandung in April 1955. Most significantly, the cabinet finally put into place an election law to hold Indonesia's first parliamentary elections in 1955. From the moment the law was passed, Indonesian politics were dominated by the election campaign, which offered the possibility of a definitive test of strength that would put an end to the incessant parliamentary jockeying.

The elections provided just the opportunity the PKI had been looking for to prove its influence and thereby make its inclusion in a coalition government inevitable. Accordingly, the party pulled out all the stops in its campaign. Realizing the significance of the rural areas, an election plan written by Sakirman (a member of the politburo) instructed party members to ensure that the individuals on the committees assisting the village headmen in creating voter lists were not unfriendly to the PKI and to focus on making the PKI logo familiar to illiterate villagers.[62] The party also toned down its socialist policy demands at the national level.[63] The PKI was still vulnerable in two areas: in religion, and in its ties to foreign communists. In 1950, when Vice President Hatta accused the PKI of being led by Stalin, Aidit replied at a public meeting, "Hatta has said that the PKI is led by Stalin. Comrades, I stand before you to verify that what Hatta has said is true. Not only the PKI, but the whole laboring class is under the leadership of Stalin."[64] At the March 1954 Congress, the PKI had even elected CCP chairman Mao Zedong and Soviet premier Georgy Malenkov as honorary members of the congress presidium, but now, following Masjumi attacks on these grounds, portraits of foreign communists were no longer in evidence and little mention was made of the PRC or the USSR.[65] Masjumi also attacked the PKI for its supposed atheism, and the party thus went out of its way not to appear antireligious. In particular, especially in Central Java and East Java, the PKI posed as the representative of the more traditional Hindu-inflected Indonesian Muslims, rather than the *santri* represented by the Masjumi.[66] In a preelection speech at a party plenum Aidit remarked, "As a weapon for division of national unity, reaction most often uses religion, creating the impression that the goal of Communists around the world is to destroy religion and interfere in the freedom of belief." In that same speech Aidit laid out the party's rationale for its defense of parliamentary democracy:

> We defend the system of parliamentary democracy not only because this system is the best way to expose bourgeois dictatorship, but also because it relates directly to the struggle of the people for their basic interests, for incremental demands. . . . There are more than few examples which prove that the masses in our country can use parliament as a form of struggle for their economic and political interests. This form of struggle would be impossible to employ if a government was formed that was not responsible to parliament, that did not guarantee the democratic freedoms of the people.[67]

The PKI's enthusiastic campaigning was duly rewarded in the first parliamentary elections, though it did not quite realize Aidit's prediction of one-third of the seats.[68] The party received some 6,176,914 votes, or roughly 16.4 percent of the total, which granted it thirty-nine seats in the new DPR—twenty-two more than at the time of the dissolution of the previous parliament. Essentially, the bulk of the vote was split fairly evenly among four parties: Masjumi; Nahdlatul Ulama (NU), an Islamic party established in the 1920s that had once joined Masjumi but broke from it in 1952; the PKI; and the PNI. This surprised observers who had thought that Masjumi would be by far the party with the largest vote, based on the assumption that the mass of rural Muslim voters would support it. The regional aspect of the vote proved to be enormously significant, however: NU, the PKI, and the PNI all derived a large majority of their votes from Central Java and East Java, which held about 46 percent of Indonesia's population. Masjumi clearly dominated the voting in the outer islands.[69] As a result, rather than providing stability to the Indonesian political scene, the elections only produced more volatility. With a parliament now dominated by four nearly equally powerful parties, at least two of whom—Masjumi and the PKI—refused to work with each other, and the regional differences laid bare for all to see, Indonesian parliamentary democracy was dealt what in time would prove to be a fatal blow. A PKI plenum after the elections concluded that the country was divided among three groups: the reactionaries, the progressives, and the oscillators, including the "left wing circles of the middle forces." Now the reactionaries had been shown once and for all that they could not attain power via the parliamentary path, so they would be left to resort to other methods, including terror and insurrection.[70] It was not only Masjumi, however, that would begin to lose faith in parliamentary democracy.

The father of Indonesian independence, Sukarno, had long since been reduced to what J. D. Legge has called a "figurehead President." The 1945 constitution, which created a strong executive presidency, was first limited by the conventions of parliamentary democracy in November of that year, and was then replaced by a new constitution in 1950 that created a cabinet-based system that further diminished the role of the president, basically limiting him to the appointment of cabinet *formateurs*. Sukarno had long resented these limitations, and he often condemned Western liberal democracy as unsuited to Indonesia. He used the occasion of the opening of the newly elected DPR in March 1956 to reiterate this opposition, contrasting Western notions of "fifty percent plus one" majority rule with a supposedly traditional Indonesian conception of *gotong royong* (mutual help), which would mean something like government by consensus.[71] With the country at a political impasse, and the economic situation deteriorating as a result, Sukarno embarked on a series of overseas visits in 1956, his first since 1945 (except for a hajj to Mecca), designed in part to raise his profile as a political leader.

After touring the United States and Western Europe between May and July 1956, Sukarno embarked on a much more controversial tour of communist countries from August through October, visiting Yugoslavia, Czechoslovakia, the USSR, Mongolia, and the PRC. His impressions from this tour were overwhelmingly positive, particularly given the willingness of the Soviets to offer aid. As he recounted in his autobiography, "Years ago I asked the USA for a loan. Not a gift. I felt like a hungry relation whimpering at the door of a rich uncle. . . . Finally I asked [Soviet premier Nikita] Khrushchev for the one hundred million. It was bitter cold, yet he came out of the Kremlin into the street to embrace me. . . . There were no long, cold negotiations. Nor did they dictate my future behavior before giving me my crust of bread."[72] Despite the unlikelihood of Moscow being hit by a sudden deep freeze in late summer, Sukarno's impression of the enthusiasm of the Soviets for his visit was accurate. His visit to China, though not as lucrative, left an even greater impression. He was reportedly moved to tears by the scale of his reception, as hundreds of thousands lined the streets from the airport to downtown Beijing. His aide recorded that Mao and Sukarno "hugged each other as if they had known each other for a long time," and both immediately announced their admiration for one another and proclaimed their shared ideals. On his seventeen-day tour around the country, Sukarno was deeply impressed by China's stability and the spirit of its people.[73]

In his first public speech back in Indonesia, on October 28, Sukarno spoke of how impressed he was by China, saying "we made a very great mistake in 1945 when we urged the establishment of parties, parties, parties."[74] Two days later he announced that he had his own conception of Indonesia's political path forward, which he would elaborate in due course.[75] Unsurprisingly, some have attributed Sukarno's turn toward his Guided Democracy plan in large part to the impressions from his visit to the USSR, and especially the PRC.[76] Yet Sukarno's press attaché on his trip, Ganis Harsono, tells a different story in his memoirs. Harsono writes that Sukarno's plan in visiting the USSR was to deliberately disrupt Indonesian politics by taking actions that were outside his constitutional authority. Specifically, he signed both an aid agreement and a joint communiqué with the Soviets without first consulting the DPR, intentionally exceeding his authority. When confronted about this by the leaders of five Indonesian political parties on September 13 in Belgrade, Sukarno feigned innocence, saying he was just trying to do what was best for the country. According to Harsono, "from the Kremlin in the Russian heartland he began his grand design that brought him finally to the apex of absolute power."[77]

For his Soviet hosts, Sukarno's visit also provided an excellent opportunity to advance their own agenda. A top secret report prepared in advance of Sukarno's visit by the Soviet Foreign Ministry for Mikhail Suslov, the Kremlin's new chief ideologist, presented the Indonesian leader as a potentially useful ally and one who could be influenced in a positive direction. Sukarno had admirably refused to speak against communism on his recent visit to the United States, was firmly anti-imperialist both at home and abroad, and was well-versed in both the classics of Marxism-Leninism and Russian literature. At the same time, he gave a lot of significance to religion as a political force and had two key weaknesses: vainglory and women. The report noted that he specifically loved giving large public speeches and "finding himself in the company of beautiful women."[78] This was someone Moscow could work with.

Sukarno had also developed his own ideology of Marhaenism (which was officially adopted as the ideology of the PNI, his former party and the party of most prime ministers in the period 1952–1957) by 1953. Marhaenism, similar to ideologies that would be developed in other postcolonial states, centered on the idea of typical Indonesians—not necessarily members of the proletariat, but those sufficiently poor to stand for the oppressed and deprived masses. Marhaenism sought to advance their interests not through class struggle, since Indonesia was said not to have the class structure of standard Marxism, but instead through a collective attempt to raise Indonesia's standard of living.[79] The Soviets saw this ideology as, on the one hand, an admirable expression of concern for the interests of the laboring people, but on the other—and especially as practiced by the PNI governments in power—as reflecting the fears of the national bourgeoisie regarding a true class struggle, a danger represented by the rise of the PKI.[80] Seen optimistically, though, as reported to Suslov in the immediate aftermath of Sukarno's visit, "there is in it much that is unclear, confused, but there is also something that gives the PKI the chance to find a basis for cooperation."[81]

This would be particularly true if the scales of the Indonesian economy and social structure were tipped more in favor of the PKI, and that is where Soviet aid came in. Over the previous year, the Soviet embassy in Jakarta had repeatedly emphasized that Indonesia was not doing enough to develop its heavy industry, and that as long as it failed to do so, it would remain a semicolony.[82] On the eve of Sukarno's visit, the Soviet ambassador to Indonesia, D. A. Zhukov, wrote a report on the prospects for industrial development in Indonesia based on the recently developed five-year plan for 1956–1960. Looking at the list of proposed objectives, he wrote, "The Soviet Union could offer Indonesia financial and technical aid in the construction of a number of important industrial objectives for the country," specifically referencing hydroelectricity, metallurgy, and geological exploration, among others.[83] The economic attaché of the embassy, one A. Ivanov, wrote that considering the role already played by the Western powers in Indonesia, "On the results of the economic cooperation of our country with the Republic of Indonesia will greatly depend the foreign political course of the Indonesian government."[84]

The Soviets were not just looking to gain political favor through aid, however. They were specifically interested in the development of state-led heavy industry, which would both enable Indonesia to oppose the West in foreign policy as well as strengthen the role of the working class in Indonesian politics. This Soviet interest was evident in the negotiations over aid that went on both before and after Sukarno's visit. In August 1956 an Indonesian trade delegation had supplied their Soviet counterparts with a list of fourteen different objectives of the new plan.[85] A month later, the Indonesian minister of planning (and future prime minister) Djuanda submitted a new, shorter list. His Soviet counterpart asked why the new list no longer included hydroelectric stations and survey work on nonferrous metallurgy, in which the Soviets had been interested, and Djuanda responded that these were not the highest priorities for Indonesia at the moment.[86] Ultimately, however, the Soviets made sure that these items were included in the communiqué on the signing of the aid agreement, in exchange for which they conceded to the Indonesians on the terms of repayment.[87] It was important enough for Moscow to help Indonesia build heavy industry that it was eager to provide aid on unusually generous terms, and it hoped that Sukarno's visit would lay the foundation not only for a foreign policy relationship but for the transformation of the Indonesian economy.

By the time of Sukarno's return to Indonesia, then, both the PKI and the Soviets were facing a difficult dilemma: Should they continue to support parliamentary democracy in Indonesia, or throw in their lot with

Sukarno, who seemed determined to take Indonesian politics in a different direction? The years of parliamentary democracy had treated the PKI well. Membership had grown exponentially, and the party's influence had grown even more, with the PKI now firmly established as one of the largest political parties in the country; previous experiences with anything less than democracy had not been kind to the party. At the same time, however, it seemed that the more powerful the PKI became, the more determined its coalition partners, especially the PNI, were to keep it from the summit of power. Would the PKI ever be able to break through on its own? Though Sukarno's history with the PKI was checkered, particularly due to the events of 1948, he seemed to have a basic leftist orientation in both foreign and domestic policy and increasingly seemed to take a friendly attitude toward the PKI. Should the PKI abandon its promotion of democracy and the parliamentary path in the hopes of riding Sukarno to power?

For the Soviets, Sukarno represented a chance to make Indonesia into an ally on the world stage, as well as a possibility to get the Indonesian economy moving—in a socialist direction, no less—after years of stagnation and mismanagement by rotating cabinets of the bourgeoisie. But Sukarno was ultimately bourgeois himself or, whatever he was, he was most certainly not a communist. Could communism be built in Indonesia with the help of a radical bourgeois nationalist? Given his prominence in the national independence struggle, could it be built without him? And there was one more concern for Moscow: there were reasons to begin doubting the reliability of the PKI. At a PKI plenum following the Twentieth CPSU Congress in Moscow, where Khrushchev gave his secret speech on Stalin, Aidit said it was necessary to "exhibit greater tact in relation to the name of Stalin, taking into account the particularities of the East."[88] This was reportedly preceded by a visit to Beijing, where Aidit had discussed the "cult of personality" with the Chinese leadership. As divisions between Beijing and Moscow began to appear, maybe it would not be such a bad idea for Moscow to use Sukarno to hedge its bets on the PKI as well.

From Guided Democracy to *Konfrontasi*, 1957–1963

On February 21, 1957, Sukarno finally unveiled his new *konsepsi* (conception) of Indonesian politics, which had been highly anticipated since he first hinted at it in October 1956 upon his return from China. In the intervening period, the internal political situation had deteriorated further. Another cabinet had fallen, political wrangling undermined the new one before it even took power, the military sought to play an increasingly important role in politics, and dissatisfaction in the outer islands was reaching the point of rebellion against the Jakarta government.[89] Sukarno again attacked Western parliamentary democracy as being unsuited to Indonesia, proposed in its place a *gotong royong* cabinet that would include members of all parties that had a certain minimum number of seats in parliament, including the PKI, and advocated the creation of a National Council composed of "functional groups" in society that would advise the cabinet and be led by the president.[90] Though Sukarno had many supporters, the reaction to his *konsepsi* was far from unanimous approval. The ensuing political turmoil brought down the most recent government on March 14, and the future of the Indonesian political system, including the role of parties, the DPR, the president, the military, and others, was gravely in doubt. In this environment, the stances of both domestic and foreign actors would play a role in determining the eventual fate of the Indonesian political system, which by the end of 1959 would include a strong presidency, a weakened party system, and soon the dissolution of the parliament. Both the PKI and the Soviet Union, despite their reasons for wanting to maintain the parliamentary system, would ultimately find grounds for supporting Sukarno's accumulation of power, a stance that the latter in particular would ultimately come to rue in 1965.

Moscow's priority was the transformation of the Indonesian economy along socialist lines, which meant state-led investment in heavy industry and the reduction of the Western economic presence in the country. It would soon come to see Indonesia's parliamentary system as an obstacle to this vision, imagining instead that a more streamlined and centralized political process under the left-leaning Sukarno offered better opportunities. In the meantime, Soviet observers in Indonesia kept pointing out the potential significance of Soviet economic involvement. Indonesia possessed some 20 percent of the world's tin, but it lacked the ability to process it, and most of the profits went to Western firms. Accordingly, the Soviet embassy in Jakarta suggested that Moscow offer to build a processing plant, writing, "Considering the special significance of tin in the world economy and the existing possibilities to limit the control of imperialist monopolies on this important type of resource, as well as helping liberate Indonesia from foreign dependence and broadening the state sector of its national economy, it would be preferable not to wait for a proposal from the Indonesian government and put forth our own initiative on this issue."[91] The embassy made a similar proposal with regard to Indonesia's oil industry, recommending that the "responsible Soviet organizations through GKES [the Gosudarstvennyi Komitet po Vneshnim Ekonomicheskim Sviaziam, or State Committee for Foreign Economic Relations] of the Council of Ministers of the USSR make contact with the Indonesian Ministry of Industry to clarify the willingness of the Indonesian side to cooperate on the matter of the reconstruction of the oil industry in North Sumatra on the basis of the General Agreement, concluded between our countries on 15 September 1956."[92] There was no shortage of possible avenues for Soviet aid, and many on the Soviet side were eager to help.

As tantalizing as the possibilities were, the problem was that the Indonesian side was dragging its feet on economic cooperation with the Soviet Union. The General Agreement of 1956 was politically explosive in the polarized Indonesian political situation of the time, and parliamentary opposition held up its ratification for a year and a half.[93] The economic stakes were raised even farther when, as a result of the deteriorating state of Dutch-Indonesian relations due to the impasse over West Irian, nearly all Dutch enterprises in the country were taken over by the end of 1957.[94] The takeovers had been largely spontaneous and disorganized, but now it was up to the government to decide what to do about them. For both the PKI and the Soviets, the potential now certainly existed to enact a definitive transformation of the Indonesian economy under state control. With the takeover of the tin and oil industries, the Soviet embassy again saw them as "the kernel, around which can be developed a domestic Indonesian mining industry" and urged that Moscow actively approach the Indonesian government about Soviet involvement.[95] But the parliament and its bourgeois parties were standing in the way.

Accordingly, Soviet evaluations of the main Indonesian political parties became significantly more negative at this time. While Masjumi, the PKI's chief antagonist, took the lead in opposing Soviet aid, NU and the PNI, the PKI's erstwhile coalition partners, looked for other ways to scuttle the aid agreement.[96] The Soviet embassy reported that the PNI had turned decisively to the right since 1957.[97] The Partai Sosialis Indonesia (PSI; Socialist Party of Indonesia)—a descendant of the party once led by Sjahrir and Sjarifuddin in the late 1940s, which had come to embrace something akin to Menshevism, advocating for the growth of a capitalist economy in Indonesia to prepare the ground for an eventual socialist revolution—was now seen as "the most evil enemy of Marxism and the international Communist movement."[98] When growing regional dissatisfaction led to open armed rebellion in the outer islands in late 1957 and early 1958, including many prominent leaders of Masjumi and the PSI backed by American military aid with US Central Intelligence Agency involvement, the Soviets decisively concluded that the party system was now being used as nothing more than a Trojan horse for the preservation of imperialist influence.[99] As the Soviet embassy reported, "Imperialist forces, interested in the preservation and strengthening of their position in Indonesia, speak out against national unity, broadening and supporting the creation and existence of various types of reactionary political parties and organizations," which had become "a serious obstacle" to progress.[100]

For the PKI, which had far more to lose if the adoption of Sukarno's *konsepsi* proved to be the wrong choice, matters were not quite as simple. In the immediate aftermath of Sukarno's speech, the party provided the most enthusiastic foot soldiers for the *konsepsi*, painting slogans on the streets of Jakarta and other cities.[101] But at this point it was not yet clear how thoroughgoing the reforms would be, and for the PKI this seemed primarily an opportunity to gain the cabinet portfolios that coalition politics had thus far denied it. Yet once the parliamentary system and the very existence of political parties—especially in the wake of the regional rebellion—began to come into question, the PKI vehemently defended both.[102] The problem was that Indonesian politics was increasingly coalescing around two poles, one represented by Sukarno, and the other represented by Masjumi, the PSI, and parts of the military, and it was the latter that sought to defend the parliamentary system. Much of the latter camp also wanted to destroy the PKI, and so the party needed to support Sukarno since only Sukarno could protect it. The PKI seemed to have three choices left, none of them optimal: defend parliamentary democracy alongside its erstwhile enemies, support Sukarno's creation of what would come to be known as Guided Democracy, or devote its energies to illegal activities, possibly even including guerrilla insurgency.

By 1959 the main issue in the transformation of the Indonesian political system had come to center on a new constitution. The elected Constituent Assembly had been debating for years to little effect, deadlocked in particular over the issue of whether a new constitution should declare Indonesia to be an Islamic state and what that would entail. Sukarno now put forward a proposal to return to the Constitution of 1945, which

invested the presidency with supreme executive authority. This was recognized as likely the death knell for parliamentary democracy, and it at
first was a bridge too far even for the PKI. Following Aidit's return from
a visit to Moscow in the spring of 1959, however, the PKI changed course
and decided to support the adoption of the 1945 constitution, though
there is no direct evidence that it was the Soviets who prompted the
change.[103] When the Constituent Assembly failed to support Sukarno's
proposal with the necessary two-thirds majority in July 1959, he dissolved
the assembly and enacted the 1945 constitution by presidential decree.
On August 17, 1959, the fourteenth anniversary of independence, Sukarno delivered a speech that would come to be known as the Political
Manifesto, laying out a new system based on the 1945 constitution. It
would be a *gotong royong* government focusing on *nasionalisme* (nationalism), *agama* (religion), and *komunisme* (communism) and thus known
by the acronym Nasakom, and it would be directed toward a state-led
economic order known as Indonesian Socialism.[104]

Why did the PKI ultimately go along with this? The answers seemed
to be evident at the Sixth PKI Congress, held only a few weeks after Sukarno's speech. First of all, the holding of the congress itself was one clue.
The military, which had promulgated an order on July 1 banning all political demonstrations, had sought to prevent the holding of the congress,
but Sukarno insisted that it be allowed and spoke at it himself, denouncing
anticommunism.[105] This was more than a mere tactical decision, however.
The main report of the congress, delivered by Aidit, declared that "the
PKI accepts Guided Democracy, understanding by this, that it is a type of
democracy, though not Popular Democracy, but democracy directed
against liberalism. The positive side of Guided Democracy is that it is
against military and unilateral dictatorship on the one hand and against
liberalism on the other." Sukarno's *konsepsi* of Guided Democracy was
said to be "the answer of the Indonesian people at the current time directed to ensuring that the crisis of liberal democracy ends with the victory of the people." In promoting this idea the PKI asserted that it expected to be represented in a Nasakom cabinet, but that this did not mean
turning the government into an instrument of class struggle. Rather, the
Indonesian bourgeoisie was too weak to conduct class struggle and thus
the main task was for the national bourgeoisie, the workers, and the peasants to unite in a struggle against the imperialists to liberate Indonesia
from its semicolonial state.[106] For the PKI, Guided Democracy could work

because it united all the patriotic elements of Indonesian society and pol
itics at a time when class struggle was still premature.

Not all of the PKI leaders were on board with this. Rumors of dissension within PKI ranks were rife after the party switched its position on
the constitution, and it seemed that even Lukman might have opposed
Aidit's current line. Alimin, the last major holdover from the previous PKI
leadership, published a brochure in 1958 (which the party suppressed)
that accused the PKI of having abandoned the class struggle altogether.[107]
As the party report at the congress warned, "Among the party cadres
there are still unclear notions of primary and secondary contradictions
in contemporary Indonesian society, and lack of understanding that in
certain conditions antagonistic contradictions can become nonantagonistic, at the same time that nonantagonistic contradictions can become
antagonistic."[108] But the new party line was not simply a surrender to Sukarno. Aidit told Giuseppe Boffa, an Italian communist who attended the
congress, that Sukarno needed the party as much as the party needed him,
especially because the PKI claimed to command the loyalty of 40 percent of
the army's troops. Njoto even told Boffa that the Political Manifesto had
been written in part by the PKI.[109] In any case, the party was taking another measure that should have had the effect of securing its position in
the country. The other major initiative announced at the congress was an
attempt to connect more with the peasantry. This meant studying rural
conditions, sending party members out into the countryside, enrolling more
peasants as members, and focusing more on rural issues.[110] While the
party was allying itself with Sukarno in Jakarta, it also hoped to build a
stronger base throughout the country that would both give it greater political weight and ensure it against disaster.

As the PKI cautiously embraced Sukarno's introduction of Guided Democracy, this moment signaled the high point of Indonesian-Soviet relations. Sukarno visited a number of socialist countries in 1959, including
the USSR, and the Soviet embassy saw him moving ever closer to the socialist camp.[111] Then, in February 1960, Khrushchev finally came to Indonesia. The visit produced a joint communiqué that displayed a lot of
common ground in foreign policy, but the most significant part of it was
the signing of a new aid agreement that included a new Soviet credit of
$250 million, though the old one had barely been touched. This new aid
agreement specifically emphasized that the Soviet credit was to be used
mainly for the metallurgy, chemical, textile, and agricultural industries,

as well as for building a nuclear reactor—that is, according to the Soviet embassy, "for the development of the key areas of the economy without which one cannot ensure the economic independence of the country."[112] Now that Sukarno was in charge of a more streamlined state machinery and had declared his goal to be socialism, the Soviets hoped that their plans for the Indonesian economy could begin to be realized.

But how could they invest so much hope in a bourgeois radical like Sukarno who, for all his talk of Nasakom, was still keeping the PKI at arm's length? At the request of the Soviet Foreign Ministry, the Soviet embassy produced a report on Sukarno's Indonesian Socialism program, noting that despite its non-Marxist nature and lack of class struggle, the program was focused on "justice," the "liquidation of oppression," and the "destruction of enslavement."[113] Contrary to other instances where the Soviets saw "nonscientific socialism" as a threat,[114] the fact that this ideology had taken hold in Indonesia was seen as a positive indication for the progress of socialism worldwide, and Sukarno was credited with attempting to adapt socialism to Indonesian reality. Indonesian Socialism was claimed to incorporate a number of "real" socialist ideas, including the elimination of the exploitation of man by man, economic planning, and the leading role of the state. It also contained problematic elements— notably, its focus on belief in God—but these were considered understandable concessions to Indonesian conditions. To remedy these problems the author of the report recommended, "In unofficial conversations with Sukarno during his time in the USSR [he visited again in 1961], support the positive sides of Indonesian socialism, especially those about economic construction. . . . At appropriate moments underline that in the current historical period any ideas which express fear of communism will spark great dissatisfaction among the popular masses against their authors, and that communism is inseparable from socialism."[115] For the Soviets, then, Sukarno's ideological heterodoxy was not necessarily an insuperable obstacle to his leading the construction of socialism in Indonesia, and they were eager to help.

Unfortunately for Moscow, and despite all the talk about socialism, it would soon turn out that Sukarno was much more interested in foreign policy than in economics. Indonesian leaders tried their best to convince the Soviets that this was not the case in order to maintain Soviet support at a time of increasing confrontation with the West. Ruslan Abdulgani, deputy chairman of the newly created Supreme Advisory Council and one of the chief interpreters of the president's ideology, told Soviet ambassador

Boris Mikhailov in December 1960, "We began with the idea of Pancasila, then we crossed to socialism 'à la Indonesia,' then we started to talk about 'Indonesian Socialism.' Now I am already talking about scientific socialism, and in the future in this context it will be appropriate to speak directly about Marxism."[116] Similarly, Foreign Minister Subandrio told Mikhailov that Indonesia was undergoing a serious socialist revolution that the West opposed, that Sukarno was relying on the PKI, and that Indonesia's experiment was important because "neither [Jawaharlal] Nehru or [Gamal Abdel] Nasser has similar conceptions" and Indonesia was revealing itself as a "country of spiritual maturity" in its construction of socialism.[117] On paper, efforts were made in 1960 to make Sukarno's Indonesian Socialism program look real. An ambitious Eight-Year Plan was published in eight volumes, seventeen parts, and 1,945 clauses to celebrate the date of Indonesian independence.[118] A land reform law was enacted on September 24, 1960, to provide some relief to peasants from their obligations to their landlords, though very little was done to enforce it.[119] It was not an auspicious beginning for Indonesian Socialism.

The Soviets soon realized that there was very little practical effort behind the ideology and policies. When Abdulgani spoke of Indonesia's turn toward "scientific socialism," Mikhailov responded by asking what the government was doing about the shortages of rice.[120] A Soviet embassy report on the state of the Indonesian working class in May 1961 concluded that "the situation of the working class in Indonesia is continuing to deteriorate and is now worse than it was before the August 1945 revolution," adding, "the point of the program of Sukarno's government relating to the provision of laborers with food and clothing remains a promise on paper."[121] Eventually the Soviets would determine the fundamental source of the problem. A report on Indonesia's economic situation in 1962–1963 noted that the nation's military typically received 40 to 50 percent of the state budget, and in 1962 it had received 80 percent. As the author pointed out, "The irresistible and rapid rise of military expenditures appears as the most serious obstacle to the reappropriation of resources in the budget in the interests of material production and faster social-cultural progress."[122] The Soviet ambassador even told his mystified Australian colleague that he thought Indonesia should have no armed forces at all and should concentrate on building a "decent economy."[123]

Compounding the problem was the fact that the relative importance devoted to the military and foreign policy, as opposed to the economy, was opening a division between the PKI and the Soviets. While the Soviets had supported Guided Democracy in the hopes that it would help pave the way to socialism, the PKI had done so with the idea that, in Indonesia's current state, the nationalist revolution took precedence over the socialist one, and this made the priority of foreign policy a natural outcome. At a party plenum in December 1960, Aidit had openly declared that "the fundamental principle that we must hold in the conduct of the national struggle is the subsuming of the class struggle to the national struggle."[124] Lukman, in a programmatic May 1961 article in the PKI's *Harian Rak'iat,* interpreted the documents from the Moscow meeting of eighty-one communist parties held in November 1960 as licensing this PKI policy. He wrote that while in Europe the task was to unite all workers and laborers, in Africa, Asia, and Latin America it was to unite the workers with the nationalists, since nationalism in the developing world fell under Lenin's category of progressive nationalism. Consequently, "if we examine the content of the policies of the 'state of national democracy' [included in the Moscow Declaration of 1960], it turns out that it is identical with the program of the government of *gotong royong,* for the creation of which the PKI is fighting."[125] Lukman, who had attended the Moscow Meeting as the representative of the PKI, was asserting that the PKI, as all communist parties, had the right to determine its own course in finding the road to socialism in Indonesia.[126]

The Moscow meeting of 1960 would be the last international communist gathering attended by both the Chinese and Soviet Communist Parties, and it was the last moderately successful attempt to restore unity to the movement. In context, the PKI's stance in favor of the equality and independence of each communist party appeared to signal a tilt toward Beijing in the growing Sino-Soviet rift. Though it would take roughly three more years before the PKI would definitively side with the PRC, the party's tilt took place just as Sino-Indonesian relations were beginning to recover from their nadir. Beijing's policy toward Indonesia was complicated by the presence of some two million ethnic Chinese who tended to occupy a privileged economic position in the country, thus making them a target for ethnic resentment and violence.[127] This caused problems for the PKI as well, since, as the US embassy put it, "The Chinese in Indonesia with few exceptions are the 'bourgeoisie' of Marx' definition . . . the existence of Red Chinese usurers squeezing the poor peasants is an ideological absurdity from which the PKI cannot extricate itself."[128] The military also began to worry that the ethnic Chinese could become a fifth column that would help Beijing subvert Indonesia from the inside.

The citizenship status of these ethnic Chinese had been a bone of contention between the two countries since independence, but the situation reached a crisis point in late 1959 after the military introduced measures intended to drive ethnic Chinese out of the countryside.[129] After two Chinese women were murdered by Indonesian soldiers, however, Beijing and Jakarta stepped back from the precipice and gradually reduced tensions.[130]

Accommodation with Indonesia on the issue of ethnic Chinese was the beginning of a new effort on the part of Beijing to woo Jakarta. In July 1960 Khrushchev had suddenly removed all Soviet experts from the PRC, and the latter was now looking for international support as its Soviet alliance broke down. Indonesia, a large Asian country that was in the throes of an anti-imperialist campaign to incorporate West Irian, seemed like a promising potential ally. Unlike the Soviets, the Chinese took a dim view of the prospects for socialism in Indonesia, but they saw a glimmer of hope with regard to its anti-imperialism.[131] Chinese foreign minister Chen Yi visited Indonesia in April 1961, and Sukarno followed with a visit to China in June. In Beijing, Mao tried to egg Sukarno on by claiming that Nehru was trying to take the leadership of the anti-imperialist movement from him.[132] Though it paled in comparison to Soviet aid pledges, the PRC also gave Indonesia a $30 million credit for machinery and technical assistance.[133] While these moves signaled Beijing's reemergence as a player in Indonesia, it still had a lot of ground to make up vis-à-vis its competitors in Moscow and Washington.

Fortunately for Beijing, the PKI was also moving in its direction, albeit slowly and carefully. While the PKI asserted the equality and independence of communist parties, it still affirmed the leading role of the CPSU in the international communist movement, and its relations with Moscow had historically been closer than those with Beijing. The Twenty-Second CPSU Congress, held in October 1961, disturbed the PKI. Khrushchev took the opportunity to denounce Stalin even more strongly than he had in 1956, and he attacked the Albanian Communist Party, which was seen as a proxy for the Chinese. After the congress, Aidit and the PKI delegation traveled from Moscow to Beijing, where Mao told them that "Khrushchev is so reckless that he can do anything." Aidit continued to assert the Soviet position as head of the socialist camp, but he made a speech defending Albania, which he had refused to denounce at the congress.[134] Though the PKI was not eager to make enemies of powerful countries, it was clearly determined to chart its own path.

As Indonesian politics in 1961–1962 came to focus ever more intensely on the campaign for West Irian, with increasing saber-rattling on Sukarno's part, the PKI took the lead in mobilizing for the nationalist cause. Sukarno had to a large degree staked his prestige and the fate of Guided Democracy on the success of this campaign, and the PKI provided his loudest and most militant supporters.[135] The Soviets, hoping that a successful conclusion to the West Irian campaign would allow Sukarno to turn his focus on the economy, provided the military aid that allowed Sukarno's rhetoric to appear as more than just empty threats. In the process, Moscow even earned the admiration of many Indonesian military leaders, including Abdul Haris Nasution, the Indonesian defense minister and bête noire of the PKI, which saw him as the likeliest instigator of a military coup.[136] Massive Soviet military aid would lead to greater Soviet involvement with the Indonesian armed forces, including the training of officers in the USSR and the stationing of Soviet officers in Indonesia. While this was not the relationship that the Soviets had envisioned, it was more than enough to scare US president John F. Kennedy, who took the initiative in pressuring the Netherlands to settle before it came to war. In the elegant phrasing of former US secretary of state Dean Acheson, "the real interest of the West, including the Dutch, was not in ascertaining the doubtfully existent wishes of naked and illiterate Papuans about a sovereignty which they did not understand, but to prevent, for the sake of Australia, New Zealand, and the Philippines, a Communist takeover of West New Guinea through the collapse or other stratagem of Sukarno."[137] On August 15, 1962, an agreement was reached that was designed to eventually transfer West Irian to Indonesian sovereignty.

The years of the West Irian campaign had been disastrous for the Indonesian economy. Rampant escalation in government spending, nearly all of it going to the military, had produced catastrophic inflation. By March 1963 the black market rate for the Indonesian rupiah was 1,250 to the US dollar, at a time when an average worker earned only one thousand rupiah per month. The majority of the peasantry had largely cut itself off from the cash economy as a result, and as a consequence food was becoming scarcer in the cities. Indonesia could not afford to import many of the basic goods necessary for daily life, and this was only compounded by the fact that it had now acquired a vast territory with a poverty level higher than that in the rest of the country. Meanwhile, the nationalized Dutch enterprises had nearly all ended up in the hands of the military, which cut the government off from possible sources of revenue to be used for anything else.[138] At a session of the PKI Central Committee in March 1963, Aidit declared that Indonesian industry was on "the precipice of total catastrophe."[139] Clearly something had to be done to rescue the economy, and now Sukarno faced a choice. The USSR had been eager to help Indonesia build socialism and had even proved willing to provide massive amounts of military aid; now it was hoping that Sukarno would focus on the economy. But an economic turn toward Moscow would upset powerful constituencies both at home and abroad. The United States had also been hoping that Sukarno would turn his attention to economic development, and the Americans were busy putting together a rescue package for the Indonesian economy.[140] But the PKI—the only political force that Sukarno had to balance the military—was dead set against the acceptance of an American aid package. Finally, Sukarno could find a way to keep the mobilization going: if he found a new foreign policy cause around which to mobilize the country, he could maintain his regime in power without having to stabilize the economy. While Moscow and Washington wanted him to choose economic development, Beijing wanted him to launch a new anti-imperialist crusade.[141]

The New World Order in Flames, 1963–1965

On March 28, 1963, Sukarno seemed to turn his attention to the economy. His speech, which came to be known as the Economic Declaration called for a focus on immediate items of material consumption and improving productivity through better management and regulation, but did not go into much greater detail.[142] Aidit, seeking to further cement the PKI's relationship with Sukarno, immediately instructed all local party organizations to support the declaration. The Soviet embassy was much more skeptical, seeing it as yet more evidence that serious capital investment would be further delayed in favor of short-term measures.[143] On May 26, while Sukarno was away in Tokyo, the government of Prime Minister Djuanda introduced a series of measures, belatedly endorsed by Sukarno, that were largely in line with recommendations from the International Monetary Fund and seemed designed to pave the way for a large American aid package. These measures included the dismantling of price controls and subsidies, elimination of export duties, the revision of exchange rates, fiscal austerity, and some pension and wage hikes to balance price rises.[144] The austerity program inflicted immediate pain, and the PKI led the way in opposing them, accusing Djuanda of betraying Sukarno's Economic

Declaration. Aidit's private reaction was even more telling. In June he told East German diplomats that Djuanda and others who enacted the May 26 resolutions clearly wanted to turn Indonesia toward the "imperialists." Even so, he thought that the rhetoric of the "modern revisionists" (i.e., the Soviets) was also contributing to a "liberalizing tendency" and that Moscow was not dissatisfied with Djuanda's program. As for Sukarno, Aidit suspected that he was playing a more clever game: he might be using the regulations to both discredit Djuanda and stoke anti-imperialist sentiment in the country.[145]

Aidit might have been correct on his last point. Since the first conference of the Non-Aligned Movement in Belgrade in September 1961, Sukarno had been promoting a radical altering of the global power structure in favor of Africa, Asia, and Latin America, which he called the New Emerging Forces, to replace the Old Established Forces of Europe and North America.[146] As the Australian embassy wrote, "Sukarno is seeking to present himself as the spokesman of the whole anti-Western world."[147] In November 1963 Sukarno used the new sports stadium in Jakarta built by the Soviets to hold the first Games of the New Emerging Forces, which he hoped would replace the Olympics, though few countries sent their top athletes.[148] More significantly, Sukarno hoped to convene a Conference of the New Emerging Forces, which would replace the UN. This was music to the ears of the leaders in Beijing, as the PRC was excluded from the UN (and the International Olympic Committee) at this time; had recently broken with its superpower ally; and was also trying to construct an anti-imperialist coalition in Africa, Asia, and Latin America.[149]

This Sino-Indonesian understanding crystallized on the issue of Malaysia. The United Kingdom had assembled the Malaysian Federation from its former colonies on the Malay Peninsula and the northern part of the island of Borneo, but Sukarno had come to see it as a vehicle for maintaining imperialist influence in the region and containing Indonesia.[150] On February 13, 1963, he declared a policy, *Konfrontasi* (Confrontation), against Malaysia.[151] Though the ultimate aims of the policy were unclear, the Philippine government was also concerned about Malaysia, and the United States sought to organize some sort of negotiated settlement through the summer of 1963. For the Chinese, who similarly saw the creation of Malaysia as an act of Western containment, Sukarno's *Konfrontasi* was a gift.[152] Chen Yi and Liu Shaoqi visited Indonesia in April 1963 to meet with Sukarno and Subandrio, hoping to strengthen their resolve against Malaysia and use it to build their anti-imperialist alliance.[153] The discrepancy between Beijing's enthusiasm for *Konfrontasi* and Moscow's ambivalence was clear. Chen and Liu had come to balance the visit of Soviet defense minister Rodion Malinovsky to Indonesia, but the latter had not mentioned Malaysia once in public during his visit. Given the centrality that this issue would take on in Sukarno's anti-imperialist program, it is little wonder that the British embassy in Jakarta reported that Malinovsky's visit "was remarkable for the sparsenesss of the exchanges of compliments with which such occasions are usually larded here, and it has left no obvious residue of goodwill."[154] Though Moscow had recognized Indonesia's desire for West Irian as legitimate and provided the arms to make good on its claims, the Soviet leaders were not as convinced about the justice or wisdom of *Konfrontasi,* and they saw it as one more excuse to avoid devoting resources to the economy.

The Soviets also had more fundamental disagreements with the ideological direction that Sukarno was taking.[155] Sukarno's view of the world saw the primary conflict as between North and South, imperialism and anti-imperialism, rather than between East and West, communism and capitalism. It also seemed to identify the USSR, a superpower with a permanent UN Security Council veto, as part of the Old Established Forces. While the Soviets had grown accustomed to petit bourgeois ideological heresies arising in the postcolonial world, the rise of one so consonant with Maoism in such a large and strategically significant Asian country was particularly problematic. Adding to the problem was the fact that the PKI seemed to share this ideology.

While it certainly served the PKI to back Sukarno's *Konfrontasi,* the PKI had actually attacked the proposed Malaysia Federation as far back as July 1961.[156] This fit in with the PKI's official prioritization of the nationalist struggle over the class struggle, which now came to mirror the views of both Sukarno and the CCP on an international level. At a party plenum in December 1963, this alignment was made explicit, and the party declared that "there is no doubt that the contradiction between oppressed nations and imperialism is the main one."[157] The PKI now directly took on the CPSU, which at the Twenty-Second Congress in 1961 had adopted a program to build communism in the USSR by 1980. The PKI declared that "the attempt to achieve an abundance of material consumer goods contradicts proletarian internationalism, since the majority of peoples live in poverty and oppression. . . . The program of building communism is a subjective program, which weakens the revolutionary movement on a global scale."[158] In a conversation with the Soviet embassy,

Aidit said that he understood "proletarian internationalism" to mean that socialist countries should maintain their population at a subsistence level while devoting all surplus resources to the peoples of oppressed nations.[159] Privately, Aidit told the Chinese embassy that he thought the Soviets were really constructing capitalism.[160] The PKI had not only prioritized the struggle of South versus North over East versus West but had gone so far as declaring that domestic Soviet policy was in conflict with the interests of world revolution.

In February 1964 the Soviets sent a CPSU delegation to confront the PKI leaders about their pronouncements at the plenum.[161] Ironically, this time it was the Soviets who asked the Indonesians what gave them the right to criticize other communist parties. Unsurprisingly, the discussions did not improve the situation. While the Soviet delegation decided not to break with the PKI in the way that the CPSU had broken with the CCP, it began to look for ways to split the PKI and undermine its leadership. The delegation reported on differences within the leadership, paying close attention to who attended what meetings and who said what at them.[162] Njoto was thought to be the most definite pro-Chinese supporter, while Sudisman was more pro-Soviet, and Aidit could be swayed with the right sorts of carrots and sticks. Almost a year earlier, Aidit saw what was happening and told the visiting editor in chief of *Pravda* that "your comrades are trying to find 'dissenters' in our Party." He had begged for Soviet support, saying that he was trying to hold the politburo together because some were saying, "Let's take power by force of arms, like they did in Cuba," and he had gotten the politburo to decide that "we can and must prove that in Indonesia, a peaceful path to power is possible."[163] Now it seemed that the PKI had swung decisively toward Beijing, and the Soviets were no longer willing to offer support. From this point on the Soviets would approach the PKI less as a brother party than as another hostile element of an increasingly problematic Indonesian regime that they hoped to manipulate and undermine.

The remainder of 1964 would see an intense diplomatic struggle among the PKI, the PRC, Sukarno, and the USSR. None of the four seemed to completely trust any of the others, but aside from the Chinese and Soviets, who were now in a state of open rivalry, none felt it could afford to completely neglect its relationships with the others. The visit of Anastas Mikoyan, Khrushchev's deputy as chairman of the Council of Ministers, at the end of June well illustrated this dynamic. Mikoyan's main objective was to get Indonesia to endorse Soviet attendance at the Second

African-Asian Conference, scheduled to take place the following year, ten years after the first such conference in Bandung.[164] A preparatory conference had been held in Bandung in April, and the Indonesians had neglected to invite the Soviets, possibly at the instigation of the Chinese. Meanwhile, Sukarno's goal was to get the Soviets to openly endorse his policy of *Konfrontasi* against Malaysia, which would hopefully lead to more military aid and debt relief.[165] Both sides had mixed success at best. Mikoyan publicly proclaimed support for *Konfrontasi,* but behind closed doors he encouraged Sukarno to adopt a more "realistic" conciliatory policy toward Malaysia.[166] When Subandrio suggested changing the language of the joint communiqué from "Soviet people" to "Soviet government" in supporting the struggle against Malaysia, Mikoyan refused.[167] Meanwhile, though Mikoyan claimed he got Indonesian support for Soviet attendance at the Second Bandung Conference, the Chinese did not think so, and Indonesia's public position did not change.[168] Subandrio and Sukarno then followed Mikoyan's visit in the next few months with visits to Moscow, seeking arms and debt relief—largely succeeding in the latter while failing in the former.

Mikoyan's visit also had another goal: forcing the PKI back into line. In an eerie foreshadowing of events to come, Mikoyan told Aidit that seven thousand Indonesian military officers had been trained in the Soviet Union, that there were fifteen hundred Soviet military experts currently in Indonesia, and that while the Soviets had held back so far, "if the Soviet Party counterattacks, the Indonesian bourgeoisie will have a change in attitude, and it will not be good for the Indonesian Communist Party."[169] It was certainly very unusual for one communist party to threaten another with retaliation from the local bourgeoisie, but Aidit claimed not to be intimidated. (Ironically, Aidit would later tell the Soviet embassy that he saw the number of navy and air force officers trained in the USSR as a reason to have confidence that they would not oppose the PKI, buttressing the PKI's own efforts to win over the rank-and-file infantry.)[170] Meanwhile, the Chinese Foreign Ministry specifically instructed its diplomats not to respond to any provocations from Mikoyan during his visit.[171] Perhaps the PKI and the Chinese felt they were on the winning side, and it was Mikoyan whose actions spoke of desperation.

That the Soviets saw their position in Indonesia deteriorating is evidenced by the change in policy that followed Khrushchev's removal in October 1964. The new leadership under Leonid Brezhnev and Aleksei Kosygin gave full-throated support to Sukarno's confrontation with

Malaysia, and promised to supply Indonesia with any military help it requested. Yet the Soviets always seemed one step behind Sukarno. When he withdrew Indonesia from the UN on January 7, 1965, in protest over Malaysia's joining the Security Council, the Soviets could not support the move.[172] Meanwhile, the Chinese called it the "first spring thunder that awakens the world."[173] The PKI was unimpressed by the new Soviet leadership as well, telling the Chinese embassy that Brezhnev and Kosygin seemed "arrogant and stubborn [傲慢固执]."[174]

While the PKI might have felt itself to be winning the battle against the modern revisionists, it was becoming increasingly frustrated with its lack of progress in the government. The PKI had endorsed Guided Democracy and loyally supported Sukarno in the hopes that his program of Nasakomization would be realized—meaning that the PKI would be given influential posts in the cabinet. This had not happened, however, and Sukarno seemed to be willing, and perhaps intending, to put it off indefinitely. Now the PKI would attempt to advance matters by turning its attention to the villages, where it would champion the cause of poor and landless peasants by leading *aksi sepihak* (unilateral actions) against landlords in the countryside. At the December 1963 PKI Central Committee plenum, Aidit called for "radical land reform" that would go beyond the land reform law to seizing land by force and distributing it free to peasants.[175] In March 1964 Aidit told the East Germans, "Of decisive significance for the further leadership and development of the struggle [for Nasakomization] is the winning of the peasants, a task to which the PKI is presently devoting the greatest attention, to which the reaction is now turning as well."[176] The new policy seemed to reflect a new approach to gaining power that would combine political struggle in the center with more militant struggle in the countryside. As Aidit told the Central Committee, "Our cadres are aware of the fact that all national democratic revolutions in Asia that have won victory and have been able to follow up victory with speedy Socialist construction have been able to do this first and foremost because of the integration of the Marxist-Leninist parties and the peasants of the countries in question. The Cuban Revolution also won because of this."[177] Clearly the example of the PKI's increasingly close Chinese allies was becoming more significant.

The PKI's offensive in the countryside did not meet with the success the party hoped for. Attempts to seize land sparked a backlash from Islamic groups, who often found themselves defending lands held by religious leaders, mosques, and *awqaf* (religious endowments). The increasingly bloody confrontations caused Sukarno to call representatives of the ten remaining legal political parties to Bogor Palace on December 12, 1964. Sukarno engineered a compromise that would end the *aksi sepihak*, as well as ban an anti-PKI political group, the Body for the Promotion of Sukarnoism (BPS). This attempt to restore political stability would not last long. As the British embassy reported

> If Soekarno hoped by the rather facile maneuver of the Bogor Declaration and his subsequent opportunist dissolution of the BPS to put an end to the row between the PKI and the non-PKI, he failed. The upshot has been to leave the PKI riding high and the other side in disarray, and the rift in the country as wide as ever. Watching Soekarno is like watching a man at the circus riding two horses together. The animals have been badly trained and are now running further and further apart. If Soekarno is not to fall in the sawdust he has soon got to stick to one—and it will be the horse on the left.[178]

The PKI was not as confident as the British about which horse Sukarno would choose.

The year 1965 was violent and pivotal for the Cold War in Asia. American ground troops came ashore in South Vietnam. The Sino-Soviet split reached its apex, and the collapse of China's foreign policy strategy to build an anti-imperialist Afro-Asian coalition would set the stage for the explosion of the Great Proletarian Cultural Revolution the following year. War between India and Pakistan transformed the geopolitical configuration of South Asia. And in Indonesia, the fifth most populous country in the world—which sat astride the sea lanes between the Indian and Pacific Oceans and where the world's third largest communist party seemed to be closer to power than any other nonruling communist party in the world—the volatile political situation that had been building for at least a decade reached a bloody and tragic climax.

Much has been written about the events of 1965 in Indonesia, and it would be beyond the scope of this chapter to attempt to recapitulate all of them in detail.[179] Much about these events also remains unknown and is a matter of great dispute, not only among scholars but within contemporary Indonesian society, where the narratives and interpretations of the events of 1965 hold great moral and political significance. Rather than attempt a comprehensive narrative, the present discussion will limit itself to a few points that newly available materials in China and Russia can help illuminate.

While in 1964 the PRC, the PKI, Sukarno, and the USSR were still trying to find ways to work with each other, at least for instrumental reasons, the divisions became starker in 1965. Despite the continuing deterioration of the Indonesian economy, already exacerbated by the termination of almost all American aid following Sukarno's March 1964 public outburst at the US ambassador ("to hell with your aid!"), he seemed willing to let the aid relationship with Moscow deteriorate as well.[180] Though various Indonesian officials kept telling their Soviet counterparts that Sukarno was still interested in the planned aid projects, the resources that Indonesia was supposed to provide did not materialize, Soviet equipment arriving in Indonesian ports was mysteriously held up or damaged, and, according to the Soviet ambassador, the Indonesians no longer even bothered asking for extensions on their debt; they just stopped paying.[181] With hostility and suspicion on both sides, it looked like the aid relationship might collapse completely. As Subandrio told Chen in August 1965, it was quite possible that in the coming days either the Soviets would publicly abandon Indonesia or Sukarno would tell Moscow "to hell with your aid," just as he had done with Washington.[182] Though the PRC was not in a position to replace Soviet economic aid to Indonesia, Beijing did provide a new $50 million credit in 1965, and Chinese trade with Indonesia now exceeded Soviet trade, leading the Soviet ambassador to conclude that Indonesia was, in fact, trying to make the PRC its primary economic benefactor.[183] There was at least one form of aid Indonesia wanted that Moscow had refused and Beijing could provide: nuclear weapons. The PRC had tested its first nuclear weapon in October 1964, and now Subandrio told Chen that Indonesia also wanted the bomb but had been denied it by the Soviets.[184] Chen responded by promising Subandrio that China would increase its economic and military aid, and the following month the Indonesians sent a delegation to the PRC that visited nuclear facilities, among others. As the head of the Indonesian delegation told his Chinese hosts, "If Indonesia had nuclear missiles, American imperialism would not dare attack."[185]

Relations between the PKI and the Soviets nearly came to the point of a complete break, and the Soviets started cultivating other forces in Indonesia, including certain military officers and rival political parties. In April the Soviet ambassador recommended expanding ties with the PNI and even Islamic groups and parties.[186] In particular, the Soviets began cultivating relations with the Murba Party, a small group led by former acolytes of Tan Malaka that the USSR had once labeled Trotskyite but was now considering building into a replacement party for the PKI.[187] The PKI leaders were well aware of Soviet machinations to build up the Murba Party, and complained about it to Mao.[188] Aidit even protested to the Soviet embassy, "However bad you think the Indonesian Communists are, they are closer to you than the Murba and other such parties."[189] Ultimately the Soviets stepped back from the brink and did not back the Murba Party, but it was telling that they even considered it at a time when they were accusing China of splitting the communist movement.

These political shifts might have had an impact on the events that were to follow. While an anti-Western foreign policy was popular and understandable given Indonesia's history, now it seemed to have taken sides not only in the Cold War but also in the Sino-Soviet dispute. The Soviet Union, which had close ties to the Indonesian military, seemed a far more stable and desirable patron to much of the non-PKI political establishment in Indonesia. Sukarno's increasingly open identification with Beijing, culminating in his August 17, 1965, declaration of a Jakarta–Phnom Penh–Hanoi–Beijing–Pyongyang axis, frightened military leaders who saw their positions threatened by the proposal for a "fifth force," a popular militia championed by the PKI, which had also originated from Beijing.[190] The break between the PKI and the Soviets might have had a similarly destabilizing impact. As long the Soviets still held some influence in the PKI and PKI leaders looked to maintain their relations with Moscow, voices in the party calling for patience and restraint—based on the gradual, nonviolent path to power promoted by the Soviets—held more weight in the party. Once the Soviets were seen to have betrayed the PKI, it became significantly more difficult for anyone inside the party to advocate for what seemed like revisionist policies.

What exactly happened on September 30, 1965, and the days that followed has long been the subject of intense debate. Nevertheless, it seems increasingly clear that the killing that night of six top Indonesian generals and the subsequent declaration of a Revolutionary Council led by Untung bin Syamsuri was at least in part organized by the leaders of the PKI to decapitate its military opponents. This is supported by the careful research of John Roosa, who concludes that the plan was put in motion by Aidit, working with a group of military officers led by Sjam, who was in charge of the PKI's Special Bureau, its covert arm.[191] It does not seem that the PKI was trying to remove Sukarno; rather, it was likely hoping to eliminate competitors for his eventual succession. The plot was put down within hours by units led by Suharto, and despite the publication of a

Harian Rak'iat editorial supporting the Revolutionary Council on October 2, the PKI mounted little effective resistance to Suharto. But the conclusion that the PKI leadership ultimately chose to remove its opponents by force only prompts a deeper question: Why would the PKI, the most powerful political party in the country, with over three million members of its own and possibly over twenty million in affiliated organizations, and which had managed to effectively create a triangular alliance with Sukarno and Beijing, risk it all in a violent confrontation with Indonesia's armed forces?

Three factors seem to have a played a crucial role: the PKI's frustration with its political progress and a growing belief that power could only be achieved through violence; a belief that the PKI was now large and powerful enough, with enough support in the military itself, to take power; and a possible expectation of outside assistance. Soviet documents relating to the coup should be treated cautiously, since it is possible that the Soviets were influenced by the information put out by Suharto's forces—and, in any case, by this point they were quite hostile to both the PKI and the PRC. Nevertheless, it is also likely that the Soviets still had informants inside the PKI and therefore had better information than the Americans, British, and others, and their top secret communications would be less likely to be influenced by propaganda. According to the top secret report of the Soviet ambassador following the coup, in the wake of the PKI's massive forty-fifth anniversary celebrations of May 1965, the PKI leaders "decided to begin a premature forcing of the struggle for power."[192] This decision was prompted by the PKI's "overestimation of the 'revolutionary-ness' of the situation in the country, too much attention paid to the parades and demonstrations of strength by the PKI, including in the ranks of the military," and an overestimation of Sukarno, who was, after all, a "petit bourgeois left liberal," and a "temporary fellow traveler [*poputchik*], especially in the struggle against the military forces."[193] Aidit himself had told a delegation of Soviet academics in March 1965 that the Central Committee of the PKI was becoming increasingly doubtful that a "dictatorship of the proletariat" could be established in Indonesia without a civil war.[194] The PKI action was a tremendous disappointment for Moscow, because "Until the events of September 30 the PKI in Indonesia disposed of rare possibilities for coming to power without an armed uprising or, at least, with minimal casualties and losses." According to the ambassador's report, "this process [of political development in Indonesia] could have continued to the benefit of the PKI, had its leadership not, under the influence of Chinese schismatics, departed from fundamental Marxist-Leninist positions, and not crossed over to the schismatic platform of the CCP leadership."[195]

Despite the clearly polemical tone of the Soviet ambassador's report with regard to the role of the Chinese, it does seem that Chinese leaders were, at minimum, informed of the PKI's plans in advance, at a time when they were also beginning to become disillusioned with Sukarno.[196] In a conversation with Aidit on August 5, 1965, Mao, referencing the concerns over Sukarno's health, said to the PKI leader, "It is possible this year, next year, or the year after you will have to seize power. First, do you dare seize power?" Aidit laid out a fairly accurate picture of the events two months later: "If the first possibility [a military attack on the PKI] occurs, we plan to establish a military committee, whose left wing would hold the top position but would also include centrists in order to confuse our enemies. It would make the enemies unable to discern its true nature, and therefore the center-right-leaning regional military commanders would not oppose us right away. If we raise the red banner right away, they will oppose us immediately. The leader of this military committee would be an underground member of our party, but he would identify as a centrist. The term of this military committee should not be too long. If it is too long, good people will turn bad. After the military committee is established, we would immediately arm the workers and peasants."[197] No evidence from the Chinese archives has yet come to light confirming any active Chinese support for the PKI's plan. A secret report from the Soviet embassy in Jakarta, however, said that PKI members told them that China offered military aid to the PKI, and a report from the Southeast Asia division of the Soviet Foreign Ministry claimed that the Chinese supplied arms in advance to the coup participants.[198] Though these reports cannot be taken as definitive, given the fact that Aidit told Mao in advance about the plot, it does seem likely that, at very least, Aidit expected Chinese support to be forthcoming.

Despite all the plotting and speculation from the Chinese and Soviets— as well as the Americans and British—in the immediate aftermath of the coup, none of the four outside powers seemed to know exactly what was happening or had a plan in place to deal with it. At the time of the coup, Chaerul Saleh, formerly a member of the Murba Party, and Ali Sastroamidjojo, the former prime minister and PNI leader, were in Beijing, and their hosts were still talking about ways to continue cooperation with Indonesia.[199] Meanwhile, Brezhnev, Kosygin, and Mikoyan sent a letter to

Sukarno urging that the political turmoil not damage Soviet-Indonesian relations, while a Central Committee resolution decided "not to take any steps on our side that might be perceived as support for one of the groups struggling for power in Indonesia." Moscow also hoped that "the military circles, in the event of their securing power, would be interested in strengthening Soviet-Indonesian relations."[200] Meanwhile, after a few days of indecision, the Americans and the British soon figured that this was their big chance to deal the PKI a decisive blow, and they began to worry that the military would not take full advantage without their prodding. The British political adviser to the commander in chief in Singapore wrote to the Foreign Office, "Confused though the situation in Indonesia may be, it seems clear that during the past few days the army have had an opportunity to break the power of the PKI that will not recur. It is also becoming increasingly apparent that they may be letting this opportunity slip through their fingers. . . . It is not in our interests to see the PKI recovering its influence and preparing itself for the day when it will be strong enough to seize power. I submit that we should not miss the present opportunity to use the situation to our advantage. I, of course, agree that we should not indicate support for any particular group in Indonesia, but I recommend that we should have no hesitation in doing what we can to surreptitiously blacken the PKI in the eyes of the army and the people of Indonesia."[201] The American role in the subsequent massacres has been well-chronicled.[202] Though estimates vary widely, over the coming months roughly half a million communists and suspected communists would be killed, including Aidit, Lukman, and Njoto. While the Chinese, Soviets, and others planned for the revival of the PKI, just as it had been revived after 1926 and 1948, this time it would not recover.

A shock of the magnitude of the destruction of the PKI could not but have significant repercussions for communists around the world. The PKI as a party and Indonesia as a country had been Beijing's most important allies in the Sino-Soviet split, and with the demise first of the PKI and subsequently of Sukarno, the PRC's chances of leading a meaningful segment of the international communist movement virtually disappeared. Outrage in mainland China against the persecution of communists and ethnic Chinese in Indonesia inflamed popular passions and was turned into fuel for the radical mobilization of the Cultural Revolution, which gained steam throughout 1966. As Zhou Taomo writes, "The PRC propaganda machine depicted the turmoil in Indonesia as part of a 'vicious anti-China, anti-Chinese wind all over the world' that required the Chinese people to further advance their revolution." Association with the policy of collaborating with bourgeois leaders like Sukarno was used as part of the justification for the persecution of Liu Shaoqi and the consolidation of Mao's power.[203]

The USSR, which maintained relations with the Suharto regime and even continued some of its aid projects under Suharto's so-called New Order, evinced unseemly glee in its use of the PKI's demise as a cautionary tale for any who were tempted to follow the siren call of Maoism. At a Soviet party plenum in December 1966, Brezhnev declared that the PKI had taken an "adventurist, putschist tack" under Aidit's leadership and that the destruction of such a vast party was "the price they paid for leaving the international communist movement and following China." Two months before the coup a PKI delegation had come to Moscow, and Brezhnev warned it about the consequences of the path the party was on. But then, according to Brezhnev, the delegation went on to Beijing, where it was instructed to organize an armed putsch. Ultimately, according to the Soviet general secretary, it was the Chinese who were responsible for the disaster.[204]

But simply blaming the Chinese would not be enough. Part of the reason that the PKI had taken a violent path was because many of its leaders had become frustrated with their lack of progress toward achieving political power through other means. The Soviets might have imagined that had the PKI simply been more patient, it would have attained power eventually. But the Aidit leadership was in place for fifteen years, and for most of that time it had followed Moscow's lead pretty faithfully. What lessons could the Soviets learn from the tragic experience of the PKI that they could apply elsewhere? There were many other parties struggling with some of the same issues as the PKI, including an underdeveloped agrarian economy, the prevalence of postcolonial nationalism, the prominence of religion in politics, and the presence of a charismatic leader.

For starters, the experience of the PKI would spark a Soviet reevaluation of the role of Islam in the process of socialist revolution. The PKI had perpetually found itself subject to the accusation that it was against religion, a potentially fatal flaw in the world's largest Muslim nation. PKI leaders tried to deal with this by appealing to a syncretic religious tradition, emphasizing their tolerance, and trying at times to work with Islamic parties, particularly the NU. In a speech on September 27, 1964, Aidit had threatened to punish anyone engaged in antireligious propaganda, even remarking, "Whoever speaks against religion is not a communist."[205] The Soviet embassy criticized this, saying that, of course, communists must be careful in a Muslim country, but threatening expulsion for those who speak against religion was too much.[206] In his report on the events of September 30, the Soviet ambassador followed the time-honored Soviet tradition of criticizing others for one's own mistakes. He wrote that, in PKI strategy, "There had not been sufficient value given to the purely religious Muslim factor in the country, keeping in mind that the absolute majority of the people are deep believers."[207] A few years later, Alla Ionova, the leading Soviet scholar of Indonesian Islam, wrote a monograph that explored in depth the role of Islam in national politics and the ways in which it had been used to defeat the PKI.[208] Meanwhile, in January 1966, the deputy head of the International Department of the CPSU, Rostislav Ul'ianovskii, wrote an article in the theoretical journal *Kommunist* arguing that religious views that were not fanatical or counterrevolutionary were not an obstacle to socialism, and that socialists should find ways to work with religious activists.[209] The Soviets would begin to pay greater attention to Islam not only as a possible obstacle to socialism but also as a means to serve the purposes of socialism, treating it as a potentially positive force in the national liberation movement.[210]

The experience of trying to engineer a transition to a socialist economy under a radical petit bourgeois nationalist like Sukarno was also instructive for Moscow. Someone like Sukarno, despite his anti-imperialist outbursts and occasional flirtations with socialist ideology, would always be untrustworthy, unwilling to truly take decisive steps that would undermine the class interests of his bourgeois supporters; at crucial moments he would likely betray the revolution. Even before that point, Sukarno was driven to increasingly desperate flights of nationalist fancy because of his fundamental unwillingness to tackle the serious work of economic transformation.[211] This did not mean that the Soviets, or local communist parties, should not work with nationalist leaders of Sukarno's ilk. In many countries such arrangements were unavoidable, and in any case, making enemies of all such postcolonial charismatic nationalist leaders would be a fatal error in the Cold War competition. The PKI had gone too far in its optimistic reliance on Sukarno, however. A delegation of Czechoslovak engineers touring rural Indonesian in 1963 had remarked on this phenomenon among the PKI rank and file, writing that "President Sukarno should be the defensive shield of the Party. Among the masses, the Party is becoming the defensive shield of Sukarno."[212] In the end, according to the Soviet ambassador, Sukarno had turned out to be nothing more than a petit bourgeois left liberal and a "temporary fellow traveler [*poputchik*]."[213] Therefore, the limitations of such figures had to be kept in mind, and they should never be mistaken for the real thing—that is, an actual Marxist Moses who could lead his nation to the socialist promised land. The true vehicle for socialist revolution was the party, not radical bourgeois leaders, and should remain so.

Sukarno's dominant position, however, stemmed in part from another Soviet error: support for his destruction of the parliamentary system and his creation of Guided Democracy. It will be recalled that the Soviets were earlier and more enthusiastic supporters of the transition to Guided Democracy than the PKI leaders themselves. This was the most evident criticism in ex post facto Soviet academic critiques, though once again it was either the PKI or Sukarno that was blamed for the mistake, not Soviet policy makers.[214] According to one collective work put out by the Orientalist Institute under the editorship of Ul'ianovskii, the PKI misunderstood Sukarno's intentions and put too much faith in his benevolent intentions when it should have defended parliamentary democracy.[215] The Soviet shift evidenced in these works from 1969 to 1970 in favor of the benefits of a democratic system that allowed for the legal operation of the communist party over a (noncommunist) authoritarianism was well timed. Across the Pacific Ocean from Indonesia, a self-declared Marxist was about to become the democratically elected president of Chile. Moscow's strategy, shared with the Chilean Communist Party, would be centered on adherence to the constitution and the preservation of the democratic system.[216]

The experience of the PKI was also illustrative of the relations between communist parties in what the Soviets and others referred to as the "international communist movement." As the largest nonruling communist party in the world, the PKI continually asserted its independence and its right to chart its own theoretical and political path. When the Soviets accused PKI leaders of siding with the Chinese in 1964 by criticizing the CPSU's party program, Aidit responded by saying that the PKI leaders intended to also go to Beijing and criticize the Chinese for their ambitions to build communism.[217] At the same time, the PKI leaders actively sought out Soviet advice on their own domestic political strategy. One of their stated goals in visiting the USSR in 1961 was to get Moscow's advice on their relationship with Sukarno.[218] It was a relationship not merely defined by the question of independence or lack thereof from Moscow (or Beijing); it also imposed obligations and restrictions on the Chinese and Soviets. As frustrated as the Soviets became with the PKI, they ultimately stopped short of actually allying with the Murba Party or creating an alternative communist party. The relationship operated neither as a patron-client arrangement nor as an alliance between equals. Instead it looked more like a franchise system, in which the local communist leaders were basically licensed to operate the local franchise of the international communist movement, while headquarters in Moscow looked after the interests of the brand as a whole.

2

DEMOCRATIC COMMUNISM

Allende's Chile and Peaceful Transition

To Salvador Allende, who is trying to obtain the same result
by other means. Affectionately, Che.

—Che Guevara, dedication of his *Guerrilla Warfare*
as personal gift to Salvador Allende

"Ours will be a revolution, Chilean-style, with red wine and empanadas" announced Chilean president Salvador Allende Gossens at a press conference soon after assuming office.[1] In an era of militant revolutionary iconography—young leaders in army fatigues, Kalashnikov-toting Viet Cong, millions waving copies of Mao Zedong's Little Red Book containing quotes such as "power comes from the barrel of a gun" and "a revolution is not a dinner party"—the Chilean revolution stood out as the shining example of what became known as peaceful transition. While its Leninist origins became a matter of endless debate and speculation, the concept of peaceful transition had only become a central element of Soviet policy along with the introduction of the notion of peaceful coexistence at the Twentieth Congress of the Communist Party of the Soviet Union (CPSU) in 1956, which was more famous for Nikita Khrushchev's "Secret Speech" exposing Joseph Stalin's crimes. Peaceful coexistence entailed eschewing military confrontation in favor of economic competition with the capitalist world on the international scene. Peaceful transition was its domestic counterpart, prescribing the achievement of socialist revolution through peaceful domestic political competition, particularly but not solely through electoral means rather than armed insurgency. Mao and his fellow leaders in the People's Republic of China (PRC) rejected the concept of peaceful transition, asserting that revolution could only be achieved through armed struggle, or a "people's war"; the debate over whether revolution could only be accomplished through violence became central to the Sino-Soviet split that rent the international communist movement in the 1960s. The Partai Komunis Indonesia (PKI; Indonesian Communist Party) had seemed for a while to be the great exemplar of the peaceful path until its top leaders tragically opted for a seizure of power on September 30, 1965, that Moscow blamed on the nefarious influence of Beijing.

The explicit justification for the promotion of this model was the danger of small, local wars escalating into a world war, but there was also an element of recognition of changes in the capitalist world. With Western Europe recovering rapidly from the devastation of World War II, the chances of an immediate seizure of power, particularly by the French and Italian Communist Parties, seemed to be receding. As the capitalist world in general boomed economically in the 1950s and 1960s, the appetite for militant struggle among workers who were increasingly prosperous and benefiting from an enhanced welfare state began to disappear. Some on the left sought to resolve this difficulty by summoning alternative "proletariats." Herbert Marcuse, taking his cue from the American political scene in the 1960s, famously offered students and oppressed minorities as alternatives, invoking sexual as well as economic oppression in the process.[2] Soviet theoreticians, however, were having none of this, and they attacked Marcuse with a particular vehemence.[3] Soviet policy instead remained committed to the idea of a revolution, at least in the developed capitalist world, led by communist parties and working classes. This was necessary not only for the revolutions within the capitalist countries themselves but because the Soviet global conception of revolution depended upon the idea that national liberation movements in the developing world needed the leadership of the international working-class movement in order to follow a "noncapitalist path" to a socialist future. In Soviet writings, the international working-class movement was always labeled first in historical significance over the national liberation movement.[4] Peaceful transition was thus an essential element of the evolving Soviet conception of the world revolution against capitalism.

For the Chinese, however, peaceful transition was a further manifestation of Moscow's lack of revolutionary will; it was simply another way for Moscow to lessen the chances of a confrontation with the West, and it therefore showed the Soviet Union's willingness to betray the oppressed peoples of the world for the sake of an accommodation with its fellow white, industrialized nations. Any new state or party that had not gained power through violent means would inevitably fall victim to neocolonialism because the ties with the former colonial power, as well as the power of local elites, would remain intact. Chinese diplomats closely monitored Soviet promotion of the peaceful transition model and labeled any other parties or countries that promoted it as revisionist.[5] The PRC found a strong ally for its approach in the Cuban leadership, which had taken power through violent means and without the participation of a local communist party that had been committed to the parliamentary path. Both Beijing and Havana promoted Cuba as a model for the rest of Latin America. But the predominant view among the other communist parties in Latin America was strongly committed to the Soviet line of the peaceful path, which led to resentment of Cuban interference in their internal affairs and, ultimately, a harsh divide between Cuba and the other Latin American parties.[6] The continuing Cuban efforts to ignite armed revolt on the mainland strained Cuban-Soviet relations to the breaking point. While the Soviet leadership was reluctant to go as far as labeling Cuba an adversary, like the PRC, by 1967 Leonid Brezhnev admitted that it had become hard to see the difference between the two.[7] The Cultural Revolution in China only exacerbated the tension between Beijing and Moscow over the notion of the peaceful path as Beijing began an unprecedented effort to promote the most militant aspects of Maoist thought just at the time that revolutionary energies were exploding in the capitalist world outside the staid control of the established, Soviet-oriented communist parties. Moscow tried to stem the tide by infiltrating such militant organizations as the Black Panthers with loyal communists, but as the Soviet ambassador to the United States, Anatoly Dobrynin, wrote to Andrei Gromyko in March 1970, Maoist and Trotskyite groups were multiplying too quickly to be controlled.[8] Dobrynin could offer little in the way of strategies to stem the tide besides efforts to increase the "average American's" fear of China.[9] Without an authentic revolution to match the dramatic images of events taking place in Algeria, Congo, Cuba, and Vietnam, among other places, there was little that the Soviets could do to recapture the revolutionary imagination of Western students and the developing world for the peaceful path.

It was in this context that Chile suddenly came to the fore. The Partido Comunista (PC; Communist Party) had been committed to the peaceful path long before 1956 because of a history of electoral success through cooperation with other leftist parties.[10] During the early years of the Sino-Soviet split, the party had been such an enthusiastic supporter of the Twentieth Congress line that, during the brief period in late 1964 after the removal of Khrushchev when it seemed possible that the new Soviet leadership might try to reconcile with the Chinese Communist Party, the Chilean party's general secretary, Luis Corvalán, told a visiting Soviet delegation that if the USSR did reconcile with the PRC, Chile would not be able to follow.[11]

Meanwhile, the Frente de Acción Popular (Popular Action Front), which had joined the PC and the Partido Socialista (PS; Socialist Party) since the latter's reunification in the late 1950s, had nearly won the presidency through the candidacy of Allende in 1958; by 1964 it had caused those on the right and in the center to ally in order to prevent a leftist victory. Consequently, by 1970 few countries had a longer tradition of electoral success on the part of Marxist parties or a more realistic chance of putting the peaceful path into practice. When this eventuality finally came to fruition with that year's election, the Soviet leadership was well aware of its significance. At a party plenum in March 1971, while introducing the foreign policy section of the address that he intended to give at the upcoming Twenty-Fourth CPSU Congress, Brezhnev remarked,

> In connection with the situation in Latin America, space is allotted to the recent victory of the forces of National Unity [Unidad Popular, or UP] in Chile. For obvious reasons at the congress this will be talked about rather guardedly, but here in our auditorium it is possible to add that the coming to power of communists and socialists through the constitutional path—if, of course, they manage to hold on to power and realize their declared program (in substance a program for building socialism)—it will have immense principal significance and could seriously influence the further development of many Latin American countries.[12]

Despite the closed nature of the plenum, the Chilean regime became aware of Brezhnev's remark.[13]

And yet, as Brezhnev noted, success was far from assured. The new UP government was composed of a coalition of parties with different political agendas that would somehow have to be unified for the government to be effective. Parties outside the ruling coalition—primarily the Partido Demócrata Cristiano (PDC; Christian Democratic Party) and the Partido Nacional (Nationalist Party)—controlled the majority of seats in

MAP 2.1
Chile in 1970.

both houses of Congress, the Chilean Senate and Chamber of Deputies, throughout Allende's tenure in power. The Chilean system staggered the presidential and congressional elections, meaning that, until 1973, Allende governed with the Congress that had preceded his accession; furthermore, since only half of the seats in the Senate were up for election, the achievement of a majority would have been nearly impossible. But the opposition, as the Christian Democrats and Nationalists came to be known once the two largely coalesced by the beginning of 1972, never managed to gain enough seats to impeach Allende, and so relations between the administration and the Congress remained hostile but stalemated. There were also forces on the extreme left that had never bought into the notion of the peaceful path but retained an outsize political influence both inside and outside the UP. Finally, there was the matter of Allende himself, a heterodox character from the Soviet perspective, who seemed to think that Chile was not following anyone else's path but instead charting its own, a "Chilean path" that constituted "a second model of the transition to a socialist society," the first being the dictatorship of the proletariat.[14] Consequently, it remained to be seen not only if the UP government would survive but exactly what kind of government it would turn out to be and what that would mean for the model of peaceful transition the world over.

The Chilean experiment was therefore one that held tremendous significance for the possibilities for socialist revolution around the world. Success could mean a chance of breaking through the de facto division of the world imposed in the late 1940s and instead charting a path forward for revolution in capitalist countries, particularly in Latin America, as well as France and Italy. Success would also mean disproving the Chinese argument that revolution could only be made by force of arms. For Moscow, however, danger remained in the fact that the Chilean experiment could prove something altogether unexpected given the variety of ideological positions inside the UP and the lack of Soviet control. For Beijing, the Chilean case provided an intriguing dilemma: on the one hand, it seemed to provide a test case for the Soviet theory of peaceful transition, but on the other, Allende's Chile followed an anti-imperialist Third World foreign policy and became tremendously popular in the developing world, precisely at the time that China was trying to recover diplomatically from the Cultural Revolution. Complicating matters further was the fact that many political actors on the far left in Chile, inside and outside the government, drew inspiration from Maoism in their attempts to accelerate the revolutionary process.

80

For Allende and the UP government this meant that while they had predicated their hopes for success on receiving extensive support from the socialist countries, in the end both Beijing and Moscow supported the Allende regime only to the extent that it served their respective global agendas. The Soviets, in close concert with the PC, particularly through the involvement of the German Democratic Republic (GDR), attempted to mold Allende's policy to fit the line of peaceful transition, slowly implementing socioeconomic reforms while trying to build an enduring political base for the regime among the middle classes, the military, and the media. The Chinese, on the other hand, supported Allende in his anti-imperialist foreign policy, particularly in his confrontations with the United States, but never took seriously his program of socialist revolution, and ultimately they had little trouble maintaining relations with the subsequent military regime under General Augusto Pinochet. The result was a mirror image of the fallout after the failed Indonesian coup of 1965, when the USSR maintained relations with Suharto while the PRC cut off relations with Indonesia. These ideological divisions were not simply imposed from outside, however. Rather, they reflected real disagreements within the UP coalition and the broader Chilean Left. The ideological divides within the UP over issues such as the resort to arms, the speed of the revolution, the relative weight of the peasants versus the workers, and the relationship to so-called bourgeois reformists ultimately prevented the government from producing a coherent plan and following through on it—something that both East Berlin and Moscow identified as the fundamental failures of the regime in their respective postmortems. In the context of the bitter ideological divisions among socialist countries in the 1960s—chiefly between the PRC and the USSR, but including Cuba, North Vietnam, Romania, Yugoslavia, and others—these disagreements between left-wing politicians inside Chile took on new levels of hostility and political significance. They not only made it difficult to get sufficient external support without alienating potential allies but also polarized political debates by turning differences about policies into litmus tests of who or what was considered revolutionary. The effect of this polarization on the UP government, and its role in the fall of the regime, are evident in the mutual hostility and suspicion that characterized relations between the constituent parties in the UP because they sabotaged each other, and Allende, in the battle to implement their particular revolutionary visions. Without the achievement of internal political unity and cooperation in the implementation of a political agenda, along with the committed support of foreign socialist powers, Chile's UP government stood little chance of facing down a determined opposition.

The Chilean Left in the 1960s

In the decade before the election of Allende, the Chilean Left presented a picture of variety and possibility with few analogues elsewhere. Despite the prohibition of the PC from 1948 to 1958, the country had a stronger tradition of democracy, as well as political diversity and participation, than any other in Latin America at the time. This produced a political scene that contained two self-proclaimed working-class parties with significant electoral support, the PC and PS, which had been electoral allies since the formation of the Frente de Acción Popular in 1956. In addition, there were two large centrist parties increasingly committed to fundamental socioeconomic reform—namely, PDC and the Partido Radical (PR; Radical Party). To the right, the Conservative Party and Liberal Party seemed to be losing support, as they were obliged first in 1964 to support the candidacy of the Christian Democrat Eduardo Frei Montalva in order to avoid an Allende victory and later to merge and form the Partido Nacional. To the far left, Chinese and Cuban influence helped to produce motley groups composed largely of students and intellectuals, some of them former or current members of the PC or PS who rejected the electoral path altogether. The latter situation did also occur, however, in many other Latin American countries. What distinguished the Chilean situation were three factors. First was the fact that, unlike in most other countries, the PC and PS actually cooperated most of the time. Second, the support of the political center for fundamental change seemed to indicate that capitalism had been rejected by the majority of the population. Third, the apparent resilience of the constitutional tradition—and, in particular, the loyalty of the military to that tradition—indicated that the results of elections would be respected and therefore revolution by electoral means would be possible.

The earliest of the parties of the Chilean Left to emerge was the PC. It had been formed at the beginning of 1922 under the leadership of Luis Recabarren Serrano, finding support primarily among the copper and nitrate miners in the north. It soon also established an electoral stronghold in the extreme south of the country, an area of the dispossessed Mapuche, as well as poor fisherman and farmers; it was from the latter that the party's later general secretary, Corvalán, would emerge.[15] From the days of the Frente Popular (Popular Front), formed of the PR and PS in the 1930s, the PC maintained a line of cooperation with other leftist parties and the pursuit of an electoral strategy. The party gained a reputation as being unfailingly loyal to Moscow, so much so that it operated as a sort of adviser for the Soviets on Latin American affairs.[16] The respect for the PC, and Corvalán in particular, in Moscow would later be reflected in the efforts put forth to rescue him from imprisonment after the coup.[17]

Yet not all members of the party were satisfied with the strategy of the leadership. The PC was riven by factionalism repeatedly in the 1950s and 1960s over the issue of adherence to the peaceful path. In a May 1957 party plenum speech expelling factional leader Luis Reinoso for attempting to lead an armed revolt against the dictatorship of Gonzalez Videla, Corvalán pointed out that Reinoso was "pretending to justify his policy by taking a foothold in certain positions of the Brazilian comrades, who, basing themselves on certain theses of the Chinese comrades, share the belief that the revolution in Latin America will inevitably have the character of armed struggle, or that this is the most recommended path."[18] This was well before the Cuban Revolution and the immense influence it would have on the Latin American Left.[19] By the time of the Twelfth PC Congress in March 1962, and with the growth of the Sino-Soviet split and the example of Cuba, dissension within the PC over the issue of armed struggle had reached significant proportions. The leadership responded by prohibiting the dissemination of Maoist literature, but a small group within the party, calling itself Espartaco (Spartacus), began publishing Chinese polemics in its own journal; this led in October 1963 to the group's expulsion from the party. By the beginning of 1966 this group of dissenters had become the nucleus of a new party, the Partido Comunista Revolucionario (PCR; Revolutionary Communist Party), which held its first congress that year and networked with similar parties across Latin America.[20] Though the PCR's significance on the Chilean political scene was negligible, its influence on the PC itself was not. The leadership of the PC under Corvalán had tied its own political power and credibility to the notion of the *vía pacifica* (peaceful path), and it was very aware of how easily alternative positions could find support within the party. The speech of politburo member Orlando Millas at that same Twelfth Congress pointed to the difficulties for the regional party committees in propagating the peaceful path in the face of rank-and-file members who "do not ad-equately understand this thesis."[21] The party leaders were predominantly from the upper and middle classes, and they understood their vulnerability to radical appeals among the rank and file.

The PS, meanwhile, was a very unusual creature, one without parallel in the rest of Latin America. It had been formed in 1933 by Marxists opposed to the Comintern—ironically, on the issue of the peaceful path, which they supported.[22] Unlike the PC, the PS was not formally governed by the principles of Leninist party discipline, and consequently the party was often fractured and individual members were difficult to control. By the late 1950s, however, a series of splits and reconciliations within the PS had produced a party generally considered to be to the left of the communists. Both the Sino-Soviet split and the Cuban Revolution had produced different effects on the PS than on the PC, and in October 1960 the general secretary of the PS, Salomón Corbalán González, wrote a letter to the PC leadership saying, "The example of Cuba is intensely impacting the popular conscience and is opening the eyes of the masses."[23] At a party plenum a year later, he declared his support for the PS line of creating a Frente de Trabajadores (Workers' Front), arguing that the Cuban Revolution had shown that class confrontation, rather than collaboration, was the way to achieve revolution. At the same time, a group within the party led by Allende's future foreign minister, Clodomiro Almeyda, evinced open sympathy with the Chinese position.[24] The general secretary of the PS from 1961–1965, Raul Ampuero, was more supportive of the electoral path, and the Twentieth Congress of the PS in February 1964 affirmed the strategy of pursuing the peaceful path through the candidacy of Allende. But Allende's defeat that year spelled doom for the electoral path within the PS. At the subsequent party congresses in Chillan in 1965 and Linares in 1967, armed struggle was declared the sole path of revolution, cooperation with the PDC or the PR was rejected, and the radical line of the Havana-led Organization of Latin American Solidarity (OLAS) for guerrilla warfare was affirmed. In theory, if not yet in practice, the PS seemed to have abandoned the electoral strategy of the PC.

Despite these obvious sources of tension, however, the collaboration between the communists and socialists continued. The communists consistently pushed to deepen that collaboration, seeking to move beyond a mere electoral alliance toward the formation of a unified political program and, eventually, a unified party.[25] Perhaps uniquely among the world's communist parties, the PC acknowledged that the PS was also a legitimate workers' party and it even refused to discuss "whether the vanguard of the proletariat is the Communist Party or the Socialist Party."[26] Given that the PC had the confidence of Moscow, this meant that the PS was also treated in an uncommonly comradely way by the Soviets and their allies. A high-level Soviet delegation led by politburo member Andrei Kirilenko, along with an East German delegation, attended the PS Congress in Linares in 1967. For the following year, Corvalán arranged an invitation by the CPSU for a PS delegation to visit Moscow, a rare case of the Soviets establishing interparty relations with a noncommunist party in a country that had a communist party in good standing.[27] As the election of 1970 approached, both the CPSU and Sozialistische Einheits Partei (SED, Socialist Unity Party, the ruling party of the GDR) maintained increasingly close contacts with the PS, in coordination with the PC.

The unusual level of ties between the PS and the Soviet bloc did not, however, mean that the latter completely trusted the former. The continued adherence of the PS to its line of armed revolution, its support of OLAS, its studied neutrality in the Sino-Soviet split, and its condemnation of the Warsaw Pact invasion of Czechoslovakia made sure of that. Furthermore, there were fears—which would recur repeatedly during the period of the UP regime—that the socialists were trying to dominate the coalition and subordinate the communists.[28] When in late 1968 the PS asked the GDR to give it equipment so that it could publish its mouthpiece, *Ultima Hora,* on its own rather than through the PC, the East Germans worried that granting publishing autonomy to the PS would give "the adventurist and ultraleft current in the Chilean workers' movement significantly stronger possibilities for the distribution of its damaging opinions."[29] They decided not to help, which was ironic because the PC's own printing press had been the result of a fifty-thousand-dollar donation from Beijing back in 1960.[30] The prominence of the PS within the UP coalition then confronted the Soviets and their allies with a problem: they could neither trust nor control the PS, but they could not ignore it.

One of the most disquieting elements of the PS for the PC and its Eastern European allies was the sympathy of many of its members for the extreme left, particularly the Movimiento Izquierda Revolucionaria (MIR; Leftist Revolutionary Movement). The latter was largely composed of radical students, and it had been formed under the leadership of Miguel Enriquez Espinoza and Luciano Cruz Aguayo in 1965 after Enriquez had been expelled from the PS for objecting to the electoral line affirmed by the party at the Twentieth Congress in 1964. Enriquez visited China in 1966 and Cuba in 1967, following which the MIR had consistent contact with Havana; some of its members received military training in Cuba. In 1969 the MIR began conducting armed actions around the country, employing small *grupos politico-militares* focused on raising funds for itself and organizing poor peasants to undertake land seizures. While the organizational ties between Cuba and the MIR were extensive, the program published by the MIR in *El Rebelde* in November 1968 hit some unmistakably Chinese notes. In arguing that revolution would not come about through economic competition, the MIR asserted that reformism and revisionism were betraying the world proletariat and that "the crisis of humanity finds its concrete expression in the crisis of the world leadership of the proletariat." The Soviet ambassador in Chile, sending a translated version of this program back to Moscow, underlined two particularly revealing passages. In the first, the MIR asserted that "peaceful coexistence, whether active or passive, is a temporary agreement between socialist bureaucrats and imperialism directed toward freezing or disrupting revolution."[31] Then—in a direct threat to the USSR common in Chinese propaganda at this time, but far beyond the Cuban position—the MIR declared that "in socialist countries, controlled by reformism or revisionism, we support the revolutionary people, and not their bureaucratic leadership, which is deforming the process of the building of socialism, and has abandoned revolutionary Marxism."[32] At the time this program was published, Havana had publicly supported the Warsaw Pact invasion of Czechoslovakia, and the improvement of Cuban-Soviet relations was well under way.

The importance of the MIR was magnified not only by the sympathy it engendered within the PS but because of the personal ties between the movement and Salvador Allende. Allende's nephew, Andrés Pascal, was one of the leaders of the movement, and Allende's favorite daughter, Beatriz "Tati" Allende, who was married to a Cuban intelligence agent in the embassy in Santiago, became a close adviser of Enriquez.[33] The sympathies of Allende himself for violent revolution were well known and evidenced, among other things, by Che Guevara's dedication of his book *Guerrilla Warfare* to Allende;[34] Allende's expressed willingness to meet reactionary violence with revolutionary violence as expressed to the famous French revolutionary thinker and writer Régis Debray;[35] and Fidel

Castro's gift of the submachine gun, with which Allende would ultimately kill himself during the coup.[36] The estimation of Allende's ideological purity and political reliability—or lack thereof—would be a major factor in the strategic calculations of the PC and its allies in East Berlin and Moscow.

The Chilean Left, then, presented a confusing picture for outside socialist powers. For the Soviets there was an electorally powerful coalition with a commitment to Marxism and a real chance of winning, but one whose key ingredients were ideologically suspect. Consequently, Soviet support for the UP coalition in power would depend on close contact with Allende and leading members of all parties in the coalition, especially the communists and socialists, who met with officials from the Soviet embassy on a nearly weekly basis. The Soviets used these meetings to evaluate the regime's progress and determine who was ascendant at any given moment and what that meant for the political direction of the regime. In the absence of Chinese documentation, Beijing's attitude toward the various elements of the UP coalition is more difficult to determine. Allende, Almeyda, Enriquez, and PS general secretary Carlos Altamirano had all visited the PRC during the 1960s, but the documents related to their visits are still classified. But subsequent Sino-Chilean conversations held after the establishment of relations with the PRC in 1970 and available in the Chilean Foreign Ministry demonstrate that the PRC did not take any of the groups on the Chilean Left seriously as a true revolutionary party. The conduct of small Maoist groups in Chile in relation to the UP regime expressed not only rejection of the revolutionary claims of the latter but the belief that the Via Chilena was ultimately a scheme to divert the true revolutionary energies of the people from their proper direction.[37] It seems that Chinese policy therefore had a dual character, corresponding to two different imperatives. The first was the need to discredit the peaceful path, and the behavior of the Maoist groups within Chile reflected this impulse. At the same time, the PRC's need to extend its influence in the developing world meant that it had to maintain good relations with the UP, and so the PRC increased aid and trade ties. The Soviets seem never to have quite figured out exactly what Chinese policy was in relation to the UP, but they were certain, albeit almost surely mistakenly, that Beijing was extremely active and somehow responsible for the fall of the regime. Their enduring suspicion of the dynamics within the regime meant that they would ultimately choose not to step in with the economic aid necessary to ensure the regime's survival.

The Dream Becomes Reality: Unidad Popular in Power

When Allende was elected on September 4, 1970 by the narrowest of margins in a three-way contest, the first question on everyone's mind was how long the regime would survive or even, indeed, whether Allende would actually be allowed to assume his position. Given that the constitution stipulated that if no candidate received a majority of the popular vote, the election was to be decided by the Congress, many wondered if Allende would perhaps be denied the fruits of his victory via legal means, even though tradition held that the winner of the popular plurality was always confirmed by the Congress. In the meantime, while the administration of US president Richard M. Nixon plotted ways to prevent Allende from assuming power, Cuba and Peru, led by a left-leaning military junta under General Juan Velasco Alvarado, offered to defend the new UP government militarily if necessary.[38] Despite the machinations of Washington and some on the Chilean Right, the chances of Allende being voted down were slim.[39] This is precisely what Allende himself told the Komitet Gosudarstvennoi Bezopasnosti (KGB; Committee for State Security) right after the election, which was then passed on by KGB chief Yuri Andropov to the Central Committee of the CPSU.[40] The reason was that the PDC represented the decisive faction and, given the leftist positions assumed by its presidential candidate, Radomiro Tomic, during the election and the increasingly anti-capitalist mood within the party, its members were unlikely to unite with Nationalist Party members to deny Allende the presidency.[41] Nevertheless, the PDC did make use of its leverage to force Allende to agree to a series of conditions intended to preserve democracy and forestall any attempts at establishing a dictatorship of the proletariat, including pledging fealty to the constitution; provisions to maintain freedom of the press and prevent the politicization of the armed forces; and promising not to put the portfolios of foreign affairs, defense, or the interior in the hands of the communists.[42] Given the minority position of the UP within the Congress and the necessity of constitutional amendments to fulfill some parts of its campaign promises, Corvalán asserted that "Chilean legality" would constitute an "obstacle" to the implementation of the UP agenda.[43]

Allende therefore faced a number of difficulties that cast doubt on the potential success of his presidency, including the heterogeneous nature of his coalition, the constitutional constraints, and the minority position of the UP in congress. From the Soviet perspective, the fact that he represented a party that looked more toward Beijing and Havana than Moscow presented further cause for concern. Worse, on the eve of the election, the PC gave the Soviet embassy an exceedingly negative evaluation of Allende, saying that he "is by character a very self-obsessed person, who rates himself extremely highly. However, he is a political activist who is already on his way out of the arena, losing influence among the people. Our friends [the PC] generally characterize him as a 'mummy' (i.e., something outdated and conservative)."[44]

Nevertheless, the Soviet leadership, as well as scholars and officials involved in Latin American affairs, were quite taken with the revolutionary implications of the election even though they were cautious about the UP's chances for success: Brezhnev had pointed in a March 1971 plenum to the potential influence of the Chilean example in other countries. Immediately after the election, the Soviet ambassador in Chile wrote, "This victory of the leftist bloc, created on the initiative of the Communist Party of Chile, was an important step in the life of both the Chilean and other Latin American peoples, enabling the deepening of the anti-imperialist process on the Latin American continent and reflecting the growing influence of the international communist movement."[45] N. I. Zorina, writing in *Latinskaia Amerika,* a scholarly journal published by the Institute of Latin America in Moscow, in an article titled "Chile: A New Stage of History," claimed that the election held the possibility of a "global development of the revolution."[46] (The journal's editorial board included Nikolai Leonov, one of the KGB's main Latin America experts.)[47] In an article toward the end of 1971 in *Mirovaia Ekonomika i Mezhdunarodnye Otnosheniia,* the primary Soviet foreign affairs journal, Zorina went even further, declaring that "the parties of the UP bloc, having come into the government, represent the interests of the working class, the laboring peasantry, numerous middle strata, intelligentsia. And they have arrived in power with a program of revolutionary transformation, dedicated in the final account to the building of socialist society."[48] Given the acknowledged heterogeneous nature of the coalition and the interests that it was said to represent, the claim that its program involved "revolutionary transformation" directed toward building a "socialist society" was a strong affirmation indeed of the ideological significance of events in Chile. The failures of the "bourgeois reformist" programs exemplified by Allende's predecessor from the PDC, Eduardo Frei Montalva, were said to indicate that the development of capitalism in Latin America had proceeded far enough that revolutionary transformation could only mean socialism:

economic and technological factors meant that wageworkers were now numerically dominant, and even students qualified as a group oppressed by local and foreign capital.[49] While the Chilean revolution was still only at the anti-imperialist and anti-oligarchic stage,[50] the willingness of influential Soviets, including Brezhnev, to hold it up as an alternative model to Cuba, a full-fledged socialist country, testifies to the importance and potential of the Chilean model in Soviet eyes. As Zorina wrote, "the movement of the Chilean revolution along the path of using constitutional opportunities and democratic traditions has exceptional ideological significance on the plane of the international struggle of the two systems. Reaction everywhere in the world uses the worn-out, but for now still effective argument: revolution is violence, it is destruction; revolution is dictatorship, it is incompatible with democracy."[51] The Chilean experiment was not only an alternative model of revolution; it was also the communist answer to anticommunism.

Internal Soviet evaluations provided an explanation for their sanguine view of the UP government. A report prepared by the Latin American division of the Foreign Ministry in August 1971 emphasized the key role that the PC had played at every stage of the process of forming the coalition, as well as the fact that the party controlled all of the most significant economic ministries. Because of this, the PC wielded "decisive influence" over the leftist bloc, which was consequently more united and becoming an even more influential political force. Allende himself now exercised "decisive influence" on the political life of the country, enabling the "development of a new stage of domestic political struggle" and opening the door to "radical socioeconomic transformation."[52] As long as the influence of the PC (rather than that of the PS) was dominant, and Allende was working closely with the communists, the Soviet leadership was optimistic about the direction of events in Chile.

As a result of this Soviet confidence, Chile and the USSR rapidly began building an edifice of economic and scientific cooperation; the two nations exchanged economic delegations in 1971–1972, leading to the signing of multiple economic agreements involving fishing, mining, wood processing, agriculture, residential construction, and the gift of a kindergarten. Moscow granted Chile over 200 million rubles (US$240 million) in credits, which included an 85-million-ruble credit in June 1972 to cover the costs of materials, equipment, and Soviet specialists for a number of industrial projects.[53] The Chilean National Commission on Scientific Research and Exchange asked to send students to Moscow to study the "economics of the transition period from capitalism to socialism."[54] Other socialist countries chipped in as well, with every single country in Eastern Europe (save Albania), as well as Cuba, offering credits to Chile.[55]

There were, however, limits to the extent of Soviet economic aid to Chile. Cuba was already a tremendous burden on Soviet finances, and the Kremlin was not willing to take on another such obligation. A US Department of State report quoted a Soviet diplomat saying that Moscow "does not want Chile to become dependent on trade with communist countries." The Soviets were concerned with the possibility that Allende might try to push the revolution too quickly, crippling the economy and damaging Chile's international standing; thus, it urged caution in such actions as recognizing Cuba and, as will be seen below, in the implementation of economic reforms.[56] Fidel Castro himself also urged caution, reflecting the judgment of the GDR that he had become a much more faithful servant of Moscow.[57] He told the new Chilean chargé d'affaires in Havana that Allende "needs to go slow, concentrating his forces on the problem of copper and leaving the construction of socialism for later." Castro joked that Cubans could not be much help economically, since they were not very good at production, but they were very good fighters in the case of attack.[58] The Cuban view of the potential of Soviet economic aid was mixed, however. When Aleksei Kosygin, visiting Cuba in November 1971, promised the Chilean ambassador the USSR's support, Castro affirmed the significance of the pledge, telling the Chilean ambassador, "You can count on the permanent help of the USSR."[59] At the same time, the Cubans told the Chilean chargé that "the USSR is on the international level in some aspects of modern technology and very backward in others," pointing specifically to copper and nickel mining among the latter—areas of particular interest for Chile.[60] The lack of technological compatibility was only one of the reasons that many of the credits granted by the USSR to Chile ultimately went unfulfilled.[61]

The Chinese reaction to the victory of Allende was positive, though nowhere near as enthusiastic as the Soviet reaction. In Moscow, the Chinese ambassador was the first person to greet the new Chilean ambassador, inviting him to a meeting immediately, which the latter took as a sign of China's desire to cultivate a special relationship with Chile. The PRC ambassador delivered a note of congratulations expressing support for "the struggle of the Chilean people under the direction of Salvador Allende in defense of their national sovereignty and for the economic development of the country."[62] No mention was made of revolution, of

FIGURE 2.1 Cuban premier Fidel Castro with Chilean president Salvador Allende on the balcony of La Moneda during Castro's lengthy visit to Cuba in November 1971. Castro urged caution, showing that he had become a reliable Soviet ally. *(Romano Cagnoni / Getty Images)*

any sort, or of socialism. Soon after Allende's assumption of power, Chile became the first Latin American country besides Cuba to recognize the PRC. The establishment of relations was not without its difficulties, however. The new Chilean ambassador in Beijing, Armando Uribe, complained that no one in the embassy could read Chinese, and that they were having trouble keeping the names of Chinese officials straight.[63] Uribe soon reported that China looked very positively on Chile because of its foreign policy stances, particularly in the United Nations (UN), and that China viewed Chile without ideological judgments or a desire to involve it in Sino-Soviet disputes.[64] Yet Uribe urged prompt action on the development of economic relations with the PRC, fearing that Beijing would not understand if Chile dithered and that "it would be interpreted as a negative political disposition toward China." This could have grave consequences, as it could lead to a "tendency to concretize the relation with Chile in accordance with a type of international policy that will certainly have very delicate ideological-political implications (disagreements with the USSR, etc., etc.) and the possibility of falling into the temptation to judge and—what is even worse—to emit public judgments, on the internal

Chilean experience, in terms conditioned by the peculiar ideological-political schemes and principles of China."[65] The Chileans were well aware of how fragile their newly established relations with China were, and they were obviously concerned to avoid getting on the wrong side of Beijing ideologically.

Despite an initial delay caused by Chile's uncertainty about what it could import from China, trade relations did begin to blossom over the course of 1971. In April the PRC sent a trade delegation led by the minister of foreign trade to Chile to investigate the possibility of buying copper and other minerals in exchange for tea, rice, and industrial equipment. The Chileans finally reciprocated in November, and a series of trade accords were signed between the two countries, including an agreement for China to purchase sixty-five thousand tons of copper per year for four years. In the meantime, China made a number of benevolent gestures toward Chile, including donations of rice, dried milk, conserves, wool, medical aid, and cash in the wake of a major earthquake that year. By May 1972—when a second Chilean official economic delegation, led this time by Minister of Planning Gonzalo Martner, visited the PRC and signed four long-term agreements, including one for an interest-free loan of $65 million—the Soviets had become very worried about the rapid growth of Sino-Chilean relations, especially as the Chilean visitors to China were supposedly undergoing "corresponding ideological manipulation [obrabotka]."[66] The East German embassy in Santiago expressed similar concerns in a missive of December 1971, imagining that Beijing was seeking to use Chile as part of a long-term plan to infiltrate Maoism throughout Latin America.[67] In a further report on Sino-Chilean relations from 1972, the GDR worried that, judging by the coverage in the Chilean press, Chinese aid was valued much more highly than Soviet aid, and the Chileans might "play the more beneficial conditions of the agreements with China against other socialist countries."[68]

Complicating matters for both the Chinese and the Soviets, however, was the fact that Allende saw himself as creating a completely new model of socialist revolution, one that he wanted to share with the world. In an interview for the Soviet journal Novoe Vremia in December 1970, Allende said, "This Chilean social process has been converted into a source of profound attraction and interest for the whole world and especially for underdeveloped peoples [pueblos subdesarrollados]," although he was, as of yet, reluctant to openly propagate it as a model.[69] This reluctance soon disappeared as the central Chilean planning agency, the Oficina de Planificación (Planning Office), organized a conference beginning on March 24, 1971, that was billed as a "roundtable" on the "Chilean path to socialism."[70] Two months later Allende told a visiting East German delegation that the Chilean model differed from the Cuban one not only in terms of the means of seizing power and that "Chile should be a better example than Cuba for the way of the peoples of South America to socialism."[71] The Soviets were concerned when, at the UN General Assembly the following year, Chile promoted its model to Latin American and countries that were part of the Non-Aligned Movement, asserting that its "political maturity" allowed it to conduct socialist transformation in the context of "respect for the constitutional and legal norms of our country, democratic pluralism, and freedom of action for opposition forces."[72] The appeal of the Chilean model was not limited to Latin America or even the developing world. Corvalán and PS leader Altamirano visited Italy in May 1971, where the Italian communists and socialists expressed a great deal of interest in the Via Chilena.[73] Later that year, French socialist leader François Mitterand visited Chile, seeking what Allende jokingly called "the papal blessing" for his own efforts at taking power through democratic means.[74] As Western European communists began to embrace the idea of allying with other leftists parties in electoral coalitions, a phenomenon that came to be known as Eurocommunism, Allende's apparent success provided a powerful impetus.

In the first year of the UP government, Allende had reason to be proud of his successes. On July 11, 1971, the Congress unanimously approved his constitutional amendment nationalizing the copper industry, which was the most popular item on his agenda. Though Allende followed an inflationary policy of raising wages while reducing certain taxes, excess capacity in the Chilean manufacturing sector meant that inflation, Chile's perennial bête noire, actually dropped to only 3.4 percent in the first three months of 1971.[75] Meanwhile, Chile's gross domestic product rose 8.5 percent, while unemployment fell to only 4 percent in 1971. Most of the benefits went to the workers, as their incomes rose 20 percent and consumption overall rose 12 percent.[76] At the same time, Allende managed to nationalize most of the banking sector, as well as many large firms. The popularity of the UP government caused vacillation within the ranks of the PDC, which proclaimed a policy of "constructive opposition" at a party council meeting in May; in July this led to the splitting off of yet another group from the PDC, the Izquierda Christiana (Christian Left),

La técnica avanza y exige tu participación responsable.
En el camino hacia el progreso de Chile, la Nacionalización del Cobre
significa abrir nuevas perspectivas y crear fuentes de trabajo.
Recursos que te permiten más y mejores oportunidades.
La Nacionalización del Cobre es un desafío al subdesarrollo.

FIGURE 2.2 Back cover photo on the nationalization of copper from *Ahora* magazine, August 24, 1971. The text reads, "Chilean copper nationalization engages you and benefits you. The technology advances and demands your responsible participation. On the road to progress in Chile, the nationalization of copper means opening up new perspectives and creating jobs; resources that allow you more and better opportunities. The nationalization of copper is a challenge to underdevelopment." *(Reproduction courtesy of the Hoover Institution)*

which soon joined the UP government.[77] It seemed possible that the Via Chilena might actually succeed.

Under the surface, however, there were troubling signs. The government was ill prepared to run so much of the economy, and by September, 47 percent of the state budget was going to finance the deficits of the state sector.[78] This was already creating problems in terms of paying for imports of basic consumer items, so much so that in October 1971 the PC leadership asked Soviet ambassador Aleksandr Basov for additional aid of $300 million per year, half of which was to be allocated to the immediate needs of the population. As Corvalán told Basov, because of the democratic nature of the regime and its narrow electoral victory, "we cannot ask the workers to 'pay' for revolutionary transformation."[79]

Even more troubling were the increasing divisions within the UP coalition itself. The very success of the UP government had led its most prominent member, the PS, to adopt an even more radical, uncompromising stance with regard to the issue of the peaceful path at a party conference in La Serena in March 1971. One Chilean scholar argues that the PS had long since abandoned electoral means for more of a Leninist path and that the UP victory actually took it by surprise.[80] Only a month after the election, the PS's communist coalition partners undermined the party's standing by telling the GDR that the PS leadership included many Trotskyites as well as "other petit bourgeois forces," adding, "In the leadership of the Socialist Party there are still strong anticommunist and anti-Soviet tendencies. For example, there are no workers in the leadership." The PC leaders expected that the PS leadership would eventually team up with the PR, and Allende himself, to battle the communists for hegemony within the UP coalition and that no "class policy can be expected from the PS leadership."[81] On the eve of the conference at La Serena, the PC leaders told their East German comrades that they expected Altamirano to be chosen as the new general secretary and that, given his "ultraleft" tendencies, this would be a "retreat" for cooperation with the international workers' movement and the Soviet Union. Nevertheless, they cautioned, "we should therefore not idealize the Socialist Party, but we should also not evaluate it negatively."[82] In any event, Altamirano was selected as the new general secretary, although the outgoing one, Aniceto Rodríguez, tried to use the UP victory to tamp down the enthusiasm for armed struggle in his final address. This provided little comfort to the PC leadership, which was quite aware of the prominence of ultraleft representatives in the new leadership.[83] A Soviet report on the PS soon after the conference concluded that "the success of the revolutionary process in Chile will depend in no small measure on how they manage to overcome the left-extremist tendencies in the UP bloc."[84]

A further cause for unease at the La Serena conference was the fact that, as the East German delegation pointed out in its report, the agenda adopted included only negative elements, as opposed to positive steps directed toward the construction of socialism.[85] According to the Yugoslav delegation's report, the PS Congress "increased the skepticism of the delegations from Eastern European countries regarding the economic policy and general policy of Allende's government."[86] This played into what the Soviets and their allies saw as a larger problem at the heart of the UP agenda—namely, that "there still exists no unified economic policy." According to the East German embassy in Santiago, there was still a lack of economic oversight and clear leadership structure, insufficient conceptualization of tasks, and no state structure to control distribution to parallel the one coming into existence for production.[87] As the Chilean economy began to unravel, this would become the chief complaint of Soviet bloc observers.

In the meantime, dissension on the Chilean far left was on the increase. The MIR, which had agreed to suspend armed actions after the election and had been lying low early in the year, now became dissatisfied once again with the pace of agrarian reform and took the lead in increasing the rate of land seizures. As the local UP committees formed during the election disintegrated in its aftermath, the political structures of the ruling coalition became detached from the provinces. Into this vacuum stepped the MIR, gaining support among local poor peasants and Mapuche, especially in the southern provinces, and forming a new organization called the Movimiento Campesino Revolucionario (Revolutionary Peasant Movement), whose slogan was "Nothing Can Stop Us." The East German embassy noted with trepidation that the MIR was now also working with the pro-Chinese PCR.[88] In addition, there were problems at the top of the government. Corvalán went so far as to tell East Berlin that Allende had tendencies toward a "personal regime" and that "he liked a little leadership [*Führertum*]."[89] As the political situation became tenser during 1972, these weak points would turn into major sources of division.

For the time being, however, things in Chile were looking up. As long as the economic situation seemed positive, public divisions within the regime were minimized; the popularity of the UP, and consequently its prospects for holding power and implementing its agenda, seemed quite good. While the economic situation held, the chances for a successful peaceful transition to socialism, led by Allende and the PC (without too much interference from the PS), were enough to keep observers in Moscow sanguine. Despite the results of the conference in La Serena, a PS delegation to Moscow in July 1971 was well received. While the Soviets noted continuing differences of opinion on the issues of armed confrontation and the push for a single-chamber legislature, they had seen in the PS an overall "evolution" in recent months toward the positions of the communists. The delegation was received at the highest level, and held a five-and-a-half-hour conversation with Brezhnev.[90] The PC was hopeful that Soviet outreach to the PS could convince it to follow the PC line, and it asked that that the CPSU increase ties with the PS.[91] At the same time, the Chilean embassy in Beijing hopefully noted what it saw as a decisive change in the Chinese attitude by the first anniversary of the UP government. An editorial in *Renmin Ribao* placed great emphasis on Chile's nationalization of copper, declaring that "the government and people continue to advance along the road of the national-democratic revolution." The Chilean ambassador wrote, "It remains clear that the revolutionary character that they have assigned to our current political process refers to a national-democratic ambition, and not a socialist one; however, it seems already recognized that we are on our way to it [socialist revolution]." He promised an analysis in a further report on "how they come here to qualify popular governments before considering them revolutionary and socialist."[92] Given the past expressions of sympathy for the PRC from Foreign Minister Almeyda, Altamirano, and even Allende himself, it was unsurprising that Beijing's evaluation of their revolutionary status would carry so much importance for the UP regime.

Toward the end of 1971 the glass seemed half full from the perspectives of all concerned, despite the lingering problems of disunity and disorganization. The Soviet Union saw a government that was taking serious steps toward socioeconomic transformation without, as of yet, putting its own status in danger, and it hoped that as time went on and the success of the policy of peaceful transition became clearer, the ultraleftist tendencies within the PS would decrease and that it would increasingly come to follow the line of the PC. In other words, in time, the "objective factors" of the success of economic transformation would cause popular opinion to coalesce around the line of the PC, and the threat from the extreme left, first in Chile and then perhaps around the world, would begin to dissipate. The Chinese, for their part, saw a Third World country that was decisively and successfully throwing off imperialist economic penetration while following an independent foreign policy directed toward solidarity with the rest of the developing world. Especially given its positive international orientation toward the PRC, the Chilean state under Allende therefore represented an excellent example of the Third World group that Beijing was trying to construct in the international arena—an effort that had been given a new impetus with the entry of the PRC into the UN in October 1971.[93] But the positive views of the UP's performance during its first year belied the deeper sources of division that lay underneath. Even its economic successes were interpreted differently by various forces within the regime. Some, led by the communists, thought that the key achievement of 1971 was rising living standards, which would broaden the regime's popular base. Others, led by the socialists, believed that the regime's success was due to its rapid nationalization program, and they sought to seize as much of the economy for the state as rapidly as possible. As the regime's economic problems grew in 1972, contributing to the rise of a stronger and more unified opposition, the instability of the UP coalition and its international relationships would become manifest.

Dissension within the Unidad Popular

By the latter part of 1971, the UP regime was at a crossroads. The implementation of policies that enjoyed broad popular and political support—and what Soviet theorists called the tasks of the "wide national front" during an anti-imperialist revolution—had been largely accomplished: copper and banks were nationalized, landed estates over eighty irrigated hectares had been confiscated, and a foreign policy oriented toward socialist and Non-Aligned Movement countries had been adopted. Now the question was how to proceed farther down the revolutionary path. On a global level, as the capitalist welfare state became entrenched and the possibility of violent seizure of power by the workers receded, the socialist revolutionary model was left with two choices: the accession of the working class to power by peaceful electoral means or the violent seizure of power by peasants, students, racial minorities, or some other "surrogate" proletariat. In Africa and Asia the working classes were often too small to make the first option realistic, while in Europe and North America there were not enough peasants to choose the second option. In Latin America, however, there were enough workers and peasants to make both options seem realistic, and this dilemma consequently produced three primary approaches within the UP coalition: open confrontation, democratic evolution, or an instrumental use of democratic processes until the "correlation of forces" favored the revolutionaries. Allende was firmly committed to the second model of the transition to socialism—namely, a democratic one (not to be confused with social democracy), which he saw as fundamentally superior to all of the other models, including the Soviet one.[94] At times, though, even he expressed doubts about whether Latin Americans were really ready for true parliamentary democracy—pointing, for example, to the enduring influence of Argentina's Juan Peron.[95] The PC viewed the democratic path instrumentally, believing it to be the safest option as long as the "correlation of forces" (which, in the discussions of the Chilean Left and their allies was often code for the alignment of the armed forces) favored the opposition. Behind closed doors the PC nevertheless spent a great deal of time figuring out how to eventually achieve the dictatorship of the proletariat and what that would look like in Chile.[96] While the approaches of Allende and the PC diverged in theory, in practice they produced similar policy prescriptions at this stage, and so Allende often joined forces with the PC against the PS. The PS, for its part, thought the time had come for the "acceleration" of the revolution, by which it meant the adoption of policies—especially a rapid, radical land reform—that would produce fervent militant support among the poorer sectors of the population in preparation for an imminent, and inevitable, violent confrontation (*enfrentamiento*) with the opposition.[97]

On August 14, 1971, Altamirano laid out the new PS platform at a party plenum. He criticized the UP government for proceeding too slowly toward socialism, accusing it of "inefficiency" and "irrationality" and exhibiting a creeping "bureaucratization" that was "not conducive to an authentic revolutionary process" and would lead to the "depoliticization of the masses." The solution to this was the direct participation of workers and peasants in government, which could not be achieved from above but could "only be achieved from below through the action and struggle of the masses." Distancing himself from the views of the MIR and others, Altamirano explained that he was against "spontaneous actions," instead advocating that the party leadership give strategic direction to the workers and peasants. As far as the economic agenda to be followed, he argued that among the two chief objectives of the UP government—namely, socializing the economy and raising living standards—the first must always take precedence; as he put it, the "battle for production" was only a secondary part of the "battle for socialization." In concrete terms, Altami-

rano dedicated the PS to measures that would speed up political and economic transformation, including the election of a single-chamber legislature,
amending the constitution to allow the president to dissolve the Congress,
the enactment of laws to expropriate large private concerns, and the ex-
propriation of all landholdings above forty hectares.[98] This agenda was
designed to divide the country into two antagonistic camps and create
confrontation.

Meanwhile, a high-level GDR delegation gave its own detailed prescription to Allende in November 1971.[99] The East Germans were particularly interested in Chile at this time because of their global competition
for recognition with West Germany, whose leading parties already had
ties with the PDC and PS. For their part, the Chileans saw the GDR, the
most advanced country in the socialist bloc, as a key potential source of
aid and advice. The chief item on the agenda presented to Allende was the
creation of a true state planning organ under the direct control of the president that could begin to implement a comprehensive economic plan. This
would also include the placement of industry under direct government
control rather than through intermediaries such as the state Production
Development Corporation. At the same time, agricultural production
needed to be planned, and the GDR recommended devolving control of it
to the provinces, where local planning organs should be created. They also
advocated the creation of a centralized government banking system and
the mobilization of the workers in production committees. In short, the
prescription of the East Germans saw greater centralization, planning, and
emphasis on production as the way forward for the UP government.
Nothing could have been further from the agenda laid out by Altamirano,
who wanted mobilization from below and radicalization of the revolution
to combat creeping "bureaucratism," but it was the East German plan
that would become the basis for policies advocated by the PC—and its
comrades in East Berlin and Moscow—in 1972.

As these divisions over whether to "expand and accelerate" or "deepen
and consolidate" the revolution rent the UP coalition, the parties decided
to hold a series of meetings in late January and early February 1972 at El
Arrayan, near Santiago, to try to hammer out an agreement. The main
issues on the agenda were whether to expropriate landholdings between
forty and eighty hectares (farmers of small- and medium-size parcels constituted 40 percent of the rural population), how to win over the middle
classes, relations with the MIR and those on the far left, and the possibility
of opening negotiations with the PDC. On the first issue, the PC won and

101

the eighty-hectare limit was maintained, but the results of debate on the next two issues were murkier. The MIR was not condemned outright and a decision was made to negotiate an understanding with it. The proposal for negotiations with the PDC was shelved for now, though it would return, with predictable results for the unity of the coalition, later in the year. The parties also decided not to propose a plebiscite to create a single-chamber parliament. Though the major decisions seemed to largely favor the PC line, the PS claimed victory as well, releasing a statement saying, "The justice of the party's positions has once and for all been recognized with respect to not holding back 'to consolidate the process,' but to deepen it, aggressively confronting the resistance of the bourgeoisie."[100] The East German embassy was mostly satisfied with the results of the meetings, especially regarding the plans to make greater attempts at winning over the "middle strata" and the defeat of the proposal to "accelerate and radicalize" land reform, but it held no illusions that real unity had been achieved.[101]

In the aftermath of the El Arrayan meetings, both the PC and the PS loudly proclaimed their views on the direction of the country. The PS leadership published an analysis in *El Mercurio* (the largest newspaper in the country and one owned by a family with ties to the opposition) declaring that "the bourgeois state in Chile is not suitable for the creation of socialism, and its destruction is necessary," concluding ominously that "in the final instance, it will be violent confrontation that will determine who is the victor."[102] On March 15, Orlando Millas, a top PC leader who would later serve as both Allende's minister of finance and minister of the economy, gave a speech at a PC plenum that was subsequently published for public consumption. In it he lamented the failure of the parties at El Arrayan to reach agreement on a broad appeal to the laboring classes, regardless of party, and to separate themselves from those on the far left, which he argued was being used by factions on the right to incorporate the PDC more firmly into an opposition bloc. He went on to condemn those on the far left in the most severe terms, claiming that it was "our revolutionary duty" to fight it. Exhorting the PC to greater vigilance, Millas remarked, "Today in our country the struggle against Marxism-Leninism is very intense and varied, and it docs not always receive an immediate and adequate response from our side. Many times this struggle appears in the form of perversions of mutilated vulgarizations, of the presentation of Maoism as a sort of final word of Marxism, or of the large-scale dedication of social resources to the publication of anti-Soviet works of [Leon] Trotsky himself." He concluded by affirming that "the most revolutionary is to fight for the success of the government."[103] While the PS was itching for battle and waiting to shed the shackles of bourgeois democracy, the PC was increasingly seeing the threat to the government from the Right as paling in comparison to the one from the Left. As the year progressed, decisions regarding which party the UP should try to come to terms with—the MIR or the PDC—would become the flashpoint for disagreement on the Left.

It did not take long before the El Arrayan agreement was in tatters and the same issues had resurfaced. At a PS party plenum in May, Altamirano proposed amending the constitution to nationalize all enterprises worth more than 14 million escudos (about US$500,000) and confiscate land-holdings above forty hectares, this time proposing a plebiscite if this proposal was rejected by the opposition.[104] The dissension within the UP coalition became so bad that at a meeting of the coalition members later that month, Allende declared his intention to resign, saying that the in-fighting had made his position untenable and that the PS, in particular, was undermining his authority in public.[105] Though this was already the fourth time since assuming power that Allende had threatened resigna-tion, Altamirano and Corvalán thought he was serious this time. Allen-de's resignation threat prompted the UP parties to convene another set of meetings in May and June in order to try to resolve their differences and agree on a path forward. As part of the new agenda, they agreed to hold negotiations with the PDC to try to get it to cooperate with at least part of the government's agenda.[106]

But the decision to open negotiations caused an explosion of anger within the PS and, on July 26—not coincidentally the anniversary of Fidel Castro's storming of the Moncada barracks in 1953 and a national hol-iday in Cuba—various elements on the far left, including the MIR, parts of the PS, and other UP parties such as the Christian Left and the Mov-imiento de Acción Popular Unitario (MAPU; Popular Unitary Action Movement), convened a People's Assembly in the southern city of Con-cepción. The prospect of a unified Left acting in opposition to the govern-ment frightened the communists and their allies. The Soviet ambassador worried that the united front of the UP parties would crumble under the pressure of the class struggle.[107] The assembly in Concepción, however, also frightened Allende. Despite his professed belief in the peaceful path, Allende resisted open condemnation of groups on the far left, particu-larly the MIR, and, according to the Cuban embassy, he continued to meet with MIR leaders regularly.[108] According to the communists, part of the reason Allende had been reluctant to condemn the MIR was that it was blackmailing him with personal information—including that of his affair with his secretary—that had been provided to the MIR by his daughter Beatriz.[109] Now, however, Allende reacted strongly, sending a letter condemning the "ultraleft" to the leaders of all of the UP parties. Allende denounced any step against the government, from any direction, as "counterrevolutionary"; the East German embassy observed that, for the first time, Allende was not only attacking ultraleft actions but also ultraleft ideology, and, "From this follows not only an organizational, but rather for the first time also a fundamentally political-ideological division from left-radicalism, which has well-known strong positions among others in the Socialist Party." Chastened, the PS initially ceded some ground. Altamirano gave a speech supporting the government on August 1, and thirty-three PS members who also belonged to the MIR were expelled from the party.[110] Then, on August 4 the police raided an encampment of the poor at Lo Hermida looking for a member of the MIR, and the shootout that ensued resulted in one dead, eleven wounded, and 160 under arrest.[111] The PS leadership quickly did an about-face, attacking government "repression" and distancing itself from UP policy.[112] While Allende seemed to be moving ever closer to the PC, those on the far left were becoming ever more militant and dragging a large part of the PS into their camp.

After the events of July and August 1972, the relations with ultraleft groups came to occupy a greater role in the divisions within the UP. In an analysis of the deep ties between the MIR and the PS, the East German embassy concluded that "Left Radicalism is presently the chief danger for the internal stability of the Unidad Popular."[113] The Soviet Foreign Ministry was similarly concerned, writing about how the activity of the MIR, along with "leftist elements of the Socialist Party," was "objectively facilitating the reaction's achievement of its goals."[114] Meanwhile, according to the PC, the Cubans were heavily involved in MIR activities, even including the secret provision of arms without the consent of Allende.[115] In August the PC sent politburo member Volodia Teitelboim to Havana in the hopes of ending this but was unsuccessful.[116] This was a problem that went far beyond Chile, however. The ideological positions of those on the far left threatened the core of the Soviet global revolutionary strategy. As one Soviet scholar wrote, "In a whole slew of theoretical constructions of left radicalism there distinctly lies a striving to create a special regional model of social transformation. Some call it the 'theory of underdevelopment,' 'sociology of underdevelopment,' others—'regional revolutionary theory,' and even 'Latin Americanized-Marxism.' It is characteristic of supporters of such views that their 'regionalism,' as a rule, is not limited within the bounds of Latin America, but encompasses within it Africa, Asia, and other underdeveloped regions of the world."[117] For the Soviets and their allies, it was not a question of whether the strategy pursued by the PC or the PS would be more conducive to achieving a lasting revolutionary transformation. Rather, the means in this case *was* the ends—demonstrating not only the futility but also the danger of the radical Left constituted for them a central objective of the Chilean experiment.

Help from Abroad

In the midst of all of this division within the UP and the indecisiveness it engendered, the economic situation deteriorated over the course of 1972. The excess capacity in Chilean industry had been exhausted and now, due in part to the lack of investment as resources were diverted to consumption, inflation jumped again—by 163 percent in 1972 according to official figures. Increasing worker absenteeism and the disorganization resulting from rapid and insufficiently planned land reform meant that both industrial and agricultural productivity were falling, which necessitated the import of ever more consumer goods from abroad, causing the balance of payments deficit to balloon. Matters were made worse by the lack of credits coming from the United States, although much of that gap had been made up by other countries, and by US copper companies' attempts to prevent the Chilean government from selling copper abroad until they felt they had been justly compensated.[118] The Soviet ambassador reported that the fundamental issue was that the UP coalition had still not come up with a unified economic agenda and that economic success "would depend on the degree of unity of action in the economic arena between the parties of the UP bloc, above all the Communist and Socialist Parties."[119] In October a massive strike begun by truckers, who feared rumors that the state was going to set up a public trucking company, was joined by storekeepers and others in the middle class who were fearful of the potential extent of nationalization. The strike nearly paralyzed the country, and Allende had to call in the armed forces to get goods moving again. The strike only ended, however, once Allende agreed to reshuffle his cabinet to include representatives of the military, seen by the opposition as their guarantor of the constitution and sobriety within the government. With the economic situation critical and the opposition becoming ever more active and united, the UP government looked to its allies abroad for salvation.

Thus far, however, Soviet support for Chile had been deeply disappointing. Despite the amount of attention the UUSR had been paying to Chile and the close degree of contact between the Soviet embassy and the UP coalition, the Soviets had done little to alleviate the economic burdens of the government, and the Chileans had noticed. As Corvalán complained openly to the Soviet ambassador, "Some comrades have grown pessimistic regarding the possibility of aid for Chile from the Soviet Union. . . . The most important thing is that the Soviet comrades believe that we are doing everything in our power for the victory of the revolution."[120] He had correctly deduced that the lack of Soviet aid was due to the USSR's doubts about the very viability of the UP's revolution. With the economy in crisis, the government in perpetual internal conflict, and Allende threatening to resign, Ambassador Basov even appealed to his superiors to do more—morally, if not financially. Pleading with Moscow, he noted that Allende's resignation "would cause catastrophic outcomes for our friends and the leftist bloc. It is clear that from our side, we need to work out measures to exert pressure on Allende, strengthening his resolve and belief in the prospects of the Chilean revolution."[121] It would be hard for the Soviets to convince Allende of something that they themselves did not believe.

In desperate straits, however, Chile turned to the Soviet Union to rescue its economy. After addressing the UN General Assembly, Allende embarked on a trip to the USSR and Cuba, as well as other shorter stops, arriving in Moscow on December 6, 1972. His primary goal was to get financial assistance to cover the growing balance of payments deficit and the $80 million needed to service short-term credits due by January 5, 1973.[122] In addition, Allende wanted to follow up on the proposal of Corvalán, who had just visited East Berlin and conferred with Erich Honecker regarding Soviet bloc purchases of copper in case the US-led boycott of Chilean copper exports continued. Corvalán had also proposed a plan to have the Soviets and their East European allies cover Chile's $220 million balance of payments deficit for 1972; this was politely rejected by the GDR, which pointed out that it was already overburdened, having given $100 million in aid that year to the North Vietnamese.[123] They did, however, agree to a $15 million credit for 1973, to be paid back in copper, as well as the purchase of another ten thousand tons of copper.[124] Allende and Corvalán then went to Moscow, holding meetings with Leonid Brezhnev, Andrei Kirilenko, and Boris Ponomarev, among others, in an attempt to cajole them into supplying the needed aid. According to a review of the visit passed by Moscow to East Berlin, however, the Soviets were skeptical of the Chilean proposal because—in a preview of what Zhou Enlai would tell Almeyda two months later—they did not see the utility of stopgap measures as long as the UP government lacked a longer-term economic plan. They advised Allende "that it would be useful [*zweckmässig*—most likely a translation of *tselesoobrazno* in the original Russian version of the report] for the UP bloc before the March 1973 parliamentary elections to publicize a real political-economic program for five or ten years to openly say which tasks the new government assumes in the interests of the laborers and which problems it is confronting."[125] They also denied the request of Gonzalo Martner, the Chilean minister of planning, for a $240 million credit because Chile had used only $2 million of the $240 million credit granted earlier. Though the Soviets did end up offering $45 million of the $80 million needed, Allende left dejected, and it was clear that Moscow was not confident enough in the Chilean regime and its president to bet heavily on them.[126]

The Chilean government did not pin all of its hopes on the Soviets, however. On November 20, when Allende was still preparing to go abroad, the Chilean Foreign Ministry sent a note to its counterpart in Beijing, appealing desperately for aid. The appeal centered upon the heightened revolutionary situation and possibilities in Chile, as well as its importance for the global anti-American struggle. The Foreign Ministry proposed shifting the next scheduled Sino-Chilean mixed economic committee meeting from Santiago to Beijing, as well as elevating the level of the delegation to include Foreign Minister Almeyda. In so doing they dangled one more carrot in front of the Chinese: "The visit to Beijing of the aforementioned governmental delegation will allow, in addition to studying ways to increase economic interchange and collaboration, the formulation of a declaration which will register the degree of coincidence that exists between Chile and China in many aspects of the international situation."[127] In effect, Chile was offering the PRC international support in exchange for economic aid. Two and a half weeks later, the Chinese accepted the proposal.[128] On January 30, 1973, Almeyda met with Zhou Enlai to discuss the possibility of aid and the state of the Chilean revolution. Zhou was skeptical of the path chosen by the UP government, saying to Almeyda, "You have made steps much quicker than ours ten years after the War of Liberation. Did you prepare the conditions for these steps?" Later Zhou clearly noted that the Chileans were moving too rapidly and that, as a consequence, they were making themselves dependent on foreign aid, the danger of which had already been demonstrated by Cuba and its obsequious behavior toward the USSR. Zhou then asked straight out why giving Chile enough aid to solve its balance of payments problem this year would not simply lead to the same problem in the future. Almeyda tried to argue that the coming year, 1973, would be the most difficult because the agricultural situation would inevitably improve, the price of copper would rise, and Chile would work on correcting its errors and "rationalizing" the economy. Zhou was having none of it and responded, "It might get better, it might get worse. What will you do if it gets worse?" Almeyda could only promise that "we will act so that it does not get worse." Zhou then shifted to the political realm, asking Almeyda about the balance of power in the military and the possibility of a coup.[129] In the end, Zhou, like the East Germans, pointed to the necessity of devoting significant resources to North Vietnam as an excuse to avoid meeting the Chilean requests, but it was clear that he did not have a lot of confidence in the Chilean revolution due to the perceived weakness and incompetence of the leadership and the lack of willingness to sacrifice. Zhou then wrote to Allende to explain that, while he had China's sympathies as a fellow struggling Third World country, Beijing was not able to provide much concrete assistance at the moment, remarking again upon the need to rely on one's own forces and to endure sacrifice.[130] The PRC did, however, provide a $48 million credit; technical specialists to help build industrial projects; and $5.2 million in immediate aid for food and medicine, including 100,000 tons of rice. This was enough to worry the Soviets, who nevertheless noted that, between Beijing and Santiago, "serious disagreements exist in their views regarding the questions of building socialism."[131]

While the UP regime was looking abroad for immediate economic relief, the PC looked for help in formulating a more coherent economic policy that would produce long-term solutions. In response to the request East Berlin sent a high-level advisory delegation, led by Ernst Höfner, the deputy finance minister of the GDR, to Chile for six months (September 1972–March 1973); its focus was on finding ways to raise production in order to lower inflation.[132] Soon after its arrival, the delegation concluded that there would likely be no economic improvement in 1973 and that the problems could only be solved with external aid due largely to the mistakes of the UP government itself—especially "ultraleft overreaching and mistakes with regard to the urban middle strata and large and middle peasants."[133] Advocating greater centralization of economic control and the use of trade unions to increase worker discipline, the delegation admitted that "without cognizance of the political situation, the political correlation of forces and the special problems of the UP, the economic questions cannot be solved."[134] The GDR soon found that its influence was having an impact, as Allende adopted the suggestion of state control over the export of copper on October 10, 1972, and the PC became more assertive in inter-party UP discussions against PS proposals to accelerate expropriations and thereby antagonize the "middle strata."[135] Basov was still very pessimistic, however, telling the GDR that Chile's economic development was stagnating because there was no unified approach to the solution of its problems. In particular, he criticized land reform initiatives because the peasants had not been given title to the expropriated land.[136] He proposed sending a group of experts to Allende himself, and the PC soon adopted this tactic, trying to arrange a meeting between the East Germans and Allende. The meeting was quite successful, as Allende accepted the necessity of basing his economic policy on "scientific foundations," but this led to increasing friction between Allende and the PS. Against the advice of the PC, however, Allende refused to push for a change in the PS leadership until after the March 1973 congressional elections.[137] Before departing, the East German delegation submitted a six-point plan, agreed to by the PC, that involved making the economy the primary issue for all UP parties; focusing on raising production and exports; establishing a system of price controls to rein in inflation; making state enterprises profitable; working out a unified economic conception within the UP; and creating a simple, unified system of state planning to direct the economy.[138] The plan dovetailed with the economic approach that the PC had been advocating since mid-1972, which was focused on reining in inflation, devaluing the currency, and improving the profitability of state enterprises; it was an approach also endorsed by the Soviet leadership.[139] These economic prescriptions contained elements of what would later come to be known as structural adjustment and, in fact, when the UP government looked into an International Monetary Fund loan later in 1973, Minister of the Economy Millas, a member of the PC, endorsed the tighter monetary policy and currency devaluation that the fund demanded.[140] Ironically, Millas asserted that it was the opposition in the Chilean Congress that would prevent such measures from being passed. As the situation between the UP and the opposition—and within the UP itself—became more desperate and polarized, the possibility of major structural change began to vanish.

Consequently, in the crucial months before the congressional elections of March 1973 finally divided the country into two camps hell-bent on confrontation, Chile's socialist allies did not come through with sufficient aid to alleviate its economic difficulties and improve the UP's political standing. The Soviets, who wanted to see the Chilean experiment succeed, thought that internal divisions between the communists and socialists would prevent the Chilean regime from proceeding along the path laid out by Allende and the PC, in accordance with the recommendations of the East German delegation. The Chinese were not as committed to UP success, so their reluctance to devote significant resources to Chile at a time when their own population was suffering was less surprising. Despite their intense differences, what is perhaps most remarkable about the Chinese and Soviet attitudes toward the Chilean regime are the parallels in their evaluations of its performance and potential. Both saw the UP leadership as divided and incompetent, simultaneously moving too rapidly with regard to nationalization and too cautiously in terms of sacrifice and mobilization, thereby antagonizing the middle classes while failing to raise the living standards of workers and peasants. Their different attitudes toward the Chilean regime, however, led Beijing and Moscow to advocate different paths for Chile. The Soviets, in close concert with their East German comrades, advocated more centralized planning and worker mobilization in order to raise production, thereby deepening the revolution and increasing support for it. The problem, in their eyes, was that the revolution was not being led "scientifically" and that ultraleft and petit bourgeois forces were too influential. The Chinese never took seriously the Chileans' claims to be moving toward socialism. Zhou therefore advocated slowing down the revolutionary process to focus on economic independence, "reliance on one's own forces," and thus achieving the anti-imperialist goals that Beijing set for all Third World countries at the time. One thing that both Beijing and Moscow could agree upon at this point, however, was that Allende did not seem like a good investment. He was not powerful enough to force the various UP parties, particularly the PC and PS, to cooperate, since each had to answer to its own base and contend with its own internal dynamics. It was not simply a matter of strongarming Altamirano and Corvalán, since even they were primarily representatives of larger groups within their parties. With internal UP deadlock

110

preventing the government from reaching out to the PDC and making the crucial connection that might have allowed the UP to divide the forces that were now gathering for its destruction, Beijing and Moscow were probably right about the prospects of the UP at this point.

The Road to the Coup

Both the UP and the opposition had been looking toward the congressional elections of March 4, 1973, as the last major electoral opportunity to escape the political stalemate before the presidential election of 1976. The opposition thought that it had an opportunity to garner two-thirds of the vote and thereby gain enough seats to impeach the president. Allende spoke of getting a majority that would allow him to amend the constitution, but as the reality of popular opinion became clearer, he decided to lower public expectations. The only correct prognostication, though, came from the head of the armed forces, General Carlos Prats, who predicted, "Everybody will win the election."[141] The opposition won about 55 percent of the vote, not nearly enough to impeach Allende, against 43 percent for the UP. This was a better result than many had predicted for the UP, and it meant that the opposition majorities in both houses of Congress actually diminished slightly. Nevertheless, the real impact of the election was its removal of the electoral path as a possible solution to the increasing antagonism between Chile's two political camps.

The Soviet view of the election results was cautiously optimistic. It was clear that the opposition's efforts had been foiled and support for the UP had increased slightly, but the bottom line was that "the unstable political balance between the government coalition and the group of opposition parties had been preserved."[142] The GDR was more sanguine, seeing the results not only as a significant affirmation of the UP but—given the fact that the UP votes had gone almost exclusively to the communists and socialists instead of the smaller parties in the coalition—as proof that those who voted for the UP this time were "determined to defend the popular government to the extreme."[143] An even more positive development from the perspective of East Berlin and Moscow was the outcome of a secret PS plenum held soon after the election. The Allende wing of the party was said to have defeated the Altamirano wing, removing three of the latter's partisans from the Central Committee. The East German ambassador speculated that Altamirano might soon be removed as general secretary, possibly in favor of Almeyda, because "the position of Altamirano has suffered a defeat, not merely ideological but also practical, in the elections."[144] At the plenum, the proposal of Altamirano to conduct the "bourgeois democratic" and "socialist" stages of the revolution in one stage was defeated, the ultraleft was condemned and the notion of PC as "reformists" was rejected. The PS even accepted the leadership of the USSR in the socialist camp "from a pragmatic standpoint," though it still refused to conduct negotiations with the PDC and focus on raising production. In return, Corvalán made some moves toward reconciliation, declaring at a PC plenum soon after, "We do not see our struggle as only through elections. We have never called our path 'legalistic' but rather revolutionary. We do not exclude the possibility of violence. It is openly said: We do not sympathize with the expression 'peaceful path'; to us it sounds pacifist."[145]

This semblance of a truce within the UP coalition was not to last, however. On June 29, a regimental commander in Santiago led a coup attempt; a poorly kept secret over the previous week, it was put down within four hours. Nevertheless, the manifestation of counterrevolution reenergized the far left which came out in defense of the regime and seized thirty thousand small- and medium-size enterprises that day.[146] Allende used the coup attempt to great effect, calling on the workers to occupy the factories, promising arms to the people, and dramatically addressing the masses from his balcony. The GDR saw the coup attempt as a good sign, interpreting the fact that the commanders of the armed forces refused to participate as proof that the regime commanded a majority within the military and seeing Allende's actions as reflecting "decisiveness."[147] Duly frightened by the prospect of a military coup, however, both Prats and the PC tried to convince Allende that the only way to preserve the regime was to come to an agreement with the Christian Democrats. Not coincidentally, on July 3, the Latin American division of the Soviet Foreign Ministry submitted a report that affirmed that "objectively" the possibility for an agreement with the PDC existed.[148] The UP regime also produced a new "emergency plan" for the economy, incorporating many of the PC's objectives in terms of organization and mobilization, but Moscow still felt the new program had a "general and nonconcrete character." The real problem, however, was the effect that the coup attempt had had on the PS. The Soviet Foreign Ministry reported that the PS was categorically against negotiations with the PDC and thought that this was not the time to concentrate on the economy; rather, it should concentrate on "the questions of preparation for armed conflict, which is seen as inevitable."[149]

At this advanced stage, neither the PC nor PS denied the necessity of preparing for armed conflict; they merely disagreed over its inevitability and how to prepare for it. On July 9, Corvalán told the East German ambassador, Harry Spindler, that armed conflict was still avoidable, claiming that the other UP parties and Allende agreed. At the same time, he said that half of the PC was working illegally to prepare for armed conflict. The PC, the PS, and even the MIR were working together to prepare the armed defense of factories and the regime, with small arms provided by Cuba.[150] Corvalán claimed that Prats had even promised to provide the parties with arms in case of emergency. In the meantime, under Prats's leadership, the UP was conducting a rapid purge of the officer corps; Corvalán also proposed the disastrous idea of an unarmed march of UP supporters, wearing red armbands, through the streets of Santiago. He expressed doubts about Allende, however, describing the latter's actions during the last coup attempt as "unclear," a fact attributed to Allende's "petit bourgeois origins," which caused him to "fear the dictatorship of the proletariat."[151]

Unlike the PC, the PS was not merely preparing in case of coup. Rather, it was actively courting confrontation. According to the PC, the PS even proposed to conduct an *autogolpe* (self-coup) by dissolving the Congress.[152] A few days after meeting with Corvalán, Spindler met with Altamirano, who appealed for arms, saying Chile was now the focus of the world revolutionary struggle. Altamirano was sanguine about the prospects for armed struggle, estimating that 45–65 percent of the soldiers and *carabineros* (police) in Santiago would support the UP and claiming that the UP already had twenty-five hundred of its own men under arms.[153] He argued that the main battle would be in Santiago, since the army needed to keep troops in the north to protect against a possible Bolivian invasion, and if troops tried to move up from the south, they could blow up key bridges. Altamirano asked the GDR to provide him with communications equipment, and he was sending prominent PS member and recent minister of the interior Hernán del Canto to Cuba, Bulgaria, and the GDR to seek weapons. When Spindler asked if the PC and Allende had been informed about this, Altamirano was evasive, saying that they had been informed in "general terms."[154] Spindler then told Basov about the conversation, and Basov told him that Altamirano had recently been visiting all of the socialist embassies with the same goal. Basov agreed that Altamirano was fundamentally correct—that Chile probably was the focus of the world revolutionary struggle and that help most likely was necessary because the UP was not sufficiently prepared for armed confrontation. Despite this, the CPSU officially responded to Altamirano's request by saying, "In view of that fact that there are left-sectarian elements in the Socialist Party and that differences of opinion between the communists and socialists remain, we always deal with the fulfillment of requests from the Socialist Party of Chile in concert with the leadership of the Communist Party of Chile."[155] Despite the gravity of the situation, the agreement of the PC leadership would not be forthcoming. As Teitelboim told the East Germans, Corvalán had written a letter to the CPSU saying,

> The provision of arms to the Socialist Party cannot be recommended in any case. It must be kept in mind that the Socialist Party is composed of heterogeneous elements, that it is not a party of a new type, and that only 15 years ago it followed anti-Soviet and anti-communist positions. The provision of arms to a force of the UP without the agreement of Allende is completely impossible. This is also stated in the letter from Comrade Castro to Comrade Altamirano. On top of that there is also no guarantee that this sort of action could be handled in total secrecy.[156]

That is not to say, however, that the Soviets completely dismissed the idea of arming the UP regime. The same answer to the PS pointed out that Moscow was willing to provide arms to the government according to the requests of Allende and Prats, who had visited Moscow in the spring and determined that Soviet weapons were just as good as Western ones.[157] As early as July 1971 Allende had already sought to switch to Soviet supply for the Chilean armed forces, and—in principle, at least—Moscow had agreed.[158] Nikolai Leonov, at the time the subdirector of the KGB's Analysis and Information Department, revealed that a high-level KGB meeting was held in the spring of 1973 to determine whether or not to provide Chile with a further $30 million in emergency economic aid. The proposal was ultimately defeated after extensive discussion because of skepticism about the regime's possibility for survival, but Leonov said that a decision was made in the Ministry of Defense to provide arms to the regime and that a ship loaded with weapons including tanks set sail in the Northern Hemisphere summer of 1973. He claimed, however, that Soviet sources inside the US Central Intelligence Agency reported that a coup was imminent and, to avoid the spectacle of Soviet arms being used to destroy the regime, the ship was diverted.[159]

Contrary to the view of many that the Soviets ultimately decided not to save Allende because of a perceived division of the world between the United States and the USSR,[160] it seems that Moscow was very aware of the significance of Chile for the world revolution and was willing and able to come to its aid. If what Leonov asserted is true, that ship had already sailed—quite literally. The question was to whom the arms should be sent. The Soviets were apparently willing to arm the government, but they were afraid the arms would be used by the military *against* the government. The CPSU, and its Chilean comrades, did not trust the PS enough to provide them with arms due to the latter's "left sectarianism." But behind this fear was a much more concrete threat: China. On August 8, 1973, the Latin American division of the Soviet Foreign Ministry submitted a report which said that the activity of the Chinese embassy in Chile had "led to the growth of pro-Chinese elements in various political parties of Chile, specifically the Socialist Party, MAPU, and MIR."[161] In a meeting with the East Germans at the end of August, Basov admitted that China's influence in the PS, while significant, was limited, but he asserted that China was providing material aid to ultraleftist groups.[162] In the context of the global Sino-Soviet conflict, the prospect of a Chilean revolution dominated by a PS that might lean toward Beijing was worse for the Soviets than a martyred revolution. That left the PC as the last possible recipient of Soviet arms. Yet the PC apparently never formally requested them. On July 10, Corvalán told Basov that while they would want weapons from Moscow, they could not see a way to receive them without the military's knowledge. At the same time, a Cuban military delegation was providing both weapons and military training to the MIR, the PS, and Allende's personal bodyguard, but the PC was afraid that this would cause a scandal for the government.[163] Ultimately, Corvalán did not believe that any amount of preparation would enable the UP to defeat the armed forces in a direct confrontation, so he hoped to deter a coup by marching the workers through the streets unarmed while seeking to ideologically subvert the military. Unsurprisingly, those policies did not prevent or delay the coup; they accelerated it. They induced anxiety in the military and the opposition about the possible subversion of the constitution by the Left without actually enabling the regime to defend itself against the military.

The last real hope of Allende and the PC to avoid a coup was to come to some sort of arrangement with the PDC. But the PS was dead set against it, and it threatened to leave the UP coalition, and thereby bring down the government, if the PDC was invited to negotiate.[164] It took the intervention of Fidel Castro to convince the PS to accept the talks and remain in the coalition.[165] In the end, the effort was futile anyway, as Allende and the PDC failed to come to terms.[166] Radomiro Tomic, the former PDC presidential candidate and erstwhile leader of the left-wing faction of the party who had worked to fashion an agreement with the government, told Basov after the negotiations collapsed that "the UP has completely exhausted its chances and its fate is decided."[167] The other strategy that Allende pursued to avoid a coup—again, despite the opposition of the PS—was the creation of a national security cabinet including representatives of the armed forces. On August 9 the new cabinet was sworn in, though without Carlos Briones, who was to be reappointed minister of the interior, because the PS, of which he was a member, objected to the cabinet's formation.[168] At the same time, Altamirano was apparently considering his own countercoup against Allende, using a detachment of marines in Santiago.[169] Once again, it was apparently the Cubans who dissuaded him.[170] With the country now paralyzed by a new strike (one more severe than the one of October 1972) and both right- and left-wing groups stockpiling arms, the supposedly "apolitical" Chilean military was the last hope of the regime. Allende created an "anticoup command" consisting of the generals Alberto Bachelet, Carlos Prats, and Orlando Urbina, as well as representatives of the PC, the PS, and the trade union federation, which even had links with the MIR.[171] When the UP-sympathizing Prats was forced from his position by a council of generals on August 22, to be replaced by Augusto Pinochet, Luis Corvalán called Pinochet "faithful to the constitution."[172] The faith of Allende and Corvalán in the military, however, would be misplaced.

The Chilean coup of September 11, 1973, may have been the most highly anticipated coup since Caesar returned to Rome. During the summer, graffiti had appeared on the Cuban embassy reading "Remember Jakarta."[173] In early August, Allende had sent a message to Castro that "Salvador Allende will only leave the presidential palace dead."[174] Castro was just as convinced that a fight was coming, but he tried to persuade Allende to at least conduct it from a more defensible position than La Moneda, the presidential palace.[175] Nevertheless, it is interesting to see what Moscow had to say on the eve of the coup. On September 5, the Latin American division of the Soviet Foreign Ministry produced one more report on Chile that already had the feel of a postmortem. At first the UP government had implemented serious reforms that "significantly undermined the bases of capitalism and imperialist dependence, created the prerequisites for the further consolidation of the revolutionary process." By late 1972, however, problems had arisen due to the falling price of copper, lack of worker disciple and the problems of the leftist bloc "expressed in its forcing the tempo of transformation without taking account of the real possibilities of the country." Some forces of the UP—chiefly, the PS—had undermined faith in the constitutional path and the MIR "practically embarked on a path of political provocation against the government." The PC did what it could to salvage the situation, but in the end the experiment failed because of the "nonfulfillment of the UP program, the lack of a clear line with respect to the small and middle property-holders, the appearance of sectarianism, and the vacillation in the adoption of decisive measures."[176] These words were actually taken verbatim from Corvalán himself, who prefaced them by telling Basov on August 23 that "we are now paying for our mistakes."[177] In short, on the eve of the UP collapse, the PC—and its allies in Moscow—attributed the coming catastrophe to the divisions within the UP itself. Soviet ambassador Basov continued to defend the line of the peaceful path, arguing that it had no theoretical problems, while blaming the UP's problems on its own inability to implement its program. Summing up, Basov declared, "The main obstacle in solving the problems, that must be underlined, is now as before the Socialist Party."[178]

And so on September 11, the Chilean experiment in democratic socialism ended. Allende was dead (having taken his own life), Altamirano had fled the country, and Corvalán was in prison. In those final few months, as the tensions within Chilean society built and the prospects of a coup became more tangible with every new day, the divisions within the UP coalition only grew. While the possibilities for a political solution to the economic crisis receded, the PS not only prepared for war but actively sought it as Allende and the PC sought to do everything to avoid it. The Soviet leadership, realizing full well what was at stake and looking for ways to help, was nevertheless more afraid of the wrong kind of revolution than a counterrevolution. We have no documents to support Soviet claims about material Chinese aid to those on the far left, who received most of their arms from Cuba, nor does it seem that Beijing actively sought to sow dissension within the coalition, but we do know that the GDR, the PC, and the USSR believed that the hand of Beijing was behind it in some way. In the absence of the deep suspicion and global political divisions engendered by the Sino-Soviet split, it might have been possible for the PC and the PS to come to some sort of agreement on a political and economic program that would have made the UP regime more effective, organized, and resilient, not to mention more attractive to potential sources of external support. In the international communist political climate of 1973, however, the communists and socialists spent much if not most of their efforts on undermining each other, and that, in the end, made it impossible for the Via Chilena to succeed.

Learning the Lessons of Chile

In certain ways, Allende became far more important in death than he had ever been in life. As they did with Che Guevara, the Soviets found Allende an extremely useful martyred hero to trot out against their enemies once he was safely below ground. For others, though, the fall of Allende was a key moment: the violence of reaction became apparent, and a generation of armed guerrillas—chiefly in Latin America, but elsewhere, as well—was born on September 11, 1973.[179] It was China's lack of reaction, however, that was perhaps the most shocking. To the surprise of many observers, Beijing maintained relations with the Pinochet regime and even continued economic aid. It was a reversal of the situation in Indonesia after 1965 where Beijing broke relations with Jakarta while Moscow maintained its relations and aid agreements with Suharto. In the aftermath of the Chilean coup, the stakes surrounding the debate over the concept of peaceful transition only grew. As the PRC continued to attack the Soviet Union for being insufficiently revolutionary, groups inspired by Che or Mao, like Sendero Luminoso (Shining Path) in Peru, took up arms against what they saw as irredeemably violent and oppressive capitalist regimes.[180] Meanwhile, Eurocommunism was on the rise in Western Europe, and particularly in Italy, where communist parties embraced coalitions with other parties on the left in the hopes of taking power through the ballot. In this context, the debate about whether the fall of the UP was due to rightist opportunism or leftist extremism took on global significance.

Allende's body was barely cold when the Soviets began planning their defense of the theory of peaceful transition. On September 20, Y. I. Kuskov of the International Department of the Central Committee of the CPSU told his East German comrades that representatives of the ultraleft were seeking to make use of Chile for their own purposes—specifically, that "the word of Mao Zedong . . . is the only way to socialism," and "we must now work out and publicize a correct analysis of the events in Chile, that the theory of the peaceful path to socialism in view of the existence of the socialist camp is correct." Kuskov went on to explain that the analysis should focus on the role and policy of the PS, especially "whether the Socialist Party had perhaps recognized Marxism-Leninism only in words."[181] On October 24 the East German politburo listened to a thirty-six-page report produced by Soviet scholars as a preliminary analysis of the events in Chile. The report pointed out many faults of UP policy, such as the disorganization of attempts at land reform, the payment of compensation in the nationalization of the banks, the failure to implement a currency reform to control inflation, and the failure to attract the middle strata. The UP government was fundamentally divided between a proletarian line represented by the PC and a petit bourgeois line represented by the MIR, the PS, and others. But there were also elements of nuance presented in the report that had not been seen in earlier Soviet analyses. The Soviet scholars argued, for example, that in the conditions of Chile, it would have been necessary to create a new "revolutionary army." That did not mean, though, that they were abandoning the peaceful path, only that there was a "dialectic between peaceful and nonpeaceful forms of revolution." This meant that both forms must always be present, but the choice of which to employ at any given time must depend upon the calculation of the objective relations of power rather than the subjective will of the revolutionaries. The latter was the source of error of those on the far left and Maoists. Above all, the Chilean experience was still an important demonstration of the possibility of revolution in both developed capitalist countries and underdeveloped countries dependent on imperialism, though "it would naturally be false to absolutize it—that is, to use it as a template [*schablonisieren*]."[182]

As time went on and the events in Chile became a subject of broad interest across the Soviet academic world, certain differences of opinion became evident. Most Soviet scholars continued to focus on defending the possibility of the peaceful path and pointing out the successes of the UP.[183] Every decision of the UP was analyzed in detail in order to figure out how the peaceful path could be successfully implemented the next time. Yet there were some who, though paying lip service to the idea of the peaceful path, clearly had drawn other lessons. Kiva Maidanik of the Institute of Latin America—whom Olga Ulianova calls "the last eternal romantic revolutionary of the Soviet Latin Americanists"[184]—has argued that since the UP program had made the choice for socialism, it would have been impossible to stop at the anti-imperialist stage and consolidate the revolution, as E. A. Kosarev suggested, since, Maidanik noted, "revolution is made under the banner of social justice, not increasing the norms of accumulation." Maidanik asserted—clearly siding with the PS against the PC in a key point of contention—that compromise with the PDC and the consequent winning over of the middle classes would have been impossible. Revolution, at least in the Third World, was to be made in the name of the workers, and the middle classes must of necessity be against it. Finally, he claimed that while it might have been possible to follow the peaceful path until the elections of March 1973, after that an alternative strategy was required. He denied any affinity with those on the far left but said that they, like a broken clock, were still right twice a day.[185] While Maidanik was largely alone in his analysis in 1974, as time went on and the Maoist danger receded while polemics with the Eurocommunists heated up, Soviet analyses of Chile would gradually move toward greater emphasis on the need to use armed force to protect the revolution. The leaders of the PC, in exile in Moscow, took their cue from the Soviet analyses, whose militant turn led to the PC's own "militarist turnabout" in September 1980 along with the subsequent training of Chilean exiles in guerrilla warfare and their infiltration into Cuba, Nicaragua, and Chile itself in the 1980s.[186]

Beijing's reaction was longer in taking shape than had been Moscow's. At first, the PRC used Chile to condemn the "aggression, subversion, control, and intervention of the superpowers against the countries of Asia, Africa, and Latin America." At the same time, it attacked the "absurd theory of the so-called 'peaceful transition' for the anti-imperialist struggle of the peoples of Asia, Africa, and Latin America, a theory that one superpower has propagated."[187] The new Chilean regime understood the understated nature of the Chinese response and especially the fact that it put the blame on the two superpowers, not the people in Chile who had actually made the coup. Chile stopped appearing in the Chinese press after September 30, 1973, and unlike other socialist countries, there were no concrete efforts undertaken, or committees formed, to aid and support Chile. Getting to the heart of the matter, the Chilean chargé d'affaires in Beijing wrote to the new junta that the PRC may have sympathized with some of the UP's policies, "but the term 'Chilean path to socialism' was never used here [in China]," and "China does not consider any Chilean party as authentically Marxist-Leninist. Perhaps it was the Socialist Party for which it had a certain cold sympathy because of its independence from the CPSU. It was, however, a strong blow for China that ex-President Salvador Allende visited Moscow while the highest authority to visit Beijing was Minister Almeyda."[188] Chile, under Allende or Pinochet, was just another anti-imperialist, underdeveloped Third World country in the eyes of Beijing, and there would be no breaking of relations, no abrogation of agreements, and no condemnations in the international sphere. The Soviets missed no opportunity to use the PRC's connections with the Pinochet regime to poison Beijing's relations with the rest of Latin America, and the postcoup conduct of the Chinese provided Moscow with an easy villain in the Chilean saga. According to Moscow, the Chinese had used the naïveté and revolutionary élan of the Chileans to gain a foothold for their own selfish purposes and then, when the time came, Beijing betrayed the Chilean revolution for a few pieces of silver (or, in this case, copper).[189]

The experience of the Unidad Popular government in Chile was a crucial episode in the history of the Marxist revolutionary project. It was the only example of an avowedly Marxist government coming to power through electoral means and seeking to implement a Soviet-style economic program based on state control of the means of production without violating—at least not openly and egregiously—the constitutional norms of so-called bourgeois democracy such as freedom of speech and political pluralism. Salvador Allende is still a hero to many, and there are streets named after him and monuments dedicated to him around the world. The importance of the Chilean case was magnified by its historical moment, at a time of global revolutionary ferment when students in the West were on the march, the rhetoric of Third World versus First World confrontation was on the rise, and the United States was still trying to fight its way out of Vietnam. For many Chile represented the way out, the "third way" that would enable the capitalist West to transition to socialism while avoiding the horrors of totalitarianism. Yet the Unidad Popular experiment in Chile was ultimately doomed by its own internal divisions, which mirrored those that had divided the international communist movement since the late 1950s.

The differences over the forms of the revolutionary transition, both inside the Chilean Left and among leftist groups around the world, certainly predated the Sino-Soviet split. The issues of peaceful transition versus armed revolution; acceleration versus consolidation of the revolution;

and the role of the workers, peasants, and middle classes in the transition were inescapable for would-be revolutionaries and reformers around the globe in the 1960s and 1970s who were trying to build a Marxist utopia in a world radically different from the one inhabited by Marx. The Sino-Soviet split, however, radicalized and politicized these differences to the point that cooperation and compromise among different groups on the left became impossible. The UP government failed to come up with a coherent political and economic program and, even in the final moments of fighting for its very existence, its constituent parts spent more time undermining each other than trying to fight their enemies.

The Chinese and Soviets used Chile to advance their respective global revolutionary agendas. For China—seeking to build a united front of Third World countries to oppose the superpowers, particularly on the grounds of economic neocolonialism and political interference in other countries' internal affairs—the Allende regime represented a positive development, though not a grand departure by any means. The Pinochet government (which, after all, did not return the copper mines to their former American owners) served many of the same purposes from the perspective of Beijing and, given the PRC's attitudes toward both nonintervention and socialist revolution in the 1970s, it would have been quite surprising indeed if it had actually broken relations with Chile. The PRC ultimately calculated that, given the benefits of trade and cooperation, as well as good relations with one more country as measured against the failure of a false socialist revolution, the reality of Chile was worth more than its symbolic value. For the Soviets, however, the symbolism of Chile was far more important than the reality of the country itself. From Moscow's perspective, the UP government was problematic for many reasons, starting with the fact that it was led by a member of the PS of petit bourgeois origins who had in the past been known to sympathize with Fidel Castro, Che Guevara, and Mao Zedong. Had Luis Corvalán, rather than Salvador Allende, been elected president, it is quite likely that the Soviet attitude would have been very different and Moscow would have been much more keen to play an active role in supporting and defending the Chilean revolution. But due to the divided nature of the Chilean Left and the jealousy with which each party guarded its power, only Allende commanded broad enough support to be the candidate of a leftist bloc, and Corvalán's candidacy was never even proposed. Under the circumstances, the massive Soviet aid that the UP government had hoped for never materialized, as the Soviets did not see Allende as a good bet. Nevertheless,

122

the symbolic value of the Chilean experiment, especially after its demise, was tremendous from the Soviet perspective and it would be employed to great effect against both those on the so-called ultraleft and the Eurocommunists and Social Democrats for the remainder of the Cold War.

While the Soviets initially sought to defend their thesis of peaceful transition from those who would use the coup as a counterexample, events in Chile would turn out to be the high point of Moscow's embrace of bourgeois democracy, at least before the era of perestroika. In Indonesia the Soviets had pushed the PKI to endorse Sukarno's Guided Democracy plan, and the disastrous consequences for the PKI led to a reevaluation, including an acknowledgment that the abandonment of parliamentary democracy had been a mistake. Now, however, parliamentary democracy had led to the UP's demise by preserving avenues of power for local opposition and their external patrons—chiefly, Brazil and the United States.[190] As Ahmed Azad, a member of the Moscow-oriented South African Communist Party, put it in an article titled "The Lessons of the Chilean Revolution," "In the struggle to break the power of the moribund classes it is dangerous to be tied down to bourgeois notions and concepts of democracy, freedom, and equality."[191] In the future, Soviet advice to other revolutionaries would account for this danger and once again bourgeois democracy would be seen as a cover for imperialist machinations. This would contribute to the strategy of the Soviet Union and the Tudeh Party in Iran in the wake of the latter nation's 1979 revolution.[192] The defeat in Chile would not inspire a complete strategic reversal, however. In addition to their embrace of constitutional democracy, the PC and the Soviets had also adopted a gradualist economic strategy, one focused on increasing production and gaining popular (including middle-class) support rather than seizing the means of production and investing in state-controlled heavy industry. This economic gradualism, paired with political control, would be characteristic of Soviet-inspired revolutionary programs in the latter part of the Cold War. Though some would seek to move faster—Mengistu Haile Mariam in Ethiopia being a prominent example—Moscow would advocate a more gradual, less coercive approach to socialist economic transition.

3

TANZANIAN *UJAMAA*

Building Socialism in a Communist World

> To summarize, the planning and control system is like a sa-
> fari. First you determine where you are, then where you want
> to go. After that you plan the route, and agree among your-
> selves on the plan. Once you have set off, you check from time
> to time that you are still on the right track.
>
> —Government of Tanzania, *Draft Planning and Control Guide,*
> October 1972

In 1967, two months after formally setting Tanzania on a socialist path
with the Arusha Declaration, President Julius Nyerere proclaimed, "It
is imperative that socialists continue thinking. . . . It is necessary that those
who call themselves scientific socialists should be scientific!"[1] Nyerere pronounced those words in Cairo, a city that had a strong claim in 1967 as
the epicenter of the Third World, because his program to build socialism
without class struggle—focusing initially on agricultural rather than industrial development and relying primarily on his country's own resources
instead of foreign aid—had brought criticism from adherents of various
forms of Marxism both within Tanzania and abroad who saw it at best
as a product of misguided idealism or, at worst, as reactionary obfusca-
tion. While the Arusha Declaration had given rise to great hope in some
corners, it would also give rise to deep skepticism in others. In Cairo,
Nyerere was attempting to make a case to the rest of the developing world
that one could seriously pursue socialism without becoming a client of
Beijing or Moscow and that ideological disagreements over the nature of

socialism should be welcomed as productive rather than seen as grounds for political conflict.

What Nyerere failed to acknowledge in that speech, however, was that the "scientific socialists" had not stopped thinking about how to build socialism in places like Tanzania. Since the late 1950s, Soviet theorists and policy makers had been aware of the practical and theoretical difficulties presented by the prospect of adapting Marxism-Leninism to the postcolonial context in which countries with underdeveloped economies, little industrial development, and weak political systems sought to advance to socialism without venturing through the capitalist stage first.[2] This gave rise to the elaboration of a theory of the "noncapitalist path of development," which became formally enshrined as the communist program for the developing world at the Moscow meeting of the international communist movement in November 1960.[3] Putting this theory into practice would prove to be tricky. Initial Soviet hopes for the construction of socialism in postcolonial Africa centered on West Africa—in particular, the countries of Ghana, Guinea, and Mali, where radical leaders espousing combinations of socialism and African nationalism were openly opposing the West and seeking aid from the East.[4] There Moscow attempted to help build a heavy industrial base in the hopes that it would produce a working class that would then form a communist party. The realization of the aid program proved more difficult than envisioned, and local leaders soon began to worry that the Soviets' long-term plans included subverting and ultimately overthrowing their regimes. Consequently, the Soviet ambassador in Guinea was expelled in December 1961, and his counterpart in Mali nearly suffered the same fate in February 1963. This method of building socialism in Africa therefore proved to be not only an economic failure but a political catastrophe as well.

This did not discourage the Soviets from seeking to build socialism in Africa, but it did lead them to consider other ways of doing so. In December 1965 the deputy head of the Africa Sector of the International Department of the Central Committee of the Communist Party of the Soviet Union (CPSU) told an East German diplomat in Moscow that while Tanzania's leftward progress was slow, "the slow tempo of this development process doubtlessly also has positive aspects, because obviously the occasionally occurring overhastiness [*Übereiltheit*] in some African countries—the experiences of Guinea, for example—will not occur in Tanzania."[5] Though neither Nyerere's rhetoric nor his policies were what the Soviets themselves had envisioned, they were curious to see the direction these policies would take, and the evolution of his ideology, in the hopes that his version of socialism, known as *ujamaa* ("familyhood," in Swahili), might provide a useful blueprint for the spreading of socialism on the continent.

The Soviets were not the only ones interested in the progress, or lack thereof, of *ujamaa*. For certain Western governments, Nyerere's eschewing of the rhetoric of class and racial struggle, and his constant emphasis on maintaining an independent foreign policy, made him seem like a beacon of hope in a continent that was, as the phrase attributed to Chinese premier Zhou Enlai famously put it, "ripe for revolution."[6] As the Canadian high commissioner in Dar es Salaam, evaluating the Arusha Declaration for the UK Foreign and Commonwealth Office (FCO) at a time when Tanzania had broken relations with London, wrote, "If Arusha succeeds, I suggest that Tanzania may well become politically one of the more stable states in Africa. . . . 'Arushaism' should serve as an immunization against Maoism or Stalinism—always provided it succeeds."[7] The Australian high commissioner wrote that "Julius Nyerere is now indeed sui generis in Africa. He has formulated in the Arusha Declaration, and in all the explanation which has followed, an ideological framework which, with all its inadequacies and impractical idealism, is coherent and consistent, almost elegant in its simplicity and relevant to the social and economic problems of Tanzania." Rejecting the claim that Nyerere was under communist influence, he added, "To search too hard for influences on Nyerere is, however, to fail to give him the credit he deserves for his own undoubted capacity—if only by African standards—for creative and original thinking."[8] These views certainly did not represent the unanimous opinion of *ujamaa* in Western capitals; as Deputy Under-Secretary of State Leslie Monson, responding to the Canadian high commissioner, noted, "There is certainly ground for believing that Arusha socialism will develop into a very nasty weed indeed and one which will permit no other plants to thrive alongside it."[9] Nevertheless, the progress of *ujamaa* was being monitored with great interest by Western governments to see whether it might inoculate Africa against communist penetration or instead prepare the ground for it.

Ironically, the foreign power that would ultimately come to play the largest role in Tanzania on the ground—namely, the People's Republic of China (PRC)—seemed to show the least interest in the actual progress of *ujamaa*. In Zhou Enlai's "Message of Greetings to President Nyerere on TANU's [the Tanganyikan African National Union's] National Conference," delivered only months after the Arusha Declaration, he wrote, "Last

126

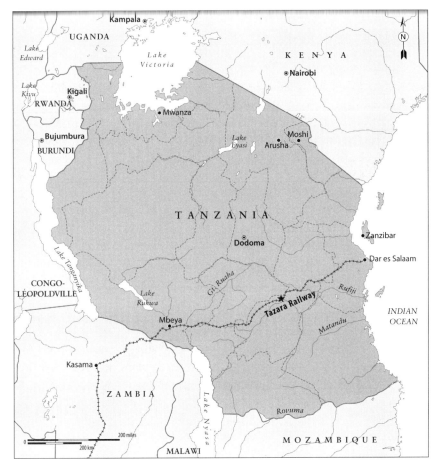

MAP 3.1 Tanzania in 1970.

February, you adopted the well-known 'Arusha Declaration' and continued to push forward the Tanzanian people's patriotic struggle against
imperialism and their cause of national construction through self-
reliance."[10] Zhou's letter mentioned imperialism five times, but it did not
mention socialism once. On Nyerere's subsequent visits to China in 1968
and 1974, discussion would largely center on the liberation struggles in
southern Africa while *ujamaa* was hardly discussed.[11] Much ink would
be spilled by the diplomatic corps in Dar es Salaam in trying to divine
what Beijing was really after in making Tanzania the centerpiece of its
African aid policy, and the specter of Chinese influence would become a

powerful factor in Tanzanian domestic and international politics independent of the actual intentions of the Chinese leadership.

As time went on, Nyerere himself became more and more interested in a different international audience—his fellow leaders of Third World countries. As the president of a poor nation trying to build socialism on its own while also fighting for the liberation of the whole of southern Africa, Nyerere increasingly positioned himself as a spokesman of the Third World on visits to places like Cuba, Sweden, and Yugoslavia, as well as in such venues as the Commonwealth of Nations, the Non-Aligned Movement, and the Organisation of African Unity. His experience in building socialism in Tanzania would provide the background for a radical critique of the international economic system, and Nyerere became one of the most vocal proponents of the New International Economic Order adopted by the United Nations General Assembly in May 1974.[12] His rising status as a leader of the Third World only enhanced his importance—and that of his socialist experiment—in the eyes of many around the world.

Tanzania's experiment in socialism also acted as a magnet for sympathetic scholars and activists in the 1960s and 1970s, many of whom came to teach at the University of Dar es Salaam, which became something of a hotbed of radical politics during this period.[13] The presence of these foreign scholars only a few kilometers from the centers of political power complicated matters by engendering a domestic leftist opposition to Nyerere and exacerbated the concerns of foreign diplomats on both sides of the Cold War divide. Their presence, however, also presents something of a dilemma for the historian, because they were both active participants in the politics of the time and at the same time its analysts and chroniclers. The work of these scholars has therefore shaped the historiographical debates on *ujamaa* and given it a focus that in large part derives from the concerns of those who participated in it: What sort of socialism was it? What did it need to be to succeed, and why did it fail?[14] A wave of new works on Tanzania by younger scholars has begun to shift the focus to questions of nationalism, political consolidation, and group identity.[15] This new focus on the historiography of Tanzania has just begun to find echoes in a reexamination of *ujamaa* itself.[16] In the process, however, some of the focus on socialism, which was inarguably central to the concerns of the historical actors being studied, has tended to recede in the face of more contemporary concerns about politics and identity.

The attempt to construct a uniquely African version of socialism in Tanzania was an inherently nationalist project, however, and one cannot tell the story of Tanzania's postcolonial national consolidation without an examination of the ideology and policies of *ujamaa*. This is particularly salient when situating Tanzania in an international context, because key foreign actors—in particular, the two superpowers, the United States and the USSR—were just as concerned with the nature of Tanzania's domestic policies and ideology as they were with its foreign policy. In fact, policy makers in Moscow, Washington, and elsewhere often took foreign policy as indicative of the true nature of domestic policy, and vice versa. This view was mirrored by Nyerere himself, for whom socialism had both a domestic and a foreign component, and he talked about sacrificing for the development of Tanzania and sacrificing for the liberation of Africa as inseparable duties of the Tanzanian people. As a consequence, ideological independence and political independence were necessarily connected for Nyerere, and the loss of one could lead to the loss of the other. The development of *ujamaa* then needs to be seen in this international context, both because of the foreign pressures it engendered and because of Nyerere's concern with the way those foreign pressures could reshape Tanzania's domestic politics and diminish its independence. Despite his socialist convictions and experiences with Western colonialism and neocolonialism, Nyerere was actually deeply suspicious of communism and therefore perpetually vigilant about letting Marxism gain too great a foothold in the country. As political and security threats mounted in the early 1970s, however, Nyerere's foreign policy concerns began to shift to the West, and particularly to the growing active or passive support on the part of North Atlantic Treaty Organization countries for the continuation of white rule in southern Africa, while interaction with communist powers, especially China, had proven much less threatening. Yet despite the leftward movement of Tanzanian politics and ideology in the 1970s, Nyerere continued to refuse to embrace Marxism fully, and Soviet views of *ujamaa* went from cautiously optimistic to deeply disillusioned, especially in the wake of the failure of forced villagization from 1973 to 1976. With Tanzania now in desperate economic straits, and with no great power patron behind it, Nyerere shifted his hopes to the Third Worldist movement for global economic equality, resisting as best he could the push for Structural Adjustment that his successor, Ali Hassan Mwinyi, would eventually embrace. In a world divided between capitalists and communists, attempting to blaze a new path to socialism in the Third World would prove a lonely and ultimately impossible task.

From Independence to Arusha, 1961–1967

Compared to its neighbors to the north, south, and west, independence came to Tanganyika (the mainland portion of what would become Tanzania) relatively peacefully. Having been a German colony before World War I, Tanganyika was never able to shift the focus of British economic interest in East Africa from its northern neighbors, and the presence of white British settlers did not present as much of an obstacle to independence as it did in Kenya.[17] What economic development there was focused almost exclusively on the production of agricultural raw materials for export—in particular, sisal—and there was little processing of these materials done in Tanganyika, let alone industries focused on import substitution. Though TANU—formed out of the Tanganyikan African Association in 1954—quickly gained wide support throughout the country, according to Cranford Pratt, "the speed with which African nationalism became a major force throughout Tanganyika cannot be explained primarily as a consequence of general processes of social change that were rapidly transforming Tanganyikan society."[18] Rather than being a movement dominated primarily by an outward-looking elite mobilized by the dislocations of a dynamic economy, TANU was formed from a myriad of groups with varied, often conflicting interests, the composition of which differed from region to region.[19] While its early years were marked by political struggle, TANU's landslide victory in multiracial elections in September 1958 led Sir Richard Turnbull, the last colonial governor, to announce that Tanganyika would develop as a primarily African state. For the next three years TANU would adopt moderate policies and cooperate with the British as the country moved toward independence. In short, Tanganyika appeared to be an unlikely candidate for a radical leftward turn.

This moderation was embodied in the figure of Julius Nyerere, TANU's nearly undisputed leader from its foundation. Only thirty-one when he was elected president of the Tanganyikan African Association in 1953, he was a chief's son who had made his way from a local Roman Catholic primary school through the elite East African educational institutions in Tabora, Tanganyika; Makerere University in Kampala, Uganda; to the University of Edinburgh in 1949. When he arrived in Edinburgh, he was met at the train station by a member of the UK Colonial Office Welfare Department, among other reasons because "people from the Communist Party cells were also at Waverley station meeting students."[20] Nyerere never seemed to lean in that direction, however, inclining instead toward the Christian socialism of his teachers at Edinburgh, particularly John MacMurray and Axel Stern. His professor of political economy, Sir Alexander Gray, concluded his 1946 work *The Socialist Tradition: Moses to Lenin* by stating that "the great need of the present day is for a prophet of liberalism . . . because liberalism at the present moment is dangerously in eclipse." Perhaps locating that prophet, the final sentence speaks of the "very great and deserved welcome accorded to Mr. [Friedrich] Hayek's warnings regarding *The Road to Serfdom*."[21] Even before Edinburgh, however, Nyerere had already been developing his theory of a socialism built on African traditions that would not require the kind of class struggle envisioned by Marxism. As Thomas Molony argues, many of the key elements of Nyerere's 1962 pamphlet *Ujamaa—The Basis of African Socialism* were present already in a letter written to the *Tanganyika Standard* in July 1943.[22] As the leader of TANU before independence, Nyerere was the chief architect of its policy of cooperation with the British authorities, insisting on the reservation of seats for Asians and Europeans in the Legislative Council, which he saw as necessary "to avoid any impression that Africans were seeking to ignore or to overwhelm the interests of the non-Africans."[23] Like TANU as a whole, Nyerere seemed to envision a path to political independence and economic development that avoided violent disruption of any kind.

It was no surprise then that newly independent Tanganyika and its moderate president were regarded with a healthy degree of skepticism in Beijing and Moscow. As late as February 1961, the Soviet embassy in Ethiopia reported that Tanganyika was one of the few colonies in Africa where the independence struggle "had not yet taken on a decisive character." This was supposedly because Tanganyika's low population density and lack of European settlers meant that land was not yet scarce. (Land scarcity was said to be the chief economic impetus for national liberation movements elsewhere.) TANU's cooperation with the British, Nyerere's promises of "race peace," and the lack of calls for fundamental economic independence all pointed to the conclusion that what was taking place was a strategic handover of control rather than a struggle for independence.[24] East Germany's Abteilung Internationale Verbindungen (AIV; Department of International Ties), equivalent to the Soviet International Department, considered Nyerere "western-oriented" and also criticized his racial policies. Instead, the East Germans imagined alternatives to Nyerere within TANU as the masses grew dissatisfied with his policies, focusing especially on the figure of Oscar Kambona, TANU's general secretary, as the potential leader of a popular revolt.[25] The Chinese were similarly concerned about Nyerere's "nonracism" (非种族主义), lack of class analysis, "illusions" about the West, and cooperation with the British, so much so that for a time they actually supported other African opposition parties in Tanganyika.[26]

Tanganyika's economic policies in its first years of independence seemed to confirm this skepticism. A three-year plan created with the help of the International Development Bank was adopted in July 1961 that paid little attention to the domination of the economy by Asians and Europeans, inciting a wave of strikes and demonstrations.[27] This came in the wake of a speech in Cologne in January of that year in which Nyerere declared, "It is clear to us that the government alone does not have enough means to enable the development of our country, and we recognize that in large measure we will consequently have to rely on private enterprise."[28] The following December, a village settlement scheme was inaugurated based on recommendations from the World Bank that envisioned highly mechanized farming, which would necessarily rely on capital and experts from the West.[29] As a whole, despite promises of "Africanization" of the bureaucracy, Tanganyika continued to be heavily reliant on British civil servants, and the middle and senior ranks of the civil service had a foreign majority as late as 1963.[30] In this context, Nyerere's publication of his pamphlet introducing *ujamaa* in 1962 seemed no more significant than the many proclamations of socialist policies by leaders in the postcolonial world that would either wilt under foreign pressure or turn out to be empty words, leading Nikita Khrushchev to ask during a speech in Sofia, "What kind of socialism do they have in mind?"[31]

Nevertheless, soon after Nyerere's pronouncement of Tanganyika's turn toward socialism, the government began seeking Soviet aid. George Kahama, the minister of trade and industry, went to Moscow seeking help in developing Tanganyikan industry, and particularly the exploitation of its mineral wealth. To try to get the Soviets to come through, he told Deputy Chairman A. I. Alikhanov of the Gosudarstvennyi Komitet po Vneshnim Ekonomicheskim Sviaziam (GKES; State Committee for Foreign Economic Relations), the institution specifically responsible for foreign economic aid, that "the Republic has made its goal the construction of African socialism. Therefore attracting private capital is undesirable. The government has decided to turn to the socialist countries, which are not interested in the exploitation of the resources of the country for their own purposes."[32] In particular, Kahama claimed that Tanganyika was planning to nationalize a British electric company, and he wanted to know if the Soviets could help run the plants after nationalization. Two months later Alikhanov received Minister of Labor Michael Kamaliza, who came to emphasize how much his government was hoping for Soviet help because of what the USSR had already done for the United Arab Republic, saying that "Tanganyika similarly intends to follow the path of progress, relying on the help of socialist countries, in particular the Soviet Union."[33] Alikhanov promised that the Soviet government would seriously consider Tanganyika's requests, and 1963 did see Tanganyika sign its first trade agreements with Bulgaria, Czechoslovakia, Hungary, Poland, the USSR, and Yugoslavia.[34] The overall picture in Moscow was still rather negative, however, and it would take a series of internal and external developments in Tanganyika and Zanzibar before communist countries started taking Nyerere's socialism more seriously.

Those developments began with the revolution that shook the newly independent island of Zanzibar, right off the Tanganyikan coast, in January 1964. While the revolution excited some on the communist side of the Cold War divide and frightened others on the capitalist side, leading in particular to the development of lasting, productive relationships between Zanzibar and the Chinese and East Germans,[35] what concerns us here is how the subsequent merger of revolutionary Zanzibar with the mainland to create the new nation of Tanzania was perceived abroad. In communist capitals, the merger was generally understood to be an attempt by the United Kingdom and the United States to bring the Zanzibari revolution under the control of their reliable friend Julius Nyerere, who was said to himself be worried about "communist influence" from Zanzibar.[36] The Soviet embassy in London claimed that the British had orchestrated the whole thing: "having lost their previous influence in Zanzibar, the English tried to stop the development of democratic changes in the country through the union with Tanganyika through Nyerere, who is known for his pro-English orientation."[37] In fact, it might have been the Soviets' own past sins that took the question of communism off the table in Zanzibar, as a US Department of State telegram reveals that none other than Sekou Toure, the president of Guinea, sent a special emissary to warn Zanzibari president Abeid Karume of the dangers of "over-dependence on Communists, citing Guinea's own experience."[38] In any case, the evidence suggests that the union was Nyerere's own idea and was not taken under the direction of London or Washington.[39] (According to one high-level Tanzanian official, it might not have even been Nyerere's idea originally, but

Karume's.)[40] Nevertheless, the seemingly anticommunist nature of the union was compounded when it led to a standoff over German diplomatic representation, since the mainland recognized West Germany but Zanzibar recognized East Germany. Bonn successfully insisted on the status reduction of East German representation, and Kambona told Khrushchev in Cairo not to make an issue of it.[41]

While the union of Tanganyika and Zanzibar seemed to portend ill for the potential of communism in Tanzania, the contemporaneous mutiny of the mainland army, which had to be finally put down by the British Royal Marines, would ultimately have the opposite effect. The soldiers were protesting the slow pace of Africanization of the officer corps, so the fact that the government had to ask for British help to put down the mutiny was particularly humiliating. Nyerere responded by replacing the British officers training the Tanzanian Army with, among others, Chinese instructors. The Americans were apoplectic over the idea of Tanzania inviting the Chinese military, and the US ambassador tried several times personally to convince Nyerere otherwise. The pressure got so intense that Nyerere exploded at a press conference in August, "Am I really expected to believe such rubbish? I do not like this. I protest against this kind of pressure. It must stop. The Chinese want to colonize Tanganyika, my foot! It is humiliating that I have to explain to ambassadors any decision accepting seven Chinese advisors. . . . India quarreled with China, but it does not question our accepting Chinese military aid. I use Israelis here. No Arab country has asked why we accept aid from Israel. But seven Chinese instructors for six months and look what happens."[42]

While the invitation of Chinese instructors rapidly turned up the temperature of the Cold War in Tanzania, Nyerere's strategy was not about balancing East and West. The British journalist Colin Legum spoke with Nyerere and reported the latter's opinion (in the clipped language of State Department telegrams) that the "West analyzes African problem in terms of its own relationship with East. It has begun to identify common interests with USSR and is much less alarmed today by Soviets than CHICOMS [Communist Chinese]. So East-West rivalry in Africa tends become CHICOM-West competition, but for Africans East-East competition more deadly and they must find way between increasingly antagonist Soviet and CHICOM interests. Nyerere also concluded Russians were greater menace in Zanzibar than Chinese."[43] These remarks shed new light on the growing Tanzanian rapprochement with China in the mid-1960s that caused so much alarm in London and Washington. Before the Third Afro-Asian

FIGURE 3.1 Tanzanian president Julius Nyerere with Chinese premier Zhou Enlai in Dar es Salaam, June 1965. It was here that Zhou described the conditions for revolution as favorable throughout Africa, Asia, and Latin America. *(Tanzanian Ministry of Foreign Affairs)*

People's Solidarity Conference, held in Moshi, Tanganyika, in February 1963, a Chinese delegation met with Nyerere, Vice President Rashidi Kawawa, and others, leading to the signing of aid and trade agreements.[44] In addition to helping train its army, China would help Tanzania build a rice farm, a textile factory, and a farm implements factory before offering to help it build a railway to the Zambian copper belt. During the next two years, first Kawawa and then Nyerere would visit China, and

135

Zhou would culminate his tour of Africa in 1965 in Tanzania with a speech expanding the area supposedly "ripe for revolution" to include Asia and Latin America.[45] But Nyerere's relationship with China during this period was utilitarian, a product of China's willingness to help out on terms more advantageous than those offered by other countries, including the Soviet Union.

China's comparative weakness on the world stage meant that it was easier for Tanzania to maintain its political and ideological independence vis-à-vis Beijing than it would have been had it relied on Moscow or Washington. Kambona told the US ambassador that on Nyerere's visit to China in 1965 the Chinese tried to make him sign a joint communiqué condemning US aggression around the world, but Nyerere refused to sign, and Zhou had to be woken up at 3:00 a.m. to approve a watered-down draft.[46] According to the Soviet Foreign Ministry, at a banquet during the visit Nyerere responded to pressure to side with China on the Sino-Soviet split by saying "we will not allow our friends to choose our enemies."[47] Despite Zhou's infamous remark on his subsequent trip to Tanzania, the United Kingdom was "not nearly so distressed with [the] visit and Nyerere['s] performance as it might have been," and was quite pleased with the negative local reaction to Zhou's speech.[48] The aid negotiations between China and Tanzania also revealed that the two sides were just as divided on domestic policy as on foreign policy, and while both proclaimed a fealty to the concept of "self-reliance," as the Soviet Foreign Ministry noted, they understood that term to mean very different things .[49]

The negotiations over the Ubungo Farm Implements factory are highly revealing in this regard. As part of an agreement on economic and technical cooperation in June 1964, China agreed to provide Tanzania with a factory to produce basic farm implements, including ox-drawn plows, *jembes* (hoes), *pangas* (machetes), and axes for Tanzanian farmers, but the negotiations hit a snag when it turned out that the projected retail prices would end up higher than those of implements currently being imported from the United Kingdom. While the National Development Corporation doubted whether pouring resources into a factory whose production would have to be subsidized by the government was a good idea, the Chinese responded that what mattered wasn't profitability but self-reliance. In a meeting with the Tanzanian treasury secretary, Chinese representatives explained that the factory "was in keeping with the Arusha Declaration of self-reliance" and "it would be a sheer waste of time to go into the profitability of the scheme as it was not profit that was aimed at but the quality of the implements and the need to supply them in quantities enough to meet the demand of the Tanzanian Agricultural policy." In response, the treasury secretary revealed his own view of how to put self-reliance into practice: "I answered that I agreed with them that self-sufficiency was our prime objective, but I added that it was in our interests also to be sure that the factory would be able to pay for itself, notwithstanding the fact that if possibilities for exports to our neighbors existed it would be advisable to take them into account, particularly as we had to realize the necessary foreign exchange with which to repay this and our foreign loans."[50] The two sides went back and forth, with the Tanzanians demanding a feasibility study to prove the factory would be economical, while the Chinese thought such considerations were irrelevant and wanted to push ahead. The minister for industries, mineral resources, and power stepped in to calm things down, observing that "it is not surprising that we are experiencing a certain amount of difficulty in our dealings with the Chinese team on this project. . . . The fact is simply that the Chinese do not understand our business practices and modes which are essentially based on the Western European fashion. It will, therefore, be quite unfair to expect the Chinese to react in the same way as an investor from a capitalist economy would in similar circumstances." Yet even he agreed that Tanzania needed to make profitability a priority, writing "whilst it is true that there will be some undesirable political ramifications if the Chinese offer is rejected, I tend to agree with you that our decisions should be based purely on economic considerations."[51] The factory would ultimately be built by the Chinese, despite the fact that its implements would be both more expensive and of lower quality than the imports they were replacing. This exchange took place in the first month after the Arusha Declaration, and it would turn out that, in the new political climate, the Chinese understanding of self-reliance would have a lot more purchase with Nyerere than these Tanzanian officials understood at the time.

The contradictions between a leadership pushing a socialist model and a bureaucracy still focused on a Western-oriented development scheme became increasingly evident in the years before the Arusha Declaration of February 1967. In its annual report for 1965, the East German consulate reported that some of TANU's principles reflected the "theory and practice of scientific socialism" but that foreigners in the government apparatus were sabotaging government decisions.[52] As a consequence, the actual economic direction of the country was still ambiguous while

Africanization was beginning to produce an African bourgeoisie. Toward the end of 1966, the returning East German consul told his colleagues at the Ministry of Foreign Affairs in a debriefing that "the progressive forces are potentially strong. The main weakness of the progressive forces are that they have no ideology and are weakly organized."[53] While Nyerere was the key, the consul considered him nothing more than a "liberal with socialist thought patterns [*Gedankengängen*]." Similarly, the Soviet vice consul in Zanzibar, in a meeting with the director of the Tanzanian Department of Planning and Development in December 1966, thought that it was the continuing influence of imperialists on the mainland, largely in the bureaucracy, that was keeping the nation from developing along a noncapitalist path.[54] Beyond the influence of outsiders, however, the Soviets also saw fundamental economic transformations as taking Tanzania away from its stated socialist path, noting that "agrarian relations in Tanganyika are under the influence of a process of social differentiation. The official policy of the government for the development of 'African socialist communes [*obshchiny*]' is not competing successfully with the capitalist path of agricultural development on the basis of private property." In particular, this was producing a "kulak" class of African farmers, especially in the north of the country.[55] While some at the top in Tanzania had good intentions, the East Germans and Soviets felt that those intentions were not backed by either a strong ideology or a strong organization and were consequently being overwhelmed by the forces of capitalism, both domestically and internationally, as well as being undermined by an ambivalent bureaucracy.

While Nyerere was disinclined toward "scientific socialism" and nervous about the influence of its foreign state sponsors, he substantially agreed with their diagnoses of why socialism in Tanzania was not making much progress. Evaluating the results of the Arusha Declaration ten years later, Nyerere would claim its primary accomplishment was that "we in Tanzania have stopped, and reversed, a national drift toward the growth of a class society."[56] Any efforts at development undertaken thus far seemed to be producing new privileged groups that pursued their own interests. When students at the University of Dar es Salaam responded to the imposition of a National Service requirement by marching on the government in October 1966, Nyerere, in an emotional speech, expelled all the protestors from the university. As the US embassy noted, "President Nyerere is faced with a problem of critical importance for the future of his country. Advanced education is obviously a crucial factor in developing a society. Given his ideologically-based rejection of the formation of a 'privileged' African class, the President must seriously consider the question: How can such education be given to a necessarily small minority of the people without inducing elitist tendencies? This [is] a head cracker which no society has yet solved, least of all the Communists with their 'new classes' and elite party."[57] Eight months before the student protest, Nyerere gave a speech titled "Leaders Must Not Be Masters" that bemoaned the conduct of the leadership, which seemed to be setting itself up as an unaccountable elite.[58] Job Lusinde, who would become one of the chief architects of the *ujamaa* policy, later remembered that party and government elites at the time began "imitating colonial government behavior" and that "we who were privileged started becoming rich," describing how a bank manager convinced him to take a loan in 1965 to build himself a new house.[59] If Tanzania was to become a socialist country, it would need a change of course that would both establish a clearer ideological direction and a stronger enforcement mechanism.

Thus, on the eve of the Arusha Declaration, Nyerere was trying to perform a difficult balancing act. He wanted to develop the country along socialist lines but hoped to avoid dependence on foreign aid providers that could demand political favors in return. He wanted to prevent the evolution toward a class society, but adopting the language of class would create precisely the divisions he was seeking to preempt. Implementing any such policy meant turning TANU, which had already been established as the sole political party in 1965, into a powerful instrument of rule, but that had to be done without turning it into a self-contained elite party. Internationally, diplomatic crises with the United Kingdom, United States, and West Germany had distanced Tanzania from the West, but Nyerere remained as reluctant as ever to embrace the Soviet Union. Domestically he was caught between a bureaucracy composed largely of Westerners or those trained in Western countries, and a nascent leftist opposition in TANU and among the university students attracted to the examples of communist countries and socialist professors. The Arusha Declaration, and the policy papers that followed it and expanded upon it, would have to establish a path to socialism sufficiently robust to resist the pull of capitalist development without abdicating Tanzania's ideological, and perhaps political, independence by embracing scientific socialism. While the theoretical task was difficult enough, the practical application of *ujamaa* with the tools available would prove nearly impossible. All the while, both sides of the Cold War divide waited to see to which side of the tightrope Tanzania would fall.

The Arusha Declaration and Its Aftermath, 1967–1970

The Arusha Declaration, adopted by TANU's National Executive Committee on January 29, 1967, and then published on February 5, laid out a vision of socialism that gave hints of scientific socialism without actually embracing it. The document, largely written by Nyerere but amended by the party, insisted that "the state must have effective control over the principal means of production" and that "it is essential that the ruling Party should be a party of peasants and workers." Yet rather than implementing a vetting process for TANU membership based on occupation or class background, the declaration ordered TANU and government leaders to divest themselves of excess resources or capitalist investments. The idea seemed to be that socialism was the product of belief achieved through a process of ideological transformation rather than a result of political struggle over material inequality. It was not that Nyerere rejected the notion of class analysis or class struggle in principle or thought that they were inapplicable to Africa; rather, the goal of the program envisioned in the declaration was to preempt the development of a class structure, since "these feudalistic and capitalistic features of our society could spread and entrench themselves." Most of the document was taken up with justifying and explaining two elements of *ujamaa* that would distinguish it from other forms of socialism: the prioritization of agricultural over industrial development and an emphasis on self-reliance. Such self-reliance was a product of Tanzania's harsh international experience since independence; as Nyerere asked, "How can we depend upon foreign governments and companies for the major part of our development without giving to those governments and countries a great part of our freedom to act as we please?"[60] The prioritization of agriculture was in part necessitated by this idea of self-reliance; since Tanzania was primarily agricultural already, the only way to earn an investable surplus without foreign aid would be through the development of agriculture. Nyerere, though, was also concerned about what prioritizing industrialization in a predominantly rural country would do to its social structure. Were the state to exploit the peasants to invest in urban areas, that would produce precisely the sort of class divisions he sought to avoid. Underlying Arusha socialism,

140

then, seemed to be a conviction that the choice of means for their social, political, and moral content was as important as the specification of the ends.

The seriousness of the shift in policy was made apparent immediately, as the government nationalized major branches of the economy nearly overnight.[61] The declaration was then followed by two targeted elaborations of policy—"Education for Self-Reliance" and "Socialism and Rural Development"—that set concrete directions for Tanzania's transition to socialism.[62] While they had some reservations, the reactions of the Soviets and their allies to Tanzania's new course were quite positive. An article in the *African Communist,* the journal of the Moscow-allied South African Communist Party, even preempted possible criticism of the declaration by noting that, "in any case, socialism in Africa must learn to speak the language of Africa. Anyone who does not recognize these things is not a Marxist but an armchair pedant."[63] Such a reaction was revealing, and it could not have been taken for granted. The Arusha Declaration was not only written without any Soviet input but broke with the Soviet doctrine of prioritizing industrial development; it represented yet another attempt to create an explicitly non-Marxist version of socialism. In addition, the declaration was promulgated at the height of the Cultural Revolution, when Soviet fears about Chinese ideological influence were at their zenith. Superficially, at least, Tanzania's socialist turn bore significant resemblances to events in China, with Nyerere himself even calling for a cultural revolution and the TANU Youth League doing its best imitation of the PRC's Red Guards.[64] The Arusha program also contained more substantive elements of the Chinese approach, particularly in its emphasis on agriculture, self-reliance, and a belief in the possibility of ideological transformations of individuals instead of seeing class as fate.[65] Despite this, the Chinese leadership was less enthusiastic about the Arusha Declaration than the Soviets were, considering it "insufficiently revolutionary."[66] Nevertheless, Tanzania's relations with Beijing were at this point certainly much closer than those with Moscow, and Nyerere would make his second trip to China in 1968 though he had yet to set foot on Soviet soil. Before the end of 1967, Tanzania would accept the Chinese proposal to build a rail link between Dar es Salaam and the Zambian copper belt, a fact that certainly did not please the Soviets. That December the Zambian ambassador in Moscow reported that "the Third Africa Division of the Soviet Ministry of Foreign Affairs, which is in charge of matters relating to Zambia, has for some time now been expressing the

141

FIGURE 3.2 Chinese engineers meeting with Tanzanian officials for the planning of the Tazara railway. The railway would be Beijing's largest aid project in the developing world during the Cold War. *(Tanzanian Ministry of Foreign Affairs)*

Soviet desire for the construction of the railway. . . . These expressions are followed by the usual questions on how the progress with the Chinese offer is going. Usually, this is followed by statements like 'Maybe the Cultural Revolution did so much damage to the Chinese economy that it makes or may make it unable to meet its commitments.'"[67] Between the ideological heterodoxy of the program and Tanzania's budding relationship with Moscow's rival for leadership of the international communist movement, the Soviets certainly had plenty of reasons to react negatively to the Arusha Declaration.

The positive reaction among the Soviets and their allies therefore testifies to the earnestness with which they sought to promote socialism in the developing world, as well as, perhaps, a certain capacity for self-deception. An internal evaluation by the East German AIV saw the Arusha Declaration as "the expression of the beginning of a new stage in the construction of the anticapitalist progressive development conception of the revolutionary-democratic leading forces of TANU." More emphatically, the author saw it as evidence of a shift from "petit bourgeois nationalism" tied with "pan-African, bourgeois democratic, and religious elements" to "acceptance of the fundamental ideas of scientific socialism."[68] While the East German consul general in Dar es Salaam was not quite as sanguine, he did see it as a program for "noncapitalist development" and as the "kernel of a social order that can be described as socialist."[69] "Socialism and Rural Development,", which appeared in September 1967, was evaluated even more positively, as it seemed to definitely mark the development of *ujamaa* along "scientific" lines. Most important, the East German consul to Zanzibar noted, "for the first time the class question is concretely and clearly worked out (differentiation process on the land and analysis of the current situation)."[70] Initial internal Soviet evaluations are hard to find, but that year Rostislav Ul'ianovskii, one of the top officials in the International Department concerned with promoting socialism in the developing world, helped put out a collective work titled *The Noncapitalist Path of Development in the Countries of Africa*. The book pointed to the Arusha Declaration as a defining moment for the development of socialism in Africa in which the importance of relying on the peasants and workers, and containing the bourgeoisie, was finally recognized.[71] Despite Nyerere's overt desire to arrest the tendency toward class differentiation in Tanzania, the East Germans and Soviets saw his very invocation of the concept as evidence of progress toward something they would recognize as socialism.

This is not to say, however, that they thought Tanzania's future progress toward socialism was assured. For starters, there were all sorts of actors influencing, or attempting to influence, the progress of Tanzanian socialism. Aside from the Chinese, who were a constant source of discussion, the East Germans saw the Israeli kibbutz as a particularly influential model and they were concerned about the role of the European social democracies; the "Fabians" and "English liberals" teaching at the University of Dar es Salaam; and the French professor René Dumont, whose book *False Start in Africa* made a notable impact on Nyerere's thinking. But there were two key issues that both the East Germans and Soviets saw as still missing from the existing pronouncements and which they thought would determine whether *ujamaa* would succeed. The first was the role of class. While Nyerere had introduced the language of class, and even spoke of TANU as a party of "workers and peasants," he had not accepted class struggle as the fundamental mechanism of political change and, until he did, his policies were doomed to fail. As a consequence of this, the TANU leadership, including Nyerere, maintained its illusions about bourgeois democracy (albeit a single-party version), and therefore failed to understand the proper role of a ruling party in the transition to socialism.[72] Even before the Arusha Declaration, the East German consul in Dar es Salaam suggested to Oscar Kambona that TANU should reorganize itself along the lines of a communist party, including the addition of a politburo.[73] Authors in the *African Communist* argued that "the vital hill to be climbed now in Tanzania's ascent to the summit of socialism is the building of a leading party of active socialist organizers, teachers, and leaders" and "what remains to be seen is whether [TANU] can act as a vanguard."[74] Reviewing the work of Ul'ianovskii and others on African socialism, Vladimir Iordanskii viewed the lack of a unified vanguard revolutionary party as one of the main obstacles on Tanzania's noncapitalist path, pointing in particular to the opposition Nyerere's policies encountered at a party conference in Mwanza in October 1967.[75] It would be along these two vectors that Moscow and its allies would measure Tanzania's subsequent progress, and the issues of class analysis and constructing a vanguard party would become heated ones inside Tanzania, both inside and outside official circles, especially as many grew frustrated with the slow pace of progress toward *ujamaa*.

The Arusha Declaration was met with ambivalence among Western diplomats, whose analysis was often exactly the opposite of that of Eastern Europeans. The British high commissioner in Nairobi thought that the declaration included "readily identified Communist terminology" and was "much more radical than African Socialism practiced in neighboring countries." In particular, he thought it represented the "Communist" concept of "concentration within the ruling party of all power—social and economic as well as political" and "the claim that the party represents only peasants and workers, and the nationalization of all major resources, irrespective of whether this can be shown to be in the national interest." As proof, he pointed to the positive reactions to it coming from Radio Moscow.[76] His Australian and Canadian colleagues in Dar es Salaam were, however, much less alarmist in their evaluations.[77] Meanwhile, the US embassy, while concerned about the "anti-capitalist vocabulary" in "Socialism and Rural Development", thought that it also contained "much practical good sense on how to get villagers to work together for their common benefit." A month earlier, the embassy noticed a piece in the *Nationalist*, TANU's English-language newspaper, that praised "a rich, hard-working farmer in Tanga region" who was "described as having sisal fields, coconut trees, a bus, a shop, and three wives—the epitome of a modern African kulak."[78] While the East Germans and Soviets were hopeful about the appearance of certain key phrases coming from the leadership but cautious because of structural barriers that remained, the Americans seemed to think that conditions on the ground were indicating that perhaps the rhetoric from the top did not need to be feared.

As the various Cold War contestants were imagining a struggle within the Tanzanian leadership over ideology, and more specifically over the adoption of communist or scientific socialist principles, it seems that the actual policy debates were more about implementation mechanisms than ideology. Denis Phombeah, visiting Leipzig as part of a Tanzanian government delegation in March 1967, told East German party leaders that the Arusha Declaration did not represent the product of any clear ideological decision and that the recent cabinet reshuffle, including the replacement of the vocal pro-Chinese Marxist Abdulrahman Babu with the British-educated Paul Bomani, was based on considerations of capability, not ideology.[79] Bomani himself well encapsulated the ideological flexibility that characterized the top Tanzanian leadership at the time of the declaration. On the one hand, Derek Bryceson, the minister of health and labor, told the Canadian high commissioner that he and Bomani had opposed Nyerere's decision to nationalize the banks; on the other hand, in November of that year Bomani, now the minister of economic affairs and development planning, went to Moscow to learn about how Soviet planning institutions worked and ask the Gosudarstvennii planovyĭ komitet (Gosplan; the State Planning Committee) to send a planning specialist to Tanzania.[80] The Soviets decided to honor his request, as Tanzania's claims to being a socialist country seemed more believable than they had in 1963.[81] A year earlier, the East German consul to Tanzania, Gottfried Lessing, had identified Bomani, along with Minister of Finance Amir Jamal and Minister of Industry, Minerals, and Electricity Nzilo Swai, as the "three decidedly reactionary ministers" in the government.[82] But by this point Bomani was in Moscow telling the deputy chairman of Gosplan, "Now the question stands, which system is more conceivable [*ideesposobna*], and can Tanzania build socialism? The imperialists assert that it is impossible, and offer us all sorts of aid on condition that we follow the capitalist path of development. Our government has categorically rejected aid on such conditions."[83] Bomani's shift reflected both a certain level of ideological flexibility as well as the authoritative position of Nyerere, whose determining influence was one of the few points of agreement of nearly all outside observers.[84]

145

The perception that there was an opening, and an ideological battle to be won, motivated the Soviets and their Eastern European allies to seek opportunities for influence in Tanzania, particularly in the form of aid. An extensive report on Tanzania produced by the East German Foreign Ministry's Africa Department in January 1968 noted that the Soviets were now viewing Tanzania, along with Somalia, as a primary focus of their policy in East Africa, which was crucial since "the influence of the socialist states with the USSR at the top can substantially enable the implementation of a noncapitalist path in Tanzania."[85] An earlier report on the Arusha Declaration had noted that it had opened excellent opportunities for East German cooperation with Tanzania—in particular, for sending experts in the planning of agriculture and industry, as well as instructors for schools and universities, to counteract the influence of Westerners teaching there.[86] Though progress on Soviet aid projects in Tanzania had been nearly non-existent into early 1967, the pace started to pick up and delegations of Soviet experts began arriving by the end of the year.[87] While in 1966 a Soviet embassy official told a Tanzanian politician that "the Soviet Union does not intend to set up a race and compete with the Chinese in Tanzania," now their geologists were conducting detailed studies along the path of the proposed Tazara (Tanzania-Zambia) Railway, which they imagined would be built by "hundreds of thousands of Chinese workers."[88] Tanzania's appetites always seemed to be a step ahead of Soviet generosity, however; when Bomani came to Moscow in November 1967 to submit a new list of aid projects for discussion, he was told that it would be better to complete the ones listed under the existing agreement first. When the Tanzanian ambassador in Moscow asked for credits to build massive state farms of the kind he saw in Uzbekistan, the GKES told him it was premature, and when the subject of large-scale Soviet aid to agriculture came up again in 1970, the Soviets said the scale of the projects was actually too small for them.[89] As the Tanzanians kept leaning on the Eastern Europeans and Soviets to provide more and more aid on increasingly generous terms, the Czechoslovaks began to suspect that the Tanzanians were using the socialist countries for leverage with the West.[90] What the Tanzanians saw as self-reliance struck the Soviets as unreasonable, particularly when Tanzania sought to establish standard contracts for all foreign experts that regulated things like salaries, vacation, and luggage allowances.[91] The problem was that the example set by the Chinese put the Soviets and other Eastern Europeans to shame. As the East German consul reported, it was not so much Chinese ideological penetration that was to be feared but the favorable impressions made by Chinese aid, seen as "valuable and selfless," with projects completed promptly and cheaply.[92] Thus, despite the hopeful signals of the Arusha Declaration and its aftermath, Moscow still found it difficult to get a political foothold in Tanzania.

Along with these frustrations over aid, over the course of 1968–1969 frustration and impatience began to build both inside and outside Tanzania over the slow pace of progress toward the fulfillment of the Arusha Declaration. The initial wave of nationalizations in trade and industry showed that the leadership was serious about the turn toward socialism, but in the first years after the declaration, it would prove much easier to nationalize industry and fight a cultural revolution than to tackle the main focus of the declaration: agriculture. While the TANU Youth League launched Operation Vijana in late 1968 in the hopes of "smashing enemies of socialism" (as its leader Lawi Sijaona declared, campaigning in particular against the wearing of miniskirts), agricultural reform had a series of false starts.[93] This was in large part because of the inherent tension between Nyerere's insistence that the formation of *ujamaa* villages (agricultural collectives whose precise definition would be the subject of much debate) be voluntary and the apparent necessity for some sort of centralized direction and investment mechanism. Consequently, contradictions abounded in the government's policy on agricultural development. Nyerere had written in his "Socialism and Development" that "it would be absurd to try and settle all these questions from Dar es Salaam" because "local initiative and self-reliance are essential," but two years later, the TANU Central Committee "decided that now a good time had come for TANU itself to be in charge of the leadership of all *ujamaa* villages everywhere in the country in order for there to be uniformity in direction and development in all parts of the country."[94] This led to the suppression of the Ruvuma Development Association, which had seemed to be the best example of precisely the local initiative Nyerere was seeking.[95] Meanwhile, despite the talk of collectives organized by the villagers themselves on the basis of self-reliance, Tanzanian officials explored the possibility of Soviet-style state farms, and Nyerere and second vice president Rashidi Kawawa even toured prison farms in early 1969, seeing them as a potential model for state farms using "tougher, more revolutionary measures" that might speed up the process.[96] To try to get the urban-oriented party leadership to focus on the task, a TANU Central Committee meeting in Handeni in July 1969 decided that committee members should go live temporarily in *ujamaa* villages, but Derek Bryceson had earlier told the head of the Soviet Economic and Technical Cooperation Mission in Tanzania, I. P. Shatokhin, that he doubted any such decision would ever be put into practice.[97] The delay in implementing *ujamaa* in the country-side was thus more about practical and bureaucratic difficulties than ideological questions per se. As the US embassy reported in 1969,

> Close but informal questioning of the Government's top adviser on *ujamaa* villages indicates that this whole question is very murky. The Government, quite frankly, has no set doctrine as to how peasant "capitalist" tendencies should be dealt with. There is healthy aware-ness that what will work with Chaggas [who lived in the vicinity of Kilimanjaro], for example, would probably be useless with Gogos [who lived in arid central Tanzania, near Dodoma], and that the whole process will be extremely long-term. Much thought remains to be done on such questions as incentives and traditional prac-tices. For example, shifting agriculture, which is anathema to the whole concept of settled, cooperatively functioning communities, is absolutely essential unless fertilizers are applied to the notoriously poor soils of Tanzania.[98]

From the perspective of the East Germans and Soviets, however, these practical and bureaucratic difficulties were the manifestations of deeper ideological problems. Specifically, they were the result of the failure to embrace class struggle and create a vanguard party. In September 1968, the East German consulate reported on growing levels of class conflict in the Mwanza region, near Lake Victoria, and the rise of a "kulak-type class," but said that the party was ideologically unequipped to handle it.[99] Four months later, the consulate complained that the Arusha Declaration was not followed up with policies in 1968, and the fundamental problem was that there was no "class consciousness" in leadership circles. As a consequence, the role of the bourgeoisie was strengthening while that of the working class was weakening, and "reactionary tendencies" were visible in the countryside. In nakedly Leninist terms, the consulate wrote, "Thus has the answer to the question 'Who—whom?' in 1968 in Tan-zania developed to the detriment of progressive forces."[100] The East Ger-mans saw the need for ideological combat as so dire that they were even sympathetic to Operation Vijana and other initiatives aimed at removing the "colonial mentality" in culture and education, despite the obvious echoes of China's Cultural Revolution.[101] Soviet evaluations of the state of *ujamaa* in the countryside similarly pointed to the lack of a clear ideology as the sources of the problems of organization and implementation. A report by a Soviet economist working in Tanzania from July 1969 concluded that there was as yet no coherent understanding of the socioeconomic nature of the villages, and as a consequence, there was a "theoretically naive understanding of the principle of just division of income and the striving to equalize its level." He added that "from the above-mentioned it follows that currently neither the theoretical prerequisites, nor the practical experience create immediate possibilities for the effective social reconstruction of the Tanzanian countryside." Ultimately, the problem of course derived from class issues: "The root cause of these difficulties is the current amorphous class structure of the society, the lack of internal unity between the state and the mass of the peasant population that it leads, as well as the extremely insignificant numbers of the working class, practically unformed as a class as of yet."[102] Though frustration and skepticism were evident, not all had yet given up hope. An Africa expert in the Soviet Foreign Ministry wrote soon after that despite the difficulties, "the social-economic transformations being realized in post-Arusha Tanzania carry a generally progressive character, and are directed toward the creation of the prerequisites for the development of the country on a noncapitalist path."[103] The East Germans and Soviets had not given up hope that Tanzanian socialism would yet produce results, but they believed that its fate would depend on the balance of class forces within the leadership and the country at large—that is, who would beat whom.

As frustration with the slow pace of change in the countryside built in 1968–1969, Nyerere and the rest of the TANU leadership would be faced with the choice of whether to wait patiently for the peasants to take the initiative in creating *ujamaa* villages or to somehow speed the process along themselves. This would put a number of central elements of *ujamaa* squarely into question: How voluntary must it be? How much central direction was necessary? How much investment was required, and who should provide it? Much of the leadership, especially Nyerere, saw these questions in practical terms; as time passed and political tensions grew, the ideological framing of the scientific socialists that the fundamental questions were really about class struggle and a vanguard party would gain more traction within Tanzanian society and officialdom. Although Nyerere sought to keep these forces at bay, his own increasing desperation about how to get the *ujamaa* project off the ground in the countryside added an extra factor in favor of a revised approach.

The Road to Forced Villagization, 1970–1973

In November 1973 Julius Nyerere announced a TANU decision reached in September that living in *ujamaa* villages was now an order.[104] By the end of 1976, some thirteen million people, or roughly 80 percent of the population, would be relocated into organized villages, and many of those people did not move willingly.[105] This seemed to fly directly in the face of one of the central elements of *ujamaa*—its voluntarism—which was a major point of distinction between this socialist program and some of the more infamous ones that preceded it. Nyerere himself had outlined the importance of voluntarism for grassroots support in his programmatic papers of 1967, but the rationale behind it, and the consequences of abandoning it, were well understood within the bureaucracy as well. Responding to a proposal to centralize the planning of *ujamaa* villages in 1970, the principal secretary for the treasury, F. A. Byabato, wrote, "Ujamaa village development to be viable let alone politically and socially meaningful must have and be seen to have a solid base of local mass support. . . . Direct participation in decision making has been and remains a basic theme of self-reliant socialism. It is the direct antitheses of channeling detailed decisions on small sums, projects, and implementation questions to Dar es Salaam."[106] It was no surprise, then, that as late as August 8, 1973, the deputy secretary general of the TANU Youth League announced that TANU and the government had no intention of forcing people into *ujamaa* villages.[107]

If the perils of forced villagization were so well understood, why did TANU ultimately decide to implement it anyway? It was certainly not for lack of consideration of the alternatives. The pace of voluntary villagization since the Arusha Declaration had been frustratingly slow, despite repeated attempts by political leaders—and especially second vice president Kawawa—to cajole people into villages. But studies on the ground showed that many peasants were unreceptive to these messages. As one observer from the Economics Department at the University of Dar es Salaam wrote after conducting field research on villages in the Rufiji District, "To them [some peasants] this shamba [farm] is no different from the shambas they were called to work in during the colonial period and they did not see where the returns went."[108] Reports described villagers refusing to work on communal farms, or devoting minimal effort, opting instead to devote their efforts to private plots. Attempts by planners to increase scale and efficiency were often frustrated because the farmers were simply unwilling to go along with them. As one Ujamaa Village Planning Team report to the Economic Committee of the cabinet on villages in Sumbawanga District explained, "The plans do not include the suggestion of encouraging further cooperation between individuals on their private plots, in addition to the communal work on the wheat shambas. This would seem to be an essential part of the development toward ujamaa. The reason it is not included is again because the farmers were unwilling to accept such a proposal." Peasant loyalty to certain forms of private property was also an obstacle; the team noted, "In calculating the requirement of oxen and ploughs, it is assumed that those already owned by individual village members will be made freely available for communal work. . . . In practice it is unlikely that many farmers will be willing to give their oxen and equipment to the village before they have finished their private work."[109] It is not hard to imagine how the problem of a peasant refusing to give up his oxen and plow to the collective would have been solved in the Soviet Union in the 1930s, but it was precisely those sorts of solutions that *ujamaa*, socialism without class struggle, was meant to avoid.

Instead the leadership believed that the answer was education. As one cooperative inspector wrote to the commissioner for cooperative development, "Education is one of the most important factors for a country to achieve political and economic development. . . . The elders also need a political knowledge in order to widen up the idea of Ujamaa villages to them, because there are some who think that the Ujamaa villages are not for the benefit of the 'Wananchi' [citizens] but for the benefit of the government. Also for this the government should try to keep an eye on those people who try to confuse the villagers."[110] TANU political education teams were sent out into the countryside to explain to the peasants the benefits of living in *ujamaa* villages in the hopes of overcoming their resistance. Naturally, education would be more effective if it were combined with demonstrated economic benefits, and there was thus much talk about ways of providing equipment, and particularly tractors, to collective farms in order to increase their productivity. The problem was that the villages themselves were often too poor to purchase tractors and too small to make effective use of them, but a mass central distribution system seemed to fly in the face of encouraging self-reliance. Instead government officials sought to adapt the Soviet system of machine tractor stations. As the Economic Committee of the cabinet recommended in 1970, "the establishment of a Tractor Hire Service by Kilimo will provide useful experience in this type of operation, which has proved effective in many countries of Eastern Europe."[111] The presence of tractors would also be its own form of socialist education, as one report observed, because "the presence of the tractors at Chumbi was a great impetus to cooperative activities. The people were working very hard so that the tractors could plough the greatest amount of land possible before they left for another village. While it would be good for every village to have their own tractors, it is better to have a number of villages collectively owning tractors for it stimulates jealousy which in turn fosters hard work."[112] As in the Soviet Union, if these tractor stations could be staffed by qualified technicians who doubled as political educators, the government could kill two birds with one stone.

The problem was that the officials in the countryside were often no more sympathetic to the aims of *ujamaa* than the peasants were. While it made sense for convinced Marxists to view the problem of reactionary officialdom in class terms, even American diplomats seemed to see it that way. Reporting on a trip through central Tanzania in 1971, two US embassy officials wrote,

> Many key government officials themselves appear extremely skeptical of the prospects for the policy, particularly in pastoral areas. . . . The background of these government officials, however, represents a caveat which should also be kept in mind in assessing their comments as reported in the enclosure: most regional civil servants are in their middle 40s or older and received their training in the tradition of the British district commissioner service; most come from particularly prosperous, small-farmer dominated regions; and like all civil servants, all are primarily concerned with action rather than ideology. A number of them, therefore, probably start with a bias against socialist agriculture which may affect their judgment on future prospects for ujamaa.[113]

If Americans noticed the problem, certainly it did not evade the attention of Soviet observers. As Shatokhin reported back to the GKES in October 1970, the success of *ujamaa* depended on the political and ideological orientation of the leaders, some of whom only pretended to support socialism, and the lack of cadres made the growth of "capitalist elements" inevitable.[114] The weak ideological preparation of both officials and peasants meant that the creation of "socialist villages," as Soviet embassy officials called *ujamaa* villages, were producing lower harvests than private farms, a problem exacerbated by the fact that the villages united both poor and rich farmers because of Nyerere's insistence on the uniqueness of African socialism vis-à-vis its European counterpart.[115] From the Soviet point of view, the refusal to take class into account was harming *ujamaa*'s progress. Nevertheless, the USSR remained invested in the project because, as Shatokhin put it, "The Arusha Declaration makes an attempt to define the path of noncapitalist development in an exceptionally backward peasant country, in which 80% of the population is engaged in agriculture," and therefore allowances had to be made and help offered when possible.[116] *Ujamaa* villages were being formed in a three-stage process, from villages where people merely lived together to villages at the highest level where all work was done together and all property held in common. Though this was not how collectivization had been accomplished in the USSR or anywhere else where Soviet influence was paramount, the Soviet embassy justified the process under Tanzanian conditions with the idea that the function of the initial forms of *ujamaa* was to smash the "patriarchal structures" of the countryside in order to lay the groundwork for introducing technology at higher forms of villagization. Shatokhin's overall verdict thus stated that *ujamaa* remained "unconditionally progressive."[117] His hope was that the resistance produced by these initial attempts at transforming the countryside would lead to more naked class conflict that would force the government to take a more "revolutionary," class-based approach.[118] In order to move things in the right direction, the Soviet embassy continually looked for ways to build ties between the CPSU and TANU in order to push the latter more toward the vanguard party model, but the problem was, according to the embassy, that the Tanzanian leadership was "striving to protect TANU from external ideological influence."[119]

By the early 1970s, however, this line of critique was being increasingly taken up by many Tanzanians as well. Revolutionary expectations had been raised, especially among the youth, and the natural target for their frustrations was the older generation that held power within TANU and the government. Criticizing the leadership for their lack of attention to class struggle and failure to create a vanguard party became a powerful way to push for more rapid change. Issa Shivji, a law student at the University of Dar es Salaam and at the center of a left-wing group publishing the journal *Cheche* (Spark), after Lenin's *Iskra,* wrote an essay titled "Tanzania: The Silent Class Struggle" in November 1970 that was seen as threatening enough to lead to the banning of *Cheche.* In it Shivji asserted that political power had been captured by a "bureaucratic bourgeoisie" that was using the state to serve its own interests; it was an argument that owed much to the venerable critiques by Leon Trotsky in *The Revolution Betrayed* and Milovan Djilas in *The New Class.*[120] Shivji advocated the transformation of TANU from a "mass party" aimed at achieving independence into a "revolutionary vanguard."[121] Others were not willing to accept the official classless position—refusing, for example, to see the peasant resistance to *ujamaa* as merely a matter of ignorance that could be solved with education. In November 1972, the *Daily News* carried an interview with a political economist with the Economic Research Bureau at the University of Dar es Salaam, Adhu Awiti, who went out into the countryside to document class differentiation.[122] She found plenty of evidence to support her case, arguing that the government and TANU bureaucrats in the villages were making common cause with the richer peasants. Directly attacking the official doctrine of *ujamaa,* she asserted that "a party or government strategy which doesn't recognize that classes actually exist cannot succeed." While many were no doubt coming to these critiques and Marxist positions on their own, there was an increasing number of Tanzanians being sent to study in socialist states, as well as a growing number of experts from socialist countries coming to Tanzania, often with the explicit intention of trying to spread ideas of "scientific socialism" alongside their technical tasks.[123]

The critiques surrounding the need for class struggle and a vanguard party were, however, not merely limited to students and professors at the university but were increasingly heard within the corridors of power. Dean McHenry, who was a lecturer at the University of Dar es Salaam during this period, wrote about a party divided between groups that he labeled "ideological socialists" and "pragmatic socialists."[124] Kingunge Ngombale-Mwiru, who held a number of high positions, including that of the director of Kivokuni College, the training school for party cadres, was often considered the head of the ideological socialists. Many in the leadership saw him as a Soviet sympathizer and a convinced Marxist-Leninist, and they feared what young party cadres were learning under his direction. While at the college, Ngombale-Mwiru worked with Issa Shivji and the former *Cheche* group, establishing an hour at the beginning of each day for students to discuss current political and social issues. As he described it, "At Kivukoni, we created a revolutionary situation," adding that "our students were very much in favor of a vanguard system." Tensions rose to the point that he was called before a Central Committee meeting in 1972, where members sought to expel him from the party on the grounds that he was trying to overthrow them. Ngombale-Mwiru argued that he didn't want to replace the party with a new one; rather, "We need a vanguard within a mass party. You need them to train your leadership. They should know better than the rank and file. . . . You can't have a serious movement while the leadership is limited to what everybody knows."[125] In an interview with the *Daily News* later that year, he argued for something similar—namely, the creation of a vanguard within a mass party.[126] This explanation did not satisfy the Central Committee, and according to Ngombale-Mwiru, it took nothing less than the personal intervention of Nyerere to save him.[127]

This political struggle within the leadership was taking place in the context of a country that felt increasingly insecure because of threats both foreign and domestic. Tanzania was on the front lines of the struggle against white rule in southern Africa, with Dar es Salaam serving as the headquarters of the Organisation of African Unity's Coordinating Committee for the Liberation of Africa. Tanzania not only hosted activists from numerous liberation organizations, from South Africa's African National Congress to Angola's Movimento Popular de Libertação de Angola (MPLA; People's Movement for the Liberation of Angola); and Mozambique's Frente de Libertação de Moçambique (FRELIMO; Liberation Front of Mozambique), but it also armed and trained their fighters, as well as acting as a conduit for people and arms going to and from places like the PRC and the USSR. Consequently it became a target for attacks by the Portuguese and Rhodesians, who sometimes launched cross-border raids against militants, and even occasionally reached into the center of the country, such as when FRELIMO leader Eduardo Mondlane was assassinated by a mail bomb at his home on a Dar es Salaam beach. The insecurity of both the country and the government was compounded with the 1971 coup in Uganda, which overthrew Milton Obote, who was quickly given asylum in Tanzania, and brought to power Idi Amin, who had designs on Tanzanian territory. The British high commissioner wrote in a report in June 1971 that the Ugandan coup was traumatic and had fundamentally destabilized Tanzania.[128] Amin's attacks on Tanzanian territory led Nyerere to declare in September 1972 that the nation could tolerate no more bombing.[129]

Largely in response to the Ugandan threat, the party published a new set of guidelines, known as Mwongozo, that, among other things, set up a people's militia to help defend the country's borders. The Mwongozo was primarily written by none other than Ngombale-Mwiru and sought to mobilize revolutionary sentiment by calling for the people to hold their leaders accountable to the standards set out in the leadership code of the Arusha Declaration.[130] This led in mid-1973 to a massive strike wave and unrest directed against those labeled *wanyapara* (exploiters) that ultimately had to be suppressed by the government.[131] It was not just factory owners who became the target of Mwongozo-inspired righteous indignation. The Asian community in Tanzania, which made up much of the merchant and landlord class, found itself under attack, as it did all over East Africa at this time, and while Nyerere emphasized that Mwongozo was not meant to be directed against any particular ethnic group, a decision to nationalize urban real estate was taken as evidence that the Asian community was an enemy of *ujamaa*.[132] On top of this, the leaders themselves were given reason to feel personally insecure.; Abeid Karume, the first president of Zanzibar and now vice president of Tanzania, was assassinated in April 1972, creating ripples of political intrigue and persecution on the island. Meanwhile, Oscar Kambona, who resigned from the party in 1967 and subsequently fled to London, was associated with attempts to encourage the overthrow of Nyerere, including the dropping of leaflets from the air over Dar es Salaam in 1972.[133] In the countryside, one of *ujamaa*'s most aggressive promoters, Iringa regional commissioner Walter Kleruu, was shot dead at point-blank range on Christmas 1971 by an angry peasant, an event that led the British High Commission to write, "We watch with interest to see if this is an isolated incident or if we are on the brink of stiffer resistance to the government socializing policies."[134] Nyerere was no doubt wondering the same thing. It all made for a picture, as the British high commissioner wrote, of a country in "deep malaise."[135]

With the nation in turmoil and progress toward *ujamaa* maddeningly slow, Tanzania nevertheless found itself enmeshed in a global conversation about building socialism in the developing world. Perhaps the high point of Tanzania's advocacy of its own socialist model came in a speech written and meant to be delivered by Nyerere, though actually delivered by Karume's successor, Aboud Jumbe, in Sudan in January 1973. Titled "The Rational Choice," it argued that socialism was not merely an ideological preference but actually the logical choice for all developing countries.[136] The Soviet embassy was quite enthused by the speech; as Ambassador Vyacheslav Ustinov wrote, "The aforementioned speech, despite its continued eclecticism and inconsistency, testifies to the positive conceptual evolution of Nyerere, in particular shows his attention to the evaluation of the revolution in our country and the conviction with which he proves that developing countries have the objective possibilities for building socialist societies."[137] Tanzanian ministers gave similar speeches promoting socialism and *ujamaa* in international settings because, as Peter Kisumo, the minister for regional administration and rural development, told one such gathering of East African leaders, "our system of Ujamaa villages seeks to promote the interest and development of mankind."[138] In March 1972 in Chile, a country in the midst of its own socialist experiment, the Oficina de Planificación (Planning Office) held an international seminar discussing Chilean socialism, and one of the papers compared the Via Chilena (Chilean path) and *ujamaa*.[139] Though Tanzania was promoting its model abroad, where it was attracting interest, the question was, as the headline of one opinion piece in the *Daily News* put it, "Are We Deviating or Setting a Precedent?"[140]

Opinions on that question within Tanzania abounded. As part of the discussion, Tanzanians examined other countries' versions of socialism with great interest, not only to see what worked and what did not but also to help make the case for whatever version of socialism they wished to see at home. The *Daily News* carried stories on socialism not just in the usual places, such as Cuba, the Soviet Union, Vietnam, the Warsaw Pact states, and Yugoslavia, but also in places like, Algeria, Pakistan, Somalia, and Sudan.[141] Particular attention was paid to policies and events in China and Salvador Allende's Chile, on which there was nearly daily coverage of everything from agrarian reform to American interference, including a speech of Allende that the *Daily News* chose to title "Our Ujamaa in Chile."[142] The peculiarity of this national conversation was strongly in evidence in an article titled "What We Can Learn from Hungarian Agriculture."[143] In a piece of misdirection worthy of playwright Arthur Miller's *The Crucible,* the article spun a tale about how the Hungarian government first sought to control agriculture using methods of central control and coercion and only began to succeed once the government learned to devolve control to the locals, pull back on mechanization and investment, and abandon coercive methods. In the context of the Tanzanian debates of 1972, the article was certainly making its case against those who were impatient and wanted the government to force matters in the countryside. Tanzania's place in the conversation about socialism meant that ideological influence was a two-way street, and the success of *ujamaa* therefore was crucial not only to the government's legitimacy at home but also to Tanzania's status abroad.

As a result, the government felt compelled to keep looking for ways to make progress in the countryside. In May 1972 TANU produced a policy statement titled "Siasa ni Kilimo" (Politics is agriculture) that tried a new approach of encouraging more "scientific" farming practices while de-emphasizing the social aspects of *ujamaa* in the countryside.[144] This came on the back of a broader decision taken by TANU's National Executive Committee in January 1972 in favor of decentralization, which meant devolving decision-making authority to local and regional officials.[145] While decentralization might have seemed to grant more room for local initiative, in practice it had precisely the opposite effect, since bureaucrats were sent from the center to take control in the regions, as Issa Shivji argued.[146] As Nyerere told the Soviet ambassador, this was precisely the point of sending important TANU figures to the regions with the hope that it would produce "more actions than words."[147] Incorporating decentralization, state planning authorities seemed to envision a sort of Rawlsian "wide reflective equilibrium" approach to planning. As the *Draft Planning and Control Guide* from October 1972 explained,

> Development is concerned, more than anything, with the needs of the people. Though the district is the first level at which formal plans are prepared, planning really starts at the village and ward levels. . . . But all development must take place within a national framework, so that local effort is in harmony with the nation's long-term goals. Initial suggestions for development projects will be approved successively by the people through their District and Regional Development Committees. They will then be referred upwards to the national level to be reconciled with, and to influence, national objectives and policies, and to be agreed by the National Assembly. This procedure leads to the development of the national framework for preparing detailed plans at each level.[148]

In practice this process tended to take the form of conversations among officials at multiple levels, and the only peasants whose voices were taken into account were those who were well connected. As a consequence, neither decentralization nor the policy statement "Siasa ni Kilimo" did

much to make *ujamaa* more attractive to the majority of peasants still refusing to move to organized villages.

On the eve of the decision to force villagization on a national scale D.
Khairullin, a Soviet expert with the GKES mission in Tanzania, produced
a report on the state of *ujamaa* that outlined its difficulties from the perspective of a sympathetic observer. While according to government sta-
tistics 15 percent of the country's population was now in *ujamaa* villages,
collective farms were yielding only 1.5 percent of the total commercial
production of the country. *Ujamaa* villages lacked both funds for investment and qualified cadres, and the peasants were concentrating their efforts on their private plots due to lack of incentives to work on the communal farms. Khairullin summed up the situation as follows: "Ujamaa
villages present a motley conglomeration of settlements of the poorest
peasants (middle peasants mainly do not want to take part in this movement, because they are not attracted by the principle of the equality of
property of the inhabitants of these villages, the lack of possibilities for
the use of hired labor, etc.), beginning from a small number of show settlements with elements of provisioning to villages epitomizing poverty,
recalling, as it says in the book 'The Creation of Ujamaa Villages in
Tanzania,' concentration camps for common criminals." Despite this, the
Tanzanian experiment was too important to be written off at this stage
and thus, after once again affirming *ujamaa*'s "progressive character,"
Khairullin told his superiors that "considering the immense significance
that the Tanzanian leadership gives to questions of the creation of villages
of collective labor, as well as the increasing aid of western countries [re-
ferring in this case to the Scandinavian countries mentioned early in the
report] and the PRC in this sphere, it appears productive to review the
possibilities of offering technical cooperation from the Soviet side to Tanzania in the development of 'Ujamaa' villages."[149] In particular, he suggested having Moscow help set up machine practice stations, along with
repairmen and educational centers, to teach locals how to maintain tractors. Before the question could be debated in Moscow, however, the Tanzanian leadership decided to order its population into villages.

In the light of previous policy failures, domestic and international turmoil, and the importance of the success of *ujamaa* for the leadership, the
decision to force villagization has to be seen less as a radicalization of the
revolution than as a retreat. It was not accompanied by the sort of mass
enthusiasm and popular mobilization that accompanied collectivization

during the First Five-Year Plan in the USSR or the Socialist High Tide in China. Instead it was implemented by the newly decentralized bureaucracy, which often saw the peasants more as benighted people in need of guidance and control rather than class allies, as the notion of TANU as a party of "workers and peasants" would suggest. Controlling the bureaucracy had already proved to be a difficult task for the leadership, so giving it more power and tasking it with controlling others might have served to solidify its authority at a time of domestic political tension. Forced villagization was also not an economic policy in the sense that it would obviously lead to growth in the short term. In practice it led to a drop in production, as most observers anticipated, including Nyerere and others who had since 1967 argued so vehemently that villagization must be voluntary. In public it was justified by the claim that the state could only provide services like health care, education, and water to people who were concentrated and easier to reach, but the state lacked the capacity to provide such services at the time, as evidenced by the fact that the decision taken in 1974 in Musoma for full primary education was not acted on until 1977.[150] Rather, it seems that the leadership had reached a point where, if it did not order forced villagization, it would have had to either abandon self-reliance and rely upon large-scale aid from a country like the Soviet Union or abandon the project of *ujamaa* altogether; this would have brought with it domestic and international political delegitimation. Forced villagization thus seemed like an act of desperation rather than one of revolutionary enthusiasm. Perhaps it was no coincidence that the decision was taken in the same month that Salvador Allende, who had refused to break with Chile's constitutional order, was overthrown in a military coup. As one letter writer to the *Daily News* saw it, "Some of those who claim to be socialists like Allende may still believe that socialism can be achieved by gaining a majority in the parliament, passing some laws and declarations and then urging the people to work hard by feeding them with some slogans."[151] Tanzania had already tried that approach. Now it was time for a different one.

Forced Villagization and Its Aftermath

Compared to previous attempts at large-scale mass collectivization of the peasantry, villagization in Tanzania was achieved with relatively little violence, though violent episodes certainly took place. Undeniable progress was also made in the provision of services and the improvement of social indicators. As Nyerere said in his 1977 speech "The Arusha Declaration Ten Years After," there were nearly twice as many primary school pupils in 1975 as in 1967, and the literacy campaign had made over five million people literate.[152] The number of rural health centers had jumped from forty-two in 1967 to 152 in 1976. And yet, as Nyerere admitted, these sorts of initiatives would only be sustainable in the long term if production increased enough to pay for them and thus, as Andrew Coulson wrote in 1982, "the acid test is in production over time; if food and cash production do not increase faster than population growth, it will be hard to provide the promised social services, or to invest in industries."[153]

In this respect, villagization was an unambiguous failure. By 1976 Tanzania was importing $63.5 million worth of food, compared with $39.6 million in 1973, which was itself a significant increase over $24.5 million in 1970 and only $12.7 million in 1967.[154] The situation was so bad that Nyerere called in the Soviet ambassador on a Saturday evening in 1974 to ask about possibly meeting with a group of Soviet geologists prospecting for gold to alleviate the state's financial problems.[155] The more people who lived in *ujamaa* villages, the worse Tanzania's food production got. These new food imports were not offset by exports of other goods; while Tanzania exported slightly more than it imported in 1967, the ratio of exports to imports fell steadily, bottoming out in 1985, Nyerere's last year as president, when Tanzania's exports were worth only 28.6 percent of its imports.[156] Initially Nyerere blamed the falling production numbers on factors like drought and declining terms of trade resulting from oil price shock of 1973, which made the purchase of equipment internationally more difficult.[157] As time went on and production remained low, he increasingly turned his attention to the disadvantage that countries like Tanzania faced in the international system, especially as the aid his country desperately needed could only be procured by betraying the ideals of the Arusha Declaration.

For many potential donors it was the government's policies that were responsible for Tanzania's predicament, and so demanding a change of course only seemed to make sense. A World Bank report on Tanzania in 1974 accused Tanzania of focusing on "social instead of productive investment," adding that "Tanzania has tipped the balance in favor of its egalitarian objectives at substantial cost of increased production and income."[158] While the World Bank imagined that its "verdict will sound the death knell of Ujamaa," diplomats on the ground were not so sure; they thought the strength of the political system would allow the government to persevere, as indeed it did for roughly another decade.[159] There were dissident voices within Western governments too. As one economist in the British Foreign Office asserted, "The policy of 'villagisation' was at least an attempt to set up viable production units, within reach of modern techniques, extension services, and markets. The fact that it has not yet succeeded does not necessarily mean that the new system should be blamed for old problems."[160] Though there was some disagreement on the economic merits of *ujamaa*, in Cold War terms it seemed problematic because, as the British high commissioner wrote, "[the Russians] have, of course, cause for satisfaction in the extent to which orthodox socialist/communist theories have gained currency in many spheres of life."[161] He could not have been more wrong.

The Soviets were anything but happy with the turn of events in Tanzania. One of the top Soviet experts on Africa and the developing world, Aleksei Kiva, wrote a damning article about *ujamaa* in the main Soviet theoretical journal of the field, *Narody Azii i Afriki* (Peoples of Asia and Africa) in the fall of 1974. Rejecting a central theoretical claim of Nyerere that the communal tradition of African agriculture would make it easier to organize cooperatives, Kiva argued that such cooperatives could be organized but would be difficult to operate effectively because simply replacing "traditional authority" with bureaucrats would just exchange one form of exploitation for another. Forcing villagization was, he asserted, a major mistake: "Success of the policy of Ujamaa-ization, in our view, will depend in large measure on the basis of preparation for transition to each new step of cooperativization, avoiding unjustified speed and—especially dangerous because of their political consequences—coercive measures."[162] Kiva contrasted Tanzania's approach with the supposedly successful experience of Mongolia, where, he explained, collectivization of the peasantry came only after feudalism had been liquidated, the position of the state sector in the economy had grown strong, and the working class had matured. While the accuracy of that portrayal is certainly debatable, the fact remained that a prominent Soviet theorist was now claiming that the noncapitalist path might be better built on the backs of individual peasant proprietors. Kiva's evaluations of the reasons for Tanzania's problems were shared by the Soviet embassy in Dar es Salaam, which reported in July 1975 on the state of the country's economy. In practice the government's hastiness had led to the misuse of resources, bad organization of labor, weak labor discipline, lack of cadres, and the growth of corruption, among other things. The embassy concluded that Tanzania was now so desperately in need of foreign aid that it was only a matter of time before the government caved and turned toward the West.[163] As far as the Soviets were concerned, the Tanzanian experiment was a failure.

Though the Soviets saw it as inevitable, Nyerere was determined to resist capitulating to the likes of the International Monetary Fund, the World Bank, and others for as long as possible. As the Tanzanian economy sunk into ever greater difficulties, Nyerere spent more time traveling abroad decrying the way that the international system was rigged against developing countries. Writing in the wake of Nyerere's tour of Yugoslavia, Romania, Mexico, and Jamaica in early 1975, the Soviet embassy in Dar es Salaam reported that "Nyerere has to a certain degree definitely succeeded in raising his personal authority in the eyes of the countries of the 'Third World' as one of its more visible leaders. This circumstance, obviously, has not insignificant meaning for Nyerere himself in the conditions of well-known misfortune in his implementation of economic measures within the country that produce negative influences on his authority, and as a theoretician and a leader of the countries of the 'Third World,' who for quite a long time has attracted the interests of developing countries as an example of possible development on the noncapitalist path."[164] Nyerere's advocacy on behalf of the developing world continued well after he stepped down as president in 1985, his speeches filling an entire volume titled *Freedom and a New World Economic Order*. His successor, Ali Hassan Mwinyi, would, however, accept a program of structural adjustment as a condition of International Monetary Fund aid. Nyerere proved unable—to use Ayatollah Khomeini's famous description of agreeing to peace with Iraq in 1988—to "drink the cup of poison" himself.[165]

Despite the economic failures of *ujamaa,* it is hard to find a leader anywhere in the world whose memory was regarded with a greater degree of genuine reverence in his homeland than was Nyerere's in Tanzania. People too young to have experienced his leadership were taught to quote almost hagiographical stories and sayings of Mwalimu (Teacher), as he was nearly universally known. In 2015 Tanzania elected a new president, Joseph Magufuli, whose campaign for the presidency largely centered upon combating a culture of corruption by turning to the ideals of the Arusha Declaration, even though, as Job Lusinde bemoaned, people seemed to recall only the ethics part of the declaration and not the economics part.[166] The image of an idealistic, incorruptible Baba wa Taifa (Father of the Country), as the nearly ubiquitous portraits of Nyerere titled him, only grew more compelling as each of his successors in turn failed to reach the same impossibly high standard, at least in the public's perception.

In the half century after independence, Tanzania enjoyed a degree of stability, peace, and cohesion that few African states could claim, and Nyerere deserved a great deal of the credit. With Tanzania being a desperately poor, newly independent state in the context of the Cold War, Nyerere's obsession with preserving the nation's political and economic independence was understandable, but preserving that independence came with definite costs. In charting his own ideological course, Nyerere explicitly sought to avoid the sort of patronage relationships with great powers that many of his contemporaries in Africa came to embrace, though it is hard to argue that many of them did better than he did by adopting such relationships. Nonetheless, few African countries could boast the same quality of leadership that Tanzania could. Though it often failed, the leadership made a serious effort to keep its bureaucracy accountable to the people, to avoid wasteful use of resources, and to balance the interests of different parts of the country and different segments of society. But the strict emphasis on self-reliance and the insistence on building its own version of socialism based on a conception of African traditions meant that, despite the best intentions, Tanzania lacked the resources to develop its economy. It could not pay for the technology or expertise that might have made its agricultural strategy effective, nor did it have the resources to build a significant industrial base.

To properly build socialism in the context of the Cold War, the resources could only have come from socialist states. While there was no shortage of socialist professors from the West who could be brought in to teach at the University of Dar es Salaam, if one wanted socialist engineers, agronomists, geologists, planners, and the like one needed to look to either Beijing or Moscow and their allies. Such a flood of experts, as Nyerere well knew, would not come without strings attached. As Chinese experts and workers began to flood in to build the Tazara (often referred to as the Uhuru or Tanzam) Railway, Nyerere told visitors that "he ha[d] not the intention of leading his country back into a colonial relationship with any power," and while the US embassy thought "his protestations on this issue are unquestionably sincere," Nyerere also "expressed occasional quiet misgivings about what all the Chinese in the country are really doing."[167] It will be recalled that Nyerere chose to work with the Chinese in part precisely because they put so little emphasis on attempting to influence

Tanzania's ideology or policy unlike the Soviets, whose ambassador reportedly would harangue Nyerere for hours on end about becoming a true scientific socialist.[168] The Soviets complained that Nyerere consistently rebuffed their efforts to turn TANU into a vanguard party, in part because he understood, correctly, that the Soviets wanted him to do so in order to make TANU more susceptible to Soviet ideological influence. In late 1974 the Soviet ambassador complained that "over the course of many years Nyerere has jealously guarded TANU from the penetration of any kind of foreign ideology, preserving it from contacts with other parties including communist and workers parties."[169] As Nyerere came to lament later in his presidency, there were no good choices for a country like Tanzania in the mid-1970s. His choice was to preserve the nation's independence and, today, at least, it seems his countrymen feel that the choice was worth it.

For the Soviets, the Tanzanian experience provided a critical bridge between their attempts to build socialism in West Africa in the early 1960s and their entanglements on the continent during the later Cold War. Just as forced villagization in Tanzania was reaching its climax, the Soviets found themselves deeply enmeshed in places like Angola, Ethiopia, and Mozambique, working with leaders and parties that explicitly claimed to be Marxist-Leninist and embraced the notion of class struggle in order to transform their own countries. In the mid-1960s the Soviets learned from their failures in West Africa by abandoning their strategy of investing in state-controlled heavy industry that would produce a working class and then a communist party. This led to their interest in the results of the Tanzanian experiment and their enthusiasm for it despite Nyerere's ideological heterodoxy and Tanzania's undesirable international alignments. But Nyerere consistently resisted Soviet influence, both in terms of political structures and economic prescriptions. Moscow then attributed much of *ujamaa*'s failure to Nyerere's resistance and the mistakes that supposedly resulted. In a critique with parallels to that of the World Bank, the Soviet ambassador wrote in a 1975 report titled "On the Noncapitalist Path of Development of Tanzania" that Nyerere had overemphasized the social aspects of his agricultural policy while neglecting the centrality of raising production.[170] The failure of the Tanzanian experiment in Soviet eyes therefore led to another reevaluation of how the noncapitalist path could be implemented in Africa. In the late 1970s, with Angola now mainly under the control of the MPLA (a fact that the latter owed largely to the intervention of the Cubans and Soviets), Moscow and its allies went in to shape the new Angolan state. In 1977 the East Germans sent a high-level delegation to Angola to teach the MPLA leaders how to run a country and an economy.[171] This time they told the Angolans not to force collectivization but instead to first work with the peasants to raise productivity, ensuring a steady supply of food to the cities, where industrial development should focus on profitability rather than self-sufficiency. Above all, the MPLA had to transform itself into a vanguard party to assure the success of the envisioned socialist transformation. The prescription handed to the Angolans in 1977 clearly owed something to the Soviet diagnosis of Tanzania's misfortunes in 1973–1976. Socialism in Tanzania might have failed, but in Moscow's eyes, Tanzania was only a bump on the road to the ultimate success of socialism in Africa.

4

LENIN WITHOUT MARX

Communism Comes to Angola

We want to build socialism in the PRA [People's Republic of Angola], but not African socialism as some assert, because neither African, nor American, nor Asian, nor Spanish socialism exists. Socialism is one, and we intend to build this socialism on our land.

—Lopo do Nascimento, December 10, 1975

The problem facing us Africans at this moment is how to transform unjust relations, usually of political and economic subordination, with the other countries and peoples of the world, without this transformation being made at the expense of the social progress that must necessarily be integrated into action to achieve freedom.

—Agostinho Neto, 1974

In May 1976 Lopo do Nascimento, the prime minister of newly independent Angola, traveled to Moscow, where he told Leonid Brezhnev and Aleksei Kosygin that just as the Soviet Union was the first socialist country in Europe, and Cuba was the first in Latin America, Angola would become the first socialist country in Africa.[1] At a time when almost every country in Africa had declared itself socialist at some point since independence, and only months after a high-level conference on "African Socialism" had been held in Tunis, this might seem to have been a strange

167

claim.[2] The Soviets themselves had been seeking ways to build socialism on the African continent for almost twenty years by this point. What Nascimento meant, however, was that the ruling Movimento Popular de Libertação de Angola (MPLA; People's Movement for the Liberation of Angola) intended to turn the new People's Republic of Angola (PRA) into a centrally planned, industrialized economy along Soviet lines, run by a vanguard party of the workers and peasants modeled on the Communist Party of the Soviet Union (CPSU). There would be no discussions of alternate versions of socialism based on African traditions, rejection of class struggle, or attempts to construct a more diffuse and open political structure. The MPLA did not intend to chart its own path to socialism as Tanzania did, nor would it seek to maintain a strictly nonaligned position internationally. Marxism-Leninism was finally coming to Africa.

There was a reason it had taken this long. In the early years of decolonization, even the Soviets themselves did not imagine that the newly independent states could be ready for the direct application of Marxist-Leninist ideology. In countries with little industry and almost no working class, the Soviets envisioned "states of national democracy" that would focus on land reform, democratization, and industrial development accelerated by foreign aid, with a political coalition led by the "national bourgeoisie" undertaking progressive reforms that would set the stage for an eventual transition to socialism. But, as it turned out in places like Ghana, Guinea, and Mali in the early 1960s, those leaders from the national bourgeoisie had no intention of being opposed and eventually superseded by political parties from the left. After the failure of this initial model in West Africa, Julius Nyerere in Tanzania offered a different model, one built around self-reliance and the primacy of cooperative agriculture as a way to bootstrap development while building national cohesion. But Nyerere openly rejected class struggle, and he refused to concentrate power in the hands of a vanguard party. The failure of his program of *ujamaa* had disabused Moscow, and many left-wing Africans, of the notion that African traditions could serve as the paradigm for a direct transition to socialism without the necessity of class struggle. Now in Angola, as well as in Ethiopia and Mozambique, new regimes that had come to power through force of arms committed themselves to building parties on the principle of the unity of the workers and peasants and maintaining an alliance with the socialist camp.

The attempt to implement full-scale Marxism-Leninism in Africa was not merely a response to these failures of earlier attempts to chart a more gradual transition to socialism along some version of the "noncapitalist path." They were also the product of war. In newly independent states such as Ghana and Tanzania, where independence had come relatively peacefully, leaders had often had experiences of political administration within the colonial regime and they sought to maintain economic ties with the former metropoles when possible. At the same time, they lacked the coercive machinery to force radical change, especially if it challenged entrenched interests such as local chiefs. But the experience of lengthy guerrilla struggles created a different set of circumstances in Angola and Mozambique. Fighting for their independence radicalized the liberation movements and pushed them to depend upon the socialist countries—and first and foremost the Soviet Union—for arms and supplies. When they finally came to power they commanded relatively competent armed forces but found a decimated economy that had been largely abandoned by the Portuguese, who were not only owners and administrators but most of the skilled laborers as well. A more radical approach was therefore the product of both ideological conviction and necessity.

That radical approach, however, was tilted more toward the political and ideological side of things than toward the economy. The Soviets' earlier attempts to skip the stage of private capitalist development by building state-owned industrial enterprises through foreign aid had convinced them of the futility of making this the primary method of development for agrarian economies. Now, in Angola and Mozambique, they encouraged the continuation of a role for private capital, both foreign and domestic, and especially in Angola's crucial oil and gas sector, as a way of enabling development without having to foot the lion's share of the bill themselves. Continued tolerance for private capital, however, meant that there were potentially dangerous political and ideological forces at play, and so it became all the more crucial to make sure that not only was a proper vanguard Marxist-Leninist party in charge but that that party was in firm control of whatever private capital was operating in the country. In the long run, that would have fateful consequences for Angola long after the regime officially abandoned Marxism-Leninism.

There was another factor that militated in favor of a small vanguard party with a tight hold on power: race. The MPLA leadership was largely composed of whites and *mestiços* (mixed-race peoples) who came from more privileged strata of Angolan society and often had the chance to get an education and even study overseas, where they then encountered Marxism-Leninism through contacts with communists in France and

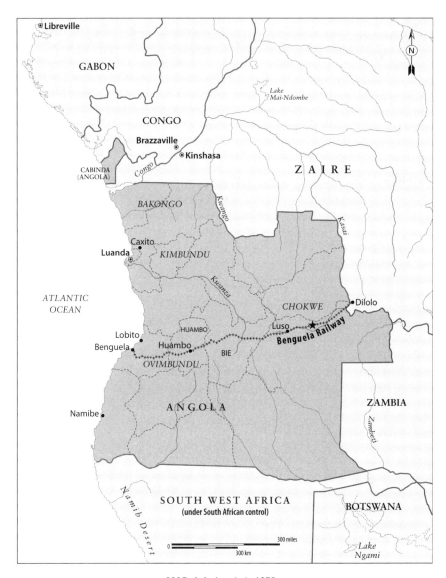

MAP 4.1 Angola in 1975.

Portugal. For the vast majority of the Angolan population, however, liberation was inseparable from the question of race. White Europeans were the oppressors, and liberation needed to mean their replacement by black Africans. The question for both the MPLA and its Soviet sponsors was thus how to promote an ideology based on class in an environment in which most people understood their oppression in terms of race. This was a problem that would lead to repeated challenges to the existing MPLA leadership, as well as to the MPLA's standing as the liberation movement of Angola by the rival Frente Nacional de Libertação de Angola (FNLA; National Front for the Liberation of Angola) and the União Nacional para a Independência Total de Angola (UNITA; National Union for the Total Independence of Angola), both of which at times adopted more of a "black nationalist" stance. As southern Africa in general—and the struggle against the apartheid regime in South Africa, in particular—became an ever more prominent front of the Cold War in the late 1970s and 1980s, the very viability of Marxism-Leninism as a tool of liberation in the struggle against imperialism depended upon finding a compelling way to deal with race. For the MPLA it was a question of survival, since the race question posed a potential threat to the legitimacy of the regime. While the MPLA at lower levels would at times adopt some elements of black nationalism itself, as well as ensuring that the face of the regime was always black, the race issue ultimately became a further reason to keep political power tightly controlled and oppose democratization.

Angola Erupts, 1960–1966

The Portuguese had first made contact with the Kongo kingdom of what is now northern Angola as early as 1484, but it was not until the Scramble for Africa in the late nineteenth century that Portugal attempted to exercise control over the vast expanse of territory occupied by Angola today. The necessity of protecting its vast African claims from more powerful and dynamic European rivals in the early twentieth century led Lisbon, beginning in 1910, to devote tremendous resources to military occupation and economic exploitation of the colony, and especially the building of railroads for the export of cash crops—particularly coffee and cotton. While agriculture accounted for 80 percent of Angolan gross domestic product and 70 percent of exports by 1960, the colony would soon also become a major supplier of oil and diamonds.[3] Despite the fact that foreign firms, particularly American and German ones, accounted for an increasingly large percentage of the economic activity in Angola, the right-wing authoritarian regime in Lisbon held on more tightly than most to colonial rule because, as the most important regime mouthpiece regarding colonial policy editorialized, "Africa is for us a moral justification and a 'raison d'être' as a power. Without it we would be a small nation; with it we are a great country."[4]

The political imperative behind Portugal's maintenance of its colonial empire gave Portuguese colonialism a somewhat different character from colonial rule in the rest of the continent. In 1951 Portugal's colonies were integrated administratively with the metropole as overseas provinces. In contradistinction to other imperial powers—and most particularly the governments in Pretoria, South Africa, and Salisbury, Rhodesia (now Harare, Zimbabwe), with which they would soon be allied—the Portuguese pursued an explicitly integrationist model, claiming that their goal was the creation of a multiethnic Portuguese civilization defined by language and culture. In practice, however, this conception of a diverse civilization proved to be a barrier to integration, as the population of Portuguese colonies was divided into three groups—namely, white European settlers, *mestiços,* and Africans. In 1950 there were 78,826 Europeans, 29,648 *mestiços,* and 4,036,689 Africans in Angola, although active encouragement of immigration would increase the number of Europeans fourfold by the early 1970s.[5] Africans, representing the vast majority of the population, could only obtain citizenship by attaining "civilized" status, which required Portuguese literacy, employment, and a lack of a criminal record, while *mestiços* were automatically granted citizenship. As only 0.7 percent of Africans managed to attain such status by 1950, there were ample grounds for antagonism between Africans and *mestiços,* a fact that would weigh heavily on the conduct of the liberation struggle. Though these divisions were ostensibly eliminated and all Africans were granted Portuguese citizenship in 1961, in practice this had little effect other than doubling their tax burden, since educational and economic opportunities for Africans were nearly nonexistent. Such opportunities in Portuguese Angola were so rare, in fact, that tens of thousands of Bakongo refugees from northern Angola emigrated to the Belgian Congo, whose opportunities were, in the words of one scholar, "comparatively attractive."[6]

It was in this context that Angolans began to agitate for independence. Under the leadership of Mario Coelho Pinto de Andrade—an Angolan of mixed racial background who had studied philology in Lisbon and social science at the Sorbonne and was a prolific writer of poetry and prose—a group of Angolans in Europe, under the tutelage of the Brazilian and Portuguese Communist Parties, formed the Angolan Communist Party in October 1955 with some two hundred members. Their initial goals were liberation from the colonial yoke, the creation of a party based on Marxist principles, and a coalition with other progressive forces in the country.[7] The party was very small, however, and it had trouble finding new members, so its core of young leaders, including Luandan poet Viriato da Cruz, founded the MPLA in December 1956. Cruz, despite being a convinced Marxist, came up with the name in order to avoid any overt communist leanings that could prejudice the MPLA's search for external support.[8]

The nascent MPLA faced two basic difficulties. The first was that its founders originated in that vanishingly small segment of Angolan society that was able to obtain a high-level education, often in Europe, which meant that they were disproportionately white and *mestiço,* with ambitions of leading an independence struggle in a predominantly black country. The second was that these same founders were tied organizationally and ideologically to communists in Lisbon and Paris—a result, in part, of the fact that, under the conditions of the Portuguese dictatorship, it was the communists who were the most committed anticolonialists. At a time when the leading lights of African socialism—people such as Gamal Abdel Nasser, Kwame Nkrumah, and Julius Nyerere—attempted to jealously guard their nonaligned position internationally while keeping Marxism-Leninism at arm's length domestically, this meant that the Angolan liberation movements, who needed external support to fight for their independence, were forced to take sides in the Cold War. For the MPLA's leaders, whose origins made the communist countries their natural allies, this need for aid would make it very difficult to maintain their political and ideological independence from their sponsors (chiefly in Moscow), though they certainly tried. The result was a fraught and complicated relationship between the MPLA leadership and the Soviets, one in which both sides constantly sought out alternatives but ended up stuck with each other.

The situation was complicated further by the presence of a competitor liberation movement based primarily among the Bakongo population, which changed its name to the União das Populações de Angola (UPA; Union of Peoples of Angola) under the leadership of a thirty-six-year old Léopoldville-educated Bakongo named Holden Roberto in 1958. While the UPA would come to be seen as a pro-Western movement, in part due to its receiving funding from the US Central Intelligence Agency, it presented a problem for the MPLA because, especially in the early 1960s, it was winning the battle for official African support between the two movements. Roberto represented the UPA at Nkrumah's Pan-African Congress in 1958, where he met not only Nkrumah but also Frantz Fanon, Patrice Lumumba, Sekou Toure, and others who persuaded him to abandon the project of reconstituting the Bakongo kingdom and push for a united and independent Angola.[9] Roberto decided to focus the UPA's efforts on military struggle, which after July 1960 was enabled by close ties with the leaders of newly independent Congo-Léopoldville who provided his movement with bases; supplies; political influence; and access to the lengthy, heavily forested, and thinly controlled Angolan-Congolese border. Following the onset of armed struggle in northern Angola in February 1961, the UPA combined with the smaller Democratic Party of Angola to form the FNLA, leading to the creation on April 5, 1962, of the Govêrno Revolucionário de Angola no Exílio (GRAE; Revolutionary Government of Angola in Exile). Due to the greater ability of the FNLA to conduct armed struggle, the following year the newly formed Liberation Committee of the Organisation of African Unity (OAU) recommended that its members recognize the GRAE and funnel all aid exclusively to the FNLA.

Meanwhile, the MPLA's initial forays into gaining external support were directed more toward Europe, where its leaders were located, than toward Africa. The MPLA was represented neither at the first Afro-Asian People's Solidarity Conference in Cairo in late 1957 nor at the All-African People's Conference in Ghana in late 1958, but Andrade and Cruz both attended the Afro-Asian Writers' Conference in Tashkent, Uzbek SSR, earlier that year.[10] MPLA representatives did attend the Second All-African People's Conference in Tunis in 1960, and the movement subsequently set up its headquarters in Conakry, Guinea, much farther from the action in Angola. That summer Cruz led an MPLA delegation to the German Democratic Republic (GDR), Czechoslovakia, the USSR, and the People's Republic of China (PRC) in July. Though he told both Moscow and East Berlin about the MPLA's newfound embrace of armed struggle,[11] this was still the era of Soviet promotion of peaceful coexistence, and military aid was not forthcoming. Cruz had more success in Beijing, where his hosts, led by Foreign Minister Chen Yi, were satisfied that he sympathized with them in their dispute with the Soviets.[12] At the height of the Great Leap famine, however, the Chinese aid offer was modest, consisting of the

equivalent of twenty thousand US dollars, an allowance for office supplies, and agreement to accept ten people for military training.

The situation would change, however, with the eruption of violence
in Angola in early 1961 and the nation's sudden emergence on the international agenda. On February 4, 1961, several hundred Angolans armed
primarily with knives and clubs attacked Luanda's main prison with the
ostensible aim of freeing political prisoners. The MPLA would subsequently claim credit for the attack, though evidence for that claim is scant,
and Cruz subsequently admitted to the East Germans that the MPLA had
little to do with it.[13]

With Angola now squarely on the international agenda, the Soviets
took a closer look at the MPLA. In April 1961 the head of the Second
African Division of the Soviet Foreign Ministry, created that year to deal
with sub-Saharan Africa, produced a report touting the MPLA as the
"most progressive organization in Angola" and quoting its program
calling for "the initial defense of the interests of the peasant and working
masses, who account for almost the whole population of Angola, and
union with all progressive forces of the world." An extensive analysis of
the program of this small, relatively new organization that had only just
begun what would be a fifteen-year liberation struggle focused on the finer
points of its economic and political program, including calls for a planned
economy, development of light and heavy industry, state control of trade
and industrial development, agrarian reform and nationalization of land,
and even a surprisingly detailed plan for cooperative farms. This Soviet
Foreign Ministry report declared that the program "expresses the interests of the broad masses of Angola," but a lengthy discussion followed,
and the report noted that "from the available evidence, the MPLA does
not play a fundamental role in the struggle of the Angolan people," acknowledging that it was the UPA that was far more active in leading the
struggle on the ground. The report also admitted that the MPLA's constituency was basically the youth and the intelligentsia, "and to a certain
degree representatives of the working class and peasantry." Despite this,
it was clear that the USSR must support the MPLA, especially because
the UPA was supposed to be financed, in part, by the Americans.[14] Soon
after the conference, Khrushchev promised his support to the MPLA via
the Soviet embassy in Conakry.[15] The MPLA first appeared on the list of
parties to be financed primarily by Moscow through the International Aid
Fund to Left Workers' Organizations in 1962, to the tune of twenty-five

thousand dollars.[16] The East Germans were even more sanguine than the Soviets regarding the MPLA, saying that it had succeeded in uniting all of the progressive forces of Angola and that its "main support" (*Hauptstürtzte*) was the peasants and workers. According to the East German Foreign Ministry, "from [the MPLA's] program and the statements of their leaders one can understand that they are substantially imbued with the Marxist line of the communist forces."[17] The East Germans were convinced enough of the bona fides of the MPLA to give them two aid packages totaling 104,000 marks (about twenty-six thousand dollars at the official exchange rate) in 1961, including medicine and motorcycles but no weapons. For 1962 East Germany envisioned increasing ideological work on the MPLA and inviting Mario de Andrade to Berlin.[18] Meanwhile, the Chinese went in the other direction. When Cruz came to the Chinese embassy in Conakry asking for money to purchase arms in the Congo, the Foreign Affairs Institute, contradicting Cruz's report, mentioned that the UPA was actually doing most of the fighting and the result was that the Ministry of Foreign Affairs decided to express encouragement for the Angolan struggle but deny Cruz's aid request.[19] As far as the Chinese were concerned, what seemed to matter was who was doing the actual fighting; in the available documents, no analysis seems to have been made by the Chinese of the economic program of the MPLA.

The ideological affinity between the MPLA and the Soviets went beyond just economics; it also reflected a shared vulnerability on the issue of race. As the Sino-Soviet split heated up in the early 1960s, the Soviets found themselves accused of being just another white, imperialist power whose support for revolution in the Global South was suspect. Meanwhile, the competition with the FNLA forced the MPLA to come to terms with its own image as a movement of *mestiço* intellectuals in exile who were reluctant to fight. In response, the party held a meeting of its Committee of Directors in May 1962. The meeting adopted the principle of removing *mestiços* from the leadership and Cruz, who had been the most active of the MPLA leaders, was among those removed. There are differences of opinion as to how this change was accomplished. John Marcum, an American scholar who toured Angola in this period as a leading figure of the American Committee on Africa, which supported the FNLA at the time, wrote that this was a major defeat for Cruz by a movement seeking to rid itself of both its *mestiço* leadership and its Marxist orientation.[20] Jean-Michel Mabeko-Tali, the only non-MPLA scholar thus far to have had extensive access to MPLA documents, claims instead that

Cruz voluntarily resigned his position in order to make the movement more competitive with the FNLA on racial grounds.[21] In any case, Agostinho Neto, the erstwhile honorary president of the MPLA, escaped from prison and convened the first party congress of the MPLA in December 1962, where the principal of nonracialism was reaffirmed and the leadership structure changed once again. Cruz was not returned, but three *mestiços,* including the pro-Soviet Lucio Lara, were added to the Committee of Directors. Andrade and Cruz, who had headed the MPLA in Neto's absence, were both disillusioned with the results of the conference and now largely disaffected.[22]

Under Neto's leadership the MPLA took a different tack on the race issue from the one Cruz had been pushing. On a visit to East Berlin in June 1963, Neto pitched the MPLA as an explicitly postracial movement encompassing all progressives regardless of race or religion. It condemned the "racist" nature of the FNLA, which it said conducted its own struggle on a "tribal" basis.[23] Neto continued on to Moscow, where he asked for and received military and financial aid, before returning to Africa, where the MPLA formed a new organization, the Democratic Front for the Liberation of Angola, based on the principles of unity as opposed to the "tribalism" and "racism" of the FNLA.[24] The Soviet Foreign Ministry now began to parrot Neto's accusations, accusing the FNLA of fomenting tribal discord.[25] Neto's new line on the racial issue, and the split within the MPLA that it caused, was also reflected in the MPLA's international position. Though he dabbled with the prospect of visiting China in the fall of 1963 after his tour of the Eastern Bloc, Neto did not actually make it to Beijing.[26]

In fact, Neto solved the racial problem in a way that was uniquely useful to Moscow. Though he was married to a European, which was a political liability, Neto—unlike many of his competitors for leadership of the MPLA—was fully black and yet committed to the idea of a nonracial Angola and a class-based liberation struggle. As Eduard Mondlane, the president of the MPLA's ally, the Frente de Libertação de Moçambique (FRELIMO; Liberation Front of Mozambique), told the Soviet Committee for Solidarity with the Countries of Asia and Africa (SCSCAA) during the Khartoum Conference of 1969 (where Moscow officially baptized its allies in southern Africa), Neto "was one of the ones rather more distant from scientific socialism, and despite this he came with the following proposal, saying 'I do not know how you [the USSR] will do it, but we need to work out a system that will arm us, antiracists, against ideological racism, that will give us theoretical postulates—a political textbook that would be sufficient to oppose to the whole racist system, not in a general methodological form, but how the state should look, how to reconcile two communities, how to arrange the coexistence of the white and black man.'"[27] An ideological bulletin distributed by the MPLA in 1967, containing quotes from Neto, explained the difference between racial and class-based visions of anticolonial struggle: "For some colonialism is a form of domination of blacks by whites, of Africans by Europeans, and for them the problem of struggle for national liberation does not go beyond a crusade to liberate our land from foreign invaders. . . . Colonialism is fundamentally a variant of the exploitation of man by man, the struggle for national liberation is the struggle of the exploited masses against such exploitation."[28] The bulletin went on to discuss the revolutionary imperatives of social transformation after independence, quoting a recent Neto speech on the topic of neocolonialism. The Soviets' Achilles heel in the developing world was the racial question, and Neto was someone who not only offered protection on the issue because he was black but shared the fundamental Soviet claim that revolutions needed to be about issues of class and economics rather than race.

Yet the congruence on key ideological issues did not mean that the Soviets and Neto were content to be locked into an exclusive relationship. Particularly in the wake of the OAU Liberation Committee's decision in July 1963 to recognize the GRAE, the Soviets investigated the possibility of building a relationship with Holden Roberto. Roberto appealed for aid to the USSR on December 4, 1963, and GRAE foreign minister Jonas Savimbi spoke to the East German representative in Cairo, telling him that many within the GRAE were suspicious of the Americans and wanted to establish ties and receive support from socialist countries that "selflessly support the struggle of the African people."[29] Savimbi even proposed sending a GRAE delegation to the various socialist capitals, starting in East Berlin. The delegation left for Europe in April 1964, but by this time Savimbi and others had become disaffected due to Roberto's leadership style, and he told the East Germans that American influence within the GRAE was growing.[30] Despite the OAU decision, the USSR refused to shift its support to the supposedly American-supported FNLA.[31]

At the same time, Neto sought to establish his own relationship with Beijing, hoping at a minimum to deny a possible source of support to his rivals both inside and outside the MPLA. The Chinese took much more seriously than the Soviets the possibility of shifting their support to the

FNLA, ultimately only deciding not to invite Roberto to Beijing for fear of offending left-wing opinion throughout Africa, especially among their rebel allies in the eastern Congo.[32] While this was being considered, the MPLA made repeated efforts to sabotage the visit, arguing both that Roberto was working on a rapprochement with Moscow and that Moscow was using the possibility of a Chinese rapprochement with Roberto to hurt Chinese standing in Africa.[33] Neto now decided to finally go ahead with his visit to Beijing, which he had postponed several times in 1963, but the Chinese reduced the number of the delegation's members from twenty to three.[34] The Chinese embassy in Cairo was still skeptical of the MPLA in advance of the visit, reporting that the party's leaders neglected the struggle at home and ran to "revisionist" countries for aid and direction while Roberto was leading the real fight.[35] Neto finally arrived in Beijing on June 19, saying all the right things about anti-imperialism and agreement with China, attributing previous differences to "misunderstandings."[36] Meeting opposition from his Chinese interlocutors, Neto even claimed that "the MPLA's real inclination is toward China's revolutionary line . . . but current concrete difficulties do not allow the movement to openly oppose certain countries."[37] Seeing that the Chinese were not buying this position, Neto changed tactics, instead acting repentant toward the end of his visit and claiming that the Chinese had managed to change his mind. After a session devoted to the Sino-Soviet split, Neto declared that "only now have I begun to recognize the struggle necessary when I return to the country, it is already late, but we can still succeed, we need to increase criticism of the mistakes we have made, having leaders leave the struggle at home to go abroad is a mistake."[38] At this point the declarations of faith and goodwill by Neto and his comrades seemed to have had some effect on their Chinese hosts who reported that Neto's determination to renew armed struggle seemed genuine. While Beijing did not enter into an exclusive relationship with Neto by cutting off ties to Roberto and Cruz (the latter, in fact, visited Beijing again one week after Neto left),[39] relations between Neto and the Chinese had at least been somewhat improved, opening the way for Chinese aid and training of MPLA fighters.

Despite the improvement in Sino-MPLA relations, Soviet support would loom ever larger as the needs of the MPLA grew. The overthrow of the pro-French government in the Republic of Congo by a left-wing regime led by Alphonse Massamba-Débat in August 1963 had allowed the MPLA to relocate its headquarters to Brazzaville. Now, with the support of its new Congolese allies, the MPLA managed to open a new front in the small enclave of Cabinda, a piece of Angola to the north of the Congo River that was separated from the rest of the country but easily accessible from the MPLA's headquarters in Brazzaville and its training camp in Dolisie. Aid to sustain the fight, including arms and training, came mostly from Moscow, and between 1964 and 1967 financial aid through the Soviet International Aid Fund to the MPLA jumped from forty-five thousand dollars to $145,000, with the MPLA's ranking on the aid funding list jumping from forty-third to seventeenth.[40] Meanwhile, Chinese aid during these years was scattered and unreliable, with Portuguese intelligence reports in 1965–1968 detailing Chinese aid to Cruz's faction, the FNLA, the MPLA, and the newly created UNITA, which had been founded by Jonas Savimbi in 1966.[41] A new aid player, Cuba, briefly entered the scene, after Che Guevara visited Brazzaville and met with Neto in 1965. Cuban soldiers and instructors in Brazzaville helped to train the MPLA, even attempting to lead two columns in 1966 south to the Angolan mainland. The columns had little success running the gauntlet of the hostile Congolese, FNLA, and Portuguese, however, and by 1967 Cuba's attentions shifted temporarily away from Angola.[42] Thus, in spite of its attempts to diversify its sources of support for the MPLA all roads ultimately led back to Moscow.

Moscow's embrace would prove to be an uncomfortable one, however. The Soviets imagined that their aid entitled them to a significant, if not determinate, voice in MPLA strategy, as well as to the loyalty of the party vis-à-vis geopolitical rivals and on issues of international importance. Agostinho Neto much preferred giving orders to taking them, and his dictatorial style engendered a continual lineup of challengers to his political dominance of the MPLA. These challengers, in turn, would look for outside support, and Neto had to prove his loyalty in order to secure the continuing support of his patrons, especially in Moscow. The resulting dynamic would prove to be unstable, and though it was almost stretched to the breaking point in 1974, ultimately the Soviets and Neto needed one another too much to allow for a complete break. This interdependence was fed by Cold War politics, which made it difficult to cultivate multiple sources of support for liberation movements, as well as by the racial politics in Angola that continually threatened to undermine the legitimacy of a multiracial organization promoting a class-based ideology in a region dominated by the politics of racial oppression.

The Struggle Moves East, 1966–1974

By 1966 the situation in Africa, which had been in rapid flux in 1961, had ossified. After the independence of Northern Rhodesia as Zambia in late 1964, the progress of decolonization had stalled, leaving most of the southern part of the continent under either Portuguese or white minority rule. It had become clear that the Portuguese regime had no intention of surrendering its colonies and that, with enormous sacrifices including military expenditure constituting 40–50 percent of its budget, as well as fitful and reluctant support from some of its North Atlantic Treaty Organization allies, it could succeed in keeping the anticolonial revolts under some measure of control.[43] The independence of Zambia had altered the picture somewhat, as there was now a new independent African country from which to access the Angolan interior. The MPLA set up an office in Lusaka to head its Third Military Region with the intent of covering the new eastern front on March 18, 1966, planning eventually to link the northern and eastern fronts. But the government of Zambia, dependent upon Portuguese goodwill to allow its copper exports to reach the sea via the Benguela Railway through Angola, exercised a dampening influence on the pace of military activity in the east, and the high hopes for the new front quickly evaporated.

Frustration with the continuing failure to make meaningful military progress toward liberation soured the MPLA-Soviet relationship. The Soviets increasingly blamed the MPLA leadership and its choice of tactics for the party's inability to inflict significant losses on the Portuguese and capture and hold populated territory. A top-secret Komitet Gosudarstvennoy Bezopasnosti (KGB; Committee for State Security) report from June 1970 sought to explain the failure of the MPLA's armed struggle by saying that it had overestimated the potential of guerrilla warfare and "underestimated the necessity for the creation of an effective underground organization in the cities."[44] The Soviet ambassador to Tanzania echoed this critique, writing that "the leaders of these national liberation organizations [he was also addressing FRELIMO and the Zimbabwean African People's Union, or ZAPU] still do not sufficiently clearly understand that one cannot count on military victory over regular and well-armed forces of the enemy on this basis without including all forms of armed and political struggle."[45] As late as March 1974, on the eve of the Lisbon coup that would pave the way for independence, the Soviet ambassador in

Brazzaville was complaining that the MPLA was still neglecting political and underground struggle among workers and soldiers in the Portuguese colonial army.[46]

While on the surface this critique seemed merely tactical and strategic, it also contained an element of the ideological, since it implied that the MPLA was in practice following a Maoist strategy of guerrilla warfare in rural areas instead of conducting political struggle in urban ones. At the height of the Sino-Soviet split, such heterodoxy could not but worry Moscow, and the Soviets carefully followed the MPLA's tentative steps to build a stronger relationship with China in these years. In June 1969 the MPLA sent a representative to Beijing asking for twenty-two thousand dollars and permission for a leadership delegation to visit the PRC, though the Chinese were not terribly receptive at the time.[47] The following year the KGB detected increasing receptiveness on the part of the Chinese toward the MPLA overtures.[48] KGB chairman Yuri Andropov reported that the MPLA was seeking military and material aid from Beijing, asking China to stop supporting UNITA and expressing sympathy for PRC policies. Agostinho Neto, when asked about this by the Soviet ambassador in Zambia, said that the MPLA had not yet received any military aid from the PRC and that, of course, it understood that the majority of its aid came from the USSR.[49] But, he explained, it seemed that now the focus of Soviet aid to African liberation movements had shifted to Guinea-Bissau instead, and that since Soviet resources were understandably limited, it made sense for the MPLA to seek additional help elsewhere. In other words, the MPLA had its own explanation for why guerrilla warfare was not going as well as had been hoped, and in part that was due to insufficient support from Moscow.

Within the MPLA there appeared to be a deeper disconnect between the fact that while the lion's share of the support came from Moscow, the sympathies of the rank and file lay elsewhere. Part of this might have been attributable to the eclectic nature of the party's training program. One captured MPLA fighter told the Portuguese in 1967 that, in the MPLA training camps, political education included instruction in Marxism from Soviet textbooks, but the military training revolved around the study of Maoist tactics.[50] Some MPLA fighters had undergone training in the PRC, and the image of the Chinese revolution remained alive and useful for those who were dissatisfied with Neto's leadership, perceiving the confluence of a postracial ideology and a tilt toward Moscow as evidence of revisionism. According to Portuguese sources, the increasing reliance of the MPLA on the USSR was causing dissatisfaction among certain leaders who did not have confidence in continued Soviet support.[51] The leader of the African Party for the Independence of Guinea and Cape Verde, Amilcar Cabral, saw the Sino-Soviet split as a convenient tool for those dissatisfied with Neto's leadership to express their discontent.[52]

In July 1971 Neto led a delegation to the PRC, his first visit since 1964, and was received by Zhou Enlai.[53] While South African intelligence claimed that Beijing agreed to provide arms to the MPLA, Neto told the Soviet embassy in Brazzaville that no such agreement had been reached.[54] Nevertheless, a September 1971 letter from MPLA militants captured by the Portuguese reveals that, in the wake of this visit, MPLA members were instructed that China was "now our friend [*ja e o nosso amigo*]."[55] Other factors contributed to the increase of Chinese influence within the MPLA as well. MPLA commanders were now being trained, along with their comrades from FRELIMO, the African National Congress, and others at a camp in Iringa, Tanzania. With the breaking of ground on the Tazara Railway in 1970, Chinese workers flooded into Tanzania, and Iringa soon had fifteen Chinese instructors teaching Marxism-Leninism, guerrilla warfare, and the experience of the Chinese revolution.[56] The works of Mao Zedong were still being used for training, as they had been since the 1960s.[57] Now, however, new trainees just returning from the PRC were influenced by the principles of the Cultural Revolution,[58] and they became the inspiration behind the Movimento de Reajustamento (Readjustment Movement) introduced by the MPLA in late 1972 in order to restructure the movement. This gave a greater voice to more junior officers, particularly on the eastern front, in order to defang some of the resentment that was building up within the movement.[59] By 1972 Portuguese intelligence even reported that, within the MPLA rank and file, sentiment was far more pro-Chinese than pro-Soviet, though this verdict was likely exaggerated.[60] The increase in Chinese influence nevertheless helped catalyze rank-and-file pique against the leadership and, combined with the dissatisfaction that leadership already felt with the level of support coming from Moscow, the stage was set for a crisis that would nearly sever the MPLA-Soviet relationship.[61]

In addition to contributing to disagreements over strategy between Moscow and the MPLA, the opening of the eastern front in 1966 had an important impact on the internal dynamics of the party. The ethnic differences between the Chokwe and Ovimbundu fighters in the east and the largely Mbundu and *mestiço* leadership in faraway Brazzaville were compounded by allegations that the MPLA leadership was favoring the northern front over the eastern one in terms of distribution of resources, particularly arms.[62] This would produce the greatest threat yet to Neto's leadership and would cause the Soviets to temporarily stop aid to the MPLA. Tensions between the Neto-led Brazzaville leadership and the forces of the eastern front under the command of Daniel Chipenda, a charismatic Ovimbundu officer almost a decade younger than Neto, exploded in the wake of a reconciliation agreement signed by the MPLA and the FNLA in Kinshasa, Zaire, in December 1972. Chipenda and others saw the agreement—which created the Supreme Council for the Liberation of Angola, with Holden Roberto as president—as including unacceptable concessions by the MPLA.[63] While Neto certainly had his reasons for believing that the MPLA would get the better of Roberto and the FNLA, the main purpose of the agreement from the MPLA's perspective was clear: to enable it to access Angola from Zaire and thereby shift the focus of the battle to the northern front.[64] For those under Chipenda's command on the eastern front who had borne the brunt of the fighting for the last six years, this was the spark that would ignite a mutiny.

Matters came to a head in May 1973 when the Neto-led MPLA leadership issued orders to arrest Chipenda and his leading lieutenants on the grounds that they were conspiring to overthrow and kill the current leadership. Chipenda fled to Lusaka, where he was protected by the Zambian government, while clashes took place on the eastern front near the Angolan-Zambian border between fighters loyal to Chipenda and those loyal to Neto.[65] This time the Soviets would not be as quick to support Neto as they had been in the past. Reporting on events in Angola to the Soviet Central Committee, Viktor Kulikov, the chief of the General Staff, largely blamed Neto for the turn of events, saying he had ignored the national question in the formation of his leadership and instead of dealing with the causes of the conflict was seeking to end it by force.[66] In response, the Central Committee directed the Soviet ambassador in Zambia to meet with both Chipenda and Neto and to feel them out on the issue of reconciliation, underlining that Moscow had always fulfilled the MPLA's aid requests but that the continuation of the split would make it difficult to do so.[67] Chipenda received some assistance from Moscow, and the Soviet ambassador in Lusaka continued to invite him for "confidential" conversations.[68] Kulikov even raised the possibility of talking to Holden Roberto.[69]

It seems possible, if not likely, that if a group of Portuguese officers had not staged a coup on April 25, 1974, the Neto-Soviet relationship, and possibly the entire MPLA-Soviet relationship, would have ended completely. In the beginning of 1974 Moscow finally did cut off aid to the MPLA, though this was so damaging to Neto that he did not even tell the MPLA *aktiv* (a Russian term to describe the collective of most active members) about it at a meeting in Dolisie, Congo, in February 1974.[70] Neto's pessimism, however, was on display in a speech he gave at the University of Dar es Salaam that month, in which he declared, "In our days the socialist camp is split, the struggle of uncompromising ideological conceptions is weakened, and the relations of solidarity, which made this camp an 'iron bastion,' are destroyed. . . . We must be realistic, the national-liberation struggle in Africa has no firm base in the international arena."[71] It was not just the Soviets who seemed to be abandoning Neto. The presidents of the neighboring countries—Kenneth Kaunda of Zambia, Marian Ngouabi of Congo, Mobutu Sese Seko of Zaire, and Julius Nyerere of Tanzania—tried to reconcile Chipenda and Neto, but their efforts led to increasing disillusionment with Neto. On April 18 the Soviet representative in Tanzania asked Nyerere whether he would recommend that Moscow resume aid to the MPLA. Nyerere answered that he was on his way to Lusaka with Neto to meet with Kaunda and would give a final verdict once he returned, but that "in Angola there is only one organization which is able to conduct armed struggle—that is the MPLA. We need to give this organization and its leadership all possible aid and support. The leadership of the organization is not chosen by its friends, but by the organization itself."[72] Five days later Nyerere returned to Dar es Salaam and told the Soviets that Neto was behaving incomprehensibly and was the primary obstacle to reconciliation: "I am telling you openly, that I had great difficulty holding back and not telling Neto everything I thought. I wanted to advise him right there in the airport to resign his post as leader and go back to practicing medicine, where he could apparently do more for humanity." Referring to his remarks five days earlier, he told them, "Now, after the trip to Lusaka, I am starting to doubt the correctness of such a position, and I am asking the question are we correct in acting this way, are we helping the MPLA or just Neto personally, an individual who does not want to help create the atmosphere necessary for the restoration of unity in the organization."[73] Given that Kaunda was sheltering Chipenda, Mobutu had long supported Roberto, and Ngouabi

FIGURE 4.1 Julius Nyerere and Agostinho Neto, from the magazine of the Organização das Mulheres de Angola, February 1974. Neto visited Tanzania at a time of strained relations, looking for support as he battled for control of the MPLA, less than three months before the overthrow of the Portuguese dictatorship. *(Reproduction courtesy of the Hoover Institution)*

was hoping to annex the Angolan enclave of Cabinda to his country, the loss of Nyerere's confidence could have meant the end of the road for Neto.

Ironically, Neto would be saved by the Portuguese military, which overthrew the regime of Marcello Caetano in a coup only two days after Nyerere pronounced his damning verdict. Given the rapidity with which events would then move in both Angola and Portugal, the Soviets would see the difficulty in trying to build up a new movement to compete for power in the soon-to-be independent Angola. The need to bolster the MPLA would be particularly pressing because of another development that had taken place in 1974: Chinese rapprochement with Zaire, and a resulting significant increase in Chinese aid to the FNLA, which now looked like the most militarily formidable of the liberation movements. The Chinese promised massive military aid, including some 120 instructors who would arrive at the FNLA's training camp in Kinkuzu, Zaire, in 1974. Roberto followed a visit to Beijing with one to Romania, where

FIGURE 4.2 Deng Xiaoping and Holden Roberto, from the FNLA's *Events* magazine, March 6, 1974. On the eve of independence the FNLA seemed to be the strongest, militarily, of the three liberation movements, as the PRC sent instructors to train its fighters at a camp in Kinkuzu, Zaire. *(Reproduction courtesy of the Hoover Institution)*

Nicolae Ceauşescu also promised to aid the FNLA.[74] Though China did not cut off ties or military aid to the MPLA at this point, the sudden shift in its relations with the FNLA, and the MPLA's present state of chaos, made the FNLA suddenly China's main ally in Angola.

Throughout this period of struggle China's position remained relatively constant. It was willing to support whichever movement seemed to be conducting serious guerrilla warfare, and it was not terribly interested in the supposed political and economic programs that a given movement said it would implement upon independence. The Soviet Union, however, had chosen to take a more involved position, loyally supporting the MPLA from 1961 because of its Marxist ideology and continually intervening to protect the position of Agostinho Neto, who shared the Soviet view that national liberation movements should be fundamentally about class, not race. Now, though, it seemed that Neto's refusal to account for issues of racial and tribal identity in distributing power had perhaps fatally harmed the MPLA, and all those years of loyal support might be for naught. Moscow ultimately would not abandon Neto, but it would take a more active role in building the structure of the MPLA and, eventually, the Angolan state, with an eye toward the implementation of mechanisms of political control and ideological indoctrination that would prevent the emergence of such splits. The Soviet Union, and also Neto, would learn to pay more attention to identity issues both in terms of trying to better integrate the leadership and appeal to popular anger and to immediately and violently crush any overt race- or ethnic-based challenges to the MPLA leadership by tarring its promoters with the charge of Maoism.

From Coup to Civil War, 1974–1976

Though Portugal's military proved able to keep insurgencies in its three African colonies at bay, ultimately the cost proved unsustainable. On April 25, 1974, the Caetano regime in Lisbon was overthrown by the Movement of Armed Forces, composed primarily of junior officers, making General António de Spínola, who had recently authored a book calling for a political solution to Portugal's colonial wars, the new president. While initially the new Portuguese government hoped to maintain some sort of loose political ties with its African colonies, the realities of the Portuguese political and economic condition, the animosities of an extended war, and the ascendance of the Portuguese Communist Party (PCP) and the left wing of the Movement of Armed Forces, made such an outcome highly improbable, leading General Spínola to resign in September. It was clear that Portuguese colonial rule would be coming to an end as soon as some sort of arrangement could be made for the transfer of power.

Guinea-Bissau had already declared its independence in 1973 and, in Mozambique, FRELIMO commanded a dominant position. It was Angola, with its ethnic divisions and internecine conflict, that provided the most difficult problem. Each of the Angolan movements had its supporters and detractors. The FNLA, generally considered the strongest militarily at this point, offered a noncommunist option that Western governments could support, though its organizational discipline left something to be desired. UNITA seemed to be the most popular among the white population of Angola, possibly because of its history of understandings with the Portuguese.[75] Meanwhile, the MPLA had close ties to the PCP and other left-wing forces back in Portugal, and in particular had the support of the

Portuguese high commissioner in Angola, Admiral Rosa Coutinho, also known as Red Rosa.[76] In particular, Melo Antunes, the Portuguese minister of decolonization, told the MPLA at a meeting in Algeria that the Lisbon government saw the FNLA as a Trojan horse for American influence, and thus the MPLA had its complete support, including a secret agreement to allow the MPLA to use Portuguese airports, roads, and military transport.[77] Yet, in addition to the Chipenda revolt (now known as the Revolta do Leste, or Eastern Revolt) on May 11, 1974, another group of dissident MPLA members went public with a manifesto attacking the "presidential absolutism" of Neto. This group would come to be known as the Revolta Activa, and it was led by Mario de Andrade and Joaquim Pinto de Andrade, consisting of a number of largely educated white and *mestiço* senior figures within the movement.[78] With the MPLA now broken into three parts, it was no wonder that, as one representative of ZAPU told the Soviets, the MPLA was in no position to exercise decisive influence in the country.[79]

With independence now on the not-too-distant horizon, it was time for the MPLA and its allies to try to put the movement back together as quickly as possible. Moscow, through its ambassador in Brazzaville and others, tried to get the various MPLA factions to reunite, but in June the Soviet Central Committee sent Neto a telegram reaffirming its support for the MPLA.[80] The presidents of the African host countries of the MPLA—Congo, Tanzania, Zaire, and Zambia—pressured the three MPLA factions to convene a congress that, after two months of delays, was held in Lusaka in August 1974 on terms imposed by the four presidents. The congress ended, however, with Neto's faction marching out and the rump congress, dominated by Chipenda supporters, electing him the new president of the MPLA.[81] A month later Neto convened his own conference, reestablishing some semblance of control over the MPLA. Given that Chipenda traveled to Kinshasa after the Lusaka conference to talk about forming a united front with Roberto, while the Revolta Activa (which was quite small, in any case) seemed amenable to coming to an arrangement with Neto, Moscow took the new congress as sufficient cause to throw its support behind Neto again and abandon the hope of reuniting the movement.[82]

The MPLA's frantic search for external support had begun immediately after the coup, with Neto visiting the GDR in May to seek aid. Though this was the period when Soviet aid to Neto was still suspended, the East Germans nevertheless agreed to give the MPLA financial aid and civilian goods (certain goods such as meat, socks, and cigarettes had already been sent to Vietnam).[83] The first country to supply arms was the MPLA's most consistent ally, Yugoslavia, which sent a ship that arrived in Pointe Noire on August 15, while the congress of Lusaka was still in session.[84] Once Neto reestablished control of the movement and the Soviets had decided to support him once again, Moscow went into high gear, drawing up an agreement with the MPLA for the supply of heavy weapons in December that involved transporting them through Congo.[85] Congolese president Ngouabi soon assented, though the Soviet ambassador in Brazzaville reported to Moscow that the task of leading the MPLA to victory would not be easy.[86] In February 1975 Portuguese intelligence reported that Soviet arms were arriving in Luanda by truck, and a ship with arms was expected soon.[87] Notably, considering how events would turn out, Cuba was the laggard among socialist countries in aiding the MPLA, and it did not begin doing so until late July.[88]

Meanwhile, the FNLA, with the help of North Korea, the PRC, Romania, and Zaire, was busy arming and training a projected army of fifteen thousand.[89] FNLA units moved into Angola in July and August and established an occupied zone in the north by late September. UNITA eschewed military action in favor of a call for a coalition of the three movements, at the same time trying to reassure whites that they would be safe in an independent Angola.[90] Though an MPLA-UNITA coalition might have been a realistic and promising alternative, offering both groups the potential of overwhelming popular support and a compromise that would have headed off the coming international free-for-all, the MPLA had already decided at the Conference of Cadres in September 1974 that it would not share power, affirming its status as the "sole legitimate representative of the Angolan people."[91] Jockeying for position soon led to armed clashes between the FNLA and MPLA, though, and the OAU, attempting to stop the violence, managed to get Neto, Roberto, and Savimbi to sign an agreement in Mombassa, Kenya, on January 5, 1975, pledging to cooperate peacefully and begin negotiations with the Portuguese. Those negotiations resulted in the January 15 Alvor Agreement, which established a provisional government composed of representatives of the three movements, along with a similarly constructed army, and setting the date for independence as November 11. The new government took power in a ceremony described by the South African consul general as "farcical," with each of the three movements dressing its representatives in uniforms that can only be described as aspirational: the FNLA in Mao tunics, the

MPLA in safari suits, and UNITA in suits and ties.[92] Cooperation among the three movements would not last, and the country soon began to slide toward civil war.

Each side prepared for the coming battle for control, stockpiling weapons, occupying positions in Luanda, and trying to expand and rally its base. The United States soon joined the fray, agreeing to send three hundred thousand dollars to the FNLA just a week after the Alvor Agreement. Neto returned to Luanda on February 4 (the fourteenth anniversary of the start of the armed struggle), and a SCSCAA delegation was there to meet him and report back to Moscow. A top MPLA official and future prime minister, Lopo do Nascimento, in conversation with the Soviet delegation, compared the provisional government to the one led by Alexander Fyodorovich Kerensky in Russia in 1917.[93] A large group of MPLA members left for Moscow that month, only to return as the crack Ninth Brigade, just in time to stop the FNLA from taking Luanda in September.[94] Armed clashes began in Luanda just weeks after the provisional government took power, and despite a new agreement signed between Neto, Roberto, and Savimbi at Nakuru, Kenya, on June 21, the situation continued to deteriorate. In the memorable phrase of the South African consul general on June 26, "there is no beer, there is no bread, there is no hope."[95]

Under the circumstances, a second Soviet delegation to Angola reported that civil war looked "inevitable."[96] With China, the United States, and others now aiding the MPLA's enemies, the USSR could either double down on its investment or watch years of support for the MPLA go for naught. In a heated diatribe during a SCSCAA meeting in June, Petr Manchka, a longtime Soviet Africa expert, laid out what was at stake for the Soviets in Angola:

> The issue is, down which path will go this big and important African country, important for us, where we are interested both politically and economically. Our forces are weak politically, maybe, and our further support is needed. Militarily, it is difficult to say. It seems to us that the issue is a very serious international imperialist conspiracy. . . . Now the popular liberation organization of Angola (MPLA) and the leader of this organization, Agostinho Neto, who was never our favorite, but we did not choose, we did not have a choice and it is not our right to choose (it is not our territory), he was chosen by the Angolan people and one has to account for

this. We cannot criticize him. He is a pro-Soviet person, but once it became clear, that specifically those people who support and sympathize with this organization might come to rule the country, they [the imperialists] decided to give battle, not to allow to come to power this organization, which has been supported over many years by whom? Soviet people, and other soviet powers, the world socialist fraternity [*sodruzhestvo*]. This is the substance of the question. We have invested in this matter colossal material means, allow me not to give a number, over the course of thirteen years, and of course it would not be good for us if we waste these means, but also in the moral-political sphere. Angola is Angola. And now, as it seems to us, in this place the forces of socialism and capitalism are concentrated.[97]

Manchka's view of the situation was, if anything, overly pessimistic; on July 9 the MPLA drove the FNLA out of Luanda. Nevertheless, the MPLA decided to send a delegation to the socialist countries in July and August seeking more military aid, and the East Germans and Soviets were happy to oblige; though each step of Soviet escalation required a new round of geopolitical calculation, ultimately Moscow could not afford to lose.[98] Cuba now sprang into action as well, agreeing to send, beginning in August, nearly five hundred instructors to train the MPLA army.[99] With an FNLA column advancing on Luanda by late July, the civil war was now a fact, and each of the interested international actors was obliged to place its bets.

One international actor, however, made a different choice: with the independence of Angola now officially assured and the realization that it would take a massive effort to affect the outcome of the civil war, the Chinese went home. Though it seems unlikely, the Chinese foreign minister claimed in September that his country had stopped sending arms to Angola once a date for independence had been set, and on October 27, Chinese military instructors in Kinkuzu officially left for China.[100] Certain scholars have tried to paint Chinese and Soviet actions in Angola during this period as motivated primarily by a battle between them for predominance in southern Africa, and some contemporary observers certainly saw it that way.[101] But the actions of neither Beijing nor Moscow easily fit this pattern. The Chinese apparently sought to prevent Angola from becoming a Soviet base in Africa, but they continued to maintain relations with all three liberation movements during the run-up to independence, and Lucio

Lara of the MPLA visited Beijing in June.[102] China reportedly assured him that it favored a government of all three movements, a position consistent with Chinese policy going as far back as 1964. In some ways, the United States did function as a sort of Chinese proxy in Angola,[103] but Beijing chose to try its best to maintain its public image as a disinterested supporter of anti-imperialism, without any imperial inclinations of its own, as Deng Xiaoping had famously presented it at the United Nations the previous year.[104] Similarly, it is hard to read Moscow's actions as directed specifically against Beijing. There was certainly a great deal of concern in Moscow about Chinese involvement,[105] but Soviet support for the MPLA did not jump in response to the arrival of Chinese instructors for the FNLA in June 1974, and it did not fall when Chinese instructors left in October 1975. While one cannot take Manchka as a spokesman for the Soviet government, his primary concern seems to have been the possibility of capitalist imperialists stealing the fruits of the USSR's long years of struggle and the potential significance of establishing a major Soviet-oriented left-leaning state in Africa. A report prepared by the Moscow State Institute of International Relations for the Soviet Foreign Ministry in January 1976, at the height of the war, also seemed to view the PRC as a minor factor in Soviet calculations in Angola.[106] Yet while the Soviets were not as concerned with the actions of the government in Beijing as contemporary observers believed, they were very concerned with the presence of Maoism, and Maoists, in the newly independent PRA.

In the meantime, the war had to be won, and what had been a battle between Angolans armed by foreign powers soon became a battle between Cuban and South African regulars. A lot of ink has been spilled arguing over who invaded first—Cuba or South Africa—but both countries, along with numerous others, had been militarily involved in Angola for at least ten years by this point.[107] Though the invading South African column advanced rapidly, the MPLA never ceded the capital, which it had taken on July 9, and with the continual arrival of Cuban troops and Soviet support, along with the ending of American involvement with the Clark Amendment on December 19, the tide quickly turned and the MPLA had effectively won the war by March 1976. The presence of South African troops changed the diplomatic picture radically, and while the potential recognition of an MPLA government had been a matter of concern in Moscow on the eve of independence, by mid-February the OAU and the vast majority of African states (forty of them by February 20) had recognized the PRA.[108] The FNLA and UNITA had not been completely destroyed, and the civil war in Angola would flare up again, finally ending only in 2002 with the killing of Jonas Savimbi. With the central part of Angola now decisively under its control, however, the MPLA could commence the enormous task of rebuilding Angola.

Creating the Angolan Party-State, 1974–1977

The open military conflict against the FNLA and UNITA and their foreign supporters attracted most of the attention from both contemporary observers and subsequent scholars, but the MPLA's tasks in establishing its political dominance at home, even within the capital of Luanda, were no less substantial. The issues that had plagued the MPLA throughout the years of exile—its largely educated *mestiço* leadership and its ties to communist countries and Marxist ideology—would make the tasks of broadening its social base, establishing political control, and implementing a strategy for economic development extremely difficult. Defeating the FNLA and UNITA not just on the battlefield but in the field of public opinion required opening the doors of the MPLA to the young, militant inhabitants of the *musseques* (slums) on the outskirts of Luanda. But doing so meant exposing the MPLA leadership to demands that it was not willing or able to satisfy. The alternative was to rely ever more heavily on the Soviets, as well as their Cuban—and, later East German and Bulgarian—allies. But as the MPLA was already reliant on Havana and Moscow for military help, overreliance on them in the political and economic spheres threatened to strip the nascent regime of its autonomy. Caught between a rock and a hard place, the MPLA tried to combine a tightly controlled, closed, and secretive political regime with an economy that was partly state controlled but still open to foreign investment in key sectors in the hopes of both reducing its reliance on communist aid and building political relationships with the noncommunist world, including the United States. That last part failed, in part because the United States refused to engage politically as long as there were still Cuban troops in Angola. Meanwhile, this new strategy of combining political Leninism with a mixed economy dovetailed with the new Soviet approach to building socialism, one that sought to develop the private sector alongside the state sector. The result would be a new kind of regime: a Leninist oligarchy that treated the economy as its personal property, inviting foreign investment in the name of development, only to skim the profits to preserve political power through a system of patronage. This new state would prove to be incredibly durable, outlasting the Cold War, another decade of civil war after that, and even the boom-and-bust cycles in the oil market of the first decades of the twenty-first century.

With the fall of the dictatorship in Portugal in April 1974, the political landscape within Angola shifted dramatically. Portuguese rule had made it nearly impossible for exiled movements to maintain contacts with—let alone broaden—domestic bases of support, so the small local organizations that did exist often had little except their imaginations to instruct them on the nature of the liberation movements. With the reins of control now loosened, however, the liberation movements frantically competed to gain popular support and local allies inside Angola. The left-leaning MPLA naturally became a magnet for small groups of radical youth known as action committees, including some with Maoist inclinations and ties to the Portuguese radical left, such as the Committees of Amilcar Cabral, made up in part of radicalized Portuguese officers, and the Henda Committees, a group composed of black students that allied itself with Nito Alves, a high-ranking MPLA guerrilla hero.[109] These groups soon competed for influence within the MPLA and, given the lack of qualified, educated cadres, they occupied important positions, with the Committees of Amilcar Cabral being in charge of political and ideological mobilization on the ground, even conducting literacy campaigns in the slums of Luanda, while the Henda Committees soon came to dominate the MPLA propaganda organs. In addition to these action committees, local neighborhood groups began to form, at first spontaneously, and these gradually drifted toward the MPLA in what came to be known as Poder Popular (People's Power) committees. By the end of 1974 the MPLA in Luanda had become swollen with new members who had not been part of the organization during its years in exile, and much of the MPLA's legwork was being taken on by young people with ideas of their own.

It soon became apparent that many of the new activists were making more radical demands than the MPLA was willing to fulfill. Some, such as the newly formed Communist Organization of Angola, had clear ties to Maoists in Portugal and were consequently doctrinally hostile to the MPLA and their Cuban and Soviet allies. Others, however, simply saw the anticipated liberation in starker racial terms than the MPLA would allow. Nito Alves, a young, charismatic activist who had been isolated, fighting in the Dembos forest in northern Angola during the war years, rose to prominence at the MPLA cadres' conference in September 1974 with a speech declaring a "struggle against the bourgeoisie."[110] Alves identified the bourgeoisie as whites and *mestiços,* however, and demanded that even whites born in Angola be denied citizenship unless they had fought for liberation, while *mestiços* be required to apply for it, against current MPLA policy. This point of view was continually expressed by a popular Angolan radio program, *Kudibanguela,* which the first secretary of the Soviet embassy in Luanda, Boris Putilin, described as a font of "black racism."[111]

It did not take long before the MPLA leadership decided to crack down on those with ultraleftist ideas within the movement. In September 1975, right after the successful defense of Luanda from an invading FNLA column, the MPLA held its Second Week of Struggle for People's Power, which turned out to be an exercise in enforcing the leadership's line on wayward elements.[112] The Communist Organization of Angola went underground, while the Henda Committees, after internal convulsions, moved along with Alves to a more pro-Soviet model. The problem was much bigger than the action committees, however. During a gathering of Poder Popular committees in December, the MPLA claimed that "left-extremist elements had infiltrated the people's commissions" and were sabotaging the MPLA from within.[113] On a visit to Moscow in January 1976, at the height of the war, the Angolan minister of foreign Affairs, José Eduardo dos Santos, complained about groups with "Maoist tendencies," and the MPLA began "reorganizing" the Poder Popular committees already in December, placing its own loyal members at the top of the hierarchy.[114] In February the stopping of the airing of *Kudibanguela* led to massive demonstrations of students and workers in front of the presidential palace in Luanda that was instigated, according to the MPLA and the Soviet embassy, by the "agitation of extreme left elements."[115] In the middle of fighting the FNLA and UNITA, backed by Zairian and South African troops, respectively, the MPLA was under attack by the Angolan population that was under its control.

In an attempt to impose control on the Poder Popular committees, the MPLA began conducting purges, and it passed a new law officially making the committees arms of the MPLA. The law called for elections to the committees to be held in May, with only MPLA-affiliated organizations allowed to nominate candidates and with voting criteria based on political activity. In the words of the Soviet embassy, "these kinds of limitations had the goal of not allowing the infiltration of counterrevolutionary elements in the organs of popular power."[116] To a certain degree, this effort at domestication worked and the committees became tools of MPLA control. As South African intelligence reported, "In factories and firms, workers' committees have been elected to operate alongside directors and administrators. Committees organized people to clean the streets. Committees distributed rice or beer. Even the women who sell bananas, vegetables, and cigarettes in the streets have been organized."[117] Despite this, however, the profound economic dislocation caused the political situation in the country to continue to deteriorate, with the labor movement taking the lead in conducting antigovernment strikes, and the MPLA was forced to postpone the elections.

The National Union of the Workers of Angola had, over the course of late 1974 to early 1976, gone from being an enemy of the MPLA to its ally, and then back to being a source of difficulties for the regime. According to Neto, in the fall of 1974 the unions, still dominated by white Portuguese settlers, struck to prevent the granting of independence, a reactionary move that Neto compared to the striking of Chilean truckers against the regime of Salvador Allende.[118] By October 1975, however, the whites had largely fled, leaving the unions now in the hands of black Angolans, and a national conference of laborers was convened in Luanda to refound the unions "on a new democratic basis." The new National Union of the Workers of Angola prioritized the "liquidation of capitalist exploitation and the problem of wages," but with the subsequent outbreak of international war, the union tabled these objectives temporarily in support of the MPLA slogan "Increasing Production Means Victory." Once the war turned in the MPLA's favor, the workers quickly returned to focusing on wages, and now that many abandoned enterprises were in the hands of workers committees, it was easy to almost completely paralyze the Angolan economy in the early months of 1976. As the Soviet embassy reported about the striking and demonstrating workers, "This group has been ignited by reactionary and left-extremist elements calling the workers to disobedience and destruction of equipment, putting into question the policy of the MPLA and PRA government."[119] Both politically and economically, the MPLA found itself confronted by a crisis of legitimacy, whose roots it saw as fundamentally ideological.

The war had also changed the MPLA. When the Soviet ambassador in Tanzania asked Neto in September 1974 if he had any concrete programs for the postindependence Angolan economy, Neto emphasized the importance of preserving private property, both foreign and domestic, and stressed that the government's priorities would be health, education, and social provision.[120] The MPLA produced a new economic program two months later that Boris Putilin labeled a "step to the right," one that limited the state role to merely reviewing the conditions of foreign concessions in the country.[121] Yet while the MPLA had once attempted to avoid too close of a public association with any foreign power and taking too dogmatic a line on the construction of scientific socialism, the war, as the Soviet embassy in Luanda reported, had "radicalized" the MPLA and moved it significantly to the left. The MPLA was now, not surprisingly, openly pro-Cuban and pro-Soviet, and it was beginning to plot its own transformation into a vanguard party.[122] The newly appointed prime minister of the PRA, Lopo do Nascimento, declared in a speech on December 10, 1975 that "we want to build socialism in the PRA, but not African socialism as some assert, because neither African, nor American, nor Asian, nor Spanish socialism exists. Socialism is one, and we intend to build this socialism on our land."[123] Building socialism was not a task that the MPLA could undertake on its own, and given the new closeness of the MPLA to Moscow, it was time for the USSR and its allies to come to the rescue. As the Cuban commander Flavio Bravo told an East German delegation on a visit to Angola in February 1976, Angola could be an important catalyst for the African revolution and, especially given the remaining influence that dissident socialist powers such as China, Romania, and Yugoslavia retained within the MPLA leadership, this would be a perfect example for the USSR and its allies to demonstrate the viability of their model of revolution in Africa.[124]

A massive economic aid effort was soon underway. During the Twenty-Fifth CPSU Congress that February, which Nito Alves attended as a representative of the MPLA, a side meeting was held of representatives of Council for Mutual Economic Assistance countries to decide on a plan of economic aid to Angola.[125] The MPLA set the terms for the transformation of the economy with a nationalization law on March 3, allowing the government to take control of certain enterprises in order to create a state-controlled sector, but given the limitations of the state at this time it would still continue to allow for the existence of private property and foreign enterprises which followed the law.[126] Nascimento then visited Moscow in May to sign cooperation agreements.[127] Following this, a Soviet delegation, including Petr Manchka, toured Angola in July to begin planning for the transformation of the country. Before leaving, Boris Ponomarev, head of the International Department, instructed the delegation that "the party in Angola should be an initiator of Marxist-Leninist parties on the African continent," while Brezhnev said their three main tasks included "strengthen[ing] the people's power from top to bottom . . . create a party, make the masses feel the results of the new rule, put the economy right."[128] As these instructions indicate, the task was not merely to transform the economy but also the political and ideological structure of the country.

Socialist aid and advice began pouring in. A Soviet trade union delegation arrived to advise the Angolan labor union, and the Soviet embassy suggested sending a Komsomol delegation as well to work with Angolan youth.[129] Even Bulgaria sent a delegation to study the question of agricultural development.[130] While the Soviet embassy in Luanda was busy dividing up the tasks of working out agreements in everything from political and academic exchanges to fishing and diamond mining, Neto led an MPLA delegation to Cuba in July, where the MPLA and the Cuban Communist Party signed an extensive agreement on training and cooperation.[131] The amount of influence exercised by socialist countries over the infant regime alarmed South African intelligence, which produced an exaggerated description of the situation:

> Pres[ident] Neto is surrounded by Cuban advisers. There are almost no black Angolans on his personal staff, and very few white Portuguese. The only prominent group of black Angolans near Dr. Neto is his palace guards. The Cubans now control the Ministry of the Interior and the Angolan secret police, known as the DISA (Directorate of Intelligence and Security) along with the customs and immigration services. The Cubans also share control of the Finance Ministry and the Banco de Angola with the Russians. The Russians have established direct and exclusive control of the Ministry of Defence. Therefore, the Russians and Cubans between them decide what the MPLA can import, how much money should be printed, who should enter and leave the country, and what individuals and groups can and cannot do. In yet another sphere—crucial to all Marxist regimes—the Cubans appear to have a predominant voice: the Government's programme for the political mobilisation of "the masses." It is already clear that President Neto does not have the determining voice.[132]

Though Neto's power—to the occasional disappointment of his socialist allies—still remained paramount, to many Angolans this did not seem to be the independence for which they had fought. Some wanted the Cuban troops and advisers gone sooner rather than later, some wanted more immediate economic benefits in terms of higher wages and shorter hours instead of the crusade for "production," and some simply wanted to see more black faces in positions of power. Consequently, with the temporary end of the war and the beginning of rebuilding, and despite the MPLA's efforts to establish control over the Poder Popular committees, unrest broke out throughout the country. Workers went on strike, driven by the disorganization of factories whose experts had left and the inability of the government to pay their salaries.[133] When local workers tried to replace whites and *mestiços* with blacks in factories, the MPLA leadership denounced them as "opportunists."[134] Even worse for the regime, many of these calls opposing the new policies were coming from within the MPLA itself.

The MPLA leaders, however, had a ready explanation for this dissatisfaction—one that implied its own solution. In February 1976 Carlos Rocha, the MPLA's new minister of economics, who had been trained in the GDR, gave the East Germans a class analysis of Angolan society that included a lumpenproletariat that was vulnerable to "left-extremist influence" considering it the "main danger" for the current work of the MPLA. Pointing to the demonstrations in Luanda earlier that month, Rocha said that this danger came in the form of "'black racism' from the left."[135] A month later, a visiting member of the Central Committee of the PCP made the same argument to the Soviets, noting that "left extremist elements used the slogans of the MPLA, giving them a racist coloring."[136] On June 22 Rocha got even more specific about the nature of this danger. He told a visiting East German delegation that China had been trying to split the Angolan liberation movement ever since 1962 and that Maoists were behind the workers' strikes, but that the PRA understood the danger and knew how to deal with them because "the MPLA has taken the lessons from the events in Chile, especially in relation to the activities of the left-extremist groups, which in reality paved the way for [Augusto] Pinochet."[137]

Accordingly the MPLA began a massive campaign of propaganda coordinated with targeted repression. The remaining members of the Revolta Activa, now conveniently labeled Maoists by the leadership, were arrested in April.[138] On June 20 Neto gave a speech to the first graduating class of MPLA cadres, instructing them to "defend the ideology of the working class" and emphasizing that "'workers' are all of those workers, independent of the color of their skin, who have workers' ideology."[139] In July the elections for the committees of Poder Popular, which had been delayed since May, were held, producing an acceptable result, and a newspaper titled *Poder Popular* was created to disseminate government ideology to the committees.[140] Now the MPLA leadership's attention turned toward its next target: the trade unions. Following the Soviet model, the idea was to turn the trade unions from organizations whose purpose was to defend the interests of the workers into ones whose function would be to make the workers obey the will of the regime, especially with regard to labor discipline and raised productivity. The trade unions had been fighting government control, a fact that the government attributed to "left-extremist elements" who were putting the construction of socialism in Angola in danger.[141] In response, the MPLA organized a new conference of Angolan workers in October that effected a government takeover of the unions and brought the strikes under control.[142] In addition, factories that had been run by worker's committees were now placed under the control of state administrators. The crusade against Maoism and leftist extremism was proving a useful tool for the MPLA to build all of the trappings of a Soviet-style party-state.

The party-state that would be built served multiple purposes from the Angolan and Soviet perspectives. For the Soviets, a Leninist-style party with a clear ideological orientation and selective membership, organized on the principle of democratic centralism, and in control of a powerful security apparatus was the best way to guarantee the future socialist orientation of the country. This was particularly important because their previous experiences building socialism in Africa, first with state-controlled industrialization in West Africa in the early 1960s and then with Tanzania's agrarian cooperative self-reliance in the early 1970s, had led the Soviets to a paradoxical conclusion: private property and investment, both domestic and foreign, would be necessary for a while in order to build socialism. This was a combination of self-interest (it removed some of the burden of development from Moscow's shoulders), as well as a sort of rediscovery of the Menshevik idea that, at a certain stage, private investment really was necessary to develop the forces of production. Ironically, then, one of the chief advantages of building a Leninist party was that it would be able to combat ideological challenges coming from the Left as it embraced this pragmatic economic approach. As a report to the East German politburo following the visit of Prime Minister Lope do Nascimento in 1977 concluded, "The creation of a Party will above all lead to a strengthening of ideological work. Of particular importance is the confrontation with Maoist, petit bourgeois, and left-extremist forces."[143] The creation of such a party was also supposed to ensure that the continued tolerance for private property would not overwhelm the economy or lead to undesirable ideological influences taking hold among the vulnerable population. In Mozambique, where a similar process was underway, a Soviet embassy report from December 1976 in advance of the ruling FRELIMO party congress made this point explicitly: "These transformations [transformations of a "general democratic nature"—i.e., not explicitly socialist], which are a necessary intermediate stage for the transition to socialism, together with the not yet profoundly affected private capitalist bases of ownership, therefore open certain possibilities for the spontaneous development of capitalist tendencies in the economy, and could enable the dispersal and strengthening of bourgeois ideals in social consciousness. . . . It is precisely because of this that FRELIMO today devotes so much attention to the specific principles and conceptions of political and ideological leadership."[144] The strong hand of a Leninist vanguard party was crucial to making sure things did not get off track, either to the left or to the right, during this vulnerable transition phase.

For the Angolan leadership, the creation of a strong party-state was about the preservation of their own state autonomy, not least from the potential infringements of their Soviet benefactors. As Neto's wife told a close aide of President Tito of Yugoslavia in April 1976, the MPLA had not—despite the massive Soviet aid that had helped them win the war—forgotten the Soviet termination of aid and the "abandonment of Dr. Neto" in 1974.[145] The Angolans were well aware that Soviet aid could be withdrawn at any time, and that it came with a number of strings attached. As a Yugoslav delegation reported after visiting Luanda in December 1976, the Angolans believed that the Soviets were trying to strengthen their influence, and in order to control the degree of Soviet influence, the Angolans were thus prioritizing their relations with the West, and in particular the United States, in hopes that the incoming administration of President Jimmy Carter might be more accommodating.[146] It did not hurt that Angola's main source of foreign currency, and the quickest industry to recover production levels after independence, was the American-dominated oil industry.[147] The Angolan leadership decided not to try to expropriate such essential foreign enterprises but merely to try to negotiate somewhat better terms, since, as Neto told Tito on a visit to Belgrade in April 1977, "I am aware that socialism cannot be built in poverty."[148] Neto's priorities were made clear in a letter to Council for Mutual Economic Assistance in October 1976 when he wrote that, for Angola, socialist transformation would for now mean "the creation of a powerful economic base, raising the living standards of the people, strengthening the defense capability of the country, the indoctrination of the workers in the spirit of the ideas of socialism, the preservation of revolutionary vigilance against internal and external enemies, the strengthening of unity among revolutionaries, and the creation of a political part on the principles of Marxism-Leninism."[149] The immediate goal for the Angolan leadership, and the purpose of creating a Marxist-Leninist party, was not actually to facilitate the state takeover of the economy; it was to create a powerful tool for the political and ideological control of the state and the population, one that was strong enough to stand up to both its enemies and its friends.

The culmination of this effort to build a vanguard party came in October 1976 when Neto finally visited Moscow. On October 8, Neto signed the Treaty of Friendship and Cooperation with the USSR, as well as an agreement on party relations between the CPSU and MPLA.[150] During the visit, Brezhnev specifically told Neto that Angola needed to build a political party "on the principles of Marxism-Leninism."[151] Following Neto's return to Luanda, the Central Committee of the MPLA held an important plenum which revamped the government. Neto's powers were increased and Nito Alves was eliminated from the government through the abolishing of the Ministry of the Interior, which he headed. The plenum scheduled an MPLA congress for the following year that would establish a "vanguard party of the working class" and adopted an "Action Programme" that declared that "the only road leading to the establishment of People's Democracy is the scientific socialism of [Karl] Marx, [Friedrich] Engels, and [Vladimir] Lenin." Finally, the plenum called for even closer ties to Cuba and the USSR.[152] Angola was well on its way to becoming the showcase for the latest version of how to build socialism in Africa.

In preparation for the upcoming congress and the planned transformation of the MPLA into a Marxist-Leninist party, an East German delegation arrived in January 1977 to give a six-week series of seminars on ideology and economic planning to the upper echelon of the party. In the words of Lucio Lara and Carlos Rocha, the plan was that "through the seminar, for the first time a wide circle of leading cadres will become familiar with Marxist-Leninist theory and praxis, especially in the area of leading and planning the economy."[153] The seminars offer a detailed picture of the Soviet model for the "states of socialist orientation" in the developing world as it had evolved by the mid-1970s.[154] Rather than focus on building heavy industry, the seminars identified the "main diffi-culties" in the "direction and planning of agriculture, transportation, and trade."[155] Private trade was not to be eliminated but was merely to be controlled, and state control was to expand first and foremost through the financial sector. Instead of forced collectivization, the state was sup-posed to work with the peasants to first raise productivity, thereby en-suring a steady supply of food to the cities. The primary consideration in the development of industry, meanwhile, was profitability. Had Angola become independent in the early 1960s and asked for (and received) Eastern Bloc and Soviet advice and support at that time, the picture would likely have differed considerably. A much greater emphasis would have been put on large industrial projects with collectivization of agriculture and elimination of private trade also being placed on the agenda. The seminars concluded with a weeklong class for thirty-five leading political cadres on the leading role of the workers' party and the practice of democratic cen-tralism. The Soviet model, as demonstrated in Angola, had moved toward considerably more economic flexibility on the issue of social control of the means of production while placing ever more emphasis on top-down party control.

Before the vanguard party could be created, however, the MPLA had to deal with one more split. Nito Alves had been born not far from Lu-anda in 1945, a generation after the senior MPLA leadership, and in 1966, driven by rumors and dreams of the independence struggle, he hiked to the Dembos forest, where a hardy group of MPLA fighters were con-tinuing the struggle despite being cut off by the Congolese, FNLA, and Portuguese from external support and MPLA headquarters. Though he had no secondary education, Alves studied the one text available to him in that forest, *The Fundamentals of Marxism-Leninism,* which had been brought back by a fellow fighter from his training in the USSR.[156] After the Portuguese coup, Alves encountered the rest of the MPLA for the first time, and he rose to prominence with a fiery speech at the Conference of Cadres in September 1974. Though initially taken with Maoism and the Chinese revolutionary struggle, the Chinese support for the FNLA in 1974–1975, and his own visit to Moscow for the Twenty-Fifth CPSU Con-gress in February 1976, turned him into a pro-Soviet fanatic. Alves's ora-torical skills made him a star in the *musseques* of Luanda during the battle for public opinion in 1975, and he had a talent for mobilizing popular anger in the most Manichean terms. To be anti-Neto, anti-MPLA, or anti-Soviet was to be against Angola. Neto made Alves the head of the Interior Ministry, where he essentially became the Maximilien de Robespierre of the Angolan Revolution, seeking out and destroying those who were not sufficiently devoted to the cause. The repression of the Maoists and left-radical committees became his project. Once the war had been won, however, he turned against those within the MPLA itself whom he considered unreliable, insufficiently revolutionary, corrupt, or tainted by vestiges of colonial privilege—especially whites and *mestiços*.

The Soviets became enamored of Alves, who not only appeared to be the most ideologically committed to "scientific socialism" but also seemed to solve the problem of the shaky racial identity of the MPLA leadership. Raul Castro visited Angola in May 1976 and met with the top Angolan leadership, following which he met with Soviet officials in Angola. In his conversation with the Soviets, Castro speculated on who would replace Neto, who was known to be in ill health, if something should happen to him. According to Castro, "if something unfortunate should happen to Neto, power in the country would be taken in the hands of two people who are both white: [Lucio] Lara, the leader of the MPLA, and [Iko] Carreira, the leader of the army."[157] Castro's solution was to promote Lopo do Nascimento as the successor, but the Soviets seemed to have other ideas, especially because they saw the racial and ideological cleavages in the leadership overlapping. The following month the Soviet ambassador in Luanda told his East German colleague that the leadership could be divided into two groups, one serious about Marxism-Leninism that included Alves and Nascimento, among others, and a second group that saw socialism as "premature," led by Carreira, Lara, and Rocha. According to the Soviet ambassador, "A differentiation on the basis of race is noticeable. One group under [Nito] Alves Bernardo Baptista has concerns about all nonblacks [*Andersfarbigen*] in the leadership. They are opposed by a group of 'mulattoes.'"[158] During the liberation struggle the Soviets had been very concerned about "black racism" as a threat to the MPLA, the idea of a class-based revolutionary ideology, and their own position as a largely white power in Africa. Now that it seemed that the threats to the socialist Angola they desired came from inside the MPLA rather than outside it, Moscow switched gears and saw the leading proponent of such "black racism" as perhaps the best hope for the realization of its revolutionary ambitions.

It was not long before the backlash to Alves's inquisition came from those senior leaders of the MPLA who had something to fear (led by Lara and Rocha), and Alves's Interior Ministry was eliminated in the MPLA plenum of October 1976. Through Neto's personal intervention, however, he was not yet expelled from the Central Committee. The plenum called for an investigation into his activities, though, and its results were a foregone conclusion: on May 20, 1977, a new plenum was summoned to hear the report, and Alves was expelled from the Central Committee. Once again, only Neto's intervention prevented him from being arrested. Meanwhile, Alves and his supporters were organizing their counterattack, with evident Soviet support.[159] One week after the plenum he and his followers launched an attempted coup that failed in large part due to Cuban soldiers rallying around the president.

Despite his knowledge about Soviet support for the coup, Neto did not publicly criticize the Soviets, instead going to Moscow in September to patch up relations. The Soviets duly condemned the putsch, and Neto told them officially that Alves had been motivated by "Maoist ideas" and "black racism."[160] Behind the scenes, however, Neto had learned a different lesson from the failed coup. As the Yugoslav International Department reported, "It seems that the Angolan leadership understood the attempted coup as a certain kind of warning and pressure to make certain corrections in its internal and external actions which would make it acceptable for current and long-term interests of the Socialist Camp."[161] This new adherence to Soviet wishes would be evident at the upcoming party congress, though in the long term it could hardly have made the MPLA leadership more trusting of Moscow. But the failed coup did further the process of the centralization of political power in Angola, based not only on Soviet wishes but also on the desire for self-preservation of Neto and his comrades. Within Angola the repression that followed the failed coup was massive, covering the entire country with hundreds, perhaps thousands—and, according to certain anti-MPLA sources, tens of thousands—of victims. The repression definitively turned Angola into a police state and ended the stage of popular mobilization and pluralism that had characterized the MPLA in 1974–1975. Ironically, the repression of the "Nitistas" fell along lines similar to those they had been pushing. One of the characteristics of "Nitista" dissidence had been its "tendency to confuse 'race' and 'class,'" and now provincial party committees persecuted specifically those who were educated and had been privileged under colonialism. In the province of Huila, one political leader declared anyone who had finished the fifth grade a "class enemy."[162] The challenge to the regime might have been stopped, but the victory was Pyr-

rhic. The animosities that Alves had channeled turned out to be pervasive within the regime itself.

From December 4 through December 10 the MPLA finally held its first
congress, officially transforming itself into a Marxist-Leninist "workers'
vanguard party" now known as the Movimento Popular de Libertação
de Angola—Partido do Trabalho (MPLA-PT; People's Movement for the
Liberation of Angola—Labor Party), restructuring the party along Leninist
lines and adopting Marxism-Leninism as its official ideology.[163] Cadres
were soon being trained on ideological, political, and technical matters
by Bulgaria, Cuba, East Germany, the USSR, and Yugoslavia to ensure
that the new MPLA-PT had a core of cadres with a proper grasp of
Marxism-Leninism. What had become a mass party was now transformed
into a selective elite: by the end of 1978 the MPLA-PT had only around
eight thousand members, which grew to about thirty-three thousand by
the end of 1981.[164] Despite this, the MPLA-PT continued to seek to tighten
political and ideological discipline, including a 1981 offensive in the wake
of the party's Extraordinary Congress known as the Generalized Offensive
against Liberalism and Disorganization.[165]

While the concentration of political power and the enforcement of
ideological orthodoxy continued apace, stranger things seemed to be happening in the economy: in the late 1970s it was not approaching the declared goal of restoring 1973 levels of production, and war was likely not
the reason, as the most authoritative historian of the economy in this period argues that military expenditure did not become a serious problem
until 1980 at the earliest.[166] Despite extensive aid agreements with the
Bulgarians, Cubans, East Germans, Soviets, and Yugoslavs, involving
thousands of experts on the ground (420 from Bulgaria alone by 1981),[167]
socialist aid seemed to be making little progress. On a visit to Bulgaria in
October 1981, new Angolan president José Eduardo dos Santos told General Secretary Todor Zhivkov that Angola's experience with agriculture,
the chief area of Bulgarian assistance, "was not very positive."[168] That
same year, Lucio Lara traveled to Belgrade to complain to the Yugoslavs
that their aid was too expensive (i.e., involved excessively high interest
rates) and was not matching the hopes of the Angolans.[169] Overall, its new
alliances and commitment to Marxism-Leninism had done little to change
Angola's foreign trade. In 1978, 64 percent of its exports went to the
United States and 19 percent to Western Europe, while 61 percent of its
imports originated in Western Europe and 14 percent from the United

States, numbers that were all similar to what they had been before independence. Although there was much discussion with its socialist allies about increasing aid to further the objectives of socialization and industrialization, in practice Angola in the late 1970s went in another direction. While some 85 percent of enterprises had been nationalized by mid-1977, most of them were small- and medium-size enterprises that had been abandoned by their Portuguese owners. Even so, in December 1978 President Neto declared that private ownership of small enterprises would be allowed. Then, in July 1979, Angola adopted its new Law on Foreign Investment that offered surprisingly attractive terms, including a promise of no nationalization for the next ten to fifteen years, transfer abroad of profits up to 25 percent of capital invested, and exemption from, or reduction of, various taxes and customs duties.[170] Though very little foreign investment materialized at this time, Angola's approach to economic development, as a Marxist-Leninist country in good standing with the Eastern Bloc, revealed how far the actual practice of socialist construction, and Soviet advice, had come from the early 1960s plans of state-led industrialization. And while the MPLA-PT would not officially abandon Marxism-Leninism as a state ideology until 1990, mechanisms and institutions would by then already be in place that would make the political and economic transitions much less radical and disruptive than the ideological shift would imply.

When states that considered themselves Marxist-Leninist started appearing in Africa in the mid-1970s, many were not sure how seriously to take those claims. It was one thing, perhaps, to talk about socialism or a noncapitalist path of development, but how could states claim to be Marxist-Leninist without much of a working class or even a cohort of committed Marxists? It was no wonder that observers debated, in the words of one scholar, whether "the Marxism-Leninism of the Angolan and Mozambican regimes is so much window-dressing" or if "the commitment to Marxism is a serious one."[171] The persistence of civil war in Angola and Mozambique, as well as in Ethiopia, made it hard to judge the true intentions and capabilities of these regimes with regard to the transformation of their economies along socialist lines. In any case, the debate did not last long, because by the time these regimes declared themselves Marxist-Leninist, the Cold War was already approaching its latter stages, unbeknownst to contemporaries. By the end of 1978 the PRC would begin its own experiment with market reforms, and in the mid-1980s both Angola and Mozambique would start to adopt more heterodox economic policies. Then, just a few years later, the Cold War ended, Namibian independence meant the withdrawal of Cuban and South African troops from Angola, and the MPLA officially rejected Marxism-Leninism in favor of social democracy, dropping the PT from its name. The brief experiment with Marxism-Leninism in Africa, such as it was, was over.

Or was it? As of 2021 the MPLA had still never relinquished power in Angola, though it had to fight a second civil war against UNITA that ended only with the death of Jonas Savimbi in 2002. José Eduardo dos Santos, educated in the Soviet Union and married to a Soviet citizen, remained president from 1979 to 2017, only to be replaced by João Lourenço, someone chosen by the MPLA elite because he seemed not to threaten their positions, much like Santos himself after Agostinho Neto's death in 1979. The same was true of FRELIMO in Mozambique, and there were aspects of similarity in other countries in the region where liberation movements had held on to power long after independence, such as with the South-West African People's Organization in Namibia, the Zimbabwean African National Union—People's Front in Zimbabwe, and the African National Congress in South Africa. Though much had changed in Angola since the end of the Cold War and the Angolan Civil War, especially due to the vast amount of oil wealth that flooded into the country in the early twenty-first century, political and economic reforms that would create opportunity for all Angolans; guarantee freedom, competition, and accountability in the political sphere; and provide for the health, education, and welfare needs of a desperately poor and rapidly growing population were still aspirational.

While the formal period of Marxism-Leninism in Angola might have been brief in comparison with other places in Eastern Europe or East Asia, it nevertheless left a lasting legacy. Post–civil war Luanda was known for a time as the most expensive city in the world for expatriates, a place where MPLA elites and generals hired Portuguese to administer their companies and live in ten-thousand-dollar-per-month flats while they themselves bought mansions on the Portuguese coast. It was a city where the wealthy dined on lobsters flown in from Europe while farmers just outside the city had no way to get their produce to market. It seemed to be the very paradigm of an elite kleptocracy, the farthest thing imaginable from a state committed to the workers and peasants. And yet, the institutional foundation of this state had been laid in the early years of independence, with the help and support of Bulgaria, Cuba, East Germany, the Soviet Union, and Yugoslavia. The focus on the creation of a highly centralized party, one that relied on a powerful military and security services, facilitated the continuation of the MPLA's stranglehold on power. More interesting, perhaps, is that the choice to continue to create room for private capital in order to facilitate development, and even encourage foreign investment (especially in the key sector of oil and gas), meant that the very strategy for socialist development endorsed by Moscow paved the way for the rentier-state oligarchy that the MPLA became. Furthermore, it was not just an accident that the party elite monopolized the economy. It was rather essential that, if for a period the existence of private capital remained crucial to the process of development necessary for the transition to socialism, that private capital be controlled by those who could be trusted politically and ideologically. Thus, the identity of the political and economic elite was a structural requirement. As for the concentration of wealth, that too had a justification that echoed the discussions of the 1960s and 1970s about how to transition to socialism. As one senior MPLA cadre argued, "The country needs to develop the cosmopolitan elites it never had . . . which presupposes allowing them access to wealth and power. . . . It may not please you to hear it, but Angola needs rich, strong, and powerful families that can stand up to international competition. To have a republic of better fed poor people, all with the third grade, is not a viable model for us."[172] Even kleptocracy, then, could justify itself on the grounds of national development. Marxism-Leninism in Angola, once interpreted as political Leninism with economic Menshevism, had successfully transitioned to Leninist capitalism.

5

OPIATE OF THE MASSES, OR STIMULANT?

Socialism, Religion, and Revolution in Iran

> *Prime Minister Mehdi Bazargan:* It is you who taught us
> how to make revolution. In Iran we know the Russian
> Revolution of 1917 well.
> *Soviet Ambassador Vladimir Vinogradov:* Indeed, there is
> much in common between the Iranian Revolution and the
> February Revolution of 1917 in Russia.
> *Bazargan:* And why not the October [Revolution]?
>
> —Conversation of February 14, 1979

The creation of the Islamic Republic of Iran (IRI), an enduring, modern theocratic state in what had seemed to be a developing, secularizing country, was greeted by what Stephanie Cronin calls "universal bafflement."[1] The idea that clerics could take over and run a country was considered unbelievable by observers on both sides of the Iron Curtain, even as it was taking place before their very eyes. Typical was the view of the British Foreign Office in August 1979, as theocracy was being codified constitutionally: "If the fundamentalist approach is pressed to its logical conclusion these people will reject it sooner or later."[2] Eight months later, with the constitution adopted and the institutions of the new regime already beginning to function, the East German embassy concluded that "the utopian conceptions of Khomeini of an exploitation-free society on the basis of Islam do not represent a viable model for society in Iran in the twentieth century."[3] Such incredulity was, perhaps, not surprising. As Mohammad Beheshti, one of the founders of the Islamic Revolutionary

211

Party (IRP) told a British diplomat in late 1979, "they were trying to create something totally new in the history of man."[4]

It was ironic that this unprecedented act of creation took place in Iran. Perhaps no other country in the world in the twentieth century had been as obsessed with the notion of foreign "models." As a declining empire trying to modernize in order to preserve its independence against the depredations of rival imperialist powers in the nineteenth century, Qajar Iran had looked to the Ottoman Empire and its Tanzimat reforms. Subsequent thinkers led by Jamal ad-Din al-Afghani added Meiji Japan to Ottoman Turkey as models for how to resist the West.[5] During the great wave of revolution in the early twentieth century that swept through Russia, Turkey, Mexico, and China between 1905 and 1911, Iran adopted its first constitution, modeled on the Belgian one. After Reza Shah Pahlavi was crowned in 1925, he looked to Kemalist Turkey as a model for how to create a strong, modern state while some of his opponents, including the creators of the first communist party in Asia, looked to the Soviet Union instead. After World War II, the shah would eventually attempt his White Revolution based on American models of modernization, while many of his opponents would eventually abandon the Soviet model for others: Albanian, Algerian, Chinese, Cuban, Vietnamese, Yugoslav, and the like. Iranians debated whether Iran was an example of successful modernization stuck in a cul-de-sac of dependent capitalism or if it was still semifeudal and semicolonial. Much of the political and economic discourse in Iran before 1979 could be summed up in the question, which model fit Iran best?

For the Soviet Union, Iran represented tantalizing opportunities in a difficult geopolitical context. On the one hand, in few countries of the developing world did the possibility of communist revolution seem as attainable as in Iran. In many ways Iran seemed much like China. It, too, was a former empire with a long, proud, and independent history, caught between imperialist powers who divided it into spheres of influence without formally colonizing it. In China this historical circumstance had allowed the communists to ride to power on a nationalist wave by discrediting the functioning national government as imperialist puppets.[6] Iran also had a large and growing working class, one both acutely sensitive to the international environment and with a potential chokehold on the local economy because of the prominence of the oil industry.[7] Proximity to Russia and the Soviet Union had led to significant Russian influence in the development of the Iranian Left, and the presence of the Soviet mili-

MAP 5.1 Iran in 1979.

tary had aided the creation of Soviet republics on Iranian territory after both world wars.[8] On the other hand, because of Iran's strategic location and its oil resources, Western powers—specifically, the United Kingdom and the United States—had repeatedly intervened in Iranian politics, making it clear that Iran was not a place where they would tolerate Soviet expansionism.

Accordingly, the Iranian Left found itself in a bind, facing a regime strongly backed by the United States, while the Soviet Union was hesitant to support it despite its long history of association with Moscow (which discredited it in the eyes of many Iranian nationalists). Fred Halliday, for one, has argued that the fault of the Iranian Left, not just in 1979 but throughout its history, lay in being "repetitive of international

Left analyses of its time, often without critical reflex or engagement with the society it was located in."[9] There is a significant degree of truth to that, but what makes the Iranian case unique was the way in which broader conceptions present among the international Left, including the "noncapitalist path of development," the "wide national front," "popular democratic revolution," and Third Worldist ideas of anti-Westernism and cultural authenticity combined to produce a situation in which much of the Iranian Left made a decision to support the creation of theocracy. This was the product, in part, of a Soviet reevaluation of the role of religion in politics, a significant departure from existing Marxist theory inspired by events elsewhere in the developing world, from Indonesia to Somalia and Pakistan to Vietnam. Meanwhile, the Islamists who would eventually come to power in Iran were themselves in large part products of this very same discourse. Far from representing simply a fundamentalist reaction against modernity, the founders of the IRI instead developed their ideology in large part as a response to the increasing popularity of Marxism in midcentury Iran. In various ways they argued that Islam was better suited to fulfill the tasks of national self-assertion, economic development, and the achievement of economic justice than was secular Marxism. In a sense, then, the IRI represented Islamism's supersession of Marxism as the anti-imperialist ideology par excellence in the Middle East.

The Soviet Reevaluation of Religion

One of communism's chief vulnerabilities in the Third World was its association with atheism and its perceived hostility to religion. Anticommunists made much of both Marxism's ideological commitment to materialism and the reality of Soviet persecution of religion as a way of reducing communism's appeal in countries where not only were religious belief and religious authority widespread but attacks on local religions were already associated with colonial intrusions. As a consequence, Soviet foreign policy had to find ways of getting beyond its "opiate of the masses" image if it was to gain traction in the anticolonial struggle where religion often played a prominent role. Vladimir Lenin and the Comintern at times sought common ground with religious forces in the colonial world—for example, in supporting the Indonesian Communist Party's cooperation with Sarekat Islam, the leading Indonesian nationalist organization, in the 1920s. But such collaborations were often unstable, as the Indonesian experience demonstrated, and the Comintern still generally saw religion as a reactionary force that supported existing political authority.[10] The Soviet approach to religion in the colonial world at this point was thus that—given the presence of a common imperialist enemy—collaboration could occasionally be useful, but there was no need to fundamentally reevaluate the Marxist understanding of religion's essentially reactionary nature.

In the aftermath of decolonization, however, the question of how to relate to religion became far more complicated. It was no longer a matter of merely cooperating against a common imperialist enemy for nationalist ends. Now it was a question of domestic politics: how to relate to religious institutions and religious political parties and how to interact with a religious population in order to promote progress toward the building of socialism. Rostislav Ul'ianovskii, the deputy head of the International Department of the Communist Party of the Soviet Union (CPSU) and one of the chief promoters of the noncapitalist path of development, addressed these issues in the party's theoretical journal *Kommunist* in January 1966. Ul'ianovskii argued that "the religious views of parts of the population do not create an insurmountable obstacle for the construction of socialism" and that Marxists-Leninists needed to "find a common language" with religiously motivated activists.[11] He claimed that treatment of the church in the Soviet Union was due to unique historical circumstances—namely, the church's support for the monarchy, its alliance with the forces of counterrevolution, and its ownership of vast tracts of land. Similar to Lenin's distinction between the nationalism of oppressed and oppressor nations, Ul'ianovskii distinguished between Buddhism and Islam (as religions of the colonized) and Christianity (as the religion of the colonizer). He pointed to Soviet accommodation of Islam in Central Asia by way of illustration, though the reality of Soviet rule there did not match his rosy representation.[12] The prominence of religion in the developing world was thus not to be seen as necessarily an impediment to the progress of socialism.

Despite Ul'ianovskii's position, not all Soviet observers were equally sanguine about the role of religion in the politics of the developing world. Liudmila Polonskaia and A. D. Litman argued later that year in the leading journal of Soviet Orientalists, *Narody Azii i Afriki* (Peoples of Asia and Africa) that religion had played an important role in the anticolonial struggle because colonialism had preserved a "medieval" way of life for peasants and artisans, who consequently created an "idealized" image of precolonial existence. This produced nationalist movements based on conceptions of "religious renaissance" and "utopian socialism" that identified with figures like Mohandes K. Gandhi in India and Mohammad Iqbal, a theorist of Islamic politics known as the spiritual father of Pakistan. While these movements had played an important role in the past, they argued that secularism was on the rise in the developing world, associated with leaders such as Mustafa Kemal Ataturk and Jawaharlal Nehru, the latter of whom asserted that economic problems had nothing to do with religion and that religion was actually harmful to the moral and spiritual development of nations. Though they claimed that reactionary forces might seek to use religion for their own ends and that religious beliefs made it more difficult for revolutionary democratic forces to sow the seeds of scientific socialism, they nevertheless agreed that religion conceptions were "not always immediately tied to the interests of one or another class and political group." While advancement of religious ideas of social justice or national self-assertion could not be taken as ipso facto positive, the ultimate role that religion would play was up for grabs. According to Polonskaia and Litman, the key to determining the political function of religion was not an analysis of the religion as a whole but rather what traditions within the religion were being invoked and for whose interests they were being invoked.[13]

This opened the door to a broader debate on whether religion would play a predominantly progressive or reactionary role and how communists should relate to it. The Institute of the Peoples of Asia held a roundtable, "Religion and Contemporary Social Thought of the Peoples of the Foreign East," where some scholars supported Ul'ianovskii's position on treating religious forces as possible allies while others argued that religion was primarily an instrument of reaction and had even played a schismatic rather than unifying role in nationalist movements in places like India and Indonesia. Soviet Orientalists disagreed over whether secularism was a rising trend that should be supported or whether the predominant ideological tendency was actually toward a sort of "Islamic reformation" that would have important differences from its Christian counterpart. Drawing on their specific regional expertise, Alla Ionova pointed to the reformationist approach of the dominant Islamic party in Indonesia, Nahdlatul Ulama, while Elena Doroshenko, a chief Soviet scholar of Iranian Islam and politics, argued that in Iran Shi'ism had always played a role in Persian nationalist consolidation and that the Shi'ite ulama, or clergy, had played an increasingly progressive role in Iranian politics since the early 1960s.[14]

This Soviet reevaluation of the role of religion even came to encompass the supposed religion of the colonizers—Christianity. The changes in Catholic religious practice in the early 1960s enacted by the Second Vatican Council, held from October 1962 to December 1965, and Pope John XXIII's encyclical *Mater et Magistra*, which focused on the church and social progress, raised eyebrows in Moscow. Writing in the top Soviet foreign policy journal *Mirovaia ekonomika i mezhdunarodnye otnosheniia* (World economy and international relations) in January 1966, M. Andreev dismissed the encyclical and the church's reforms more broadly as confirming the sacredness of private property and not going any further in terms of worker rights than the Fordist social welfare systems of the West. Nevertheless, he argued that the church's attempts to gain influence among the workers were not to be underestimated, and the very fact that the church was paying such attention proved that all was not well in the capitalist world. Andreev also noted the rise of "rebellious" priests in Latin America—led by the Colombian Camilo Torres—who were fighting for land reform and the nationalization of key areas of the economy and not shying away from open cooperation with communists.[15] By the time of the International Meeting of Communist and Workers Parties in Moscow in 1969, this reevaluation of religion had made its way into the formal doctrine of the movement, as the assembled parties adopted a statement saying that tensions in the capitalist world had "created the possibility of a union on antimonopolistic and anti-imperialist bases of the revolutionary workers movement with the broad masses of believers."[16]

As such a statement indicates, however, this reevaluation still had its limits. It was focused on the mass of believers, not clergy or religious thinkers and activists, and it only went as far as the early stages of revolution ("antimonopolistic" and "anti-imperialist"), not seeing religious people as potential allies in the actual construction of socialism. In the early 1970s these impressions began to change. The increasing prominence and militancy of liberation theology in Latin America caught the eye of Soviet scholars, one of whom, Irina Grigulevich, published a monograph on the subject in late 1972 titled *Miatezhnaia Tserkov' v Latinskoi Amerike* (The rebellious church in Latin America).[17] Irina Zorina, a Soviet news correspondent in Salvador Allende's Chile, thought that Grigulevich's analysis had not gone far enough; reviewing the book in *Mirovaia ekonomika i mezhdunarodnye otnosheniia*, Zorina remonstrated that Soviet authors needed a deeper analysis of the "mechanism" by which some priests, standing close to the masses, come to "express their protest against social violence in conditions of backwardness." Regarding these radical priests, Zorina added, "Grant that the specific mechanism of the formation of their ideology, arising from spontaneous social protest, limited political experience of the participants, and the strong pressure of the official propaganda apparatus transforms their programs, makes their slogans, as a rule, rather distant from scientific socialism. The relations of Communists to Left Catholics, their striving for dialogue with them, is not determined by these disagreements, but by the effort to find forms of mutual practical work and struggle for the resolution of those intense social contradictions which exist in reality."[18] Writing at a time and a place where the Chilean Communist Party, with Soviet backing, was desperately trying to come to an agreement with the Christian Democratic Party that would save Allende's government, Zorina's words reflected a real practical shift in the role allotted to religious actors in the process of revolution.

While liberation theology was still on the margins of Latin American politics, more momentous shifts were taking place in the Islamic world. The loss of the Six-Day War in 1967 and the subsequent death of Egyptian president Gamal Abdel Nasser had signaled the decline of Pan-Arabism and with it the Soviet view that secularization might be the dominant rising trend in the Middle East. It was clear that the role of Islam in politics was growing, accompanied by a rising tide of so-called Islamic socialism. On October 21, 1969, General Mohamed Siad Barre led a military coup in Somalia, and the newly ensconced Supreme Revolutionary Council declared a year later that Somalia's ultimate goal was the construction of scientific socialism.[19] Siad's choice of scientific socialism was explicitly framed, however, as consonant with Islam and the Islamic values of egalitarianism, especially because the domestic opposition focused on Islam as the reason Somalia could not accept the new policy. The Soviet embassy in Mogadishu, where Moscow had a long-standing military relationship, took an interest in helping Siad win over resistant clergy, inviting them to tour the Soviet Union and meet with Soviet Muslims, in addition to providing guidance and propaganda for convincing domestic religious audiences.[20] The CPSU International Department subsequently took an interest in publishing a book, *The Historical Choice of Somalia,* to help propagandize that nation's experience in choosing socialism. Tasking the Soviet Institute of Africa with producing the volume, Ul'ianovskii sent along materials on the subject of socialism and Islam, including speeches by Siad himself.[21] According to Siad, "Only a blind person would not see that all of these principles affirm [*otstaivaiut*] socialism. If Islam, as a spiritual faith, is the moral basis of these principles, then socialism is the socioeconomic system that fulfills them in practice, and the theory of scientific socialism is the plan of construction of such a system. On the contrary, all other socioeconomic systems contain elements of tyranny and exploitation that contradict the teaching of the Prophet."[22] The fact that the Soviets were using such speeches to promote socialism in the Islamic world demonstrates how far they had come in terms of accepting the possibility of a positive role for religion, and Islam in particular, in the process of revolution.

In fact, Moscow was coming to believe that it had little choice but to accept both religious allies and religious doctrine as part of progressive politics in the developing world. Liudmila Polonskaia, the Soviet South Asianist who was less sanguine about the role of religion in 1966, wrote in 1973 that it was inevitable that the "discrediting" of capitalism and the "idealization" of the precolonial era would lead to religion playing an important role in the conception of capitalist alternatives in the developing world. Departing from her earlier concerns about the reactionary uses of religion, Polonskaia now took the opposite tack, arguing that it was a mistake to classify religious actors as "reformers" or "traditionalists" because even many so-called traditionalists were opposed to the "spiritual enslavement" of the West. Taking seriously the ideas of Islamic modernizers about how Islamic legal concepts might be employed to create a more just economic and political system, Polonskaia even avoided the use of terms such as "utopian" or "petit bourgeois" that Soviet authors typically employed to distinguish "pseudo-socialisms" from the real thing. One reason for this shift was evidently geopolitical. The United States had also noticed the rising political prominence of Islam, and was trying to turn it in an anticommunist direction, as evidenced by the Third Islamic Conference of Foreign Ministers in Jeddah, Saudi Arabia, in 1972, where an anticommunism resolution was passed. It was little wonder that Polonskaia now pronounced that "the filling of old religious forms with new content is an inevitable stage of the development of progressive social thought of the young states of Asia and Africa."[23]

Soviet interest in religion's role in the politics of the developing world continued to grow in the 1970s.[24] Monographs, articles, and conferences attested to this interest, including a large conference held only days before the shah's departure from Iran on December 25–26, 1978. Titled

"The Place of Religion in the Idea-Political (*ideino-politicheskaia*) Struggle of Developing Countries," the conference brought together the Council on Religious Affairs; the Institute of Africa; the Institute of the Countries of Asia and Africa; the Institute of the Countries of the Near and Middle East; the Institute of Ethnography; the Institute of Philosophy; the Moscow State Institute of International Relations; the Orientalist Institute; the journals *Narody Azii i Afriki, Aziia i Afrika segodnia* (Asia and Africa Today), and *Voprosy filisofii* (Questions of Philosophy); and numerous other entities.[25] Presiding over the conference was none other than Liudmila Polonskaia, and the chief papers were given by scholars of South and Southeast Asia. Over the course of the previous dozen years, Soviet scholars and policy makers—led by the CPSU International Department's Rostislav Ul'ianovskii, who bridged the two worlds—had not only gotten past the idea that religion was an obstructionist or reactionary political force but had arrived at the conclusion that it was an inevitable and important tool for the promotion of progressive politics in the developing world. While some religious institutions and actors, especially the Catholic Church, were still regarded with suspicion, religion's association with anticolonial movements and discourses of "cultural authenticity" and anti-Westernism were seen as evidence that religious actors could be trustworthy political allies.[26] The willingness to work with religious actors in the name of socialism had already manifested in Soviet policy in Chile, Somalia, and elsewhere, but the real test of religion's progressive role would come in a place that had been largely absent in this discourse: Iran.

The Development of the Left in Iran

In no country outside the former Russian empire was the development of leftist movements more tied up with Russia than in Iran. It was Iranian émigrés, mostly of Azeri and Armenian descent, who came work in Baku or to study in Tiflis, who first absorbed socialist and Marxist ideas at a time when Russia was pushing into northern Iran and the Russian presence was already so prevalent that the supply disruption from the Russian Revolution of 1905 was a major cause of the unrest leading to Iran's subsequent Constitutional Revolution.[27] According to one estimate, there were a half million Iranians in southern Russia by 1905. Some of them formed an exclusively Azerbaijani branch named Himmat in Baku in 1904 in the wake of the Second Congress of the Russian Social Democratic Workers' Party that coordinated with the Baku Committee of the party.[28] Another group was founded by Russian-educated Armenians in the northern Iranian city of Tabriz, and was named the Tabriz Social Democratic Group.[29] Though these organizations and others associated with them were suppressed in the wake of the failures of both the Russian Revolution in 1905 and the Iranian Constitutional Revolution in 1911, their memberships and legacies would set the stage for a revival in the wake of the Russian Revolution of 1917.

In 1917, former members of the Himmat reconstituted themselves as the Adalat Party in Baku, which joined the Comintern in 1919 and then in June 1920 founded the Iranian Communist Party (ICP) at a congress on Iranian soil, in the Caspian port of Enzeli, only weeks after the pronouncement of the Gilan-based Soviet Socialist Republic of Iran. The republic, which was founded through the Jangali Movement of Mirza Kuchek Khan, was composed of nationalist populists who sought to rid the country of the Entente armies and to implement agrarian reform. The founding took place, however, only after Bolshevik forces landed in Gilan and quickly sought to put the ICP in charge of policy, thus displacing the local nationalist movement of Kuchek Khan. The ICP attempted a radical land reform that quickly alienated local elites, and its failure led the Soviets to distance themselves from the Soviet Socialist Republic of Iran, choosing rapprochement with Tehran instead. One Comintern envoy in Iran, Yakov Blumkin, was likely exaggerating when he said, "My 'Persian tale'? There were a few hundred of us ragged Russians down there. One day we had a telegram from the Central Committee: 'Cut your losses, revolution in Iran now off.' But for that we would have got to Tehran."[30] Nevertheless, the episode set a clear precedent for the Iranian Left; it would often be seen as little more than a tool of Russian or Soviet policy, to be discarded as soon as the higher-ups in Moscow had changed their minds.

After Reza Khan, the head of the Russian-trained Iranian Cossack Brigade, took power via coup in 1921, the remnants of the Iranian Left were thoroughly repressed by a centralizing, modernizing dictatorship that modeled itself after that of Kemal Ataturk in Turkey. The nucleus of a Marxist group in Iran, this time mostly ethnic Persians educated in Germany, was arrested in May 1937 and imprisoned, and it was these people who would form the core of the new Tudeh Party in 1941 once the British and Soviets had removed Reza Khan (by then the shah) for his German sympathies.[31] During the war, and in the spirit of the Grand Alliance, the Tudeh Party was essentially a popular front organization, but as the war drew to a close it held its first congress in 1944 with an eye toward constituting itself as a proper Marxist-Leninist organization.[32] At the end of the war the Tudeh Party was the most influential political organization in Iran, counting more than twenty-five thousand members and over three hundred thousand sympathizers, including "workers, women, intellectuals, artists, military officers, students, teachers, professionals, the urban underclass, and even some peasants."[33] Immediately after the war, the party offended Iranian nationalists by supporting Soviet-backed separatists in Iranian Azerbaijan and Soviet claims for an oil concession in northern Iran.[34] It still remained the best organized and arguably most powerful political organization in Iran for much of the late 1940s and early 1950s, despite being officially banned in February 1949, but its early opposition to the oil nationalization policy of the National Front and Prime Minister Mohammad Mossadeq damned it in the eyes of many Iranians. Soviet postwar policy was predicated on the idea that "the world situation in the postwar epoch will be colored by Anglo-American contradictions," and at some point Britain might even be forced to side with the Soviets.[35] Accordingly, the Soviets saw Mossadeq's attempt to nationalize oil as a way of kicking out the British in favor of the more dangerous Americans, even going so far as to speculate that Mossadeq was an American agent, and the Tudeh Party was to oppose Mossadeq on this basis.[36] The party changed its tune in late 1952 and early 1953, but this came too late for many Iranian nationalists, especially when it failed to activate its secret military organization, which was three hundred Iranian military officers strong in early 1952,[37] to oppose the coup in August 1953. With the return of the shah, the Tudeh Party was repressed again, its leaders fled to the Eastern Europe and the USSR, and its influence in Iran was essentially broken.

For a period in the late 1950s in which the shah's anticommunist efforts were at their height, exemplified by the creation of the Sāzemān-e Etelā'āt Va Amniyat-e Keshvar (SAVAK; Organization for Security and Intelligence of the Country) in 1956, Soviet policy was largely limited to rescuing individual Tudeh Party leaders. In the early 1960s the shah's White Revolution, inspired by the administration of US president John F. Kennedy's promotion of modernization, ignited even more Soviet hostility as the shah seemed to be moving ever closer to Washington, possibly even leading Nikita Khrushchev to order the assassination of the shah, according to the account of Vladimir Kuzichkin, a former Komitet gosudarstvennoy bezopasnosti (KGB; Committee for State Security) officer in Tehran who defected to the United Kingdom.[38] The alleged attempt only failed because one person failed to hold down the detonator long enough. Yet as the 1960s wore on, the shah wanted to create some room for maneuver vis-à-vis the United States, and the Soviets, now convinced of the stability of the regime to their south, sought to build a productive relationship and gain what influence they could.[39] A secret report prepared by the Soviet embassy in Tehran in 1967 and sent to the East Germans asserted that Iran was sincerely interested in improving relations with socialist countries and outlined what the German Democratic Republic (GDR) might consider trading with Iran.[40] The Soviets themselves initiated a significant program of economic aid and cooperation with Iran in 1965, headlined by the construction of the Isfahan metallurgical complex, that continued right up to the Iranian Revolution of 1979.[41] While Moscow reaped the benefits of better relations with Iran, Iranians opposed to the shah now saw the Soviet Union as a supporter rather than an enemy of the regime; consequently, opposition to the shah inevitably took on an anti-Soviet cast.

The Iranian-Soviet rapprochement coincided with the Sino-Soviet split and the fracturing of the Global Left, largely over the question of armed struggle versus peaceful coexistence and peaceful transition.[42] The eclipse of the Tudeh Party and Soviet influence over the Iranian Left therefore led to a search for new models, of which there was no shortage: Ahmed Ben Bella's Algeria, Fidel Castro's Cuba, Ho Chi Minh's Vietnam, and Mao Zedong's China, just to name a few. Of the many groups that were formed, however, three were dominant. The Feda'iyān-e-Khalq, a Marxist-Leninist organization tied to neither the Soviets nor the Chinese, opened the era of guerrilla attacks on the shah's regime with an assault on the Siyakhal gendarmerie post in February 1971.[43] The Feda'iyān was composed of several factions, one of which included renegades from the Tudeh Party led by Bizhan Jazani, who would die in prison in 1975. Disillusioned with both the Soviets and the Tudeh Party, Jazani also rejected facile Maoist analyses that labeled Iran a semifeudal and semicolonial country, instead arguing that it was an example of a new phenomenon, "dependent capitalism," in which feudal elites had been displaced during the shah's White Revolution by the forces of the so-called comprador bourgeoisie.[44] Jazani asserted that although socialist revolution in Iran was still premature, the proletariat needed to lead a coalition of the "people" against the "elites," and that the way to gain this leadership was by conducting "armed propaganda," symbolic violence against the regime that would awaken the people. But armed struggle, largely to the exclusion of political agitation, soon became the primary focus of the Feda'iyān under the influence of Masoud Ahmadzadeh. Ahmadzadeh and his collaborators, rather than emerging from the Tudeh Party, learned their Marxism from the writings of Latin American guerrillas, including Che Guevara and the Brazilian Carlos Marighella. Though the Feda'iyān leadership was largely wiped out by the SAVAK in 1976, the organization rapidly reconstituted itself as the movement against the shah's regime grew, and it played a key role in the final battles against the last defenders of the regime in February 1979.[45] The divisions over strategy and ideology, in part emerging from the debates between the followers of Ahmadzadeh and Jazani, would continue to plague the Feda'iyan, ultimately contributing to the splitting of the organization in 1980.

The other two most important organizations began together as the Mujahideen-e-Khalq (MEK), which was officially established in 1965, before the Feda'iyān-e-Khalq, though it did not attempt its first armed action until August 1971. The MEK's ideology combined Marxist economics with Islamic values and narratives, claiming that true Islam was a revolutionary egalitarian ideology that needed to be rescued from clerical domination.[46] Though the group was often associated—and associated itself—with both Ali Shari'ati and Sayyid Mohammed Taleqani, it was actually founded and its ideology developed by a group of middle-class university students in predominantly technical fields who were not themselves religious scholars.[47] The tension between the Islamic and Marxist elements of its ideology produced a split in 1975 between Muslim and Marxist wings, and the majority at the time formed the Mujahideen-e-Khalq (Marxist-Leninist), or MEK(ML), which changed its name to Peykar in 1978. The MEK(ML) identified as a Maoist organization, and by the time of the 1979 revolution it saw both the USSR and the People's Republic of China, in the wake of the latter's rapprochement with the United States, as hopelessly revisionist. Instead it looked to Enver Hoxha's Albania as its ideological lodestar. Meanwhile, the kernel of the Islamic Mujahedeen, which would retain the name and quickly rebuild as the shah began releasing political prisoners under international pressure in 1977–1978, was formed in prison under the leadership of Massoud Rajavi, a former Tehran University law student from a small town in the eastern province of Khorasan. It was Rajavi's organization that would ultimately provide the greatest challenge to the consolidation of clerical rule.

Thus, on the eve of the 1979 revolution, the Iranian Left was weighed down by a high degree of ideological fracture and a legacy of subservience to foreign interests—particularly those of the Soviet Union. Additionally, the opposition organizations inside Iran had been thoroughly decimated by the SAVAK and, while the universities provided an endless supply of fresh recruits, experience and leadership became scarce commodities. The Tudeh Party leadership, albeit out of touch and discredited, remained largely intact in the GDR and USSR, broadcasting radio programs into Iran from Bulgaria.[48] The revolution, a rapid and unexpected development that the Left did not initiate, would therefore represent an immense challenge to the Left's theoretical and organizational capabilities, and failure would mean decimation on a scale the shah had never managed to achieve.

The Rise of Revolutionary Islamism

While the Iranian Left found itself suppressed as the main target of the shah's police state, opposition to the shah increasingly came from a new source: the ulama and the religious seminaries. This was particularly evident as the White Revolution reached its climax in 1963, when some of the ulama, led by the new *marjā-e-taqlid* (source of emulation), Ayatollah Ruhollah Khomeini, openly opposed the shah's reforms, leading to large-scale protests culminating in violent repression on June 5, 1963. Though some saw the religious opposition to the shah's reforms as simply a reactionary attempt to oppose modernizing measures such as allowing women to vote, along with protecting the ulama's own economic interests (especially land ownership), the events of 1963 proved to be an important turning point in terms of overtly Islamic actors assuming the mantle of antishah, anti-imperialist, and even anticapitalist opposition. It was easy for external observers to underrate the significance of the religious opposition. The rising, educated middle-class residents of Tehran (where most foreign observers lived) were apparently abandoning Islam, but there was a larger question: Where in the world had religious actors successfully led a progressive revolution? Even according to Liudmila Polonskaia, the role of religious actors in the national liberation movement was a product of the survival of preindustrial economic formations and the "idealization" of the precolonial period. What Polonskaia had failed to see, however, was that in some cases, including that of Iran, the growth of Islamic opposition was not a premodern survival but a response to the rising popularity of secular Western—and, particularly, Marxist—systems of thought. As Hamid Dabashi writes, referring to a succession of Iranian thinkers, "All proponents of the 'Islamic Ideology' in Iran, from [Jalal] Al-e-Ahmad to [Abolhasan] Bani-Sadr, each in his own way, considered Marxism as a chief ideological competitor."[49] An eclectic group of religiously inspired thinkers in Iran saw Marxism as a challenge and sought to use a combination of Islam and Iranian history and culture to develop an ideology that would not only preserve Iran's traditions but would succeed politically and economically where Marxism had failed. As such, this was not merely the reaction of an antiquated social and religious structure trying to turn back the tide of modernity. On the contrary, it was an attempt to incorporate and supersede Marxism in constructing an alternative and superior modernity.

Dabashi begins his discussion of what he labels "the Islamic Ideology" with the work of Jalal Al-e-Ahmad, the quintessential voice of anti-imperialism in Iran in the second half of the twentieth century. Yet it seems that Dabashi might have started his analysis one thinker too late. The man that Al-e-Ahmad regarded as his mentor was no Islamist, nor even necessarily an Iranian nationalist; he was Khalil Maleki, a Marxist—one of the Fifty-Three imprisoned by Reza Shah Pahlavi in 1937 and later one of the leaders of the Tudeh Party. Maleki led an oppositional faction in the party and then instigated its split in 1948. He did not openly disavow Marxism, but he did reject the Tudeh Party's subservience to Moscow and, more significantly, rejected the Soviet Union as an exemplar of Marxism. Years before Khrushchev's Secret Speech, Maleki did not just condemn Joseph Stalin, terror, and the cult of personality. His criticism was far more fundamental: the Soviet Union was both colonialist and capitalist. It was colonialist in its relationship to other communist parties and states, and it was capitalist because—far from eliminating the exploitation of man by man, as it claimed—it was in fact built on the extreme exploitation of workers and peasants for the enrichment of a new ruling class. Instead of imitating the Soviet model, Maleki advocated the formation of a "Third Force" composed of the countries in what Mao would later call the Intermediate Zone between the superpowers in order to "protect their own national and social character and identity."[50]

As that last point illustrates, Maleki's Third Force was about more than just finding the perfect economic model. It was also about cultural identity, which he did not necessarily see as merely secondary to economics. While Marxism treats economics as fundamental and issues of culture, religion, and social and ethnic identity as secondary or epiphenomenal, many Third World anti-imperialist thinkers sought to incorporate economics within a more holistic approach that prioritized national dignity and cultural self-assertion along with economic prosperity.

Jalal Al-e-Ahmad, born in 1923, grew up in a religious family and acutely felt the pressure of Reza Shah Pahlavi's secularizing reforms before turning to the Tudeh Party and Marxism in the 1940s. Having rejected Marxism, though, he turned to literature, and his major work *Gharbzadegi* (Westoxification), published in 1962 and coining a term that would permeate all of Iranian political and cultural discourse, traced the source of Iran's oppression by the West far beyond the modern era of capitalism and imperialism and all the way to Alexander the Great and beyond.[51] Al-e-Ahmad's analysis focused on the cultural and social alienation of the Iranian elite from Iran's people, culture, and history. Ironically, the country he saw as a model for Iran of modernization without cultural assimilation was Israel: "For me as an Easterner, Israel is a model, [better] than any other model, of how to deal with the West."[52] Cultural self-assertion, rather than Islam specifically, was at the core of Al-e-Ahmad's agenda, and that is perhaps the reason why his diagnoses were much more specific than his prescriptions.

The man who would use Islam—particularly, Iranian Shi'ite Islam—as the frame for a revolutionary anti-imperialist agenda more successfully than any other was Ali Shari'ati, often seen as the chief theorist of the Iranian Revolution. Shari'ati's significance can perhaps best be illustrated by the fact that the massive crowds that filled the streets of Tehran and other cities in December 1978 and January 1979 held aloft portraits of two men: Ayatollah Khomeini and Ali Shari'ati.[53] While much of the literature on Shari'ati focuses on the content of his revolutionary ideology, and particularly the way he sought to appropriate Marxism in an Islamic context, he was first and foremost an orator who sought to move and mobilize his audiences, and for this he employed the language and emotional currency specific to Shi'ite Islam. The core stories of Shi'ite Islam—those of Ali, Husayn, the Battle of Karbala, Zaynab, and others—and their ritual reenactments provide the distinctive tropes of the religion: suffering, sacrifice, and struggle against overwhelming odds in the name of justice. As Dabashi notes, "The indigenous Persian-Shi'i language, properly charged with strategically crucial ideological notions, would be immensely powerful in potentially mobilizing a sizeable constituency, nostalgic about a past it may or may not have, anxious about a future it could or could not have."[54] All that remained was to rescue these tropes from the quietist purposes they had served for so long, which Shari'ati did by constructing an alternative Shi'ism, with reinterpreted concepts and re-purposed language, that he called "Alid Shi'ism" and contrasted with the establishment Shi'ism of the ulama, which he termed "Safavid Shi'ism."[55] What was seen as noble suffering in Safavid Shi'ism could easily be turned into revolutionary heroism in Alid Shi'ism, a useful notion when many of those inspired by it, such as the young students joining the MEK, knew that they would likely face torture and death at the hands of the SAVAK. In Shari'ati's telling, Husayn became the model of the perfect man who, not coincidentally, also served as the template of the perfect revolutionary.[56]

While Shari'ati's reading of Islam provided the mobilizing narrative for revolution, Ayatollah Sayyid Mohammad Taleqani used Islam to provide an economic counterargument to Marxism. Unlike the younger, French-educated Al-e-Ahmad and Shari'ati, Taleqani, later known as the Red Ayatollah when he was on Khomeini's Revolutionary Council, was born in Tehran in 1910 to the family of a prominent cleric and had a thorough, traditional education in Qom. After the removal of Reza Shah Pahlavi in 1941, however, Taleqani returned to Tehran and taught at the Hedayat Mosque to an audience of urban students and professionals who were increasingly attracted to Marxism and the Tudeh Party.[57] Consequently, Taleqani saw his main task as battling the attraction of Marxism by providing an Islamic critique of and alternative to it. In his major work, *Islam and Ownership,* first published in 1951, Taleqani sought to expose the inadequacy of Marxism's materialist basis for its understanding of society: "Those who think or believe that by considering only one isolated desire or bond, i.e., economic relations, they have diagnosed social ills and have proposed cures are like magicians and snake charmers who having a single magic or prescription claim to possess cures for all the diseases in the tribe and can exorcise demons or charm any snake." Instead Islam would seek to fix humankind holistically by relocating economics within ethics and reducing the drive for excessive consumption that he saw as a disease imported from the West, thereby negating the drive for infinite profit. While this would eliminate capitalist exploitation, Taleqani asserted that the state should not remove individual property that had been acquired through one's own labor and creativity because absolute ownership belonged only to God, and so an Islamic economic system would not fall prey to the state-based exploitation that Maleki had identified in the Soviet Union. Class struggle, for Taleqani, was neither inevitable nor desirable; rather, it was "the outcome of the deviation of individuals and society from the principles of truth, justice, and the notion of transgression and as a result of colonialism and oppression which is taking root."[58] While Marxists would no doubt criticize the idealism of Taleqani's vision, it not only came from the same sources of cultural and religious tradition mined by Al-e-Ahmad and Shari'ati but also was not tied to the negative example of Soviet communism.

Taleqani's vision of Islamic economics was largely shared by a man who would become one of the top officials in charge of shaping the IRI's economic policies, Abolhasan Bani-Sadr. Born in a small village near Hamadan in 1933, and the grandson of a distinguished cleric, Bani-Sadr would later leave Iran to study finance and economics at the Sorbonne, where he eventually joined Khomeini's circle before the revolution, reportedly being the first to call Khomeini "Imam."[59] His close relationship with Khomeini helped ease his path to being elected the first president of the IRI in January 1980, though it did not save him from impeachment amid the increasing political turmoil in June 1981. Perhaps the most apt description of Bani-Sadr comes from Nuredin Kianouri, the first secretary of the Tudeh Party, who a week after Bani-Sadr's inauguration as president told Hermann Axen, the member of the ruling Sozialistische Einheitspartei Deutschlands (SED; Socialist Unity Party of Germany) politburo in charge of foreign policy, that Bani-Sadr was a "Muslim Franco-Maoist."[60] Adopting Taleqani's idea of protecting private property accumulated through labor, Bani-Sadr argued that both capitalist inequality and the attempt to create equality artificially under communism were based on violence and relations of dominance. Replacing relations of dominance with equality before God, Bani-Sadr sketched a theory he called monotheistic economics (*eqtesad-e-tawhidi*) through which the state would serve merely a regulatory, balancing role rather than a dominating, controlling one, aided by the disappearance first of the Western vice of overconsumption and subsequently of class divisions. In order to remove Iran from relations of dominance in the international sphere, Bani-Sadr wanted to replace dependence on the export of oil with an agrarian economy. He then advocated unleashing the revolution on the world, with Iran spearheading an Islamic "permanent resurrection" that would rid the world of violence and economic exploitation.[61] When the new government of the IRI organized a conference in September 1979 to figure out what an Islamic economy might look like in practice, it was Bani-Sadr who represented the interests of the clergy and the vision of an economy based on "Islamic justice."[62]

Although these nationalist and Islamic thinkers were for the most part short on specific economic policy prescriptions on the eve of the revolution, they nevertheless had several advantages over their Marxist opponents. Their ideological prescriptions were built upon deeply entrenched cultural and religious traditions that provided a language, a cultural context, and an infrastructure for reaching large numbers of people in Iran. Given the history of the Left's ties with the Soviet Union, they were both able to use nationalist anti-imperialism to attack the Left and the reality of Soviet communism to discredit its ideological prescriptions. More fundamentally, they had the advantage of coming second—of being formed, in large part, in reaction to the position of their opponents. Elena Doroshenko sees the clergy as playing a predominantly conservative role supporting the regime and their influence as being in decline even among their "petit bourgeois" base. Barely mentioning Taleqani in her 1975 book *Shi'itskoe dukhovenstvo v sovremennom Irane* (The Shi'ite clergy in contemporary Iran), Doroshenko pays little attention to the economic ideas of Islamic writers.[63] Yet in a sort of ideological inversion of Leon Trotsky's "law of uneven and combined development," these Islamic thinkers were able to build in proposed solutions to the demonstrated failings of Marxism. Once the terrain of debate shifted to include religion, clerical thinkers had a structural advantage over the leftists of the mujahideen who sought to reinterpret Islam in light of Marxism. As Ervand Abrahamian writes, "Who is better equipped to judge what is true Islam? The ulama who have spent a lifetime studying the Koran, the hadiths, the shari'a and the previous Muslim scholars? Or intellectuals, from foreign universities, with degrees in engineering, modern sciences, and, at best, Islamology?"[64] With even nonclerical intellectuals increasingly identifying Shi'ism as the core of Iranian identity and its main tool for opposing the West, even the discourse of nationalism and cultural authenticity would ultimately work against opposition to the IRI. Regarding nationalist intellectuals in what he has called "the dilemma of authenticity," Negin Nabavi observes, "That much of the language used against them had been of their own making meant that they did not know how to react effectively."[65]

The February Revolution

Both the organizations on the left and the workers of Iran played important roles—with the former having considerable influence over the latter—in the events that led to the flight of the shah and the return of Khomeini in early 1979.[66] The Iranian working class formed a larger percentage of the population in 1979 than the Russian working class had in 1917, "well over 50 percent of the economically active population," according to Asef Bayat.[67] While the initial stages of protest were dominated by liberal intellectuals and Islamic organizations, the shah's position was made untenable by a successful general strike that started in June 1978 and gathered steam, being joined in September by oil refinery workers in Abadan, Isfahan, Shiraz, Tehran, and Tabriz; by late October it had essentially paralyzed the Iranian economy, including "almost all the bazaars, universities, high schools, oil installations, banks, government ministries, post offices, railways, newspapers, customs and port facilities, internal air flights, radio and television stations, state-run hospitals, paper and tobacco plants, textile mills, and other large factories."[68] Mansoor Moaddel claims that it was the participation of the workers in 1978, in addition to the coalition of ulama, *bazaaris* (merchants), and students from the 1963 protest movement, that made it impossible for the shah to suppress the protests this time.[69] While they were by no means dominant, leftist organizations did play a significant role in mobilizing workers, particularly in the all-important oil industry.[70]

When it came to military clashes, however, only the Feda'iyān and Mujahideen had the military capabilities to confront the forces loyal to the government of Shahpur Bakhtiar, the prime minister left in charge by the departing shah. The armed climax of the revolution in February 1979 was brief but violent. In the immediate aftermath, one prominent Tehran journalist told the East German ambassador that while Khomeini's camp was poorly organized and unprepared for the takeover of power, which it had expected to happen more gradually, the Left disposed of the most disciplined organizations in the country, with the Feda'iyān alone including some fifty to one hundred thousand armed men.[71] The Soviet ambassador suspected that the Iranian Army agreed to a cease-fire so quickly on February 11 only because both it and the incoming revolutionary leaders were afraid that continued fighting would lead to a seizure of power by the Left.[72] Both Khomeini and his chosen prime minister, Mehdi Bazargan, were very aware that they had to build up some kind of armed force of their own and disarm the left-wing forces, and they had to do both quickly.

Khomeini returned to Iran only on February 1, two weeks after the shah's departure, because of Bakhtiar's closure of the airports. In the meantime, a steady stream of Iranian politicians came to see him as the acknowledged leader of the revolution in his exile near Paris in order to plan a postrevolutionary regime, including most prominently Karim Sanjabi, the leader of the reconstructed National Front, who agreed with Khomeini on establishing a regime based on Islam and democracy.[73] Upon his return Khomeini refused to acknowledge or negotiate with Bakhtiar's government. Instead he established his own Revolutionary Council to pull the strings during the transitional period. On February 5 he named a provisional government, led by Mehdi Bazargan, a French-educated engineer and a devout Muslim who had long been one of the most active figures in the various successor movements to Mossadeq's National Front.[74] Bazargan and his cabinet of largely Western-educated Islamic technocrats had responsibility for policy, but they had little actual power to implement anything. Real power in the regime still resided with Khomeini and the Revolutionary Council, which increasingly controlled the ad hoc local committees (*komitehha*) that had come into being during the revolution as well as the newly created Pasdaran, or Revolutionary Guard. The situation thus resembled that of Russia in 1917, when the provisional government had responsibility but little power and was at the mercy of the Petrograd Soviet, which had some power but very little responsibility. Accordingly, the Soviet ambassador titled the chapter in his memoir that begins with the departure of the shah "Dvoevlastie" (Dual power), the term that had been used in 1917.[75]

The Soviet Union, like most international observers, was quite late to realize the seriousness of events in Iran in 1978 and express its support for the revolution, but by the fall it became clear to all that the status quo ante would not be restored and Moscow—and its protégés in the Tudeh Party—would need to begin planning for what would come next. As Klaus Wolff, the East German ambassador in Tehran, reported in October 1978, the shah had alienated all sectors of society—the bourgeoisie, *bazaaris,* peasants, workers, and ulama—and full reestablishment of control was impossible.[76] In November, responding to requests from the Tudeh Party leadership, the Soviets desperately sought to find an ally willing to resume the party's radio broadcasts to Iran that the Bulgarians had stopped in 1976, even broaching the idea of broadcasting from Mongolia.[77] For now, though, the weak position of the Tudeh Party inside Iran made any immediate attempt to seize power inconceivable. Rather, the party would need a considerable period of peace and legality to build its influence.

To prepare its return to a postshah Iran, the Tudeh Party held a conference of its executive committee from January 13 to 16, 1979, at which Iraj Eskandari was removed as first secretary in favor of Nuredin Kianouri.

Kianouri had been pushing the party's executive committee to call for the overthrow of the shah, and he was thought to be more "active" and "dynamic," a reasonable description since he had been part of the splinter group that tried to kill the shah in 1949.[78] According to Ehsan Tabari, the Tudeh Party's leading ideologist, Eskandari had favored an alliance with the National Front and Ayatollah Mohammad Kazem Shariat-Madari that would cooperate with Khomeini on the basis of reciprocity.[79] Eskandari himself told the Prague-based international communist journal *Problemy mira i sotsializma* (Problems of peace and socialism) in a November 1978 interview that while the Tudeh Party welcomed the participation of the ulama in the revolution, it would be another matter if there was serious talk of a theocratic state.[80] Consequently, the choice of Kianouri, supposedly orchestrated by someone within the Soviet Union, was also one in favor of alliance with Khomeini.[81] The fact that some veteran Tudeh Party members disagreed with party policy under Kianouri would remain a source of tension, and in August Kianouri asked his East German and Soviet patrons to convince Reza Radmanesh, who had been first secretary before Eskandari, to release a statement supporting the policy.[82] Nevertheless, the direction adopted at the conference was cautious, and the East Germans were worried about Kianouri's ability to get along with others.[83] Soviet officials advised the Tudeh Party at this time to become more active, but to be careful not to give the shah, the United States, and other possible enemies the chance to attack the party or use it to rally support against the revolution, thus endorsing the party's fundamentally cautious stance.[84] Kianouri himself did not return to Iran until April, after undergoing training in the Soviet Union from the CPSU International Department. Meanwhile, the Soviets tried to establish contacts with the leftist organizations that actually had played a role in the revolution, the Feda'iyān and Mujahideen, but both organizations asked for immediate weapons deliveries and then declined further contact.[85] The Tudeh Party would remain Moscow's only lever on the Iranian Left.

Encouraging the Tudeh Party to seize power was unrealistic, however. As an East German report acknowledged, "In view of the mass terror and decades-long strong anticommunist indoctrination of the people, the progressive and democratic forces do not have decisive influence over the movement."[86] The Soviets and the Tudeh Party therefore had no choice but to select political allies from the available options. The theory of the "state of national democracy," adopted at the International Meeting of Communist and Workers Parties in 1960, might have dictated that, at this

233

stage of the revolutionary process, the state should be led by the "national bourgeoisie," represented in this case by the technocrats of the Bazargan government.[87] But poor experiences with such governments, and in particular the example of Allende's Chile, made this an unpalatable option. Instead the Soviet ideological reevaluation of the role of religious actors, particularly given their potentially progressive role as representatives of the oppressed, opened another path. In the context of revolutionary Iran, both the Tudeh Party and its patrons in East Berlin and Moscow saw the ulama as a progressive force, and consequently a natural ally of the party at this stage of the revolution. In a report passed on to the East Germans in January 1979, the Tudeh Party leadership said of the ulama that "its demands for struggle against the monarchy and foreign paternalism [*Bevormundung*] as well as its statements for the fulfillment of the social demands of the broad popular masses objectively carry in the present confrontation over Iran's political future a progressive character."[88] Back in East Berlin, the Near and Middle Eastern Sector of the GDR Foreign Ministry, despite being somewhat confused about the nature of Shi'ism (of which it identified Baha'ism as a sect), went even further: "The development of political ideas on the basis of Islamic Law, which is accepted by the broad popular masses, and the radical slogans for the elimination of the shah's regime are factors that show that the clerical opposition under Khomeini in the present situation plays a progressive role in the development of Iran. In furthering the struggle, the need grows for the clergy to develop ideas [*Vorstellungen*] for the further socioeconomic development of the country."[89] As a consequence, the Tudeh Party saw Khomeini's role as progressive, too, and embraced him as the leader of the revolution.[90]

The subordination of the Tudeh Party to the leadership of Khomeini and his allies was only meant to be temporary. In part, this was a built-in feature of the communist notion of "states of national democracy": as the revolution progressed, the ruling coalition would shift to the left and the workers and peasants would displace the national bourgeoisie at its head. This had not always turned out to be the case elsewhere and had led to frustration in places like Egypt under Gamal Abdel Nasser and Anwar Sadat. In Iran, though, the very fact that it was the clergy who were in power made this shift all the more certain, since neither the Tudeh Party leaders nor their European patrons imagined that the clergy could hold power for long. A senior Tudeh Party official told the East Germans that "the Khomeini-led petit bourgeois forces are incapable of solving the pressing problems of the second stage of the revolution on political and

Our objective is the destruction of the
super powers.   Imam Khomeini

Jihad-e- Sazandegi (Jihad for Construction), External Liaison Section, P.O. Box: 13/331, Tehran, The Islamic Republic of Iran

FIGURE 5.1 Propaganda poster of Ayatollah Khomeini.   *(UK National Archives, ref. FC08/5131)*

above all on economic grounds, and don't have the necessary cadres. The attempts of Khomeini to achieve everything with the help of Islamic fanaticism and the religious devotion of the popular masses will make it objectively impossible to solve the tasks of the revolution according to the true interests of the Iranian people."[91] In principle, the East Germans and the Soviets agreed with this position, with the caveat that Islamic rule might only be viable for a short period. An East German Foreign Ministry evaluation in September 1979 concluded that "it is becoming ever clearer that the attempt to realize a sociopolitical concept based on early Islam in a country with relatively advanced capitalist development must fail in the long term."[92] Soviet ambassador Vladimir Vinogradov was somewhat more cautious, remarking, "Naturally, a theocratic state in Iran can have no 'eternal duration' [ewige Dauer]. The ability of Shi'ism to deflect the still uneducated masses of poor peasants, workers, and small merchants from their class interests, though, should not be underestimated."[93] The alternative to cooperation with the clergy was worse because, as the East German embassy reported in July, "confrontation with the clergy would mean confrontation with the laboring masses."[94] Consequently, despite its doubts about the economic viability of Islamism, the Tudeh Party leadership, in an open letter of July 24, 1979, clearly identified Khomeini's agenda with that of the "urban and rural laborers, that is the workers, peasants, artisans, students, and small merchants."[95] The thinking was that, for now, Khomeini represented the "progressive" elements of society, but he would soon lose their support, which would instead fall into the Tudeh Party's lap like a ripe apple.

The embrace of Khomeini also made sense geopolitically. In a conversation with East German politburo member Hermann Axen on January 25, 1979, Boris Ponomarev, the longtime head of the International Department of the Soviet Central Committee, laid out the Soviet approach to Iran. According to Ponomarev, events in Afghanistan, Angola, Cambodia, Ethiopia, Mozambique, Vietnam, Yemen, and elsewhere had shown that "socialism is on the offensive and imperialism is on the defensive." Consequently, Stalinist logic dictated that the resistance to socialism must increase as victory approached. It would be expected that the United States would fight to retain such a crucial ally as Iran. Ponomarev therefore saw the likely threat to the revolution as following the pattern of Chile in 1973: "There is a real danger of a military coup, a military dictatorship. The reactionary forces are gathering themselves. Bakhtiar is a man of the military. The opposition is very strong. The military and the Americans are still afraid that with the construction of a military dictatorship like in Chile the opposition could turn out to be stronger than the military."[96] At the time, given that Bakhtiar was still in power, the military was still intact, and elements of the US administration were in fact considering a coup, Ponomarev's comparison with Chile in terms of the potential for an American-aided putsch was not wholly unreasonable.[97] Meanwhile, Ponomarev saw Khomeini himself as a contradictory figure: he seemed to be for positive relations with the Soviet Union, but he had also said that Marxism had no place in Iran. In foreign policy, at least, support for Khomeini seemed to promise a reorientation of Iranian policy away from the United States and an exit from the Central Treaty Organization.[98] Moscow even expected the new regime in Iran to support the communist regime in Afghanistan, however, and this was an early indication that Soviet leaders did not understand the difference between their version of anti-imperialism and Khomeini's.[99]

The lessons drawn by the Soviets from the fall of Allende would strongly bolster the case in favor of allying with Khomeini rather than other liberal or leftist alternatives. This analogy would come up repeatedly in Soviet and Tudeh Party communications. Initially the focus of Soviet blame in the wake of the September 1973 coup was placed on those to the far left—in particular, the Chilean Socialist Party, which had eagerly sought confrontation with the opposition instead of seeking to chart a middle course by compromising with friendly sections of the bourgeoisie represented by the Christian Democrats and building a safe electoral majority, the strategy favored by the Chilean Communist Party and pushed by Moscow.[100] The importance of the Chilean episode and the force of the Soviet critique made this a political template for Soviet allies around the world. As time went on, however, emphasis was increasingly put on the ability of the revolutionary forces to defend themselves, eventually precipitating a turn in the policy of the Chilean Communist Party in exile in Moscow in favor of guerrilla struggle back in Chile.[101] While the Tudeh Party initially was in no position to fight on its own, this analysis dictated that, rather than compromise with "democratic" bourgeois liberals or those on the far left, the party should instead rally around the revolutionary coalition led by Khomeini as the best guarantee against a coup attempt led by the US Central Intelligence Agency.

Accordingly, at a Tudeh Party plenum in February, Kianouri emphasized that the main danger to the revolution now lay in the attempt of the liberal bourgeoisie to freeze the process of transformation by installing bourgeois democracy and "furthering the old catastrophic capitalist development pattern" in Iran.[102] He invoked Chile as an example of the danger that faced the Iranian Revolution from a potential alliance of the bourgeoisie, the remnants of the old regime, and foreign imperialists if the revolutionary coalition failed to hold together. The East German Foreign Ministry endorsed the strategy, writing that fissures between the Islamists and the bourgeois liberals around Bazargan were already appearing, with Khomeini demanding the "rapid improvement of the social position of the popular masses and criticiz[ing] the hesitant advance of Bazargan's government against 'Western influence,'" Therefore "the decisive test of power [*Machtprobe*] between the different political forces is still ahead," and clearly foreign policy—that is, the strength of one's anti-imperialism—would be a main determinant regarding whose side to take.[103] In early May, a high-level report laid out this line of thinking in explicit terms:

> The polarization of the political and social forces is accelerating. Although the leftist forces are gaining influence, they do not at the current time have sufficient prerequisites to take over the leadership of further social development. They are therefore concentrating on the creation of democratic conditions for the gradual preparation of a true alternative to the bourgeois forces, which are currently already established as the beneficiary of the popular uprising and are using all means to allow only those political changes which serve the interests of the bourgeoisie as a class. The conspiracy of these forces with parts of the old power structure as well as with foreign reaction cannot be excluded. The progressive forces support therefore all measures of Khomeini and the "Revolutionary Tribunals" that serve to smash the old state and repression apparatus.[104]

As the report makes clear, the official strategy of the Tudeh Party was to unite the Left under its leadership and then ally that union with Khomeini's forces for as long as necessary to defeat the bourgeoisie and forestall a Chilean-style coup. In this context, support for Khomeini and clerical rule was justified due to the fact that the bourgeoisie only opposed Islamization because "they feared that this form of society would not leave enough room for the rapid development of capitalism, for the dominating influence of the bourgeoisie and its profit drive."[105]

This was not the only strategy the Tudeh Party could have adopted. Others on the left had already taken a more judicious approach to the nascent IRI. The Feda'iyān, the largest organization on the left, had already begun to oppose Khomeini in March over the issue of a referendum called on whether or not to declare an Islamic republic. While the Feda'iyān decided to boycott the vote because Khomeini would only allow yes or no options, turning it into a vote for or against the revolution, the Tudeh Party campaigned in favor of declaring an Islamic republic. Alternatively, the party could have supported Bazargan against Khomeini, or joined an actual leftist union (likely dominated by the Feda'iyān) that could have thrown its weight behind either Bazargan or Khomeini. The potential for the latter option was made clear in June, when the Feda'iyān, Shariat-Madari's Muslim People's Republican Party, the National Democratic Front, the National Front, and the Mujahideen united to demand a constituent assembly rather than allow the provisional government to put its draft constitution to an immediate referendum.[106] The Tudeh Party instead sat out the united demonstration of these parties on June 15, proffering its own proposed changes that accepted the basic structure.[107] The following month, the party published an open letter in its main organ, *Mardom,* criticizing both the "left-extremist groups" for acting as an "obstacle on the way to understanding between the true religious revolutionaries and the adherents of scientific socialism" and the Bazargan government for representing the "demands of the Iranian liberal bourgeoisie" against those of the "revolutionary movement of Iran."[108] Mikhail Kriutikhin, the Telegrafnoye agentstvo Sovetskogo Soyuza (TASS; Telegraph Agency of the Soviet Union) correspondent in Tehran, supported the Tudeh Party's position, arguing that Khomeini's goal was "to make the transitional period as short as possible to prevent the counterrevolutionaries from closing their ranks and endangering the people's achievements and plans." The Feda'iyān, Mujahideen, and others who were working with the bourgeois liberals to fight the referendum were guilty of "left adventurism" and putting the revolution itself at risk. According to Kriutikhin, the Tudeh Party was right to support Khomeini by "pointing out that the method by which the constitution is adopted is of less importance than its content."[109]

In the early months of the revolution, East Berlin, Moscow, and the Tudeh Party saw Iran as having embarked upon a revolution recognized as typical of many Third World states—what official communist discourse labeled a "popular democratic revolution."[110] This revolution would begin with a class coalition comprising the bulk of the nation against the rule of imperialists, their puppets, and remnants of a feudal regime, and it would necessarily be led by nationalist or religious figures who commanded popular support. An anti-imperialist foreign policy was both an immediate dividend and an indication of the revolution's progressive nature, and it was only a matter of time until the political consciousness of the working masses evolved in the direction of the socialist Left once their economic demands had gone unfulfilled by ruling representatives of the bourgeoisie or petit bourgeoisie. The British embassy in Tehran correctly perceived the Soviet strategy, reporting that "[the Soviets] do not expect Khomeini to survive; their aim is probably to promote a left-wing takeover at the centre, not disintegration at the periphery."[111] Robin S. Gorham in the Middle East Department of the Foreign Office in London concurred, predicting, "Eventually, the failure of the government to satisfy the basic desires of the masses who have become tainted with the baubles of the West will prove advantageous to the Left Wing."[112] The primary dangers for the Soviets and Tudeh Party to avoid in the interim were either a reactionary coup or a consolidation of bourgeois power and a consequent stalling of the revolution, both likely aided by US meddling.[113] In the first months of 1979, allying with Khomeini seemed to be the best bet for this agenda.

Gathering Clouds: May–October 1979

As the struggle over Iran's political future intensified, the Tudeh Party would maintain a significantly more sanguine view of Khomeini and his circle of Islamist supporters than its East German and Soviet interlocutors. The latter paid more attention to the anticommunist and anti-Soviet rhetoric of Khomeini and other religious figures, as well as the increasing antileftist violence of the Pasdaran. They also took a much more balanced view of events in the country at large, evidenced in particular by their analysis of the Kurdish uprising, which the Tudeh Party saw strictly through the prism of Tehran politics and possible international conspiracies. On the economy, the East Germans, Soviets, and Tudeh Party saw positive signs, though some Soviet observers began to wonder if there was enough political will to go beyond bourgeois democratic measures. Overall, however, East Berlin and Moscow still endorsed the strategy of supporting Khomeini because they continued to believe in the progressive nature of the forces behind him, as evidenced by the early economic policies and foreign policy orientation of the IRI.

As early as May, Eastern Bloc observers were concerned about the direction that events were taking. The first secretary of the Czechoslovak embassy told his fellow socialist diplomats in a meeting that month that none of the capitalist countries could understand why the Tudeh Party was supporting Khomeini.[114] The increasingly anticommunist rhetoric of the regime and its supporters worried the socialists too. As the East German embassy reported just a few days later, "Just as in Western [embassies] and among representatives of nonaligned countries (though these with anticommunist motivations), but also now increasingly among comrades of brother embassies there are fears regarding the correctness of the Tudeh Party's tactics, i.e. whether the absolutely uncritical support of Khomeini really serves the revolution and doesn't push away potential allies of the Tudeh Party in the bourgeois, intellectual, and left camps."[115] The danger was compounded by the steps taken by the regime to disarm the Left. The East German ambassador wrote to East Berlin, claiming that he had knowledge of a secret order by the Revolutionary Council to the committees to disarm the forces of the Feda'iyān and Mujahideen, and

FIGURE 5.2 Ayatollah Khomeini versus Ayatollah Marx, a cartoon from the *Trouw* newspaper in the Netherlands, February 16, 1979, drawn by Tom Janssen. *(Used by permission of Tom Janssen)*

that this was supposedly part of the purpose behind the creation of the Pasdaran, as well as a new secret police organization to replace the SAVAK.[116] The East Germans and the Soviets closely monitored attacks on the left and were particularly concerned when Khomeini ordered the closure of the Tudeh Party's *Mardom* in August.[117]

The East German and Soviet views of the Kurdish situation also noticeably diverged from that of the Tudeh Party. For the Tudeh Party leaders the uprising, led by the Hizbî Dêmokiratî Kurdistanî Êran (PDKI; Democratic Party of Iranian Kurdistan), which had leftist sympathies, was only exacerbating the "atmosphere of religious fanaticism and antidemocratic measures" in the country, and a Tudeh Party representative even claimed that PDKI leader Abdul Rahman Ghassemlou was an agent of Western intelligence services.[118] In contrast, the East German Foreign Ministry provided a curiously ambiguous analysis of the Kurdish rebellion.[119] While claiming that counterrevolutionary forces were making use of Kurdish activities, the report noted that the uprising had the support of most of the population and that the PDKI was built upon "peasants, workers, small merchants, and intellectuals" and had distributed feudal holdings to poor and landless peasants. In October the Soviet ambassador told his East German counterpart that Khomeini's attempt to solve the Kurdish problem by military means was a mistake.[120] As time went on, the divide between the Soviets and the Tudeh Party over the IRI's policy toward the Kurds would only deepen, and it would parallel other divisions over the new regime's policies toward its neighbors and national minorities, especially in the wake of the Soviet invasion of Afghanistan.[121] Whereas the Tudeh Party saw Khomeini as the anchor of the revolution and anyone opposing him as counterrevolutionary, the Soviets and the East Germans saw more ambiguity in the question of who really represented the revolution in Iran.

Ultimately, however, the true test of the new regime's progressive nature in the eyes of communist observers would be its economic policies. In the summer and fall of 1979 East Germans, Soviets, and Tudeh Party leaders saw reason for optimism on these grounds. The East German ambassador viewed the nationalization of banks and large industrial concerns as evidence that the clerical leadership was taking popular demands for socioeconomic change seriously.[122] In particular, the draft of the new constitution, with its measures for limiting private property and nationalizing private capital, and talk of equality and a right to work, was seen by both the Tudeh Party and its East European patrons as evidence that the clergy was seeking to appeal to a mass base and would confront the interests of the liberal bourgeoisie.[123] This was especially significant as the Soviet Bloc embassies in Tehran saw the increasing opposition of the bourgeoisie to political Islamization as a sign that a coup attempt might be imminent. The East Germany embassy warned that "the bourgeoisie is of the opinion that the power question will ultimately be decided in Tehran, not in Qom."[124] The alliance of the Tudeh Party with Khomeini was therefore still essential, though the party was hoping to gain more power in the alliance—for example, by placing a party sympathizer at the head of the new security service, as Kianouri told the East Germans and the Soviets.[125]

While the initial economic measures taken by the regime seemed promising, could the road to socialism really proceed via a period of religious government? Soviet observers were divided on this question. Leonid Medvedko, writing in the journal *New Times* in September 1979, argued that the Islamic world as a whole had chosen the noncapitalist path of development, and that Islamic revolution was no longer directed against any particular imperialist power but instead against capitalism in general. This was especially true of Shi'ism, which came into existence as a religion of the weak and oppressed, and the Iranian revolution was, above all, a rejection of an externally imposed political and economic model. The danger was that too great an emphasis on religion and nationalism easily evolved into an instrument of neocolonialism for the suppression of progressive forces. The Islamic leaders who had supposedly successfully pursued socialist orientation according to Medvedko, including Houari Boumedienne of Algeria amd Gamal Abdel Nasser of Egypt, were the ones who saw that nothing in Islam should "conflict with the principles of scientific socialism in tackling the tasks of economic, social, and cultural development."[126]

Alla Ionova, a scholar of Indonesia, outlined what she saw as a trajectory of Islamic political reformism that did not bode well for Iran. The first step of the process of reform, she explained, was the contraposition by reformers of *ijtihad,* defined as "the principle of independent judgments within the boundaries of the texts of the Koran and sunnah," to the principle of *taqlid,* "the tradition of rigorous veneration of medieval Islamic theological authorities with its scholastic-metaphysical type of worldview." In the second stage, the camp of reformers would divide between pragmatists who would try to create ties with the West for the sake of modernization, and a more diverse camp of anti-Westernizers, ranging from more conservative economic elites to a left wing of petit bourgeois radicals with a "socialist coloring." The third and final stage, however, would result in anticommunist unity. Some conservatives would return to the principle of *taqlid* or use *ijtihad* against a rising tide of social protest. Meanwhile, the more pragmatic liberals, out of a supposed concern for a decrease in religiosity, would seek to "save" religion from politics by relegating it to the moral sphere. The process would thereby culminate in a conservative, procapitalist consensus, a notion that Ionova derived from the experience of Indonesia under Suharto.[127] With Iran seemingly in the second stage of this process, it made sense to wonder if it could avoid ending up in the third.

What all of these assessments have in common is a binary view of the world. Either the Iranian Revolution would continue along the noncapitalist path, its religious aspects diminishing along the way, or it would find its way back to the bosom of the imperialist West. The possibility of a durable anti-imperialist theocracy based on a social revolution still escaped these communist analysts. Not all observers took a similarly narrow view, however. The British ambassador met with Ayatollah Mohammad Beheshti, a cofounder of the IRP, and declared, "I came away with a considerable respect for Beheshti. . . . Beheshti himself said that they were trying to create something totally new in the history of man."[128] He was skeptical about how long this would last, however. In his end-of-year summary, he concluded, "I believe that the theocratic state now emerging will survive for the time being, running at a low but for Iranians tolerable level of economic activity; but there is increasing discontent, about economic conditions, about the role of the clergy and about minority rights and I believe that sooner or later it will be superseded, either by a military regime . . . or by a Left-wing secular regime, if the Left is able to profit from the discontent to recruit."[129] The West German embassy, far from dismissing the talk of an Islamic economy, was as early as February 18 (only one week after the victory of the revolution) trying to understand what it might look like. The embassy reported back to Bonn that it would be "neither capitalist nor communist" because it rejected the "profit orientation" of Western capitalism, but it also rejected state control of the means of production and overwhelming state influence over the economy as "un-Islamic." According to the report, "This criticism that each economic-political thought system is alien [*fremd*] accords with the feeling of the wide populace in Iran and underlines the claim of Islam to be the religion par excellence of the Third World."[130]

The leaders of the new Islamic regime saw the establishment of a more independent, egalitarian economic policy as an essential part of their revolutionary mandate. In September 1979 the IRI convened a high-level conference to figure out how an Islamic economy would work in practice. While the conference failed to provide definitive answers on the questions of the forms of property over the means of production, the scale and form of the nationalization of industry, and agrarian reform, there was a lot of substantive discussion, led by Abolhasan Bani-Sadr, about what kind of economy would be consonant with Islamic law and values. When accused of being "Marxists in robes" [*Marxisten in Kutten*], Bani-Sadr replied that the Islamic economy would recognize private property in industry and agriculture, but only so far as its means of acquisition and growth was in accordance with Islamic law, and with the caveat that the clergy reserved the right to control and influence the private sector. The head of the National Iranian Oil Company shot back, "It's not your job to get involved in things that you don't understand." The Islamists, led again by Bani-Sadr, were also firm in arguing that economic independence from the West was a central objective, even if it meant a temporary economic regression, which also put them at odds with representatives of business and the provisional government.[131] Publicly, representatives of the IRI were clear that the Marxists did not have the right answers. The Iranian minister of foreign affairs, addressing the United Nations General Assembly in October, declared that "Marx knew very little about Islam or Afro-Asian societies. The opposition of intellectuals to religion in Islamic societies resulted in the weakening of the moral force confronting imperialism. It was wrong to apply Marxist doctrines to Third World societies, and many socialist and liberal observers had as much trouble understanding the Iranian revolution as did the imperialists."[132]

In addition to the theoretical development of a third economic model based on Islam, the Islamic forces around Khomeini were skillful in their use of rhetoric and policy to convince large numbers of people that they did indeed have their economic interests at heart. Khomeini and others divided the population rhetorically into the *mostakbarin* (rich and powerful) and the *mostaz'afin* (poor), turning much of the former ruling family's wealth over to the Mostaz'afin Foundation, which was to use those assets in the interests of the poor.[133] Furthermore, there was a clear difference between the government of Bazargan and the Islamic forces on this score. As Asef Bayat writes, while Bazargan's government officially stopped the Ministry of Labor from further state employment, new revolutionary institutions, including the Pasdaran, "did absorb a good number of the jobless population."[134] Even Kianouri would later admit to Axen in June 1980 that a haphazard land reform was already underway and that "the Pasdaran are oriented against feudalism and help the peasants carry through the decisions."[135] While the overall record of progressive economic reform in the early years of the IRI was decidedly mixed, Bayat notes that "the Islamic leaders were able to mobilize the poor against the poor."[136] In the crucial early years of the revolution, the Islamists would manage to successfully contend with the left on the grounds of social justice in the struggle for popular support.[137]

Despite its concerns about the ultimate direction of Khomeini's supporters and the increasingly antagonistic policies of the regime toward the Left, Moscow still saw Khomeini as its best bet in the fall of 1979. Consequently, the Soviets reaffirmed their continued support for the Tudeh Party's strategy at the highest level. Ponomarev and Ul'ianovskii reassured Kianouri of their support in August, and the Soviet ambassador told his East German counterpart, "Even though because of [Khomeini's] age and inexperience in state affairs these complicated tasks can only be partly fulfilled, it must be acknowledged that under the present circumstances he is the only leading personality in Iran that represents certain anti-imperialist views."[138] Leonid Brezhnev himself summed up Soviet thinking on Iran, emphasizing the international angle, in a conversation with Erich Honecker during a visit to East Berlin in October to mark the thirtieth anniversary of the GDR: "In Iran, not especially positive tendencies have settled in in recent times. The leaders of the Islamic clergy have begun to persecute the progressive forces. They unsparingly suppress the actions of national minorities. . . . Our initiatives regarding the development of good neighborly relations with Iran have thus far found no practical echo in Tehran. We see all of this. However, we also understand something else: the Iranian Revolution has undermined the military-political alliance between Iran and the US."[139] As Brezhnev's statement makes clear, however, Soviet support for Khomeini was becoming increasingly pragmatic, while the Tudeh Party was ever more committed ideologically to the notion of Khomeini as the leader of the revolution.

Thus, as the political situation in Iran became ever tenser and the divisions became clearer—not only between the Islamists around Khomeini and the provisional government of Bazargan but also between both groups and the Left—the Tudeh Party found itself in a difficult and contradictory position. "Despite recent political developments," reported the SED International Relations Department about a conversation of the Tudeh Party with its East German comrades in September, "no pessimistic evaluation of the next period has been expressed." Even with this optimism and the continuing support of Moscow, however, the Tudeh Party told the East Germans in the same conversation that "the Party leadership is nevertheless preparing all measures and steps, if it becomes necessary, to go underground."[140] Some of the East Germans might have picked up on the eerie echoes of the delusional optimism of the German Communist Party in 1932 as it prepared to go underground even before Adolf Hitler's rise to power rather than unite with the socialists or stand and fight—which meant, as Arthur Koestler wrote later, that "we lost the battle against Hitler before it was joined."[141] The Tudeh Party would do the German communists one better, though: it would help Khomeini win the battle.

The November Revolution

As in Russia in 1917, it took two revolutions to bring the new regime into existence: one to remove the monarch, and a second to resolve the dual power situation that resulted. The storming of the American embassy in Tehran on November 4, 1979, and the ensuing hostage crisis broke the political stalemate that had developed between Bazargan's government and the Islamists around Khomeini, including the IRP, by leading Bazargan to resign. Though the taking of the embassy was widely thought to be a spontaneous action of students in Tehran in response to the meeting of Bazargan with Zbigniew Brzezinski in Algiers, the Soviets and the Tudeh Party thought otherwise, and not only because when the Feda'iyān had tried to storm the US embassy back in February the incoming regime had not allowed it.[142] The KGB already claimed to know who "at the very summit of the Iranian leadership" had sanctioned the taking of the embassy, which had been carried out by a trained team from the Pasdaran.[143] Kianouri told Axen that "Khomeini had already sanctioned the occupation of the American embassy before the meeting of Bazargan with Brzezinski in Algiers."[144] This defeat of the "liberal bourgeoisie" and the resulting concentration of power in the hands of the Islamists would produce significantly different reactions from Soviet and Tudeh Party leaders.

For Moscow the seizure of the embassy diminished fears of a West-backed coup and led to a reevaluation of Khomeini's role in the battle for political control in Iran. In a meeting on November 16 the Soviet Foreign

Ministry told representatives of the East German embassy in Moscow that the new polarization in Iran was increasingly between Khomeini and the "leftist democratic forces" that were pushing for an extension of the revolution rather than between Khomeini and the bourgeoisie, as had been the case earlier. The Soviets concluded, "One probably does not have to reckon with American military intervention," diminishing the relevance of the Chilean scenario; on the contrary, they increasingly feared that Khomeini would ultimately reach some sort of rapprochement with the West.[145]

For Kianouri and the Tudeh Party, the embassy seizure not only reconfirmed the anti-imperialist (and, specifically, anti-American) direction of the revolution, but the defeat of the bourgeoisie opened new horizons for socioeconomic transformation, signaling a new stage of the revolution. Kianouri still saw Khomeini's circle as representing the "progressive" elements of the revolution, comparing them to the Narodniki, the Russian Populist revolutionaries of the 1870s.[146] The Tudeh Party campaigned in favor of the new constitution, a much less democratic draft produced by the IRP-dominated Assembly of Experts and now opposed by forces led by Shariat-Madari. Party leaders interpreted this opposition as being because "they [Shariat-Madari's coalition] see particularly in the articles on 'Islamic policy,' which forbids the creation of monopolies and creates limits on property and profit, a threat to the economic and political interests of the big bourgeoisie and foreign capital."[147] In reality, opposition to the constitution also came from the Left. The Mujahideen argued that, by confirming private property and the class system, the Assembly of Experts was contradicting the principles of monotheism by practicing "social dualism."[148] Kianouri dismissed Khomeini's persecution of the Left as directed not against the Soviet Union or the Tudeh Party, which he saw properly as allies, but rather as against "pro-American communists," meaning Maoists and other anti-Soviet leftists. Instead he argued that the Tudeh Party strategy was working and that its position in the country was strengthening, despite the alarmists who worried about the banning of the party's central organs and the sacking of its headquarters. As evidence of this, Kianouri claimed that he had personally met with two members of the Revolutionary Council and that while Khomeini had not given terms for a meeting with the Tudeh Party leadership, he at least had not formally declined.[149] As strange as it may sound, the party's own optimism was nothing compared to the paranoid delusions of its opponents. For example, as the British embassy reported in early 1981, "At present the

Tudeh Party were rather playing up the mullahs, using them as a stalking horse which they could discard at will" and claiming the party had over one hundred thousand members.[150] In the meantime, the party still needed more breathing space, since it had barely any qualified cadres in Azerbaijan Province, a traditional bastion of progressive politics, and none in Khuzestan, the main oil-producing province. The key source of optimism was still that "the Tudeh Party is of the opinion that the class consciousness of the workers will soon break through the delusion [*Verblendung*] of religion."[151]

The Tudeh Party and its Eastern European patrons also began to diverge in their evaluations of the economic progress demonstrated by the regime. In contrast to its earlier optimistic appraisal of the government's economic measures, the East German embassy in Moscow reported in May 1980 that "a year after the victory of the Islamic revolution the leadership around Khomeini domestically has no positive results to boast about. For socioeconomic transformation [*Umgestaltung*] nothing has been seriously undertaken and nothing achieved."[152] A few months later, on the eve of the Iraqi invasion, after a consultation with the Soviets the East German ambassador in Moscow wrote, "The Iranian leadership still has not proposed any social program. Unemployment, inflation, difficulties in the provision for industry and the population characterize the economic situation."[153] Elena Doroshenko concluded that Khomeini's notion of an Islamic economy was more about progress in the field of social morality than about economic progress.[154] Yevgeny Primakov, the director of the Institute of Oriental Studies and a future prime minister, penned a frequently cited article in the main Soviet philosophy journal *Voprosy filosofii* in mid-1980 on "Islam and the Processes of Social Development of the Countries of the Foreign East" that focused primarily on Iran, and especially the so-called monotheistic economics, which was the title of a book (*Eqtesad-e-towhidi*) by new president Bani-Sadr.[155] Primakov presented monotheistic economics as an attempt to modernize the country using Islam without offending the interests of any of the classes that had supported the revolution, including the bourgeoisie. Though he saw political developments in Iran increasingly going in a negative direction, especially with the attacks on the Left, he still saw some hope if the Left could unify and mobilize workers to pressure the regime. The overall picture thus produced skepticism about the possibility of the current Iranian regime embarking on a noncapitalist path of development, and it led the socialist embassies to suspect that Khomeini and the IRP would eventually compromise with the bourgeoisie, producing a version of Islamic rule consonant with their class interests.[156]

The Tudeh Party, however, continued to believe that the Khomeini-led IRI was making economic progress and that transition to the noncapitalist path was still possible. In February 1980, while admitting that the current economic situation was "critical," Kianouri told Hermann Axen that significant progress had been made in the nationalization of industry and land reform, and particularly in the three months since Bazargan's resignation.[157] Four months later he told Axen that the pessimistic appraisal of the Iranian economy in the Western press was incorrect, and that land reform was in progress with the help of the Pasdaran, which was "antifeudally oriented." Kianouri even outlined a strategy to put flesh on the theoretical bones of the noncapitalist path, telling Axen that plans were afoot to create a "coordinating group" including representatives of President Bani-Sadr, Ayatollah Khomeini, the Pasdaran, and the Tudeh Party. To strengthen its economic influence within the regime, the Tudeh Party had written a book of economic proposals and given it to the government; it was also in the process of creating committees of poor and landless peasants.[158] The party therefore seemed to be following the blueprint laid out in the International Meeting in 1960 in Moscow for gradually shifting the ruling coalition to the left. Accordingly, it appealed to the socialist countries to aid the Iranian economy and support its government. Kianouri told Axen that "rapid realization of agreements [with Iran] by socialist countries would signify a great help for the progressive forces in Iran in terms of strengthening their position vis-à-vis the imperialist states."[159] He pushed the Eastern Europeans to increase economic aid to the IRI even though the Soviets had become frustrated with the lack of a new economic agreement with Iran, having sent the head of their State Committee for Foreign Economic Relations on a fruitless visit to Iran in 1979.[160] The Tudeh Party seemed ever more committed to the notion of a revolutionary transformation of Iran, initially in concert with the Islamists, and hoped for help from abroad even though the East Germans and the Soviets were growing skeptical of the revolutionary potential of Khomeini and the IRP.

While evaluations of Khomeini and the IRP were diverging, however, they all still seemed to see Khomeini and the IRP as the better option in the growing battle between the IRP and Bani-Sadr. Bani Sadr was elected the first president of the IRI in January 1980 in a landslide, a somewhat unexpected result made possible because the IRP had failed to field a viable candidate and because Bani-Sadr's personal relationship with Khomeini was very strong. The IRP, already suspicious of Bani-Sadr because he was Western-educated and not a cleric, increasingly came to worry about his political agenda, both foreign and domestic, and especially his attempt to preserve some form of democracy. The new cleavage in Iranian politics would then be between Bani-Sadr's administration on the one hand and, on the other, the IRP, which dominated the Majlis, and was led by Akbar Hashemi Rafsanjani, a cleric and member of the IRP Central Committee who would one day himself become president of Iran.[161]

For a period Khomeini's position was unclear, siding at times with Bani-Sadr and at other times with the IRP. Consequently, the Tudeh Party's position contained some ambiguity. The Soviet position on Bani-Sadr was also hesitant at first; A. Baranov of the Soviet International Department told his East German colleagues that while Khomeini's policies represented the interests of the "broad laboring masses" and the peasantry (particularly in the nationalization program and housing transfers), Bani-Sadr represented the interests of the "petit bourgeoisie," not the "big bourgeoisie" like Bazargan and Shariat-Madari, and his idealistic program of a "classless Islamic society" did have mass support. Bani-Sadr was not said to be pro-American, as Bazargan and Shariat-Madari supposedly were, but his anti-imperialism took the same form as Khomeini's—namely, in opposition to both superpowers. Ultimately Bani-Sadr would not represent a true threat because, while he was elected primarily with the hope of bringing economic improvement, the new constitution severely limited presidential powers in favor of the clergy. Baranov argued that Bani-Sadr's election was just a symptom of the clergy's failure to stabilize the country and rule on its own, and so he represented a further stage on the road to the working-class revolution that the Tudeh Party still envisioned.[162]

A month later Kianouri's take on Bani-Sadr was less ambiguous. He called him an "Islamic Franco-Maoist" who was "pathologically egocentric, aggressive, and dangerous." While he expressed support for some of Bani-Sadr's economic measures, and particularly his nationalization of foreign enterprises and land reform, Kianouri evaluated the revolutionary standing of various political actors in Iran not on specific policies but on the basis of their perceived loyalty to Khomeini, consequently calling Hassan Habibi, the IRP candidate, the most progressive choice.[163] In May the socialist ambassadors dismissed the possibility of a rapprochement between Bani-Sadr and the IRP, instead forecasting that the national bourgeoisie (both secular and religious) would soon turn against the Islamic regime, likely with Bani-Sadr as a rallying point, and would seek to re-build ties to the United States.[164] They were not optimistic about the future direction of Khomeini and the IRP, but it still did not make sense to either Kianouri or the Eastern Europeans to abandon the Tudeh Party's current strategy in favor of an alliance with an opposition led by Bani-Sadr.

As the battle lines of the approaching civil war were being drawn, this position of the Tudeh Party in support of Khomeini was rapidly becoming a far more significant factor on the Iranian political scene. In April 1980 the Revolutionary Council gave an ultimatum to the Left to leave Iran's universities, and though Bani-Sadr tried to get in front of developments by declaring a cultural revolution, it was Khomeini who then established the seven-person Council of the Cultural Revolution comprising mostly members of the IRP. The universities would be shut down for the next three years while the Islamists purged the Left from the campuses. As the battles between the anticlerical Mujahideen (with occasional support from Bani-Sadr) and the IRP were becoming more violent, the Feda'iyān was split over the question of whether to support the Mujahideen in armed confrontation with the IRP. The Feda'iyān Central Committee had already divided unofficially between majority and minority factions at its first postrevolution plenum, held in October 1979, with many in the majority maintaining close ties with the Tudeh Party, to whom they passed on an unofficial transcript of the meeting.[165] In June 1980 the minority officially broke away to form its own faction, and the remaining majority officially rejected armed struggle. While the minority identified the IRI as a regime based on a compromise between the industrial and commercial bour-geoisie, and consequently one that was no longer revolutionary, the ma-jority argued that the IRI was petit bourgeois and therefore progressive and anti-imperialist. The majority's lengthy explanation of the break in its magazine *Kar* in February 1981 also placed a great deal of emphasis on the importance of loyalty to the international communist movement, declaring that "all the groups that do not relentlessly defend the correct-ness of the communist parties against the anticommunist and antisocialist propaganda of global imperialism . . . are the groups that are targeted by the well-known reactionary cliques of imperialism for compromise."[166] Though a formal process of unification with the Tudeh Party would not be approved by the Feda'iyān majority until March 1981, it had essen-tially already accepted the party's view of Iranian politics and the IRI by this point.[167] This was important because, as Kriutikhin, the TASS cor-respondent in Tehran, reported in June 1980, while the Tudeh Party had grown to perhaps twenty-five to thirty thousand members and sympathizers by this point, the Feda'iyān had perhaps three hundred thousand sympathizers in the country at its peak, as opposed to roughly five hundred thousand for the Mujahideen. The Feda'iyān consequently had penetrated the country much more thoroughly, especially among peasants, workers, and national minorities, and Kriutikhin emphasized that "when one writes about this organization, one must state its very heartfelt relationship with the Soviet Union, its striving for cooperation with the international communist movement, as well as its irreconcilability with the Beijing leadership and its accomplices in Iran."[168] While the Feda'iyān's inexperience and "tendency toward extremism" needed to be taken into account, this fundamentally positive evaluation, combined with its acceptance of Tudeh Party leadership, dramatically increased the influence of the latter and the pro-Soviet forces more broadly.

As the Mujahideen (and, increasingly, President Bani-Sadr) on one side and the IRP (with the increasing support of Khomeini) on the other fought over the political structure of the regime, the Tudeh Party and the Feda'iyān majority sided with the IRP, seeing any opposition to the IRI—which was, after all, still holding American hostages—as objectively aiding imperialism. Though the East Germans and Soviets were no longer as worried about the possibility of a Chilean-style coup and were skeptical about the possibility that the clerical regime would embark on a noncapitalist path of development, they continued to support the Tudeh Party's strategy for two reasons. One was Khomeini's and the IRP's continued anti-imperialism and anti-Americanism, especially as compared to their confidence in Bani-Sadr's foreign policy stances. The second was that they still believed that a political victory for the Islamists could only be temporary. As the East German embassy remarked in April 1980, "The utopian ideas of Khomeini of a society free from exploitation on an Islamic basis represent no useful model for a twentieth-century society in Iran."[169] The resilience of the regime in the face of foreign threats—specifically, the Iraqi invasion of September 1980—would make them question the assumed fragility of clerical rule.

From War Abroad to War at Home

The initial impact of the Iraqi invasion was to temporarily dampen the internal conflict between Bani-Sadr and the IRP.[170] While the territorial conflict over the Shatt al-Arab, the waterway that leads to the Persian Gulf south of Basra, went back as far as the era of the Ottomans and the Sa-favids, the Iranian regime, as well as the East Germans and the Soviets, did not see the Iraqi action as any ordinary seizure of territory. As the East German ambassador reported, this was a battle between "mutually exclusive social models with ambitions to expand to other Islamic states," while Soviet ambassador Vladimir Vinogradov saw this as an attempt by Iraq to "weaken the Islamic regime" by employing the forces of "coun-terrevolution and national minorities" against it.[171] Bani-Sadr was thus not just someone clearly ideologically committed to the concept of Islamic revolution and its international expansion; his technocratic skills made him seem like the best chance the IRI had to organize competent military resistance to Saddam Hussein's forces. Early on, the GDR ambassador re-ported, Iran had put up greater resistance than anticipated, the regime remained stable, and domestic and foreign counterrevolution failed to unite.[172] Meanwhile, despite their close relationship with Saddam Hus-sein and the Iraqis, the Soviets quickly refused to take sides and supply Iraq with weapons, with ambassador Vinogradov even offering to arm Iran in a meeting with Prime Minister Mohammad Ali Raja'i on October 4.[173] Though Iran initially responded unfavorably to the Soviet offer, it helped to focus Iranian ire for the invasion on Saddam's supposed Western backers.[174]

The dampening of internal divisions would not last long, however. Once the immediate danger was averted, the IRP began to worry about the formation of a strong military under the control of the president.[175] According to Mohammad Ayatollahi Tabaar, for the Islamists "it was important that the army protected the state from Iraqi forces but not be seen as triumphant."[176] On October 11 Khomeini issued a decree designed to control the rising power and prestige of Bani-Sadr, dictating that all future decisions about the war would be taken by a Supreme Defense Council made up of eight members, including one appointed by the Ma-jlis.[177] The regime cracked down against domestic elements that were real, potential, or imaginary allies of the Iraqis against the background of the simultaneous cultural revolution taking place against the Left. This radicalization of the revolution produced a massive expansion of the Pasdaran, which was under the control of the Revolutionary Council, not the president, and would take up an ever larger part of the burden of fighting Iraq.[178]

As he watched the IRI produce institutions that made it look ever more like a functioning, powerful state, East German ambassador Wolfgang Konschel took a fresh look at the appeal and possibilities—political, economical, and cultural—of Islam as a program of governance, as well as the danger it presented for the Left:

> On the basis of his idealistic, utopian, social ideals, Khomeini cannot be considered a revolutionary in the subjective sense. His views of Islamic justice, his advocacy for the interests of "lower strata of the exploited and poor" (that do not correspond to views of scientific classes [*wissenschaftlicheklassenmässigen Ansichten*]), as well as his views against monarchy, America, and exploitation by international monopolies, nevertheless formed under the objective conditions of the Iranian Revolution an important starting point for the anti-imperialist and progressive goals of the struggle of the Iranian laborers. For the laborers whose worldviews have no scientific basis the slogans of social justice and equality, the condemnation of corruption, usury, and the propagation of chastity, moral purity and the development of small property are very attractive.

While Konschel thought the program of Islamic justice would be ineffective, it would have enough popular support to entrench itself at first, and its ultimate failure would force it to compromise with the bourgeoisie and turn on the Left. Furthermore, he noted, "Khomeini has already passed the peak of his acting as a force for domestic political integration," and without a worthy successor, the Islamic leaders would have to come up with a more concrete program that would produce new groups and leaders. Konschel saw the ongoing cultural revolution as part of an attempt to create a true intellectual center for global Shi'ism, much like Al-Azhar was in Cairo for the Sunnis. Perhaps the most interesting element of Konschel's report was its open-ended conclusion: "The preceding material is sent first of all for our own understanding and the advancement of a creative [*schöpferischen*] discussion with the department [of International Relations of the Central Committee SED] and the [Near and Middle East] sector [of the GDR Foreign Ministry]."[179] At last the East German embassy had acknowledged that they were dealing with something new that needed to be understood on its own terms.

The Tudeh Party had no such epiphany. In the face of renewed domestic conflict, Kianouri held a press conference in November 1980 declaring support of the IRI because of its fight against injustice, capitalism, and imperialism, even invoking Khomeini's un-Marxist distinction between the *mostakbarin* and the *mostaz'afin*.[180] In May 1981 the Tudeh Party organ *Mardom* published an article listing the accomplishments of the IRI, even endorsing the cultural revolution as ridding the country of Western influence and the dominance of the bourgeoisie over Iran's cultural landscape—for example, producing "progressive films whose goal is to expose imperialism and inculcate elevated human feeling that have taken the place of banal shows and films."[181] Fred Halliday, one of the keenest observers of Iran in the West, agreed with the Tudeh Party's strategy, telling the British ambassador in January 1981 that the party's support for the IRP made sense because the regime would only last as long as Khomeini lived, and the Tudeh Party, unlike the Feda'iyān and Mujahideen, was well organized.[182] As the IRP steadily gained the upper hand (and Khomeini's support) against Bani-Sadr in early 1981, the Tudeh Party became more vocal. When Khomeini dismissed Bani-Sadr as president in June, the party released a statement bidding him good riddance, asserting that Bani-Sadr had been a friend of imperialism and that it was lucky that the regime had purged him before he could do irreparable damage to the revolution. The statement expressed the hope that the next president would be unquestioningly loyal to the "Imam line."[183] Bani-Sadr, in hiding, then called for an uprising, and the Mujahideen answered the call, setting off a bomb at an IRP leadership conference that same month that killed IRP leader Ayatollah Beheshti and at least seventy others. As open war broke out between the regime and the Mujahideen (supported by the Feda'iyaā minority), the Tudeh Party condemned them both publicly as "adventurist" and "counterrevolutionary."[184] Tudeh Party support for the regime was more than just rhetorical. Intimately familiar with the workings of Feda'iyān and the Mujahideen, the party actually helped the regime physically exterminate them by revealing their safe houses, according to KGB reports.[185]

Thermidor?

By the time Khomeini finally came for the Tudeh Party leadership, in February 1983, there were very few left to speak up for it. Amazingly enough, despite the fact that the party had been preparing to go underground almost since its return to Iran in 1979—with Kianouri telling the leadership in July 1982 that the party would soon be banned in spite of its support for the regime—the arrests came as a total surprise, and roughly six thousand party members, including almost all of the top leaders, were imprisoned.[186] The leaders, including Kianouri, were then tortured and forced to confess on Iranian television to being Soviet spies, a spectacle

that went on throughout much of 1983 and 1984.[187] The Tudeh Party
was now to be led by a committee in exile directed by Ali Khavari. The
initial party plenum under his direction in December 1983 concluded that
"the policy of the Tudeh Party in view of the domestic development of Iran
was in principle correct, though in questions of organization and security
there were some serious mistakes and weaknesses."[188] More broadly,
however, the Tudeh Party leaders still did not understand what they were
dealing with in the IRI. Meeting with Ul'ianovskii in Moscow soon after
the arrests, Khavari laid out three possible scenarios for the trajectory of
events in Iran: the return of imperialist dominance, all-out civil war, or the
resurrection of a liberal bourgeois regime under someone like Bazargan.[189]
Somehow the idea that an anti-imperialist, populist theocracy might turn
out to be a viable, durable model of statecraft in the twentieth and even
twenty-first centuries had still not occurred to him as a possibility.

Whether that theocracy would fulfill the economic aspirations of those
who made the revolution that created it was a different matter. The month
before the final crackdown against the Tudeh Party, progress toward any
sort of path of noncapitalist development was dealt a possibly greater
blow: the rejection of the long-awaited bill on the revival and allotment
of agricultural land by the Guardian Council.[190] The violent confrontation with the forces on the left had not meant the end of the push for a
more egalitarian, even socialistic economic order. Many of the young activists who had helped form the IRP and supported Khomeini and his
theocratic model of the state did so in the belief that only an Islamic state
could provide a more just economic system, and justice meant a larger
state role in the economy and more redistribution. After the Majlis elections of October 1981, one of these activists, thirty-nine-year old architect Mir Hussein Moussavi, a follower of Ali Shari'ati and an admirer of
Che Guevara, became prime minister. In the Majlis he led a faction known
as the *maktabis,* named after a newsletter that sought to push the IRP
toward a more radical stance, that included roughly 120 of the Majlis's
268 members.[191] Moussavi and the *maktabis* pursued an ambitious economic agenda that included the nationalization of major industries and
foreign trade and the promotion of workers' councils, among other measures, but found themselves consistently stymied by the Guardian Council,
which included a number of more conservative, older clerics led by Grand
Ayatollah Mohammad-Reza Golpayegani.

In what was still a predominantly agricultural country, land reform
stood out as the most pressing item on the economic justice agenda. In

April 1980 the Revolutionary Council had approved a preliminary land reform decree, largely in response to spontaneous, often violent seizures of land, often aided by the Feda'iyān, that had taken place since the revolution. While in principle the law called for a comprehensive redistribution of land, in practice, the work of local land committees was inconsistent, often halted by local revolutionary courts at the urging of large landholders. In October 1981—after Rafsanjani, the speaker of the Majlis, received clearance from Khomeini—the government finally submitted a land reform bill that was more generous to the landlords, but even this failed to gain enough support because leading figures on the Guardian Council openly opposed it.[192] Finally, on December 28, 1982, the Majlis approved a land reform bill that called merely for leasing uncultivated land to landless farmers. As expected, the Guardian Council rejected it, saying that it violated the constitution because it gave too much power to the Ministry of Agriculture, and that many of the provisions violated Islamic law.[193] The hope of the radicals was that Khomeini himself would overrule the Guardian Council, declaring this to be a case of expediency in which even the provisions of Islamic law could be overridden. On January 24, 1983, Khomeini dashed these hopes. As reported by the British embassy, "Khomeini acknowledged in his speech that there were different understandings of Islam and that nearly all members of the Majlis had good intentions. But he warned against deputies being too influenced by any doctrine, whether communism or capitalism, and said that there was a danger that if the Majlis passed legislation which was then rejected by the Guardian Council people would lose faith in the Majlis."[194] Though one might wonder why Khomeini did not fear that it was the Guardian Council that would lose the faith of the people, the effect was devastating to the cause of the *maktabis*. As long as there had been a possibility that Khomeini was really on their side, there had still been hope. Now, as the British embassy reported, many of the radicals were "showing concern that the revolution may be faltering."[195]

The trajectory of the Soviet evaluation of the role of not just the Iranian revolution but of Islam as a whole in politics followed the shifting political situation in the IRI from 1981 to 1983. In February 1981, at the Twenty-Sixth CPSU Congress (the first since the fall of the shah), Brezhnev officially tried to offer an olive branch to religious believers: "In certain countries of the East in recent times Islamic slogans have been actively promoted. We communists relate with respect to the religious convictions of people who confess Islam, as well as other religions. The most important thing is toward which goals those forces that pronounce one or another slogan are aiming. The struggle for liberation can unfold under the slogans of Islam."[196] A year later, with the country in a state of virtual civil war between the regime and the Mujahideen, the picture became darker. Ul'ianovskii published a major article on Iran in *Kommunist* in July 1982, as close to an authoritative statement of policy as could be expected in a public source. In the article, he wrote that there was a part of the clergy that was "aware of the need for carrying on a consistent struggle against the united front of international imperialism headed by the US and for implementing profound social and economic reforms in the interest of the working people," and he subsequently urged leftist forces to unite to further the revolution in this direction.[197] Yet that passage was preceded by a damning critique of the economic theory put forward by the leftist clergy, in which Ul'ianovskii argued that "the understanding of 'Islamic' or 'Monotheistic' economy turns out to be a combination of principles directed toward the defense of petit bourgeois interests from the perspective of Islam." He then delineated a typology of the clergy, including the passage about the more progressively minded clergy, but when discussing the divisions among the "left democratic forces," the clergy was not mentioned. He called for a united front of the leftist progressive forces that might or might not include some elements of the clergy, but he did not mention the IRP or Khomeini specifically.[198] The British embassy in Moscow saw this as the most authoritative Soviet article on Iran since the revolution, and took it to mean that the initial Soviet optimism about the direction of the revolution was gone. Soviet experts at the Institute of Oriental Studies, meeting with officials from the American embassy in Moscow about the article, told them that the "Islamic economy" was actually about promoting the development of the petit bourgeoisie and that such regimes representing petit bourgeois interests could last for a while, pointing to the example of Sukarno's Indonesia.[199] Revealing the new Soviet views on the nature of political actors in Iran, the deputy head of the Middle East Department of the Soviet Foreign Ministry told his British counterparts that "the clergy had removed the workers and peasants from power" while arguing that there were really no fundamental differences between the Mujahideen and the Tudeh Party.[200] Unfortunately, we do not know if this meant that, in practice, the Soviets had told the Tudeh Party to shift its policy and try to help the Feda'iyān minority and the Mujahideen, which were fighting the regime, but no such Tudeh Party shift occurred.

In the aftermath of the crushing of the Tudeh Party and the failure of the land reform bill, the Soviets systematically reversed the earlier theoretical shifts that had made it possible to imagine an Islamic version of the road to socialism. Undermining the notion that Islam contained any meaningful kernels of progressivism, D. E. Eremeev wrote a sociohistorical analysis of shari'a in early 1983 in which he discussed various theories about the origins of Islamic ideology, including that it reflected the ideology of the "commercial-merchant elite of Mecca and Medina" or perhaps Bedouin slave traders. Eremeev argued that while many had pointed to shari'a's supposed lack of provision for private property in land, in the Arabian desert it was livestock, not land, that was the chief form of property, and shari'a certainly affirmed private property over livestock. "In other words, so-called social ownership of land, including pastureland, is only a mask for economic inequality," asserted Eremeev, and *zakat*, or the giving of religious alms to the poor, was nothing more than an attempt to alleviate class enmity between the haves and have-nots that was typical of many capitalist societies.[201] Dmitry Volsky, writing in the *New Times*, commented that "this truly people's revolution . . . has stalled—the political, antimonarchy and anti-imperialist revolution has not developed into a social revolution," pointing specifically to the Guardian Council's blocking of both land reform and the nationalization of foreign trade. Reversing Liudmila Polonskaia's words of a decade earlier, Volsky noted, "The Islamic overtones of the revolution of course are not an imperative of the time in the East, as the votaries of the 'Moslem renaissance' maintain at times."[202] The bitterest attack came from none other than Ul'ianovskii himself, who wrote in June 1983 in an article titled "Moral Principles in Politics and Politics in the Field of Morality" that the clergy had taken Iran on the road to despotism, and that "the fulfillment of the needs of the people should go beyond a return to archaic traditions."[203] As the British embassy remarked, "Soviet disenchantment with Iran has clearly come out of the closet."[204] It was the depth of the disillusionment that revealed the power of the original illusion.

In June 1985 the Feda'iyān majority and the Tudeh Party finally called for the overthrow of the IRI, a regime they characterized as a "medieval theocracy."[205] The following year, at a conference—the Tudeh Party's largest gathering since 1948—the party determined that the Khomeini regime had turned from revolutionary to reactionary back in 1981.[206]

Despite this, however, the party leadership still believed it lacked what Khavari described to Axen in 1984 as a "fundamental class-based evaluation of the clergy."[207] All the talk about medieval theocracies showed that the party had still not fully assimilated the lessons of the Iranian Revolution. Presenting the IRI in this way reflected a view of history in which societies could either move backward or forward along a recognizable axis of political and economic development. Such views were not limited to the Tudeh Party, or to the 1980s, however. Vijay Prashad has written that "atavisms of all kinds emerged to fill the space once taken up by various forms of socialism. Fundamentalist religion, race, and unreconstructed forms of class power emerged from under the wreckage of the Third World project."[208] To see the IRI as some sort of "return of the repressed," however, was to misunderstand both its origins and its legitimizing ideology. Instead the IRI was the product of a synthesis of Soviet-inflected Marxism, various forms of Third World movements, and a modernizing, activist version of Islam. What happened was that something new had been born: a theocracy that saw itself as progressive and committed to anti-imperialism (at least in the anti-American form advocated by the Tudeh Party) and which retained a commitment to economic development and justice, albeit more often honored in the breach than in practice.[209]

The Islamic Republic of Iran would have been unthinkable without the existence of the Soviet Union. This was not merely because of the geopolitical aspect, though it is very likely that without the Soviet Union's potential involvement, the United States would have been much more likely to interfere more forcibly in Iranian politics as it had in the past. It was also not just because of the Soviet encouragement of the Tudeh Party's strategy of supporting Khomeini and his circle against their opponents, from Bazargan to Shariat-Madari to the Mujahideen, though as Mohsen Milani has argued, "had the Tudeh chosen a different path, the fundamentalists would have probably emerged victorious, albeit after more hardship and more compromises with the moderate elements which could have decelerated the revolution's drive toward radicalism."[210] It was also because the Soviet Union's larger project of finding a road to socialist revolution in the developing world, and the practical and theoretical compromises that that entailed, made possible the very conception of something like a modernizing, anti-imperialist theocracy. Rather than viewing the Iranian political scene in the early years after the revolution as the Left versus the Islamists, it makes more sense to see a continuum on which each political actor contains some elements of both Islamism and socialism. At times the Tudeh Party could work with the Feda'iyān, the Feda'iyān could work with the Mujahideen, the Mujahideen could work with Bani-Sadr, Bani-Sadr could work with Khomeini, Khomeini could work with the IRP, and parts of the IRP could work with the Guardian Council. This was possible in large part because each actor made some calculation about the relative proportions of Islamism and socialism in each arrangement and whether or not that proportion could be ideologically acceptable. The international Left, including the Soviet Union, promoted an approach that sought to use elements of religion and nationalism, seeing them as anti-Western and anti-imperialist allies, in order to accelerate the journey of the developing world toward socialism. But this approach also opened a portal for those pursuing the opposite objective: the employment of socialist and anticapitalist rhetoric by religious and nationalist forces seeking to take control of their societies from what they viewed as the forces of secularization, Westernization, and globalization.

CONCLUSION

The Evolution of Socialism

How do we understand socialism as an international phenomenon? How does it compare to the international history of capitalism, which is increasingly a focus of historical study, or to the international histories of other political and economic forms and ideas? What makes socialism distinct is that, at least in its Marxist forms, it is self-consciously and necessarily both international and internationalist. Fred Halliday, in *Revolution and World Politics,* has identified this internationalism as endemic to the revolutionary era that began with the French Revolution of 1789, and he places internationalist ideas into three categories: utopian, calculated, and instrumental.[1] Utopian internationalist ideas are those that are incommensurate with real capabilities, calculated ideas are those that are commensurate with real capabilities, and instrumental ideas are those where the true intention is merely to use internationalism as a cover for national interest. While there is merit to such a classification, there might be a temptation to classify socialist countries' internationalism as a consequence as utopian, calculated, or instrumental. It might make more sense, therefore, to analyze the internationalist elements present in the foreign policy of each socialist country in terms of beliefs, capabilities, and interests. When the policies of two socialist countries diverge, such as the Chinese and Soviet attitudes toward the Indonesian Communist Party possibly attempting to seize power by force, it might be useful to ask whether and how much the divergence can be attributed to divergence in beliefs, capabilities, or interests.

While this scheme has some potential application to the foreign policy of almost any state, its utility in the case of socialist states that professed

263

some version of socialist internationalism is enhanced by their claim to a common ideology. Kathleen Knight, based on a study of the use and interpretation of the term *ideology* in political science during the twentieth and early twenty-first centuries, argues that political scientists have converged on a core definition of the term as "a coherent and relatively stable set of beliefs or values." While this definition emphasizes the intellectual structure of ideology, it seems to miss the function that ideology serves. Having an ideology allows one to make faster, surer judgments about the world, to delineate friend from foe, progress from regression, and to determine the normative as well as the positive value of different options. An ideology facilitates this in part by being an integrated structure, not just a set of beliefs, so that given beliefs or values can be prioritized over others based on current need in order for the ideology as a whole to continue performing this function. As Knight explains, political scientists have, in the context of American politics, come to see political ideologies as part of a spectrum, in which to claim one ideology means to delineate oneself from one's ideological opponents.[2] As long as ideological identification is determined by such spatial demarcations, it is easy to see how certain beliefs or values can be jettisoned while maintaining one's ideological identity as, for instance, a "liberal" or "conservative." It is similarly possible to imagine that if one's ideological structure identifies one as a socialist in opposition to capitalism, one can jettison certain beliefs—for instance, that markets are always in tension with central planning—without abandoning the larger ideology. Ideology therefore might be better defined as a systematically simplified way of understanding reality that facilitates judgment and action. Ideology allows its holders to identify the salient factors in a given situation and use those to determine what to do next.

This framework helps make sense of a socialist world in which different socialist countries, claiming adherence to the same ideology, could make different judgments in foreign and domestic policy without betraying that ideology. Defining themselves in contradistinction to a system of imperialistic capitalism (and believing in the ultimate victory of socialism over that system), different sets of beliefs, capabilities, and interests could produce different conclusions. Soviet belief in the necessity of avoiding full-scale war, and the utility of a uniform and cohesive international communist movement, not only matched Soviet interests but reflected Moscow's best estimation of how to maximize Eastern Bloc capabilities. China's focus on violent disruption in the developing world reflected its capabilities in terms of what sorts of aid it was best equipped to provide, as well as its interests in terms of self-preservation and geopolitical flexibility. Similar analyses could be made of Yugoslavia's global role based on its vision of a nonaligned developing world, East Germany's focus on recognition and competition with West Germany, Cuba's desire to overstretch American resources and divert Washington's focus, and even Romania's attempt to distance itself from the Warsaw Pact by building its own constituency in the developing world. These beliefs, capabilities, and interests were not constant during the course of the Cold War. To take just one example, as Cuba's relationship with the Soviet Union improved in the 1970s, the willingness of the Cuban leadership to entertain the possibility of a parliamentary path to socialism grew, as was evidenced by Fidel Castro's attempts to rein in the "adventurism" of the Chilean Socialist Party. But these adjustments of beliefs, capabilities, and interests did not therefore signal a shift in ideology. Cuba's strategy in Chile was still focused on the goal of establishing a socialist regime in Latin America as a blow against American-led imperialism. Yet as the ultimate victory of the world revolution continually receded beyond the horizon and the process of establishing socialism as a world system became ever more prolonged, the shifts necessitated by the Cold War struggle took their toll on the socialist project itself.

While the ideology was flexible, it was not infinitely malleable. In the course of this process of trial and error to develop a model of socialist development for the Third World, how to get to "social control of the means of production" and what that might ultimately mean began to shift, but not beyond recognizable bounds. For the Soviets the process began as a sort of Stalinism for export, with an emphasis on the development of heavy industry via the state sector, enabled by the provision of aid from the socialist bloc. This often dovetailed with the statist plans and inclinations of leaders in places such as Egypt or India, but as can be seen in the case of Indonesia, Soviet diplomats at times took the initiative in pushing developing countries toward such projects. Even at this stage, though, Joseph Stalin's recommendations to the Indonesian communists on the question of agricultural collectivization demonstrated a willingness to depart from the script he himself wrote. For the Soviets, a strategy of development based on state investment in heavy industry held both economic and political import, because it would create a working class, eventually leading to the creation of a communist party. For the Chinese, such a strategy was backward. Socialist economic development could not precede the political conquest of power, and Beijing's strategy in Indonesia was predicated on the latter.

In any case, Moscow's initial model of state-led industrialization accomplished with aid from socialist countries failed to produce the desired results, economically or politically. For the Soviets it was costly, both in terms of economic resources and in terms of its relations with developing countries, which did not appreciate this degree of interference. The failure of this model—in West Africa, in particular—led others to seek alternative pathways to socialist development. Tanzania countered with a model in which self-reliance replaced external aid, and agricultural development preceded industrial investment. Tanzania's socialist experiment, led by its charismatic president Julius Nyerere, made it a darling of the international Left. Socialists of all sorts came to participate in one way or another, teaching at the University of Dar es Salaam or helping out in the new *ujamaa* villages. The economic failure of *ujamaa* has had many diagnoses. The one favored by Nyerere, and by many on the Left persuaded by the claims of dependency theory at the height of the Third World movement in the 1970s, was that self-reliance, especially for a country that depended upon commodity production, was simply unfeasible given the international terms of trade.[3] The Soviets instead turned back to the market, seeing small-scale trading focused on increasing agricultural productivity, along with the attraction of foreign investment in industry—all within limits, of course—as a necessary stage on the path to a socialist future.

While this shift toward a reintroduction of the market might have seemed to some like a cynical betrayal of socialist ideals, it in fact reflected shifts that were taking place in many socialist countries, beginning in Yugoslavia in the 1950s. Johanna Bockmann has shown how Yugoslav, and later Hungarian, economists began exploring the utility of market reforms in the 1950s and 1960s, subsequently presenting their ideas to international audiences in the First, Second, and Third Worlds.[4] Yakov Feygin has shown how ideas about economic reform based on the reintroduction of market forces were even gaining currency in the Soviet Union itself during the era of Leonid Brezhnev.[5] Julian Gewirtz has detailed how these ideas helped shape the process of Chinese economic reform beginning with the famous Third Plenum of December 1978, as Hungarian, Polish, and Yugoslav economists played a prominent role in shaping the thinking of Chinese academics and policy makers in the 1980s.[6] Gewirtz's narrative challenges the idea that Chinese economic reform was a largely domestic story. This story of economic reform as arising from the pragmatic genius of the Chinese Communist Party, a story that has become very useful for the legitimacy of the regime in Beijing, is often associated with the phrase "crossing the river by feeling for the stones," attributed to Deng Xiaoping but actually uttered by Chen Yun.[7] It also contradicts the notion that the Chinese communist leadership truly intended to abandon socialism, a notion that has only grown more doubtful under the indefinite rule of Xi Jinping.[8] The introduction of market reforms in these contexts was meant to save the socialist project, not to destroy it.

The shift toward a renewed appreciation for the possible role of markets in the transition to a socialist economy was not merely the province of academics and policy makers within socialist states trying to reform their centrally planned systems. It was recognized and even endorsed by left-leaning academics in the West—above all, those who saw the Third World and its socialist experiments as the true global revolutionary vanguard. As late as 1986 Richard Fagen, Carmen Diana Deere, and José Luis Coraggio wrote, "The breakup of the European colonial empires, and assorted national liberation struggles against entrenched elites at home and hegemonic powers abroad, have moved the epicenter of revolutionary activity away from the core capitalist countries . . . this revolutionary activity . . . has been directed toward the construction of socialist alternatives."[9] Scholars examined the policies of such countries as Angola, Mozambique, Nicaragua, and the People's Democratic Republic of Yemen to figure out how this revolution could succeed. In the revealingly titled *Markets within Planning: Socialist Economic Management in the Third World,* published in 1988, Edmund V. K. Fitzgerald and Marc Wuyts looked at the problems that had resulted from the earlier attempts at state-led development and pointed out that "the response to this problematic has generally involved in recent years a greater role for markets (particularly those concerned with labour and the exchange of consumer goods from the small-producer sector), more reliance upon financial control over state enterprises rather than administration from the centre, a greater emphasis on the local organization of social infrastructure and provisioning, and more serious attention to foreign trade criteria in resource allocation."[10]

Such works, however, typically presented these sorts of policy shifts solely as the product of local experiments, assuming that this was done against the weight of opinion coming from Moscow, if indeed they credited Soviet influence at all. In this regard, the contrast between Angola and Mozambique was telling. Angola, heavily reliant on Soviet military, political, and economic support due to the existence of three competing liberation movements and the resulting foreign-assisted civil war, was receptive to Soviet policy recommendations to emphasize production over socialization as the chief economic direction. In Mozambique, Soviet influence was balanced to a degree by pro-Chinese inclinations and Frente de Libertação de Moçambique (FRELIMO; Liberation Front of Mozambique) activists were more thoroughly imbued with the model of Nyerere's Tanzania, which they had used as their rear base for mounting a guerrilla insurgency in the north. The new government there, under the leadership of Samora Machel, moved more rapidly toward collectivized agriculture, limiting private trade, and state takeover of industrial development.[11] Soviet observers criticized Machel's supposedly "weak ideological preparation" and "adventurism" and lamented the influence of both China and Tanzania in Mozambique.[12] By the early 1980s, however, given domestic economic difficulties as well as the exit of China from the African aid scene and other factors, even Mozambique had come to embrace market reforms in the name of socialism.[13] As Teodoro Petkoff, the main theoretician of Venezuela's *Movimiento al Socialismo* (movement toward socialism), said in the early 1990s, "We MASistas will eventually have to sit down to analyze previously held assumptions and reformate our version of utopia."[14]

If socialism was making room for things like markets, private property, and foreign investment, what did it still mean? Sympathetic scholars reviewing the latest experiments in socialist policy making in the Third World laid out definitions of socialism that accommodated such policies without betraying the broader ideological framework. Gordon White, in *Revolutionary Socialist Development in the Third World,* defined a socialist society as one that had "broken the autonomous power of private capital over politics, production, and distribution, abrogated the dominance of the law of value in its capitalist form, and embarked upon a development path which does not rely on the dynamic of private ownership and entrepreneurship," as well as "brought about certain fundamental transformations . . . which reflect the long-standing aspirations of revolutionary socialist movements everywhere, and the basic principles of the founding fathers of 'scientific socialism.'"[15] In other words, the key was that private capital could still exist, as long as it was not "autonomous," and the state was evolving toward a situation in which private initiative would not determine the direction of development. Fagen, Deere, and

Coraggio defined a socialist model as one where "the logic of capital, the profit motive, must be subordinated to and eventually replaced by a socially determined rationality of production and distribution," which would meet three main objectives: orienting production and distribution toward the needs of the majority of the population; "an ending of class, gender, racial, ethnic, and other forms of privilege in access to 'valued goods' such as income, culture, justice, and recreation"; and greater participation for the "popular classes" in policy making.[16] This definition allowed for greater flexibility in terms of means while at the same time expanding the ends, adding new categories of identities and new venues for redistribution to the just system that socialism was supposed to provide. Legacies of this attempt to redefine the economic architecture of socialism still echo through states built on anticapitalist revolutions. Over four decades after the beginning of China's policy of economic reform and "opening up," the Chinese Communist Party leadership is still struggling with the role of the private sector.[17] As recently as 2012, even Iran's Ayatollah Khamene'i was still making his peace with capitalism: "The mere possession of capital and its investment in the progress of the country is not a bad thing. . . . What is contemptible is that capital and capitalism form the basis of all the major decisions made in the country and drag everything toward themselves. . . . This is leech-like capitalism. This is contemptible capitalism. But if some people have capital and they use it to help the country develop—and of course they will also make some profit in this process— then that act [investment] is good, and the profit made is *halal*."[18] These legacies remain as a sort of vestigial guilt reflex within regimes even where it is no longer clear than any trajectory of socialist transformation, however remote, is still in the works.

While the focus of analysis of the development of socialism in the Third World was on economic transformation, the most enduring legacy of socialist countries' attempts to build socialism in Africa, Asia, and Latin America was actually the propagation of the Leninist model of politics. This model included a dominant single party, structured around some form of central committee with a smaller leadership group above it, which operated on the principle of democratic centralism—namely, that all party members were obligated to carry out the decisions taken at the top. This single ruling party often had units dedicated to specific policy areas that enabled policy decisions to be taken within the party and simply carried out by the government rather than having government institutions determine the direction of policy. Such single parties maintained power via control over the military, police, and mass media, as well as by setting up affiliated mass organizations for youth, women, workers, and others. Only a few states adopted and preserved this complete Leninist model, but many others adopted elements of it, some due to the direct involvement of advisers from Cuba, East Germany, the Soviet Union, or elsewhere, and others through a process of institutional imitation. The propagation of the Leninist model of politics outside formal communist parties actually came later than the attempt to promote socialist economics to the postcolonial states. Richard Lowenthal, in an essay titled "The Model of the Totalitarian State," first published in 1967 and then revised in 1976, surveyed the Bolshevik legacy and still found mostly partial or unsuccessful attempts at recreating a party-state structure.[19] By the 1980s the proliferation of Leninist regimes had become more evident. One study from 1983 asserts that "the major long-term impact of the Soviet Union on Third World socialist countries is not so much through economic relationships. . . . [B]ut through a process of institutional *Gleichschaltung,* the imprinting of Soviet-type patterns of behavior and attitude in the crucial genetic years of new socialist regimes."[20] In the cases of regimes with direct relationships to Moscow, such as Angola, Ethiopia, or Mozambique, this imprinting was accomplished by the presence of Soviet Bloc advisers who helped to set up and run many institutions of the new regimes, transmitting both the institutional structure and culture of their home regimes. More important, this was not merely an accidental by-product of an economic aid relationship. As the model of building socialism shifted from state-led industrialization to a greater tolerance for markets and foreign investment, the Soviets turned to the Leninist party-state structure as the guarantor of the ideological faithfulness of the regime. The diffusion of the Leninist political model came later in the game because it was a response to the failure of the exportation of economic Stalinism.

This legacy has remained most clearly in evidence in southern Africa. In most cases, this has meant the continuing in power of liberation movements-cum-ruling parties that were heavily supported by the Soviet Union and its allies during the liberation struggle, including the African National Congress (ANC) in South Africa; FRELIMO in Mozambique, the Movimento Popular de Libertação de Angola (MPLA; People's Movement for the Liberation of Angola); and the South West Africa People's Organization (SWAPO) in Namibia. Those parties that succeeded in coming to power during the Cold War, including FRELIMO and the MPLA, underwent a process of transformation from liberation movement to mass party to "vanguard party" under the direction of Soviet Bloc advisers, copying many of the institutions of the Leninist party-state. Those that came to power later, including SWAPO and the ANC, never formally established such single-party regimes, but they had already adopted elements of the model during the liberation struggle. In the post–Cold War era, all of these parties have moved from single-party regimes to allowing formal electoral competition but maintain what some scholars call single-party dominance, such that they have never actually lost an election in decades of multiparty competition.[21] John Ishiyama, who has studied the persistence of such parties in power in Africa, points out two key factors determining such persistence: "the more repressive a regime was prior to multi-party democracy, the more successful the successor party is likely to be," and "successor parties that were dominated by civilian leaderships, that had penetrated societies and were relatively institutionalized were more likely to survive the end of the Cold War."[22] These erstwhile Leninist ruling parties of southern Africa continue to hold party congresses, where they determine political hierarchies and lay out future policies behind closed doors, inviting delegations from other Leninist parties much as their Communist predecessors did during the Cold War. The MPLA's most recent congresses have included delegations from Cuba and North Korea, as well as from the ANC, Tanzania's Chama Cha Mapinduzi (CCM), FRELIMO, SWAPO, and the Zimbabwe African National Union—Patriotic Front (ZANU-PF).[23]

Not all such parties began as Soviet-supported liberation movements. The CCM, which was formed from the merger of Zanzibar's Afro-Shirazi Party and the Tanganyika African National Union in 1977, has ruled Tanzania since independence in 1961. Its transformation into a Leninist "vanguard party," including party departments for all areas of state policy, was accomplished in the late 1970s under Soviet tutelage despite the lack of an armed liberation struggle, and it underwent only relatively minor organizational changes with the introduction of multiparty elections.[24] The ANC, meanwhile, has in some ways become less democratic over its time in power. By 2001 "the ANC would no longer permit even internal debate about its lack of internal debate," while its adherence to the Leninist principle of "democratic centralism" is still widely criticized in South Africa.[25] While southern Africa was the site of the most direct and widespread diffusion of the Leninist party model, other examples include the Baathist regimes in Iraq and Syria and the Indian National Congress under Indira Gandhi, who, at the height of Indian-Soviet relations, cracked down on internal party democracy and attempted to impose a version of democratic centralism.[26] The Leninist model has proven a useful tool for maintaining centralized rule, controlling personnel, and keeping policy decisions out of the hands of troublesome legislatures, regardless of the ideological nature of the regime.

This last point is crucial because, as Richard Lowenthal predicted in 1976, "The future of the Bolshevik model of the single-party state in developing countries is thus likely to be most effective where the leaders using the model are most successful in emancipating themselves from the specific ideological beliefs that were linked to the model in its country of origin."[27] A study of the continued electoral dominance of the CCM in Tanzania attributed it in large part to the party's exploitation of nostalgia for its role in the liberation struggle, a factor that contributes to single-party dominance in places like Mozambique and Namibia as well.[28] Perhaps no one in southern Africa used the legacy of the liberation struggle and the discourse of anti-imperialism to hold on to power more openly and effectively than Robert Mugabe in Zimbabwe. Yet Mugabe's invocation of these themes, especially in the early 2000s, as his political and economic measures came under increasing international criticism, came after many left-wing observers perceived him as having betrayed the socialist ideals that he and his comrades had supposedly fought for.[29] John Saul, who taught at the University of Dar es Salaam in the 1960s, argued that Mugabe began "to see the class contradictions of an unequal society in merely racial terms" and the program of ZANU-PF "soon withered to become nationalism of a very weary and worn kind."[30] Mugabe's position received significant support from other African leaders, but the identities of some of his most vocal supporters were revealing. Benjamin Mkapa, Tanzania's president from 1995 to 2005 and a darling of the International Monetary Fund and the World Bank best known for his policies of privatization and liberalization, was a vocal supporter, arguing that "to us Africans land is much more than a factor of production" and "in democracy as in all other things, no one size fits all."[31] Another important public ally was Thabo Mbeki, the president of South Africa and leader of the ANC, despite the fact that the ANC had long supported Mugabe's rival Joshua Nkomo while Mugabe supported the ANC's rival, the Pan-African Congress.[32] Supporting Mugabe became yet another way for leaders of single-party dominance regimes to buttress their own legitimacy by reviving the passions of the liberation struggle against European colonialism.

CONCLUSION

What had begun in the early days of Vladimir Lenin and the Comintern as a series of compromises to gain support in the colonial world for the struggle of the first socialist state and the international working-class movement had ended up swallowing the entire movement. Lenin had argued that there was a difference between the nationalism of oppressed and oppressor nations, and that the former was objectively an ally of the global proletariat. His successors made similar arguments regarding the role of religion and religious activism, particularly in the case of Islam, as a potential force for revolutionary change. Once worried about the dangers of "black racism" and how racial consciousness in the liberation struggle of southern Africa would prevent the spread of class consciousness in places like Angola, the Soviets and their allies learned to pay greater attention to racial and ethnic dynamics, encouraging their MPLA protégés to consider these elements in their choice of leaders. Along the way, following the line of thought that whatever was anti-Western was also anti-imperialist and anticapitalist, socialist actors endorsed culture war and growing social conservatism, exemplified by Operation Vijana, where the Tanganyikan African National Union Youth League attacked women in the street for wearing miniskirts in 1968, and the Tudeh Party's endorsement of the Islamists' "cultural revolution" in Iran in the early 1980s. These compromises had been meant to facilitate national self-assertion against Western influence in order to enable developing countries to follow a noncapitalist path. Instead, too often they became the substance of the revolution, providing alternative sources of legitimacy once the economic policy elements had been abandoned.

The Cold War did not end in the developing world, now more often referred to as the Global South, in quite as definitive a manner as it ended in Europe. Where the Berlin Wall fell, the European Union and the North Atlantic Treaty Organization soon moved in, and the West sought to absorb Eastern Europe. There was no such clear moment of socialist collapse in the nations of the Global South, nor was there necessarily a mass desire to join the West, their former colonial masters, even if that had been an option. There was a wave of peace agreements, largely resulting from the unwillingness of the Americans and Soviets to continue supporting their proxies. The apartheid regime fell in South Africa; Namibia gained independence; civil wars ended, albeit temporarily, in

273

Angola and Mozambique; Vietnamese troops pulled out of Cambodia; and elections were held in Nicaragua, where the Sandinista regime met an unexpected defeat. But some regimes stayed in place, especially in southern Africa and East Asia. Some wars continued, in places like Angola, Colombia, and Peru. And some of the leaders who were defeated in the 1990s would return—perhaps most prominently Nicaragua's Daniel Ortega. With the end of the Cold War came the demise of the so-called Second World and its project of building socialism in the Third World. It is easy to write the history of Global South since decolonization as the story of First World–Third World relations, focusing on the relationships between former colonies and their erstwhile metropoles; American political, military, and economic involvement; and the activities of institutions such as International Monetary Fund and the World Bank. The project of building socialism is often treated as an afterthought—at best, merely a weak foil limited in scope and, at worst, nothing more than a bogeyman employed as an excuse for Western neoimperialism. But the attempt to build a socialist future in the Global South was real, it was more pervasive and influential than is often credited, and it has left lasting legacies across Africa, Asia, and Latin America. To ignore it is to miss a large part of the story.

ARCHIVE SOURCES

NOTES

ACKNOWLEDGMENTS

INDEX

ARCHIVE SOURCES

Bulgaria

Tsentralen D'rzhaven Arkhiv (Central State Archives), Sofia

Chile

Archivo Histórico del Ministerio de Relaciones Exteriores (Historical Archive of the Ministry of Foreign Relations), Santiago
Biblioteca Nacional de Chile (National Library of Chile), Santiago

China (People's Republic)

中国外交部开放档案 (Zhongguo Waijiaobu kaifang dang'an—Declassified Chinese Foreign Ministry Archives), Beijing

Germany

Politisches Archiv des Auswärtigen Amts (Political Archive of the Federal Foreign Office), Berlin
Stiftung Archiv der Parteien und Massenorganisationen der DDR—Bundesarchiv (Archive of the Parties and Mass Organizations of the German Democratic Republic—Federal Archives), Berlin

Mozambique

Arquivo Histórico de Moçambique (Historical Archive of Mozambique), Maputo

Portugal

Instituto dos Arquivos Nacionais da Torre do Tombo (Institute of National Archives of the Torre do Tombo), Lisbon

Romania

Arhive Diplomatice ale Ministerul Afacerilor Externe (Diplomatic Archive of the Ministry of Foreign Affairs), Bucharest

Arhivele Naționale Istorice Centrale din România (National Historical Archive of Romania), Bucharest

Russia

Arkhiv Venshneĭ Politikoĭ Rossisskoĭ Federatsii (Foreign Policy Archive of the Russian Federation), Moscow

Gosudarstvennyĭ Arkhiv Rossisskoĭ Federatsii (State Archive of the Russian Federation)

Rossisskiĭ Gosudartvennyĭ Arkhiv Ekonomiki (Russian State Archive of the Economy), Moscow

Rossisskiĭ Gosudarstvennyĭ Arkhiv Noveisheĭ Istorii (Russian State Archive of Contemporary History), Moscow

Rossisskiĭ Gosudarstvennyĭ Arkhiv Sotsial'no-Politicheskoĭ Istorii (Russian State Archive of Sociopolitical History), Moscow

Serbia

Arhiv Jugoslavije (Archive of Yugoslavia), Belgrade

South Africa

South African Department of Foreign Affairs Archive, Pretoria
South African National Defence Force Archive, Pretoria

Tanzania

Tanzania National Archives, Dar es Salaam
Tanzania National Archives, Dodoma Regional Records Centre, Dodoma

United Kingdom

National Archives, Kew

United States

Hoover Institution Library and Archives, Stanford, CA
National Archives and Records Administration, College Park, MD

Zambia

National Archives of Zambia, Lusaka

NOTES

Introduction

1. "Premier Chou En-Lai: Revolutionary Prospects in Africa Excellent!," *Peking Review,* February 14, 1964, 6; "Chou, in Tanzania: Calls U.S. a Bully," *New York Times,* June 6, 1965, 1. The subtitle of the latter article reads "Chinese Leader Says Asian, African, and Latin Areas are Ripe for Revolution."

2. Telegram, Embassy Dar es Salaam to US Department of State, June 13, 1966, RG 59, box 2695, folder Pol Tanzan-US, National Archives and Records Administration.

3. While the term "Third World" has come to be perceived as pejorative and has increasingly been replaced by other terms such as the "Global South," in the period covered in the book, particularly the 1960s and 1970s, the term "Third World" was used as a way to unite countries in Africa, Asia, and Latin America in order to project power on the global stage. See, for example, Mark T. Berger, "After the Third World? History, Destiny, and the Fate of Third Worldism," *Third World Quarterly* 25, no.1 (2004): 9–39; and Vijay Prasad, *The Darker Nations: A People's History of the Third World* (New York: The New Press, 2008).

4. See, for example, Artemy Kalinovsky, *Laboratory of Socialist Development: Cold War Politics and Decolonization in Soviet Tajikistan* (Ithaca, NY: Cornell University Press, 2018); and Gregory J. Massell, *The Surrogate Proletariat: Moslem Women and Revolutionary Strategies in Central Asia, 1919–1929* (Princeton, NJ: Princeton University Press, 2015).

5. Fred Halliday, *Revolution and World Politics: The Rise and Fall of the Sixth Great Power* (Durham, NC: Duke University Press, 1999), 265. See also Ken Post and Phil Wright, *Socialism and Underdevelopment* (New York: Routledge, 1989).

6. See Kevin McDermott and Jeremy Agnew, *The Comintern: An International History from Lenin to Stalin* (London: Palgrave Macmillan, 1996); Manuel Caballero, *Latin America and the Comintern, 1919–1943* (Cambridge: Cambridge University Press, 1987); and Alexander Pantsov, *The Bolsheviks and the Chinese Revolution, 1919–1927* (Honolulu: University of Hawai'i Press, 2000).

7. See, for example, Jerry Hough, *The Struggle for the Third World: Soviet Debates and American Options* (Washington, DC: Brookings Institution, 1986); Arthur Jay Klinghoffer, *Soviet Perspectives on African Socialism* (Teaneck, NJ: Fairleigh Dickinson University Press, 1975); Mark N. Katz, *The Third World in Soviet Military Thought* (London: Routledge, 1982); Galia Golan, *The Soviet Union and National Liberation Movements in the Third World* (London: Unwin Hyman, 1988); and Jeremy Friedman, *Shadow Cold War: The Sino-Soviet Competition for the Third World* (Chapel Hill: University of North Carolina Press, 2015), chap. 2.

8. Natalia Telepneva, "Our Sacred Duty: The Soviet Union, the Liberation Movements in the Portuguese Colonies, and the Cold War, 1961–1975" (PhD diss., London School of Economics, 2014), 181–182. See also Oded Eran, *Mezhdunarodniki: An Assessment of Foreign Policy Expertise in the Making of Soviet Foreign Policy* (Ramat Gan, Israel: Turtledove, 1979).

9. See, for example, Piero Gleijeses, *Conflicting Missions: Havana, Washington, and Africa, 1959–1976* (Chapel Hill: University of North Carolina Press, 2002); Piero Gleijeses, *Visions of Freedom: Havana, Washington, Pretoria, and the Struggle for Southern Africa, 1976–1991* (Chapel Hill: University of North Carolina Press, 2013); Philip Muehlenbeck, *Czechoslovakia in Africa, 1945–1968* (Hampshire, UK: Palgrave Macmillan, 2016); Philip Muehlenbeck and Natalia Telepneva, *Warsaw Pact Intervention in the Third World: Aid and Influence in the Cold War* (London: I. B. Tauris, 2018); Thomas P. Barnett, *Romanian and East German Policies in the Third World: Comparing the Strategies of Ceaușescu and Honecker* (Westport, CT: Praeger, 1992); Johanna Bockman, "Democratic Socialism in Chile and Peru: Revisiting the 'Chicago Boys' as the Origin of Neoliberalism," *Comparative Studies in Society and History* 61, no. 3 (2019): 654–679; Julia Lovell, *Maoism: A Global History* (London: Bodley Head, 2019); Sara Lorenzini, *Global Development: A Cold War History* (Princeton, NJ: Princeton University Press, 2019); and Benjamin Young, "Not There for the Nutmeg: North Korean Advisors in Grenada and Pyongyang's Internationalism, 1979–1983," *Cross-Currents: East Asian History and Culture Review* 7, no. 2 (2018): 364–387.

10. See, for example, Stephanie L. Mudge, *Leftism Reinvented: Western Parties from Socialism to Neoliberalism* (Cambridge, MA: Harvard University Press, 2018); Dennis Dworkin, *Cultural Marxism in Postwar Britain: History, the New Left, and the Origins of Cultural Studies* (Durham, NC: Duke University Press, 1997); Priya Lal, *African Socialism in Postcolonial Tanzania: Between the Village and the World* (Cambridge: Cambridge University Press, 2015); and Michael Kazin, *The Populist Persuasion: An American History* (Ithaca, NY: Cornell University Press, 2017).

11. Odd Arne Westad, *The Cold War: A World History* (New York: Basic Books, 2017), 5, 13.

12. Adom Getachew, *Worldmaking after Empire: The Rise and Fall of Self-Determination* (Princeton, NJ: Princeton University Press, 2020), 4.

13. Quinn Slobodian, *Globalists: The End of Empire and the Birth of Neoliberalism* (Cambridge, MA: Harvard University Press, 2018).

14. See David C. Engerman, *The Price of Aid: The Economic Cold War in India* (Cambridge, MA: Harvard University Press, 2018); and Lorenzini, *Global Development*.

15. James Mark, Artemy M. Kalinovsky, and Steffi Marung, eds., *Alternative Globalizations: Eastern Europe and the Postcolonial World* (Bloomington: Indiana University Press, 2020).

16. See, for example, Gleijeses, *Conflicting Missions;* Gleijeses, *Visions of Freedom;* Muehlenbeck, *Czechoslovakia in Africa;* Tanya Harmer, *Allende's Chile and the Inter-American Cold War* (Chapel Hill: University of North Carolina Press, 2011); and Tuong Vu, *Vietnam's Communist Revolution: The Power and Limits of Ideology* (Cambridge: Cambridge University Press, 2016).

17. See, for example, Jeffrey James Byrne, *Mecca of Revolution: Algeria, Decolonization, and the Third World Order* (Oxford: Oxford University Press, 2016); Renata Keller, *Mexico's Cold War: Cuba, the United States, and the Legacy of the Mexican Revolution* (Cambridge: Cambridge University Press, 2015); and Lal, *African Socialism in Postcolonial Tanzania.*

18. See, for example, Tobias Rupprecht, *Soviet Internationalism after Stalin: Interaction and Exchange between the USSR and Latin America during the Cold War* (Cambridge: Cambridge University Press, 2015); and Austin Jersild, *The Sino-Soviet Alliance: An International History* (Chapel Hill: University of North Carolina Press, 2014).

19. David C. Engerman, quoted in James Mark, Artemy M. Kalinovsky, and Steffi Marung, "Introduction," in Mark, Kalinovsky, and Marung, eds., *Alternative Globalizations,* 8.

20. Daniel Bessner and Fredrik Logevall, "Re-centering the United States in the Historiography of American Foreign Relations," *Texas National Security Review* 3, no. 2 (2020): 38–55.

21. Slobodian, *Globalists,* 26.

22. See, for example, Daniel Ekbladh, *Modernization and the Construction of an American World Order* (Princeton, NJ: Princeton University Press, 2010); Daniel Immerwahr, *Thinking Small: The United States and the Lure of Community Development* (Cambridge, MA: Harvard University Press, 2015); Amy Offner, *Sorting Out the Mixed Economy: The Rise and Fall of Welfare and Developmental States in the Americas* (Princeton, NJ: Princeton University Press, 2019); and Lorenzini, *Global Development.*

23. *Ujamaa,* meaning "familyness" or "togetherness," was the term used by the Tanzanian state led by President Nyerere to describe its socialist policies in the 1960s and 1970s.

24. William Wilson, "Tanzania after Arusha," memorandum to Foreign and Commonwealth Office, March 22, 1967, FCO 31/156, UK National Archives (hereafter UKNA); W. B. L. Monson to Wilson, April 1967, FCO 31/156, UKNA.

25. Sebastian Berg, *Intellectual Radicalism after 1989: Crisis and Re-orientation in the British and American Left* (Bielefeld, Germany: Transcript Verlag, 2016).

26. Vladimir Lenin, "Communism Is Soviet Power + Electrification of the Whole Country," December 22, 1920, http://soviethistory.msu.edu/1921-2/electrification-campaign/communism-is -soviet-power-electrification-of-the-whole-country/.

27. See Ezra Vogel, *Canton under Communism* (Cambridge, MA: Harvard University Press, 2014); Roderick MacFarquhar, *Origins of the Cultural Revolution,* volume 2, *The Great Leap Forward, 1958–1960* (New York: Columbia University Press, 1987); and Frank Dikötter, *Mao's Great Famine* (London: Bloomsbury, 2018).

28. Brian H. Pollitt, "The Rise and Fall of the Cuban Sugar Economy," *Journal of Latin American Studies* 36, no. 2 (2004): 319–348.

29. See Aaron Hale-Dorrell, *Corn Crusade: Khrushchev's Farming Revolution in the Post-Stalin Soviet Union* (Oxford: Oxford University Press, 2018).

30. See, for example, V. I. Lenin, "Working Class and Bourgeois Democracy," *Vpered* 3 (1905), https://www.marxists.org/archive/lenin/works/1905/jan/24.htm; Theodore Van Laue, "'Legal Marxism' and the Fate of Capitalism in Russia," *Review of Politics* 18, no. 1 (1956): 23–46; Fernando Claudin, "Democracy and Dictatorship in Lenin and Kautsky," *New Left Review* 1, no. 106 (1977): 59–76; Carl Boggs and David Plotke, *The Politics of Eurocommunism: Socialism in Transition* (Boston: South End, 1999); Alan Hunt, ed., *Marxism and Democracy* (Atlantic Highlands, NJ: Humanities Press, 1980); and Ernesto Laclau and Chantal Mouffe, *Hegemony and Socialist Strategy: Towards a Radical Democratic Politics* (London: Verso, 2004).

31. Horace D. Davis, "Lenin and Nationalism: The Redirection of the Marxist Theory of Nationalism, 1903–1917," *Science & Society* 31, no. 2 (1967): 164–185.

32. CPSU Central Committee "*50 let Oktiabr'skoi Revoliutsii*" [50 years of the October Revolution], in *KPSS v rezoliutsiiakh i resheniiakh s'ezdov, konferentsii i plenumov TsK* [CPSU in resolutions and decisions of congresses, conferences, and plenums of the CC], 8th ed., vol. 9, (Novosti: Moscow, 1972), 339. See also the discussion on Soviet reactions to the Chilean coup in Chapter 2 of the present volume.

1. Asian Axis

Epigraphs: Sukarno, Independence Day speech, August 17, 1964, https://www.cia.gov/readingroom /document/cia-rdp78-03061a000300010027-0; conversation of Dipa Nusantara Aidit with B. Il'ichev, advisor, Soviet Embassy Jakarta, December 23, 1963, F.5 O.50 D.622, Rossisskiĭ Gosudarstvennyĭ Arkhiv Noveisheĭ Istorii (Russian State Archive of Contemporary History; hereafter RGANI), p. 3.

1. Sukarno, quoted in J. D. Legge, *Sukarno: A Political Biography* (Boston: Allen and Unwin, 1972), 316.

2. Leslie Fry, to Southeast Asia Department, UK Foreign Office, January 9, 1962, FO 371/166506, UK National Archives (hereafter UKNA).

3. Regarding Sukarno and women, see I. Tugarinov, Deputy Chairman of the Committee on Information, MFA, to Mikhail Suslov, August 21, 1956, F.5 O.28 D.443, RGANI, pp. 58–65. Regarding Sukarno's interest in American films, see US Embassy Jakarta to US Department of State, "Congress of the Communist 'League for People's Culture' (LEKRA): Its Aims and Position in Indonesian Cultural Life," March 10, 1959, RG 59, 1955–1959 Central Decimal File, box 3447, folder 756D.001, US National Archives and Records Administration (hereafter NARA), p. 14.

4. UK Embassy Jakarta to UK Foreign Office, March 4, 1963, FO 371/169879, UKNA.

5. See, for example, Kersten Carool, *A History of Islam in Indonesia* (Edinburgh: Edinburgh University Press, 2017); and Kevin Fogg, *Indonesia's Islamic Revolution* (Oxford: Oxford University Press, 2020), 36.

6. See, for example, George McT. Kahin, *Nationalism and Revolution in Indonesia* (Ithaca, NY: Cornell University Press, 1952); Ruth T. McVey, *The Soviet View of the Indonesian Revolution: a Study in the Russian Attitude towards Asian Nationalism* (Ithaca, NY: Cornell University Press, 1957); Ruth T. McVey, *The Rise of Indonesian Communism* (Ithaca, NY: Cornell University Press, 1965); Herbert Feith, *The Decline of Constitutional Democracy in Indonesia* (Ithaca, NY: Cornell University Press, 1962); and Herbert Feith and Lance Castles, eds., *Indonesian Political Thinking, 1945–1965* (Ithaca, NY: Cornell University Press, 1970).

7. For more on the issue of ethnic Chinese citizenship and emigration in Indonesia and Sino-Indonesian relations, see Taomo Zhou, *Migration in the Time of Revolution: China, Indonesia, and the Cold War* (Ithaca, NY: Cornell University Press, 2019).

8. Jeremy Friedman, *Shadow Cold War* (Chapel Hill: University of North Carolina Press, 2015), 143.

9. See Stein Tønneson, "Tracking Multi-directional Dominoes," in "77 Conversations between Chinese and Foreign Leaders on the Wars in Indochina, 1964–77," ed. Odd Arne Westad, Chen Jian, Stein Tønnesson, Nguyen Vu Tungand, and James G. Hershberg (Cold War International History Project Working Paper No. 22, Woodrow Wilson International Center for Scholars, Washington, DC, May 1998), 32–43.

10. Bradley Simpson, *Economists with Guns: Authoritarian Development and U.S.-Indonesian Relations, 1960–1968* (Stanford, CA: Stanford University Press, 2008), 172.

11. McVey, *The Rise of Indonesian Communism,* 12–22, 7–11; Legge, *Sukarno,* 43–49.

12. McVey, *The Rise of Indonesian Communism,* 22; Justus M. Van Der Kroef, *The Communist Party of Indonesia: Its History, Program, and Tactics* (Vancouver: University of British Colombia Publications Centre, 1965), 6.

13. V. I. Lenin, "Report of the Commission on the National and the Colonial Questions," July 26, 1920, https://www.marxists.org/archive/lenin/works/1920/jul/x03.htm#fw3.

14. V. I. Lenin, "Draft Theses on National and Colonial Questions for the Second Congress of the Communist International," June 5, 1920, https://www.marxists.org/archive/lenin/works/1920/jun/05.htm.

15. For more on the problems caused by the PKI's stance on religion, see Jeanne S. Mintz, *Mohammed, Marx, and Marhaen* (New York: Frederick A. Praeger, 1965), 27.

16. McVey, *The Rise of Indonesian Communism,* 95–105.

17. Legge, *Suharno,* 71.

18. Tan Malaka, "Communism and Pan-Islamism," 1922, https://www.marxists.org/archive/malaka/1922-Panislamism.htm. See also Van Der Kroef, *The Communist Party of Indonesia,* 10–11.

19. McVey, *The Rise of Indonesian Communism,* 282; Mintz, *Mohammed, Marx, and Marhaen,* 40.

20. Van Der Kroef, *The Communist Party of Indonesia,* 16–17.

21. Alimin and Muso, quoted in Ragna Boden, *Die Grenzen der Weltmacht: Sowjetische In-donesienpolitik von Stalin bis Breznev* [The limits of a world power: Soviet Indonesia policy from Stalin to Brezhnev] (Stuttgart: Franz Steiner Verlag, 2006), 69. On Alimin's membership in the CPSU, see Leonid Baranov to Andrei Zhdanov, "Materialy ob Indonezii" [Materials on Indonesia], September 13, 1947, F.575 O.1 d.22, Rossisskiĭ Gosudarstvennyĭ Arkhiv Sotsial'no-Politicheskoĭ Istorii (Russian State Archive of Sociopolitical History; hereafter RGASPI), p. 56.

22. Van Der Kroef, *The Communist Party of Indonesia*, 17.

23. Van Der Kroef, *The Communist Party of Indonesia*, 31–32; McVey, *The Soviet View of the Indonesian Revolution*, 14, 16.

24. Baranov to Zhdanov, "Materialy ob Indonezii" [Materials on Indonesia], pp. 14, 26, 58, 28.

25. See Vladislav Zubok and Constantine Pleshakov, *Inside the Kremlin's Cold War: From Stalin to Khrushchev* (Cambridge, MA: Harvard University Press, 1996), 132–133; and Odd Arne Westad, *The Cold War: A World History* (New York: Basic Books, 2017), 97.

26. "Politicheskoe Polozhenie Indonezii Posle Soveshchaniia Predstavitelei Deviati Kompartii" [The Political Situation in Indonesia after the Gathering of the Representatives of the Nine Communist Parties], n.d., F.575 O.1 D.6, RGASPI, pp. 72–73.

27. E. M. Zhukov, quoted in McVey, *The Soviet View of the Indonesian Revolution*, 34.

28. Kahin, *Nationalism and Revolution in Indonesia*, 256–260, 269–272.

29. "Novyi Put' Indoneziiskoi Respubliki" [New road for the Indonesian Republic], Russian translation forwarded from V. G. Grigor'ian, Chariman Foreign Policy Commission CC VKP(b), to Vyacheslav Molotov, October 28, 1952, F.82 O.2 D.1213, RGASPI, pp. 123–141.

30. Van Der Kroef, *The Communist Party of Indonesia*, 33–34.

31. See, for example, Van Der Kroef, *The Communist Party of Indonesia*, 36–37; McVey, *The Soviet View of the Indonesian Revolution*, 38–45; Antonie C. A. Dake, *In the Spirit of the Red Banteng: Indonesian Communists between Moscow and Peking 1959–1965* (The Hague: Mouton, 1973), 8–9; and Mintz, *Mohammed, Marx, and Marhaen*, 92.

32. Boden, *Grenzen der Weltmacht*, 76–77, 79.

33. Astapenko, Third Secretary Southeast Asia division MFA, October 1, 1948, F.091 O.2, papka 2, delo 12, Arkhiv Venshneĭ Politikoĭ Rossisskoĭ Federatsii (Foreign Policy Archive of the Russian Federation; hereafter AVPRF), pp. 107, 80–81.

34. See Robert J. McMahon, *Colonialism and Cold War: The United States and the Struggle for Indonesian Independence, 1945–49* (Ithaca, NY: Cornell University Press, 2011), 251–303.

35. Report of Paul De Groot on conversation with PKI member Gondopratomo, forwarded by Iakob Goldshtein, May 5, 1951, F.17 O.137 D.754, Indonesia 1/51–11/52, RGASPI, pp. 38–40. See also Donald Hindley, *The Communist Party of Indonesia, 1951–1963* (Berkeley: University of California Press, 1963), 22–26.

36. Hindley, *The Communist Party of Indonesia*, 41–48.

37. Peter Edman, *Communism a la Aidit: The Indonesian Communist Party under D. N. Aidit, 1950–1965* (Townsville, Queensland, Australia: Center for Southeast Asian Studies, 1987), 23–26.

38. Rex Mortimer, *Indonesian Communism under Sukarno: Ideology and Politics, 1959–1965* (Ithaca, NY: Cornell University Press, 1974), 30–36.

39. Hindley, *The Communist Party of Indonesia*, 23.

40. Hindley, *The Communist Party of Indonesia*, 25, 47.

41. Mortimer, *Indonesian Communism under Sukarno*, 46.

42. Mortimer, *Indonesian Communism under Sukarno*, 50; Hindley, *The Communist Party of Indonesia*, 31.

43. V. G. Grigor'ian, to Joseph Stalin, October 17, 1950, F.82 O.2 D.1213, RGASPI, p. 1. See also Boden, *Grenzen Der Weltmacht*, 83; and Larisa M. Efimova, "Stalin and the Revival of the Communist Party of Indonesia," *Cold War History* 5, no. 1 (2005): 107–120.

44. V. G. Grigor'ian, to Joseph Stalin, report on the situation of the PKI, October 28, 1952, F.82 O.2 D.1213, RGASPI, pp. 67–70, 79–82.

45. V. G. Grigor'ian, to Joseph Stalin, resolutions of the Central Committee of the PKI titled "Sovremennoe Polozhenie Indonezii I Zadachi Kompartii Indonezii" [Current situation in Indonesia and tasks of the Communist Party of Indonesia], (translated from Chinese into Russian), June 20, 1951, F.82 O.2 D.1213, RGASPI, p. 13.

46. Boden, *Grenzen der Weltmacht,* 84–85.

47. Central Committee, PKI, to Central Committee, CCP, March 20, 1952, F.82 O.2 D.1214, RGASPI, p. 29.

48. Boden, *Grenzen der Weltmacht,* 88, 30–31.

49. Boden, *Grenzen der Weltmacht,* 89.

50. Asmu and Subekti, October 25, 1952, forwarded by V. G. Grigor'ian to Joseph Stalin on October 28, 1952, F.82 O.2 D.1213, RGASPI, pp. 65–66.

51. V. G. Grigor'ian to Vyacheslav Molotov, "Zamechaniia po voprosam, izlozhennym indone-ziiskimi tovarishchami v ikh pis'makh v TsK KPSS, v TsK KP Kitaia, a takzhe v doklade o polozhenii v kompartii Indonezii, predstavlennom t.t. Asmu i Subekti 27 oktiabria 1952 goda" [Remarks on the questions posed by the Indonesian comrades in their letters to the CC CPSU and CC CCP, as well as a paper on the situation in the PKI, presented by comrades Asmu and Subekti 17 October 1952], November 14, 1952, F.82 O.2 D.1214, RGASPI, pp. 5–6.

52. Boden, *Grenzen der Weltmacht,* 90–91.

53. Hindley, *The Communist Party of Indonesia,* 31.

54. US Embassy Jakarta to US Department of State, "The Indonesian Communist Party Congress and Political Program for the Coming Period," April 22, 1954, RG 59, box 3754, folder 756D.0111REG/1-2452, NARA, pp. 19, 24.

55. US Embassy Jakarta to US Department of State, "Annual Report of Indonesian Communist Party Leader," December 9, 1954, RG 59, box 3754, folder 756D.0111REG/1-2452, NARA, p. 7.

56. Hindley, *The Communist Party of Indonesia,* 78–80, 82.

57. Feith, *The Decline of Constitutional Democracy in Indonesia,* 128.

58. V. Vlasov, referent Southeast Asia division Soviet MFA, "Annotatsiia memorandum Khalmar Shakhta of ekonomicheskoi i finansovoi situatsii v Indonezii" [Annotation of Memorandum of Hjalmar Schacht on Economic and Financial Situation in Indonesia], April 10, 1952, AVPRF F.091 O.9, papka 5, delo 4 p. 29.

59. For more on the political fallout from the aid agreement with the United States, see Feith, *The Decline of Constitutional Democracy in Indonesia,* 198–207.

60. Grigor'ian to Stalin, report on the situation of the PKI, pp. 90–92. See also Feith, *Decline of Constitutional Democracy in Indonesia,* 237–239.

61. Feith, *The Decline of Constitutional Democracy in Indonesia,* 340, 373–382. The US embassy was very concerned about the economic consequences of the Ali cabinet's measures: "Foreign investors, including US interests, already worried under Wilopo regime, now (repeat now) jittery and confront bleak prospects even greater obstacles in endeavor to stay in business here. . . . First and probably early blow likely fall on petroleum and all foreign capital interests likely be government move toward operation of a sort if not (repeat not) outright nationalization BPM (Shell) properties in North Sumatra, in violation contractual rights and RTC agreement." US Embassy Jakarta to US Department of State, August 1, 1953, RG 59, box 3754, folder 756D.00W/1-253, NARA.

62. US Embassy Jakarta to US Department of State, "Elections Plans of the Indonesian Communist Party," July 2, 1953, RG 59, box 3754, folder 756D.0111REG/1-2452, NARA. See also D. A. Zhukov to Vasili Kuznetsov, deputy MFA, sending report of P. V. Ivanov, second secretary, and Iu. A. Sholmov, attache, November 23, 1955, F.91 O.8, papka 4, delo 9, AVPRF, pp. 22–31.

63. Feith, *The Decline of Constitutional Democracy in Indonesia,* 359.

64. US Embassy Jakarta to US Department of State, "Further Reaction to Speech of Vice President Hatta," October 31, 1950, RG 59, box 3754, folder 756D.011REG/1-2452, NARA.

65. US Embassy Jakarta to US Department of State, "Annual Report of Indonesian Communist Party Leader," p. 5.

66. Feith, *The Decline of Constitutional Democracy in Indonesia*, 359.

67. N. Bazanov to General Department, Central Committee, CPSU, translation of Aidit's speech at the third plenum of the Central Committee, PKI, August 7, 1955, F.575 O.1 D.1314, RGASPI, p. 99, 93.

68. Dipa Nusantara Aidit, interview with *New York Times* correspondent Tillman Dubrin, *Harian Rak'iat*, December 11, 1954, translated from English by Iu. A. Sholmov, attache Soviet embassy Jakarta, F.91 O.8, papka 29a, delo 1, AVPRF, p. 91.

69. Feith, *The Decline of Constitutional Democracy in Indonesia*, 434–437.

70. "Tezisy obshchego doklada TsK KPI na VI Natsional'nom S'ezde KPI" [Theses of the General Report of the CC PKI at the Sixth National PKI Congress], August 4, 1960, translated from Indonesian and sent by P. Kuznetsov to V. I. Likhachev, F.91 O.13a, papka 30, delo 4, AVPRF, p. 40.

71. Legge, *Sukarno*, 240, 242–243, 270.

72. Sukarno with Cindy Adams, *Sukarno: An Autobiography* (New York: Bobbs-Merrill, 1965), 297–298.

73. Hong Liu, *China and the Shaping of Indonesia, 1949–1965* (Singapore: NUS, 2011), 217–222.

74. Liu, *China and the Shaping of Indonesia*, 223.

75. Legge, *Sukarno*, 270.

76. Liu, *China and the Shaping of Indonesia*, 223–227.

77. Ganis Harsono, *Recollections of an Indonesian Diplomat in the Sukarno Era*, ed. C. L. M. Penders and B. B. Hering (St. Lucia, Queensland, Australia: University of Queensland Press, 1977), 153, 147.

78. Tugarinov to Suslov, pp. 58–65, 58–64.

79. For a much more detailed discussion of Marhaenism, see Mintz, *Mohammed, Marx, and Marhaen*, 55–58; and Legge, *Sukarno*, 72–74.

80. Iu. A. Sholmov, report on the PNI, June 15, 1956, F.91 O.9, papka 5, delo 16, AVPRF, pp. 118–120.

81. Olga Chechetkina, Pravda correspondent, to Mikhail Suslov, "On the Political Situation in Indonesia," September 21, 1956, F.5 O.28 D.443, RGANI, p. 88.

82. D. A. Zhukov to S. K. Tsarapkin, member of collegium MFA, December 12, 1955, F.91 O.8, papka 4, delo 9, AVPRF, pp. 33–37; A. Ivanov, attache Soviet embassy Jakarta, "Ekonomicheskoe Polozhenie Respubliki Indonezii" [Economic situation of the Republic of Indonesia], February 14, 1956, F.91 O.9, papka 5, delo 16, AVPRF, pp. 15–53 A. Ivanov, "Ekonomika Respubliki Indonezii" [Report on the economy of the Republic of Indonesia], July 23, 1956, F.91 O.9, papka 5, delo 17, AVPRF, pp. 29–52.

83. D. A. Zhukov to Vasili Kuznetsove 18, 1956, F.91 O.9, papka 5, delo 16, AVPRF, pp. 181–182.

84. Ivanov, "Report on the Economy of the Republic of Indonesia," p. 52.

85. Conversation of the Subcommission of Trade Delegations of the USSR and Indonesia on questions of economic and technical cooperation, August 10, 1956, F.365 O.2 D.27, Rossisskiĭ Gosudartvennyĭ Arkhiv Ekonomiki (Russian State Archive of the Economy; hereafter RGAE), pp. 28–33.

86. Conversation of N. I. Kolybalov, Indonesian minister of planning Djuanda, September 17, 1956, F.365 O.2 D.27, RGAE, p. 105.

87. For the text of the communiqué, see Communiqué on Soviet-Indonesian agreement on economic and technical cooperation, September 18, 1956, E, pp. 20–21; for the agreed-on terms of

repayment, see copy of the General Agreement on Economic and Technical Cooperation between the USSR and Indonesia, September 15, 1956, F.365 O.2 D.29, RGAE, p. 49; for the initial disagreement over the terms of repayment, see the conversation of negotiations between trade delegations of the USSR and Indonesia on questions of economic and technical cooperation, September 14, 1956, F.365 O.2 D.27, RGAE, pp. 100–103.

88. Olga Chechetkina to Suslov, "Politicheskoe Polozhenia v Indonezii" [The political situation in Indonesia]," p. 76.

89. For more on the Indonesian political situation in 1956–1957, see Feith, *The Decline of Constitutional Democracy in Indonesia*, 462–538.

90. Feith, *The Decline of Constitutional Democracy in Indonesia*, 542–543.

91. Iu. Shomov, second secretary Soviet embassy Jakarta, "Olovodobyvaiushchaia Promyshlennost' Indonezii" [The tin industry of Indonesia], March 20, 1958, F. 91 O.11a, papka 9, delo 1, AVPRF, p. 19. The same report can be found in F.365 O.2 D.1960, RGAE, pp. 43–49.

92. Iu. Shomov, "Neftianye Promysly Severnoi Sumatry" [The oil fields North Sumatra], June 11, 1958, F.91 O.11a, papka 9, delo 1, AVPRF, p. 130.

93. See, for example, Report on the work of the apparatus of the adviser to the Soviet embassy in Indonesia on economic cooperation for the period of February 20–April 20, 1957, F.365 O.2, delo 81, RGAE, pp. 50–58; and P. Baratovskii, Soviet embassy in Indonesia advisor on economic cooperation, to G. M. Prokhorov, temporary head of GKES division for the economies of underdeveloped countries, March 17, 1958, F.365 O.2 D.1960, RGAE, pp. 14–17.

94. Feith, *The Decline of Constitutional Democracy in Indonesia*, 582–585.

95. A. Ivanov, attache Soviet embassy Jakarta, "O Rabote Natsionalizirovannykh Predpriiatii Neftianoi I Oloviannoi Promyshellnosti Indonezii" [On the work of the Nationalized Enterprises of the oil and tin industries of Indonesia], March 30, 1959, F.91 O.12, papka 12, delo 11, AVPRF, p. 16.

96. A. Ivanov, "Obsuzhdenie i Priniiatie Zakonoproekta o Sovetskom Zaime Respubliki Indonezii" [Discussion and acceptance of the bill on the Soviet loan to the Republic of Indonesia], March 20, 1958, F.91 O.11a, papka 9, delo 1, AVPRF, pp. 34–39.

97. V. Agafanov, third secretary Soviet embassy Jakarta, report on PNI, January 20, 1960, F.091 O.16, papka 19, delo 18, AVPRF, p. 36.

98. G. Kondrat'ev, third secretary Soviet embassy Jakarta, report on the Socialist Party of Indonesia, April 12, 1958, F.91 O.11a, papka 9, delo 1, AVPRF, p. 83.

99. See, for example, P. Spiridonov, "Voennoe Polozhenie v Indonezii" [The military situation in Indonesia], April 12, 1958, F.91 O.11a, papka 9, delo 1, AVPRF, pp. 64–70. For more on the US role in supporting the insurrection, see Simpson, *Economists with Guns*, 31–36. See also Audrey R. Kahin and George McT. Kahin, *Subversion as Foreign Policy: The Secret Eisenhower and Dulles Debacle in Indonesia* (Seattle: University of Washington Press, 1997).

100. G. Kondrat'ev, "Political Parties and Social Organizations of Indonesia," F.091 O.16, papka 19, delo 18, AVPRF, pp. 1–23.

101. Feith, *The Decline of Constitutional Democracy in Indonesia*, 543.

102. Mortimer, *Indonesian Communism under Sukarno*, 71.

103. US Embassy Jakarta to US Department of State, "The VIth National Congress of the Communist Party of Indonesia," February 4, 1960, RG 59, box 2208, folder 798.001/2-260, NARA, pp. 15–18.

104. Feith, *The Decline of Constitutional Democracy in Indonesia*, 594–595.

105. US Embassy Jakarta to US Department of State, "The VIth National Congress." See also Mortimer, *Indonesian Communism under Sukarno*, 84–85.

106. "Tezisy obschego doklada" [Theses of the general report], pp. 56, 30–48.

107. US Embassy Jakarta to US Department of State, "The VIth National Congress," pp. 16–17.

108. "Tezisy obschego doklada" [Theses of the general report], p. 49.

109. Giuseppe Boffa, "Rapporto sul mi viaggio in Indonesia" [Report on my visit to Indonesia], APC MF 0465, Fondazione Gramsci Fondo, Rome, pp. 0408–0415.

110. "Tezisy obschego doklada" [Theses of the general report], pp. 99–103. See also Mortimer, *Indonesian Communism under Sukarno*, 276–291.

111. Report on trip of Sukarno to countries of Europe, Asia, and America, April 23, 1959–June 29, 1959," August 13, 1959, F.91 O.12, papka 12, delo 1, AVPRF, p. 62.

112. P. Kuznetsov, temporary chargé Soviet embassy Jakarta, "Vizit Predsediatlia Sovieta Ministrov SSSR t.Khrushcheva v Indoneziiu" [Visit of Chairman Council of Ministers USSR Comrade N. S. Khrushchev to Indonesia], March 6, 1960, F.091 O.16, papka 18, delo 2, AVPRF, p. 8.

113. V. Sigaev, third secretary Soviet embassy Jakarta, "Ob Indoneziiskom Sotsializme" [On Indonesian Socialism], April 25, 1961, F.91 O.14, papka 15, delo 14, AVPRF, p. 33.

114. Friedman, *Shadow Cold War*, 70–71.

115. Sigaev, "Ob Indoneziiskom Sotsializme" [On Indonesian Socialism], pp. 47, 48, 50.

116. Conversation of Boris Mikhailov with Ruslan Abdulgani, December 23, 1960, F.091 O.16, papka 18, delo 5, AVPRF, p. 144. Pancasila (Five Principles) was the original core of Sukarno's ideology, first announced in a speech on June 1, 1945. The five principles were nationalism, internationalism, democracy, social prosperity, and belief in God. Under Guided Democracy, all political parties, in order to remain legal, had to adopt Pancasila, which created difficulties for the PKI, though it ultimately agreed to the principle of belief in God. See Legge, *Sukarno,* 184–186. For the PKI debate on Pancasila, see Mortimer, *Indonesian Communism under Sukarno,* 92–94.

117. Conversation of Boris Mikhailov with Subandrio, December 5, 1960, F.091 O.16, papka 18, delo 5, AVPRF, pp. 112–116.

118. Mortimer, *Indonesian Communism under Sukarno,* 253–254. For a Soviet view of the Eight-Year Plan, see V. Vlasov, first secretary Soviet embassy Jakarta, "8-letnii plan general'ogo razvittia Indonezii" [8 Year Plan of General Development of Indonesia], June 17, 1961, F.91 O.14, papka 15, delo 14, AVPRF, pp. 108–119.

119. V. Agafanov, third secretary Soviet embassy Jakarta, "K voprosu ob agrarnoi reforme v Indonezii" [On the aquestion of agrarian reform in Indonesia], April 12, 1961, F.91 O.14, papka 15, delo 14, AVPRF, pp. 16–31.

120. Conversation of Mikhailov with Abdulgani, p. 146.

121. V. Sigaev, third secretary Soviet embassy Jakarta, "Polozhenie trudiashchikhsia Indonezii" [Situation of the laborers of Indonesia], May 27, 1961, F.91 O.14, papka 15, delo 14, AVPRF, p. 59.

122. Report of Iu. Gankovskii, academic secretary of the Institute of the Peoples of Asia, Soviet Academy of Sciences, to E. P. Volkov, head Southeast Asia division GKES, October 25, 1963, F.365 O.2 D.2097, RGAE, p. 19.

123. Report on conversation of Keith Charles Owen Shann, Australian ambassador to Jakarta, with Boris Mikhailov, November 3, 1964, FO 371/176453, UKNA.

124. Dipa Nusantara Aidit, political report at second plenum, Central Committee, PKI, December 1960, F.91 O.13a, papka 30, delo 4, AVPRF, p. 116.

125. M. H. Lukman, "KPI i Zaiavlenia 81-ogo Partii" [PKI and the Statement of the 81 Parties], *Harian Rak'iat,* May 23, 1961, translated from Indonesian into Russian, F.91 O.14a, papka 30, delo 2, AVPRF, pp. 17–18.

126. Dake, *In the Spirit of the Red Banteng,* 102–104.

127. Zhou, *Migration in the Time of Revolution,* 97–114.

128. US Embassy Jakarta to US Department of State, "Speculations on the Strategic Position of the Communist Party of Indonesia," August 26, 1959, RG 59, box 3447, folder 756D.001, NARA.

129. For a detailed discussion of the citizenship issue and the crisis caused by the military's measures, see David Mozingo, *Chinese Policy toward Indonesia, 1949–1967* (Ithaca, NY: Cornell University Press, 1976), 114–120, 158–192.

130. See Zhou, *Migration in the Time of Revolution,* 115–131.

131. On Beijing's doubts about Indonesia's "turn to the left," see Chinese Embassy, German Democratic Republic, to PRC Ministry of Foreign Affairs (MFA, report on conversation of embassy with the head of the Southeast Division of the MFA, German Democratic Republic, July 11, 1960, Doc 109-01505-03, 中国外交部开放档案 (Zhongguo Waijiaobu kaifang dang'an—Declassified Chinese Foreign Ministry Archives; hereafter CFMA), pp. 6–7. On the Chinese view of Indonesia's anti-imperialism, see Liu Ningyi to Central Committee, PRC MFA, Liaison Department, Peace Committee, report on the meeting of the Asian African People's Solidarity Organization Executive Committee meeting in Bandung, April 21, 1961, Doc 108-00269-05, CFMA, pp. 1–8.

132. Taomo Zhou, "Ambivalent Alliance: Chinese Policy towards Indonesia, 1960–1965," *China Quarterly* 221 (2015): 214.

133. Mozingo, *Chinese Policy toward Indonesia,* 189.

134. Zhou, "Ambivalent Alliance," 221. See also Mozingo, *Chinese Policy toward Indonesia,* 190.

135. Mortimer, *Indonesian Communism under Sukarno,* 186–198.

136. Nasution visited the USSR seeking military aid from January 2 to January 6, 1961. For Sukarno asking the Soviets to use the visit to persuade Nasution of their benevolence, see the conversation of Boris Mikhailov with Sukarno, November 15, 1960, F.091 O.16, papka 18, delo 5, AVPRF, p. 99; for Subandrio attempting the same thing, see the conversation of Boris Mikhailov with Subandrio, December 5, 1960, F.091 O.16, papka 18, delo 5, AVPRF, p. 114. For the Soviet and Chinese estimations of Soviet success in wooing Nasution, see the conversation of Zhang Hanfu, PRC deputy MFA, with Stepan Chervonenko, February 23, 1961, Doc 109-02267-01, CFMA, pp. 3–6. For more on Nasution's visit, see Boden, *Grenzen der Weltmacht,* 213.

137. Dean Acheson, quoted in Simpson, *Economists with Guns,* 46.

138. Report of Gankovskii to Volkov, pp. 17, 22–31, 19–20.

139. Foreign Division of Deutsche Noten Bank, analysis of the economic situation in Indonesia, translated from German by the Soviet embassy in Indonesia, November 2, 1964, F.365 O.2 D.2097, RGAE, p. 161.

140. Simpson, *Economists with Guns,* 87–112. For the Soviet reaction to the American aid offer, see Boris Mikhailov to Central Committee, CPSU, November 15, 1962, F.5 O.50 D.426, RGANI, pp. 163–175.

141. Zhou, *Migration in the Time of Revolution,* 136–141.

142. Legge, *Sukarno,* 331–332.

143. O. Kinkadze, second secretary Soviet embassy Jakarta, and V. Agafanov, third secretary Soviet embassy Jakarta, "K voprosu o politike osovnykh politicheskikh partii Indonezii v oblasti ekonomiki" [On the question of the policies of the basic political parties of Indonesia in the field of the economy], July 6, 1963, F.91 O.16, papka 18, delo 13, AVPRF, p. 106, 108.

144. Simpson, *Economists with Guns,* 109.

145. "Aktenvermerk über eine Aussprache mit Genossen der PKI-Führung am 13.6.63" [Record of a conversation with comrades of the PKI leadership on 13.6.63], June 26, 1963, DY 30/IV A 2/20/667, Strftung Archiv der Parteien und Massenorganisationen der DDR—Bundesarchiv (Archive of the Parties and Mass Organizations of the German Democratic Republic—Federal Archives; hereafter SAPMO-BArch), pp. 16–17.

146. Legge, *Sukarno,* 337–357.

147. Report passed to UK Foreign Office by Australian High Commission, "GANEFO—The Inseparability of Sport and Politics," December 12, 1963, FO 371/169946, UKNA.

148. For great detail on the Games of the New Emerging Forces, see FO 371/169946, UKNA, which contains a year's worth of reports from the British embassy in Jakarta on the subject.

149. Zhou, *Migration in the Time of Revolution,* 148–149.

150. C. Matthew Jones, *Conflict and Confrontation in South East Asia, 1961–1965: Britain, the United States, Indonesia, and the Creation of Malaysia* (Cambridge: Cambridge University Press, 2001).

151. For more on Malaysia and *Konfrontasi*, see Mortimer, *Indonesian Communism under Sukarno*, 208–221.

152. Zhou, *Migration in the Time of Revolution*, 138–139.

153. Conversation of Liu Shaoqi, Chen Yi, and Huang Zhen with Sukarno, Subandrio, Johannes Lemeina, and Sukarni, April 18, 1963, Doc 105-01167-02, CFMA. See also UK Embassy Jakarta to UK Foreign Office, "Account Given by Dr. Subandrio to Reliable Informants Here of the Principal Point of Discussion during Liu Shaoqi's Visit," May 3, 1963, FO 371/169884, UKNA.

154. UK Embassy Jakarta to UK Foreign Office, April 17, 1963, FO 371/169887, UKNA.

155. For Soviet analyses of New Emerging Forces versus Old Established Forces and related concepts, see Southeast Asia Division, Soviet MFA, report on Indonesia, June 2, 1964, F.91 O.17, papka 20, delo 26, AVPRF, pp. 50–60; A. Gusikov, third secretary Soviet embassy Jakarta, "New Emerging Forces," May 10, 1964, F.091 O.20, papka 32, delo 18, AVPRF, pp. 1–6; and P. Kuznetsov, temporary chargé Soviet embassy Jakarta, to S. G. Lapin, deputa MFA, report on Sukarno's Speech of August 17, 1964, August 28, 1964, F.091 O.20, papka 32, delo 18, AVPRF, pp. 64–77.

156. Mortimer, *Indonesian Communism under Sukarno*, 209.

157. Press communiqué of Central Committee, PKI, plenum, December 23, 1963, translated from Indonesian into Russian by Soviet Embassy Jakarta, AVPRF F.91 O.16a, papka 31, delo 2, p. 26. See also "Auszüge aus dem Presse-Kommunique der KP Indonesiens über den politischen Bericht des Gen.Aidit an das 2.Plenum des ZK von 23–26.Dezember 1963 in Djakarta" [Excerpts from the press communiqué of the CP Indonesia about the political report of Comrade Aidit to the second plenum of the CC from 23–26 December 1963 in Jakarta], DY 30/IV A 2/20/668, SAPMO-BArch, pp. 79–84. For the report of the PRC embassy in Jakarta on this plenum from January 4, 1964, see Doc 109-03481-01, 4–5, CFMA.

158. Press communiqué of Central Committee, PKI, p. 28.

159. Conversation of Dipa Nusantara Aidit with B. Il'ichev, secretary of Soviet embassy Jakarta, January 6, 1964, F.5 O.50 D.622, RGANI, pp. 1–2.

160. Report of PRC Embassy Jakarta to PRC MFA, January 9, 1964, Doc 109-03481-01, CFMA, p. 2.

161. For the East German report on this visit based on information from the Soviets, see "Information an die Mitglieder und Kandidaten des Politburos über grundsätzliche Diskussionen zwischen eneier Delegation der KPdSU und der Führung der KP Indonesien" [Information for the members and candidates of the politburo about fundamental discussions between a delegation of the CPSU and the leadership of the CP Indonesia], April 18, 1964, DY 30/IV A 2/20/668, SAPMO-BArch, pp. 85–89. For the Chinese version, based on information from Aidit and Lukman, see the report of the PRC Embassy Jakarta to PRC MFA, February 14, 1964, Doc 109-03481-01, CFMA, pp. 6–11.

162. "Information an die Mitglieder und Kandidaten des Politburos über grundsätzliche Diskussionen zwischen einer Delegation der KPdSU und der Führung der KP Indonesien" [Information for the politburo members and candidates on the basic discussions between a CPSU delegation and the leadership of the CP Indonesia], April 18, 1964, DY 30/IV A 2/20/668, SAPMO-BArch, pp. 88–89.

163. Report of P. A. Sativkov, Pravda editor-in-chief, to Boris Ponamarev and Leonid Fedorovich Il'ichev on visit to Indonesia to attend Afro-Asian journalists' conference, April 14, 1963, F.5 O.55 D.56, RGANI, pp. 153, 152.

164. Report of PRC Embassy Jakarta to PRC MFA, June 27, 1964, CFMA Doc 105-01231-01, CFMA, pp. 5–6.

165. See Kehr, GDR general consul in Indonesia, "Information über den Aufenthalt des Genossen Mikojan an der Spitze einer sowjetichen Parlamentsdelegation in Indonesien" [Information about the stay of Comrade Mikoyan as head of Soviet parliamentary delegation in Indonesia], July 24, 1964, DY 30/IV A 2/20/671, SAPMO-BArch, pp. 136–137.

166. PRC MFA, "苏联同亚非国家关系及在亚非地区的做法" [Soviet relations with Afro-Asian countries and activity in the Afro-Asian region], January 23, 1965, Doc 109-03652-02, CFMA, p. 10.

167. Kehr, GDR general consul in Indonesia, "Information über den Aufenthalt des Genossen Mikojan an der Spitze einer sowjetichen Parlamentsdelegation in Indonesien" [Information about the stay of Comrade Mikoyan as head of Soviet parliamentary delegation in Indonesia], July 24, 1964, DY 30/IV A 2/20/671, SAPMO-BArch, p. 137.

168. For Mikoyan's claim, see Kehr, GDR general consul in Indonesia, "Information über den Aufenthalt des Genossen Mikojan an der Spitze einer sowjetichen Parlamentsdelegation in Indonesien" [Information about the stay of Comrade Mikoyan as head of Soviet parliamentary delegation in Indonesia], p. 138. See also UK Embassy Jakarta to UK Field Office, July 2, 1964, FO 371/175260, UKNA.

169. PRC Embassy Jakarta to PRC MFA and Liaison Department, June 24, 1964, Doc 109-03481-01, CFMA, p. 32. See also PRC Embassy Jakarta to PRC MFA and Liaison Department, July 11, 1964, Doc 105-01231-02, CFMA p. 3. Aidit reported Mikoyan also saying this to the Soviet ambassador, Boris Mikhailov; see conversation of Aidit with Mikhailov, July 3, 1964, F.5 O.50 D.622, RGANI, p. 87.

170. Dipa Nusantara Aidit conversation with P. Kuznetsov, advisor Soviet embassy Jakarta, July 30, 1964, F.5 O.50 D.622, RGANI, p. 160.

171. PRC MFA to PRC Embassy Jakarta, June 30, 1964, Doc 105-01231-01, CFMA, pp. 11–12.

172. Report of PRC MFA, US/Europe Division and USSR/Eastern Europe Division, on Soviet activities in Afro-Asia, March 31, 1965, Doc 109-03652-02, CFMA, pp. 38–39.

173. Zhou, *Migration in the Time of Revolution,* 149.

174. PRC Embassy Jakarta to PRC MFA and Liaison Department, October 16, 1964, Doc 105-01606-01, CFMA, pp. 1–2.

175. Mortimer, *Indonesian Communism under Sukarno,* 295–303.

176. General Consulate, German Democratic Republic, Jakarta, "Aktenvermerk über ein Gespräch mit D.N. Aidit am 14.3.1964" [Record of a conversation with D. N. Aidit on 14.3.1964], March 19, 1964, DY 30/IV A 2/20/667, SAPMO-BArch, p. 123.

177. Dipa Nusantara Aidit, quoted in Mortimer, *Indonesian Communism under Sukarno,* 302.

178. UK Embassy Jakarta to UK Field Office, December 24, 1964, FO 371/175251, UKNA.

179. See, for example, John Roosa, *Pretext for Mass Murder: The September 30th Movement and Suharto's Coup d'Etat in Indonesia* (Madison: University of Wisconsin Press, 2006); Geoffrey B. Robinson, *The Killing Season: A History of the Indonesian Massacres, 1965–1966* (Princeton, NJ: Princeton University Press, 2019); Simpson, *Economists with Guns;* and Julia Lovell, *Maoism: A Global History* (New York: Alfred A. Knopf, 2019).

180. Simpson, *Economists with Guns,* 131–138.

181. Report of Boris Mikhailov to Central Committee, CPSU, on Soviet-Indonesian relations, April 1965, F.091 O.21, papka 33, delo 1, AVPRF, pp. 1–21; instructions of Soviet Ambassador for conversations with Indonesian leaders, May 11, 1965, F.091 O.21, papka 34, delo 14, AVPRF, pp. 7–27; E. I. Sipiagin to V. A. Sergeev, June 17, 1965, F.365 O.2 D.2187, RGAE, p. 20.

182. Report of PRC Embassy Jakarta to PRC MFA on conversation of Chen Yi and Subandrio, August 21, 1965, Doc 109-03641-02, CFMA, pp. 18–19.

183. Report of Mikhail Sytenko, September 30, 1965, F.091 O.21, papka 33, delo 1, AVPRF, p. 40.

184. Report of PRC Embassy Jakarta to PRC MFA on conversation of Chen Yi and Subandrio, p. 19.

185. Reports on Visit of Indonesian economic delegation on nuclear energy, September 20, 1965, Doc 105-01323-02, CFMA. I thank Shen Zhihua for providing me with this document.

186. Report of Boris Mikhailov, April 1965, F.091 O.21, papka 33, delo 1, AVPRF, p. 20.

187. Boden, *Grenzen der Weltmacht,* 316–321.

188. Conversation of Mao Zedong with a PKI delegation, July 4, 1965, in 毛泽东接见外宾谈话记录汇编 [Meetings and conversations of Mao Zedong with foreign guests], vol. 9, 45–54. I thank Chen Jian for providing me with this document.

189. Conversation of Dipa Nusantara Aidit with Shurygin, July 11, 1964, F.5 O.50 D.622, RGANI, p. 82.

190. For Sukarno's speech, see Simpson, *Economists with Guns,* 208; for Zhou Enlai's proposal of a "fifth force," see Dake, *In the Spirit of the Red Banteng,* 326–327.

191. Roosa, *Pretext for Mass Murder.*

192. Mikhail Sytenko to Andrei Gromyko, "Sobytiia 30 Sentiabria i Perspektivy Razvitiia Sovetsko-Indoneziiskikh Otnoshenii (Politicheskoe Pis'mo)" [The events of 30 September and prospects for the development of Soviet-Indonesian relations (political letter)], November 18, 1965, F.091 O.21, papka 33, delo 1, AVPRF, p. 55. In an annotated version of this letter sent out on December 8, 1965 by the Soviet Foreign Ministry to the Central Committee and other embassies, the line was amended to include the phrase "not without prodding from the Chinese leaders"; see A. P. Chistiakov to N. P. Firiubin, December 8, 1965, F.091 O.21, papka 33, delo 1, AVPRF, p. 150.

193. Sytenko to Gromyko, "Sobytiia 30 Sentiabria" [The Events of 30 September], p. 56.

194. Dipa Nusantara Aidit conversation with Mikhailov and group of Central Committee, CPSU, lecturers, March 15, 1965, F.5 O.50 D.713, RGANI, p. 89.

195. Sytenko to Gromyko, "Sobytiia 30 Sentiabria" [The Events of 30 September], p. 55.

196. Zhou, *Migration in the Time of Revolution,* 144–145.

197. Record of Conversation of Mao Zedong with PKI delegation led by Dipa Nusantara Aidit, August 5, 1965, in 毛泽东接见外宾谈话记录汇编 [Meetings and conversations of Mao Zedong with foreign guests], 9:65–94. I thank Chen Jian for providing me with this document.

198. B. Il'ichev, advisor Soviet embassy Jakarta, report on events of September 30 and PKI, November 4, 1965, F.091 O.21, papka 36, delo 26, AVPRF, p. 105; Report of Southeast Asia Division, Soviet MFA, on situation in Indonesia, November 11, 1965, F.091 O.21, papka 36, delo 26, AVPRF, p. 118.

199. Records of conversations of Zhou Enlai with a delegation of the Provisional People's Consultative Conference, October 1, 1965, and October 4, 1965, Doc 105-01917-01, CFMA. I thank Chen Jian for providing me with this document.

200. Central Committee resolution supporting the instructions of the Soviet ambassador in Indonesia, October 1965, F.091 O.21, papka 34, delo 14, AVPRF, pp. 66, 65.

201. Office of the political adviser to commander in chief, Far East, to UK Foreign Office, October 5, 1965, FO 371/180317, UKNA.

202. *U.S. Embassy Tracked Indonesia Mass Murder 1965,* National Security Archive Briefing Book #607, ed. Bradley Simpson, October 17, 2017, https://nsarchive.gwu.edu/briefing-book/indonesia/2017-10-17/indonesia-mass-murder-1965-us-embassy-files. See also Simpson, *Economists with Guns,* 171–206.

203. Zhou, *Migration in the Time of Revolution,* 178, 179.

204. Leonid Brezhnev, speech at CPSU plenum, December 12, 1966, F.2 O.3 D.45, RGANI, pp. 81, 82–83.

205. Report of P. Kuznetsov, temporary chargé of the USSR in Indonesia, to A. S. Chistiakov, October 23, 1964, F.91 O.17, papka 20, delo 26, AVPRF, p. 146.

206. Embassy Jakarta, report on Fourth Congress of the Sentral Organisasi Buruh Seluruh Indonesia, October 24, 1964, F.091 O.20, papka 32, delo 18, AVPRF, p. 117.

207. Sytenko to Gromyko, "Sobytiia 30 Sentiabria" [The Events of 30 September], p. 56.

208. Alla Ionova, *Musul'manskii Natsionalizm v Sovrememmoi Indonezii, 1945–1965* [Islamic nationalism in contemporary Indonesia, 1945–1965] (Moscow: Nauka Press, 1972).

209. Rostislav Ul'ianovskii, "Nekotorye Voprosy Nekapitalisticheskogo Razvitiia Osvobodivshikhsia Stran" [Certain questions of the noncapitalist development of liberated countries], *Kommunist* 1968, no. 1 (1968): 117–118.

210. For Iran, see Chapter 5 of the present volume.

211. Report of Mikhail Sytenko, September 30, 1965, F.091 O.21 Papka 33, delo 1, AVPRF, pp. 47–48.

212. Report of nine-month expedition of Czechoslovak engineers, January 25, 1963, F.5 O.50 D.513, RGANI, p. 20.

213. Sytenko to Gromyko, "Sobytiia 30 Sentiabria" [The Events of 30 September], p. 56.

214. See, for example, Aleksei Yur'evich Drugov and Aleksandr Borisovich Reznikov, *Indoneziia v Period* "Napravliaemoi Demokratii" [Indonesia in the period of "Guided Democracy"] (Moscow: Nauka, 1969).

215. A. B. Belen'skii, A.A. Guber, V. A. Zharkov, and R. A. Ul'ianovskii, *Natsional'no-Osvoboditel'noe Dvizhenie v Indonezii (1942–1965)* [The national liberation movement in Indonesia (1942–1965)] (Moscow: Nauka, 1970), 196–199.

216. For Chile, see Chapter 3 of the present volume.

217. Conversation of Aidit with Il'ichev, January 6, 1964, p. 1.

218. V. Tereshkin to Central Committee, April 27, 1961, F.5 O.50 D.347, RGANI, p. 24.

2. Democratic Communism

Epigraph: Che Guevara, quoted in Régis Debray, *Conversations with Allende: Socialism in Chile* (London: NLB, 1971), 74.

1. Salvador Allende, quoted in Paul E. Sigmund, *The Overthrow of Allende and the Politics of Chile, 1964–1976* (Pittsburgh: University of Pittsburgh Press, 1977), 131.

2. See Herbert Marcuse, *Counterrevolution and Revolt* (Boston: Beacon Press, 1972); and Herbert Marcuse, *Eros and Civilization* (Boston: Beacon, 1955).

3. See Yuri Zhukov, "Oborotni" [Werewolves], *Pravda,* May 30, 1968; and Klaus Mehnert, *Moscow and the New Left* (Berkeley: University of California Press, 1975), 58–70.

4. Jeremy Friedman, *Shadow Cold War* (Chapel Hill: University of North Carolina Press, 2015), 73–74.

5. See, for example, the report of the PRC Embassy in Cairo to PRC Ministry of Foreign Affairs (MFA), March 12, 1962, Doc 109-03220-03, 中国外交部开放档案 (Zhongguo Waijiaobu kaifang dang'an—Declassified Chinese Foreign Ministry Archives; hereafter CFMA), p. 2; and conversation of Shen Jian with Che Guevara, October 13, 1962, Doc 111-00362-03, CFMA, p. 7.

6. See the report of the PRC Embassy in Cuba to PRC MFA and Liaison Department, December 11, 1961, Doc 111-00346-03, CFMA, p. 2, and Friedman, *Shadow Cold War,* 156–158.

7. Leonid Brezhnev, speech at CPSU plenum, June 20, 1967, F.2 O.3 D.65, Rossisskii Gosudarstvennyi Arkhiv Noveishei Istorii (Russian State Archive of Contemporary History; hereafter RGANI), p. 55.

8. Anatoly Dobrynin to Andrei Gromyko, March 15, 1970, F.5 O.62 D.56, RGANI, p. 100. For more on Soviet relations with the Black Panthers and other radical organizations in the United States during this time, see F.5 O.61 D.555, RGANI; and F.5 O.62 D.558, RGANI.

9. Anatoly Dobrynin to Andrei Gromyko, March 15, 1970, F.5 O.62 D.56, RGANI, p. 112.

10. Luis Corvalán, *De lo vivido y lo peleado: Memorias* [Of what was lived and what was fought: Memories] (Santiago: LOM Ediciones, 1997), 100.

11. Conversation of Soviet delegation to Chile with Luis Corvalán and Salvador Allende, October 19, 1964, F.5 O.55 D.115, RGANI, p. 175.

12. Leonid Brezhnev, speech at CPSU plenum, March 22, 1971, F.2 O.3 D.230, RGANI, p. 9.

13. Telex, Guillermo del Pedregal to Chilean MFA, March 31, 1971, 1971 Embajada de Chile en Rusia: Oficios Telex 34, Archivo Histórico del Ministerio de Relaciones Exteriores (Historical Archive of the Ministry of Foreign Relations; hereafter AHMRE).

14. Sigmund, *The Overthrow of Allende,* 147.

15. Corvalán, *De lo vivido y lo peleado,* 7–15.

16. Jonathan Haslam, *The Nixon Administration and the Death of Allende's Chile* (London: Verso, 2005), 7.

17. Nikolai Leonov, "Soviet Intelligence in Latin America during the 'Cold War," trans. Tim Ennis, *Estudios publicos* 73 (1999): 31–32.

18. Communist Party of Chile, *Una linea inquebrantable de conducta ideologica: El Partido Comunista de Chile y el movimiento comunista internacional* [An unbreakable line of ideological conduct: The Communist Party of Chie and the international communist movement] (Santiago: Impresora Horizonte, 1963), 39.

19. See, for example, Tanya Harmer, *Allende's Chile and the Inter-American Cold War* (Chapel Hill: University of North Carolina Press, 2011).

20. *Recopilacion de documentos del Primer Congreso del Partido Comunista Revolucionario de Chile, Febrero 1966* [Compilation of documents from the first congress of the Revolutionary Communist Party of Chile, February 1966] (Toronto: Ediciones Marxistas-Leninistas, 1978).

21. Communist Party of Chile, *Hacia la Conquista de un Gobierno Popular: Documentos del XII Congresso Nacional Del Partido Comunista de Chile* [Toward the conquest of a popular government: Documents of 12th national congress of the Communist Party of Chile] (Santiago: Impresora Horizonte, 1962), 147.

22. Haslam, *The Nixon Administration,* 8.

23. Salomón Corbalán González, quoted in Ignacio Walker, *Del populismo al leninismo y la "inevitabilidad del conflicto": El Partido Socialista de Chile (1933–1973)* [From populism to Leninism and the "inevitability of conflict": The Socialist Party of Chile (1933–1973), Notas Tecnicas 91 (Santiago: CIEPLAN, 1986), 51.

24. Walker, *Del populismo al leninismo,* 51, 49. There were also some in the PS who were intrigued by the Yugoslav model of socialism, though the key supporters of Yugoslavia had been expelled from the party by the time of Allende's election in 1970. See Johanna Bockman, "Democratic Socialism in Chile and Peru: Revisiting the 'Chicago Boys' as the Origin of Neoliberalism," *Comparative Studies in Society and History* 61, no. 3 (2019): 654–679.

25. See PC, *Una Linea Inquebrantable de Conducta Ideologica,* 16; and Luis Corvalán, *Union de las fuerzas revolucionarias y antiimperialistas de America Latina* [Union of the revolutionary and anti-imperialist forces of Latin America] (Santiago: Impresora Horizonte, 1967), 16.

26. Corvalán, *De lo vivido y lo peleado,* 115.

27. "Bemerkungen zum Bericht an das Sekretariat des ZK über die Reise der Delegation des Nationalrates der Nationalen Front unter Leitung des Genossen Werner Kirchhoff nach Chile zur Teilnahme am XXIII Parteitag der Sozialistischen Partei Chiles vom 21 November bis 8 Dezember 1967" [Remarks for a Report to the Secretary of the CC on the trip of a delegation of the National Council of the National Front under the leadership of comrade Werner Kirchhoff to Chile to participate in the XXIII Party Congress of the Chilean Socialist Party from November 21 to December 8, 1967], DY 30/IV A 2/20 724, Stiftung Archiv der Parteien und Massenorganisationen der DDR—

Bundesarchiv (Archive of the Parties and Mass Organizations of the German Democratic Republic—Federal Archives; hereafter SAPMO-BArch).

28. See, for example, the conversation of Aleksandr Anikin with Czechoslovak Ambassador Stanislav Svoboda, December 29, 1966, F.139 O.21 P.5 D.5, Arkhiv Venshneĭ Politikoĭ Rossisskoĭ Federatsii (Foreign Policy Archive of the Russian Federation; hereafter AVPRF), p. 119; and the conversation of Aleksandr Anikin with the United Arab Republic Ambassador to Chile Taufik Chatillo, January 5, 1967, F.139 O.22 P. 6 D.5, AVPRF, p. 7.

29. Response to letter of Aniceto Rodriguez to Walter Ulbricht of August 15, 1968, DY 30/IV A 2/20 724, SAPMO-BArch.

30. Corvalán, *De lo vivido y lo peleado*, 108.

31. Haslam, *The Nixon Administration*, 25, 28–29, 35–36, 6.

32. Soviet ambassador Nikolai Alekseev to Soviet MFA, translation of MIR, "Deklaratsiia i Programma" [Declaration and program], February 15, 1969, AVPRF F.139 O.24 P.8 D.8, pp. 4, 6.

33. Haslam, *The Nixon Administration*, 28–29.

34. Haslam, *The Nixon Administration*, 30.

35. Régis Debray, *Conversations with Allende: The Chilean Revolution* (New York: Pantheon Books, 1971), 97.

36. Corvalán, *De lo vivido y lo peleado*, 124–125; Sigmund, *The Overthrow of Allende*, 244.

37. Report from Soviet Institute of Latin America to CPSU Central Committee, December 22, 1972, F.5 O.64 D.98, RGANI, p. 93.

38. Report of Yuri Andropov to the CPSU Central Committee, August 6, 1970, F.5 O.62 D.565, RGANI, pp. 153–154. The report contains information from Volodia Teitelboim, the PC's second in command, who visited Cuba and Peru in June and July 1970 and asked for military support in the event of challenges to an Allende victory.

39. For more on the Nixon Administration's efforts during and after the election, see Harmer, *Allende's Chile*, 56–64.

40. Report of Yuri Andropov to the CPSU Central Committee, September 8, 1970, F.5 O.62 D.565, RGANI, pp. 171–172.

41. See, for example, the conversation of Radomiro Tomic with the Soviet ambassador Nikolai Alekseev, April 11, 1969, F.5 O.61 D.560, RGANI, p. 63, in which he said that "the development of Chile cannot take place under the current capitalist and monopolist structure of its economy."

42. Sigmund, *The Overthrow of Allende*, 119–120; Haslam, *The Nixon Administration*, 61–62.

43. Luis Corvalán, quoted in Haslam, *The Nixon Administration*, 62.

44. Soviet Embassy in Chile, background report on Salvador Allende, November 21, 1969, F.5 O.61 D.560, RGANI, p. 336.

45. Nikolai Alekseev, "Pobeda levykh sil na prezidentskikh vyborakh v Chili" [The victory of the leftist forces in the presidential elections in Chile], September 27, 1970, F.5 O.62 D.565, RGANI, p. 182.

46. N. I. Zorina, "Chili: Novyi etap istorii" [Chile: A new stage of history], *Latinskaia Amerika* 1 (1971): 21.

47. For more on Nikolai Leonov, see Nikolai Leonov, *Likholet'e* [Tragic years] (Moscow: Russkii Dom, 2003).

48. N. I. Zorina, "Kharakter i perspektivy revoliutsionnogo protsessa v Chili" [Character and perspectives of the revolutionary process in Chile], *Mirovaia Ekonomika i Mezhdunarodnye Otonosheniia* 12 (1971): 59.

49. See, for example, Zorina, "Chili: Novyi etap istorii"; and N. I. Zorina, "Latinskaia Amerika v mirovom revoliutsionnom protsesse" [Latin America in the world revolutionary process], *Latinskaia Amerika* 2 (1971): 8–10.

50. See the report of MFA Department of Latin American Countries, OLAS, August 1971, F.139 O.26 P.10 D.8, AVPRF, p. 3.

51. N. I. Zorina, "Narodnoe Edinstvo i burzhuaznaia demokratiia" [Popular Unity and bourgeois democracy], *Latinskaia Amerika* 2 (1971): 43.

52. Report of OLAS on Chile, August 1971, F.139 O.26 P.10 D.8, AVPRF, p. 7, 5.

53. Report of OLAS on Soviet-Chilean economic cooperation, September 26, 1972, F.139 O.27 P.11 D.8, AVPRF, pp. 40–43; Haslam, *The Nixon Administration,* 153.

54. Report of Soviet Embassy on the Chilean National Commission on Scientific Research and Exchange, January 14, 1972, F.139 O.27 P.11 D.5, AVPRF, p. 7.

55. Report of OLAS on Chilean economic relations with socialist countries, October 10, 1972, F.139 O.27 P.11 D.8, AVPRF, pp. 48–51.

56. Haslam, *The Nixon Administration,* 74.

57. Report of GDR Embassy in Chile, "Zum Besuch Fidel Castros in Chile" [On Fidel Castro's visit to Chile], December 7, 1971, DY 30/IV A 2/20 73, SAPMO-BArch, p. 3.

58. "Llegada a Cuba. Conversacion con el Premier Ministro y con el canciller Raul Roa. Presentacion de Cartas de Gabinete" [Arrival in Cuba. Conversation with the Prime Minister and with Chancellor Raul Roa. Presentation of credentials], December 10, 1970, 1970 Embajada de Chile en Cuba: Oficios, AHMRE, p. 3.

59. November 4, 1971, 1971 Emabajada de Chile en Cuba: Telex, AHMRE. Castro told the ambassador this in a separate conversation after the meeting with Kosygin.

60. "Contesta aerogramma confidencial ECB 2" [Confidential aerogram response ECB 2], January 7, 1971, 1971 Embajada de Chile en Cuba: Oficios Confidenciales, AHMRE, p. 2.

61. Haslam, *The Nixon Administration,* 153.

62. "Cordial trato recibido de parte embajada de la Republica Popular China" [Cordial treatment received from the embassy of the People's Republic of China], April 7, 1971, 1971 Embajada de Chile en Rusia, AHMRE.

63. "Necesidades administrativas en Pekin" [Administrative necessities in Beijing], April 7, 1971, 1971 Embajada de Chile en China: Oficios, AHMRE.

64. "Actual relacion politica bilateral China-Chile" [Current bilateral politican relations China-Chile], August 16, 1971, 1971 Embajada de Chile en China: Oficios, AHMRE, p. 2.

65. Armando Uribe to PRC MFA, October 11, 1971, 1971 Embajada de Chile en China: Oficios, AHMRE, p. 2.

66. Report of OLAS on Sino-Chilean Relations, October 19, 1972, F.139 O.27 P.11 D.8, AVPRF, pp. 55–56.

67. Report of GDR Embassy in Chile, "Zur Aussenpolitik der UP-Regierung" [On the UP government's foreign policy], December 7, 1971, DY 30/IV A 2/20 732, SAPMO-BArch, p. 3.

68. Report of GDR Embassy in Chile, "Zu den Beziehungen Chile-VR China" [On Chile-PR China relations], n.d. [likely July 1972], DY 30/IV A 2/20 732, SAPMO-BArch.

69. "El Presidente de la República, ruego hacer llegar forma urgente texto transcribo a continuación a revista 'Tiempos Nuevos,' Moscu K-6" [President of the republic, please send text urgently which I transcribe below from the journal "New Times" Moscow K-6], December 16, 1970, 1970 Embajada de Chile en Rusia No. 1, AHMRE.

70. Conversation of V. Gromov with Gonzalo Martner, February 11, 1972, F.139 O.27 P.11 D.5, AVPRF, p. 14.

71. Report on meeting of GDR delegation with Allende, "Gedächtnisprotokoll über das Hauptgespräch mit Präsident Allende am 21. Mai 1971" [Memorandum of the main conversation with President Allende on 21 May 1971], May 26, 1971, DY 30/IV A 2/20 728, SAPMO-BArch, p. 3.

72. A. Vasiliev, first secretary, Belarussian UN representative, report on positions of Chile on international questions at the UN, F. 139 O.28 P.12 D.7, AVPRF, pp. 13–20.

73. Conversation of Soviet Embassy with Luis Corvalán, May 19, 1971, F.5 O.63 D.733, RGANI, pp. 64–65.

74. Conversation of Aleksandr Basov with Salvador Allende, November 15, 1971, F.5 O.63 D.736, RGANI, p. 214.

75. Sigmund, *The Overthrow of Allende*, 137–138.

76. Soviet Embassy Chile, report on Chilean economy, n.d. [likely January 1972], F.139 O.27 P.11 D.8, AVPRF, p. 4.

77. Sigmund, *The Overthrow of Allende*, 133–134, 149–151.

78. Conversation of Aleksandr Basov with Orlando Millas, September 15, 1971, F.5 O.63 D.733, RGANI, p. 160.

79. Conversation of Aleksandr Basov with Luis Corvalán, José Cardemartori, Víctor Días, Orlando Millas, and Volodia Teitelboim, October 3, 1971, F.5 O.63 D.733, RGANI, pp. 176–177.

80. Walker, *Del populismo al leninismo*, 1.

81. Report from Abteilung Internationale Verbindungen (AIV; International Relations Department) Central Committee, Sozialistische Einheitspartei Deutschlands (SED; Socialist Unity Party Germany), "Gespräche mit führenden Genossen der Kommunistichen Partei Chiles" [Conversations with leading comrades of the Communist Party of Chile], October 16, 1970, DY 30/IV A 2/20 712, SAPMO-BArch, p. 6.

82. Report of SED Delegation to Chile, "Vermerk über eine Aussprache der Delegation der SED unter Leitung von Genossen Kurt Seibt, Vorsitzender der Zentralen Revisionskommission, mit Vertetern der Parteiführung der Kommunistischen Partei Chiles am 3.2.1971 in Santiago" [Note on a discussion of the SED delegation led by comrade Kurt Seibt, chairman of the central revision commission, with representatives of the party leadership of the Communist Party of Chile on 3.2.71 in Santiago], February 10, 1971, DY 30/IV A 2/20 712, SAPMO-BArch, pp. 3–4.

83. Politburo Protocol No. 7, February 16, 1971, DY/30/J IV 2/2A 1499, SAPMO-BArch, pp. 127–137.

84. Report on reorganization of Socialist Party of Chile, June 18, 1971, F.5 O.63 D.734, RGANI, p. 26.

85. Report on reorganization of Socialist Party of Chile, 133.

86. Report of Nijadz Dizarevic, member of the executive office of the presidency of the League of Yugoslav Communists, about the congress of Socialist Party of Chile in La Serena/Chile/from January 28 to February 1, 1971, and about conversations with President Allende, Secretary General Altamirano, former secretary Rodriguez and the others, February 23, 1971, 2410/206, Arhiv Jugoslavijie (Archive of Yugoslavia).

87. Politburo Information No. 83/71, "Politik der Regierung Allende in den ersten sechs Monaten ihrer Arbeitzeit" [Policy of the Allende government in its first six months of work], June 29, 1971, DY 30/J IV 2/2J 3538, SAPMO-BArch, p. 7.

88. SED AIV, "Zur Situation in der Südprovinz Cautin" [On the situation in the southern province of Cautín], March 23, 1971, DY 30/IV A 2/20 732, SAPMO-BArch, p. 2.

89. Conversation of Walter Ulbricht with Luis Corvalán, "Stenografische Niederschrift: Gespräch des Vorsitzenden des Staatsrates, Walter Ulbricht, mit dem Generalsekretär der Kommunistischen Partei Chiles, Luis Corvalán, am 30. April 1971 in Berlin," April 30, 1971, DY 30/IV A 2/20 712, SAPMO-BArch, p. 7.

90. Telegram, Lützkendorf to Paul Markowski, October 22, 1971, DY 30/IV A 2/20 724, SAPMO-BArch.

91. Conversation of Aleksandr Basov with Luis Corvalán, July 8, 1971, F.5 O.63 D733, RGANI, pp. 93–95.

92. "Sobre un articulo aparecido en el Renmin Ribao con motive Primer Aniversario Gobierno Popular" [On an article that appeared in Renmin Ribao due to the first anniversary of the popular government], November 8, 1971, 1971 Embajada de Chile en China: Oficios, AHMRE.

93. For more on the UP regime's policy in the Third World, see Harmer, *Allende's Chile*, 84–91.

94. Sigmund, *The Overthrow of Allende*, 147.

95. Conversation of Aleksandr Basov with Salvador Allende, February 29, 1972, F.5 O.64 D.698, RGANI, p. 47.

96. See, for example, Aleksandr Basov, "Revoliutsionnyi protsess i problemy ideologicheskoi bor'bi v Chili na sovremennom etape" [The revolutionary process and problems of the ideological struggle in Chile at the current stage], May 30, 1972, F.5 O.64 D.695, RGANI, p. 32; and conversation of Aleksandr Basov with Luis Corvalán, May 9, 1972, F.5 O.64 D.694, RGANI, p. 155.

97. See, for example, Report of Nijadz Dizarevic.

98. Carlos Altamirano, *Informe al Pleno Nacional, Partido Socialista* [Speech at the Socialist Party national plenum] (Santiago: Prensa Latinoamericana, 1971), 8–10, 13, 18.

99. Report of GDR delegation meeting with Allende, "Vermerk über ein Gespräch mit dem Präsidenten der Republik Chile, Genossen Dr. Salvador Allende, am 5.11.1971" [Note on a conversation with the president of the Republic of Chile, comrade Dr. Salvador Allende, on 5.11.1971], November 16, 1971, DY 30/IV A 2/20 713, SAPMO-BArch.

100. Haslam, *The Nixon Administration*, 120.

101. Report of GDR Embassy in Chile, "Zu den Ergebnissen der internen Beratungen der Unidad Popular in El Arrayan" [On the results of the internal consulations of the Popular Unity in El Arryan], February 11, 1972, DY 30/IV B 2/20 258, SAPMO-BArch.

102. Walker, *Del populismo al leninismo*, 95.

103. Orlando Millas, *En pie de guerra: Para defender nuestra revolucion y seguir avanzado* [On war footing: In order to defend our revolutuion and continue advancing] (Santiago: Impresora Horizon, 1972), 16, 17.

104. Telegram, Harry Spindler to Paul Markowski, Georg Stibi, and Dieter Kulitzka, May 17, 1972, DY 30/IV B 2/20 354, SAPMO-BArch.

105. Conversation of Aleksandr Basov with Orlando Millas, May 18, 1972, F.5 O.64 D.694, RGANI, p. 137.

106. Conversation of Basov with Corvalán, May 9, 1972, p. 154.

107. Politburo Information No. 75/72, "Zur gegenwärtigen Lage in Chile" [On the present situation in Chile], n.d. [likely late June 1972], DY 30/J IV 2/2J 4188, SAPMO-BArch, p. 2.

108. Conversation of V. Iudintsev, Soviet embassy advisor with Luiz Fernandez Oña, October 1, 1971, F.5 O.63 D.736, RGANI, p. 177. Fernandez was actually a Cuban intelligence officer and the husband of Beatriz Allende.

109. Conversation of Basov with Millas, May 18, 1972, p. 136.

110. "Zum Brief Allendes an die Vorsitzenden der UP-Parteien sowie zu den linksextremistischen Ausschreitungen in Chile" [On Allende's letter to the chairmen of the UP parties and on the left-extremist riots in Chile], n.d. [likely late July 1972], DY 30/IV B 2/20 258, SAPMO-BArch, p. 2; Haslam, *The Nixon Administration*, 134.

111. Haslam, *The Nixon Administration*, 134.

112. Telegram, Fries to Georg Stibi, Paul Markowski, and Höltge, August 10, 1972, DY 30/IV B 2/20 259, SAPMO-BArch.

113. Report of GDR Embassy in Chile, "Zur Rolle der linksradikalen MIR im Klassenkampf Chiles" [On the role of the left-radical MIR in the Chilean class struggle], September 22, 1972, DY 30/IV B 2/20 354, SAPMO-BArch, p. 6.

114. OLAS MFA report on Chile, November 29, 1972, F.139 O.27 P.11 D.8, AVPRF, p. 94.

115. Politburo Information No. 90/72, "Zur gegenwärtigen Situation in Chile" [On the current situation in Chile], July 31, 1972, DY 30/J IV 2/2J 4232, SAPMO-BArch, p. 8. See also Harmer, *Allende's Chile*, 155.

116. Politburo Information No. 90/72, "Zur gegenwärtigen Situation in Chile," p. 8.

117. A. F. Shulgovskii, "Levoradikal'nye kontseptsii revoliutsionnogo, antiimperialisticheskogo i demokraticheskogo protsessov" [Left-radical conception of revolutionary, anti-imperialist, and democratic processes], *Latinskaia Amerika* 4 (1972): 59.

118. Sigmund, *The Overthrow of Allende,* 196, 190.

119. Aleksandr Basov, "Sovremennoe ekonomicheskoe polozhenie chili" [Contemporary economic situation of Chile], June 27, 1972, F.5 O.64 D.618, RGANI, pp. 89–102.

120. Conversation of Basov with Corvalán, May 9, 1972, p. 110.

121. Aleksandr Basov, "Krizis levogo bloka i perspektivy pravitel'stva Narodnogo Edinstva" [The crisis of the leftist bloc and the prospects of the National Unity government], May 31, 1972, F.5 O.64 D.695, RGANI, p. 56.

122. Haslam, *The Nixon Administration,* 153.

123. Conversation of Luis Corvalán with Erich Honecker, November 24, 1972, DY 30/IV B 2/20 257, SAPMO-BArch, pp. 15, 19.

124. Report on conversation of Boris Ponomarev with Luis Corvalán, December 7, 1972, DY 30/IV B 2/20 257, SAPMO-BArch.

125. Soviet report on visit of Allende, December 27, 1972, DY 30/13928 SAPMO-BArch, p. 2.

126. Corvalán, *De lo vivido y lo peleado,* 144–148; Haslam, *The Nixon Administration,* 153–154.

127. Chilean MFA to PRC MFA, November 20, 1972, 1972 Embajada de Chile en China Notas, AHMRE, 1, 4.

128. Chilean embassy in Beijing to Chilean MFA, December 8, 1972, 1972 Embajada de Chile en China Notas, AHMRE.

129. Conversation of Clodomiro Almeyda with Zhou Enlai, January 30, 1973, 1973 Embajada de Chile en China, AHMRE, pp. 2, 5, 6.

130. Chilean embassy in Beijing to Chilean MFA, February 8, 1973, 1973 Embajada de Chile en China: Telex, AHMRE.

131. Report on Sino-Chilean relations from OLAS MFA, August 8, 1973, F. 139 O.28 P.12 D.7, AVPRF, pp. 102–104. See also Salvador Allende conversation with Aleksandr Basov, February 16, 1973, F.5 O.66 D.1016, RGANI, pp. 40–41.

132. Proposal from AIV to Secretariat, Central Committees, July 19, 1972, DY 30/IV B 2/20 255, SAPMO-BArch, pp. 4–6.

133. Report of GDR economic delegation to Chile, "Information über die Tätigkeit der Beratergruppe des ZK der SED beim ZK der KP Chiles" [Information on the activity of the advisory group of the CC SED to the CC of the CP Chile], n.d. [likely September–October 1972], DY 30/IV B 2/20 255, SAPMO-BArch, p. 2.

134. "Erster Bericht über die Tätigkeit der vom Sekretariat des ZK der SED beschlossenen Arbeitsgruppe zur Ünterstutzung des ZK der KP Chiles" [First report on the activity of the advisory group sent by the CC SED Secretariat to support the CC CP Chile], October 22, 1972, DY 30/IV B 2/20 255, SAPMO-BArch, p. 3.

135. "Bericht über eine Beratung mit Gen; Cademartori über Vorschläge, die die Gruppe der Genossen der SED vorgelegt hatte" [Report on a meeting with comrade Cardemartori on the proposals put forth by the group of SED comrades], November 9, 1972, DY 30/IV B 2/20 255, SAPMO-BArch.

136. Conversation of GDR ambassador Harry Spindler, Ernst Höfner, with Aleksandr Basov, November 17, 1972, DY 30/IV B 2/20 255, SAPMO-BArch.

137. Telegram, Harry Spindler to Hermann Axen, Paul Markowski, and Georg Stibi, November 21, 1972, DY 30/IV B 2/20 255, SAPMO-BArch.

138. Secretariat Protocol No. 27, "6. Beratung des ZK der SED beim ZK der Kommunistischen Partei Chiles" [6. Consultation of the CC SED with the CC of the Communist Party of Chile], March 9, 1973, DY 30/J IV 2/3A 2305, SAPMO-BArch, p. 55.

139. Conversation of Al Lamuh Basov with Luis Corvalán, September 13, 1972, F.5 O.64 D.696, RGANI, pp. 150–151; Aleksandr Basov, "Obstanovka v Chili, perspektivy Narodnogo Pravitel'stva i vozmozhnye shagi v plane nashei podderzhki i mezhdunarodnoi solidarnoisti" [Situation in Chile, perspectives of the Popular Government and possible steps in the plan of our support and international solidarity], F.5 O.66 D.1015, RGANI, pp. 58–59.

140. Conversation of Aleksandr Basov with PC leaders, August 12, 1973, F.5 O.66 D.1019, RGANI, p. 276.

141. Sigmund, *The Overthrow of Allende,* 197, 198.

142. OLAS MFA, report on Chilean congressional elections, March 16, 1973, F. 139 O.28 P.12 D.7, AVPRF, p. 10.

143. Politburo Information No. 19/73 from AIV, "Einschätzung der Parlamentswahlen in Chile" [Evaluation of the parliamentary elections in Chile], March 26, 1973, DY 30/J IV 2/2J 4608, SAPMO-BArch, p. 6.

144. Harry Spindler to Georg Stibi, March 30, 1973, DY 30/IV B 2/20 260, SAPMO-BArch.

145. Secretariat Information, "Bericht über die Teilnahme einer Delegation des Zentralkomitees der SED an den Feierlichkeiten zum 40 Jahrestag der Gründung der Sozialistischen Partei Chiles in Santiago vom 15–21/4/1973" [Report on the participation of a delegation of SED Central Committee to the celebration of 40th anniversary of the founding of the Socialist Party of Chile in Santiago from 15-21/4/1973], May 4, 1973, DY 30/J IV 2/3J 1688, SAPMO-BArch, pp. 5–7, 9.

146. Haslam, *The Nixon Administration,*180, 181.

147. Telegram, Harry Spindler to Erich Honecker, Willi Stoph, Hermann Axen, Otto Winzer, Paul Markowski, Georg Stibi, and Korth, June 29, 1973, DY 30/IV B 2/20 261, SAPMO-BArch.

148. OLAS MFA report on the PDC, July 3, 1973, F. 139 O.28 P.12 D.7, AVPRF, p. 69.

149. OLAS MFA report on the situation in Chile, July 16, 1973, F. 139 O.28 P.12 D.7, AVPRF, p. 80.

150. GDR embassy report, "Zur Lage in Chile" [On the situation in Chile], July 9, 1973, DY 30/IV B 2/20 261, SAPMO-BArch, 1. For Cuban arms provision, see Harmer, *Allende's Chile,* 232–233.

151. "Zur Lage in Chile" [On the situation in Chile], pp. 3, 4.

152. Conversation of I. B. Puchkov, advisor Soviet embassy, with Mario Zamorano, member of the political commission of the PC, August 3, 1973, F.5 O.66 D.1019, RGANI, p. 248.

153. Telegram, Spindler to Hermann Axen and Paul Markowski, July 17, 1973, DY 30/IV B 2/20 354, SAPMO-BArch.

154. Conversation of Aleksandr Basov with Harry Spindler, July 16, 1973, F.5 O.66 D.1016, RGANI, pp. 165–166, 2.

155. "Antwort des ZK der KPdSU, übergeben von Genossen G. N. Gorinowitsch, am 23.7.1973" [Answer of the CC CPSU, passed on by comrade G.N. Gorinovich, on 23.7.1973], July 23, 1973, DY 30/IV B 2/20 354, SAPMO-BArch.

156. Secretariat Protocol No. 90, "24. Zur Lage in Chile und Unterstützung der Kommunistischen Partei Chiles" [On the situation of Chile and the support of the Communist Party of Chile], conversation of Volodia Teitelboim with Hermann Axen, August 8, 1973, August 20, 1973, DY 30/J IV 2/3A 2381, SAPMO-BArch, p. 103.

157. Secretariat Protocol No. 90, "24. Zur Lage in Chile und Unterstützung der Kommunistischen Partei Chiles" [On the situation of Chile and the support of the Communist Party of Chile], p. 103; Corvalán, *De lo vivido y lo peleado,* 147.

158. Conversation of Aleksandr Basov with Salvador Allende, July 16, 1971, F.5 O.63 D.736, RGANI, p. 89.

159. Leonov, "Soviet Intelligence in Latin America during the Cold War," 24–25.

160. See, for example, Haslam, *The Nixon Administration,* 154, which quotes Jacques Chonchol, Allende's minister of agriculture, and cites Henry Kissinger to this effect as well. Harmer,

Allende's Chile, 196–197, makes a similar argument based on remarks of the Chilean and Soviet ambassadors in the United States.

161. OLAS MFA report on Sino-Chilean relations, August 8, 1973, F. 139 O.28 P.12 D.7, AVPRF, p. 103.

162. Politburo Protocol No. 39, "8. Entsprechend einer Bitte Präsident Allende wird für 1973 eine offizielle Delegation der Sozialistischen Partei Chiles in der DDR eingeladen" [In accordance with a request from President Allende a delegation of the Socialist Party of Chile will be invited for 1973], September 11, 1973, DY 30/J IV 2/2A 1711, SAPMO-BArch, p. 103.

163. Conversation of Aleksandr Basov with Luis Corvalán, July 10, 1973, F.5 O.66 D.1019, RGANI, pp. 222, 223.

164. Telegram, Möbus, first secretary, GDR embassy Santiago, to Hermann Axen, Paul Markowski, Georg Stibi, and Alfred Patzak, July 25, 1973, DY 30/IV B 2/20 261, SAPMO-BArch.

165. GDR Embassy in Chile, "Zur Lage in Chile und zur bevorstehenden Akkreditierung des Genossen Trappen als Botschafter der DDR in Chile" [On the situation in Chile and the forthcoming accreditation of comrade Trappen as GDR ambassador in Chile], August 1, 1973, DY 30/IV B 2/20 261, SAPMO-BArch.

166. For more details on the negotiations and why they collapsed, see Sigmund, *The Overthrow of Allende,* 223–235.

167. Conversation of Aleksandr Basov with Radomiro Tomic, August 16, 1973, F.5 O.66 D.1017, RGANI, p. 108.

168. Sigmund, *The Overthrow of Allende,* 225–226.

169. Telegram, Friedel Trappen to Hermann Axen, Paul Markowski, Georg Stibi, and Korth, August 8, 1973, DY 30/IV B 2/20 261, SAPMO-BArch. See also GDR Embassy in Santiago to SED Politburo, "Zur Lage in Chile" [On the situation in Chile], August 9, 1973, DY 30/IV B 2/20 257, SAPMO-BArch, p. 2.

170. GDR Embassy in Santiago to SED Politburo, "Zur Lage in Chile," August 9, 1973, p. 2.

171. Report of GDR embassy in Chile, "Zur Lage in Chile," August 10, 1973, DY 30/IV B 2/20 261, SAPMO-BArch.

172. Politburo Protocol No. 39, "Information des Generalsekretärs des ZK der Kommunistischen Partei Chiles, Luis Corvalan, vom 28.8.1973 über einige aktuelle Aspekte der Lage in Chile" [Information from the General Secretary of the CC of the Communist Party of Chile Luis Corvalán from 28.8.1973 on certain current aspects of the situation in Chile], September 11, 1973, DY 30/J IV 2/2A 1711, SAPMO-BArch, p. 106.

173. Harmer, *Allende's Chile,* 233.

174. Conversation of Aleksandr Basov with Cuban ambassador in Chile Mario Garcia Inchaustegui, August 4, 1973, F.5 O.66 D.1016, RGANI, p. 150.

175. Harmer, *Allende's Chile,* 232–238.

176. OLAS MFA report on Chile, September 5, 1973, F. 139 O.28 papka 12 delo 7, AVPRF, pp. 107, 108, 109, 111.

177. Conversation of Aleksandr Basov and Luis Corvalán, August 23, September 3, 1973, F.5 O.66 D.1019, RGANI, p. 264.

178. Politburo Protocol No. 39 9/11/73, "Bericht über dei Teilnahme einer Delegation des ZK der SED am XIV Parteitag der KP Argentiniens und über die Übergabe der DDR-Solidaritätssendung an Präsident Allende in Santiago de Chile" [Report on the participation of a delegation of CC SED to the party congress of the CP Argentina and the giving over of the GDR solidarity message to President Allende in Santiago de Chile], September 11, 1973, DY 30/J IV 2/2A 1711, SAPMO-BArch, pp. 97, 103. The East German delegation met with the Soviet ambassador, as well as Luis Corvalán, on this trip.

179. See, for example, Tariq Ali, *1968 and After: Inside the Revolution* (London: Blond and Briggs, 1978).

180. See, for example, Julia Lovell, *Maoism: A Global History* (New York: Alfred A. Knopf, 2019), 306–346.

181. Conversation of Y. I. Kuskov with Egon Winkelmann, "Bericht über eine Konsultation mit dem stellvertetenden Leiter der Internationalen Abteilung im ZK der KPdSU, Mitglied der ZRK, Genossen J. I. Kuskow, zu den Ereignissen in Chile" [Report on a meeting with acting head of the International Department of the CC CPSU, member of the central revision commission, comrade J.I. Kuskow, on the events in Chile], September 20, 1973, DY 30/IV B 2/20 437, SAPMO-BArch, pp. 6, 12.

182. Politburo Information 10/24/73, "Die Bedeutung und die Lehren des revolutionären Prozesses in Chile: Die nachfolgende Material ist eine erste Analyse sowjetischer Wissenschaftler, die keinen offiziellen Charakter trägt, sondern als vorläufiges Arbeitsmaterial zu betrachten ist" [The meaning and lessons of the revolutionary process in Chile: The following material is a primary analysis of the Soviet scholars, that has no official character, but rather is to be treated as working material], October 24, 1973, DY 30/J IV 2/2J 4974, SAPMO-BArch, pp. 15, 14, 27, 32–34.

183. See, for example, V. V. Vol'skii, "Problemy mirnogo puti k sotsializmu" [Problems of the peaceful path to socialism], *Latinskaia Amerika* 5 (1974): 41–60; and E. A. Kosarev, "Ekonomika i mirnyi put' revoliutsii" [Economics and the peaceful path of revolution], *Latinskaia Amerika* 5 (1974): 92–111.

184. Olga Ulianova, "Soviet Perceptions and Analyses of the Unidad Popular Government and the Military Coup in Chile," *Estudios publicos* 79 (2000): 44.

185. K. I. Maidanik, "Vokrug urokov Chili" [About the lessons of Chile], *Latinskaia Amerika* 5 (1974): 116, 120–122, 132, 128.

186. Ulianova, "Soviet Perceptions," 33–34, 46–53.

187. Fernando Pérez Egert to Chilean MFA, "Contesta circular confidencial No. 28" [Confidential Reply No 28], October 31, 1973, 1973 Embajada de Chile en China: Oficios, AHMRE, p. 1.

188. Fernando Pérez Egert to Chilean MFA, "Contesta circular confidencial No. 28," p. 4.

189. OLAS MFA report on Sino-Chilean relations, July 2, 1976, F.139 O.31 P.13 D.2, AVPRF, pp. 18–23.

190. See Harmer, *Allende's Chile*, 125–132.

191. Ahmed Azad, "The Lessons of the Chilean Revolution," *African Communist* 60, first quarter (1975): 75.

192. For Iran, see Chapter 5 of the present volume.

3. Tanzanian *Ujamaa*

Epigraph: Government of Tanzania, *Draft Planning and Control Guide,* October 1972, PMO, box 327, file Ref PMC/P.100/1 Planning Guidelines 1973–4, item 19, Tanzania National Archives, Dodoma Regional Records Centre (hereafter TNA-DRRC), p. 2.

1. Julius K. Nyerere, "The Varied Paths to Socialism," in *Freedom and Socialism: Uhuru na Ujamaa; A Selection from Writings and Speeches, 1965–1967* (London: Oxford University Press, 1968), 302.

2. See, for example, Oded Eran, *Mezhdunarodniki: An Assessment of Professional Expertise in the Making of Soviet Foreign Policy* (Ramat Gan, Israel: Turtledove, 1979); Jeremy Friedman, *Shadow Cold War: The Sino-Soviet Competition for the Third World* (Chapel Hill: University of North Carolina Press, 2015); Galia Golan, *The Soviet Union and National Liberation Movements in the Third World* (Boston: Unwin Hyman, 1988); Jerry Hough, *The Struggle for the Third World: Soviet Debates and American Options* (Washington, DC: Brookings Institution Press, 1986); and

Arthur Jay Klinghoffer, *Soviet Perspectives on African Socialism* (Rutherford, NJ: Farleigh Dickinson University Press, 1969).

3. See Mikhail Suslov to CPSU Plenum, January 18, 1961, F.2 O.1 D.510, Rossisskiĭ Gosudarstvennyĭ Arkhiv Noveisheĭ Istorii (Russian State Archive of Contemporary History; hereafter RGANI), p. 20.

4. See Alessandro Iandolo, "The Rise and Fall of the 'Soviet Model of Development' in West Africa, 1957–1964," *Cold War History* 12, no. 4 (2012): 683–704; Sergei Mazov, *A Distant Front in the Cold War: The USSR in West Africa and the Congo, 1956–1964* (Washington, DC: Woodrow Wilson Center Press, 2010); and Friedman, *Shadow Cold War,* 77–84.

5. "Aktenvermerk über ein Gespräch des Genossen Rossmeisl mit Genossen Arkadaskij, Stellvertreter des Sektorenleiters für Afrika im ZK der KPdSU, am 20 Dezember 1965" [Memorandum of a conversation of Comrade Rossmeisl with Comrade Arkadaskii, deputy sector leader for Africa in the CC CPSU, on 20 December 1965], December 20, 1965, DY 30/IV A 2/20/954, Stiftung Archiv der Parteien und Massenorganisationen der DDR—Bundesarchiv (Archive of the Parties and Mass Organizations of the German Democratic Republic—Federal Archives; hereafter SAPMO-BArch), p. 64.

6. Lawrence Fellows, "Chou, in Tanzania, Calls U.S. a Bully," *New York Times,* June 6, 1965.

7. William Wilson, "Tanzania after Arusha," memorandum to UK FCO, March 22, 1967, FCO 31/156, UK National Archives (hereafter UKNA).

8. Australian high commissioner to UK FCO, "The Arusha Declaration: A Novel Approach to African Problems," September 11, 1967, FCO 31/155, UKNA.

9. W. B. L. Monson to William Wilson, n.d., forwarded April 4, 1967, FCO 31/156, UKNA.

10. "Chou En-Lai's Message of Greetings to President Nyerere on TANU's National Conference," October 15, 1967, Acc. 481, A 6/28 vol. III, item no. 196, Tanzanian National Archives (hereafter TNA).

11. Joseph Butiku (Nyerere's personal assistant who accompanied him on these visits), interview with the author, Dar es Salaam, July 20, 2016.

12. See, for example, Julius K. Nyerere, "Speech at the Inauguration of the Non-Aligned Inter-Regional Programme of Cooperation in Respect of Trade, Industry, and Transport," in Julius K. Nyerere, *Freedom and a New World Economic Order: A Selection from Speeches, 1974–1999* (Dar es Salaam: Oxford University Press, 2011), 1–11.

13. See Michelle Elise Bourbonniere, "Debating Socialism on the Hill: The University of Dar es Salaam, 1967–1971" (master's thesis, Dalhousie University, 2007).

14. See, for example, the work of John Saul, *The State and Revolution in East Africa: Essays* (New York: Monthly Review Press, 1979); Goran Hyden, *Beyond Ujamaa: Underdevelopment and an Uncaptured Peasantry* (London: Heinemann, 1980); Cranford Pratt, *The Critical Phase in Tanzania, 1945–1968: Nyerere and the Emergence of a Socialist Strategy* (Cambridge: Cambridge University Press, 1976); Dean McHenry, *Tanzania's Ujamaa Villages: The Implementation of a Rural Development Strategy* (Berkeley: University of California Press, 1979); Andrew Coulson, *Tanzania: A Political Economy* (Oxford: Oxford University Press, 1982); Michaela von Freyhold, *Ujamaa Villages in Tanzania: Analysis of a Social Experiment* (London: Heinemann, 1979).

15. See, for example, James Brennan, *Taifa: Making Nation and Race in Urban Tanzania* (Columbus: Ohio University Press, 2012); Paul Bjerk, *Building a Peaceful Nation* (Rochester, NY: University of Rochester Press, 2015); Andrew Ivaska, *Cultured States: Youth, Gender, and Modern Style in 1960s Dar es Salaam* (Durham, NC: Duke University Press, 2011); and Emma Hunter, *Political Thought and the Public Sphere in Tanzania: Freedom, Democracy, and Citizenship in the Era of Decolonization* (Cambridge: Cambridge University Press, 2015).

16. See, for example, Leander Schneider, *Government of Development: Peasants and Politicians in Postcolonial Tanzania* (Bloomington: Indiana University Press, 2014); and Priya Lal, *African*

Socialism in Postcolonial Tanzania: Between the Village and the World (Cambridge: Cambridge University Press, 2015).

17. For more on Tanzania's colonial history, see John Iliffe, *A Modern History of Tanganyika* (Cambridge: Cambridge University Press, 1979); and Pratt, *The Critical Phase in Tanzania*.

18. Pratt, *The Critical Phase in Tanzania*, 20, 22.

19. See Iliffe, *A Modern History of Tanganyika*, 523–537.

20. Julius Nyerere, quoted in Thomas Molony, *Nyerere: The Early Years* (Suffolk, UK: James Currey, 2014), 103.

21. Alexander Gray, *The Socialist Tradition: Moses to Lenin* (London: Longmans, Green, 1946), 513–514.

22. Molony, *Nyerere*, 68–70.

23. Pratt, *The Critical Phase in Tanzania*, 44.

24. V. Kabanenko, referent Soviet embassy in Ethiopia, report on Tanganyika to Soviet Ministry of Foreign Affairs (MFA), February 16, 1961, F.653 O.4 P.1 D.2, Arkhiv Venshneĭ Politikoĭ Rossisskoĭ Federatsii (Foreign Policy Archive of the Russian Federation; hereafter AVPRF), pp. 16, 17–19.

25. AIV report, "Information über die Lage in Tanganyika" [Information on the situation in Tanganyika], April 16, 1962, DY 30/IV A 2/20/963, SAPMO-BArch, pp. 6–7, 8.

26. See the report of the PRC MFA to PRC Embassy London on visit of Denis Phombeah to Beijing, June 27, 1960, Doc 108-00218-01, 中国外交部开放档案 (Zhongguo Waijiaobu kaifang dang'an—Declassified Chinese Foreign Ministry Archives; hereafter CFMA), pp. 8–9; and the report of PRC Embassy Tanganyika to PRC MFA and Peace Committee, December 14, 1962, Doc 108-00834-03, CFMA, pp. 6–8. See also Alicia Altorfer-Ong, "Old Comrades and New Brothers: A Historical Re-examination of the Sino-Zanzibari and Sino-Tanzanian Relationships in the 1960s" (PhD diss., London School of Economics, 2014), 96–140.

27. "Information über die Lage in Tanganyika" [Information on the situation in Tanganyika], April 16, 1962, DY 30/IV A 2/20/963, SAPMO-BArch, p. 6.

28. Julius Nyerere, quoted in a report from I. Ermachenkov, Soviet embassy in West Germany, to Soviet MFA on visit of Nyerere to West Germany, January 30, 1961. F.653 O.4 P.1 D.2, AVPRF, p. 46.

29. For more detail, see "Achievement in Rural Settlement Since Independence," *Nationalist* (Dar es Salaam, Tanzania), February 22, 1968.

30. Pratt, *The Critical Phase in Tanzania*, 130–131.

31. Nikita Khrushchev, "Speech in Sofia," *Pravda*, May 20, 1962.

32. A. I. Alikhanov, diary entry, September 3, 1963, F.365 O.2 D.397, Rossisskiĭ Gosudartvennyĭ Arkhiv Ekonomiki (Russian State Archive of the Economy; hereafter RGAE), p. 93.

33. Michael Kamaliza, quoted in A. I. Alikhanov, diary entry, November 22, 1963, F.365 O.2 D.397, RGAE, 96–97.

34. GKES report on economic situation and foreign trade relations of Tanganyika, August 1964, F.365 O.2. D.3163, RGAE, p. 38.

35. See, for example, Altorfer-Ong, "Old Comrades and New Brothers," 45–95; and Bjerk, *Building a Peaceful Nation*, 206–227.

36. "Einschätzung über die gegenwärtige Lage in der Vereinigten Republik Tanganjika und Sansibar" [Evaluation of the current situation in the united republic of Tanganyika and Zanzibar], May 27, 1964, DY 30/IV A 2/20/964, SAPMO-BArch, p. 26.

37. Report of I. Saprykin, attaché of Soviet embassy in UK, on question of creating United Republic of Tanzania, June 9, 1964, F.653 O.4 P.1 D.2, AVPRF, p. 19.

38. Telegram from US Department of State, stamped by Dean Rusk, on coup in Zanzibar, May 22, 1964, RG 59, box 2694, folder Pol 23-9, US National Archives and Records Administration (hereafter NARA).

39. Bjerk, *Building a Peaceful Nation,* 222–224.

40. Butiku interview.

41. Report from UK Embassy in Washington to UK Foreign Office, May 28, 1964, FO 371/176521, UKNA.

42. Julius Nyerere, quoted in report of US ambassador in Dar es Salaam William Leonhart to secretary of state Dean Rusk, September 1, 1964, RG 59, box 2691, folder Pol 15-1 Tanzan, NARA.

43. US Embassy Dar es Salaam to US Department of State, August 29, 1964, RG 59, box 2690, folder Pol 15 Tanzan, NARA.

44. Report of Liu Ningyi to PRC Central Committee on visit of delegation to Tanganyika, January 29, 1963, Doc 108-00320-02, CFMA, pp. 1–4.

45. Fellows, "Chou, in Tanzania, Calls U.S. a Bully."

46. Telegram of US ambassador, Dar es Salaam, William Leonhart, to secretary of state Dean Rusk, July 27, 1965, RG 59, box 2688, folder Pol 1 Tanzan, NARA.

47. Report of Z. Zaikin, deputy head of third Africa division of the Soviet MFA, to CPSU Central Committee, April 4, 1968, F.5 O. 60 D.458, RGANI, p. 22.

48. Telegram, US Embassy London to US Department of State, June 11, 1965, RG 59, box 2689, folder Pol 7 Tanzan, NARA.

49. See report of Zaikin to CPSU Central Committee, April 4, 1968, p. 20.

50. Treasury secretary to National Development Corporation on meeting with Chinese representatives, February 25, 1967, Acc. No 596 213 14 NDC D/3822 (A), TNA.

51. A. M. Maalim to general manager, National Development Corporation, March 7, 1967 (response to letter of March 2, 1967), Acc. No 596 213 14 NDC D/3822 (A), TNA.

52. General consulate of German Democratic Republic (GDR) in Tanzania, "Jahresbericht 1965 der Generalkonsulats der DDR in der VRT" [Annual report of the GDR general consulate in the URT for 1965], January 3, 1966, DY 30/IV A 2/20/963, SAPMO-BArch, pp. 112–113.

53. GDR MFA to AIV, report of General Consul Gottfried Lessing, October 3, 1966, DY 30/IV A 2/20/963, SAPMO-BArch, p. 224.

54. Conversation of Iu. Iakovlev, vice consul, with Ahmed Rashid, director of the department of planning and development, December 1, 1966, F.365 O.2 D.2963, RGAE, p. 69.

55. M. Amirdzhanov, first secretary Soviet embassy in Dar es Salaam, report on agrarian relations in Tanganyika, June 10, 1964, F.653 O.7 P.3 D.5, AVPRF, p. 70.

56. Julius K. Nyerere, *The Arusha Declaration Ten Years After* (Dar es Salaam: Government Printer, 1977), 2.

57. Telegram, US Embassy Dar es Salaam to US Department of State, November 30, 1966, RG 59, box 2693, folder Pol 23-8 Tanzan, NARA.

58. Julius K. Nyerere, "Leaders Must Not Be Masters," in *Freedom and Socialism,* 136–142.

59. Job Lusinde, interview with the author, Dar es Salaam, Tanzania, July 7, 2016.

60. Julius K. Nyerere, "The Arusha Declaration: Socialism and Self-Reliance," in *Freedom and Socialism,* 232–233, 241.

61. See Dean McHenry, *Limited Choices: The Political Struggle for Socialism in Tanzania* (Boulder, CO: Lynne Rienner, 1994), 131.

62. See Julius K. Nyerere, "Education for Self-Reliance," in *Freedom and Socialism,* 267–290; and Julius K. Nyerere, "Socialism and Rural Development," in *Freedom and Socialism,* 337–366.

63. Toussaint, "Tanzania's New Revolution," *African Communist* 29, second quarter (1967): 30.

64. "Create a New Tanzanian—Nyerere," *Nationalist* (Dar es Salaam, Tanzania), August 17, 1968. For more on the TANU Youth League and the so-called Tanzanian cultural revolution, see Ivaska, *Cultured States.*

65. For more on Chinese, Cuban, and Soviet approaches to this issue of creating socialist consciousness, see Yinghong Cheng, *Creating the New Man: From Enlightenment Ideals to Socialist Realities* (Honolulu: University of Hawai'i Press, 2009).

66. See the report of Zaikin to CPSU Central Committee, April 4, 1968, p. 22.

67. Zambian chargé d'affaires in Moscow to Lusaka MFA, December 5, 1967, MFA 1/1/103 Loc: 508, item 151, National Archives of Zambia.

68. Martin Breetzman, "Zur Entwicklung in Tansania" [On developments in Tanzania], n.d. [likely June–July 1967], DY 30/IV A 2/20/963, SAPMO-BArch, p. 342.

69. Gottfried Lessing to GDR MFA, AIV, September 25, 1967, DY 30/IV A 2/20/963 SAPMO-BArch, p. 372.

70. Eberhard Kunz to GDR MFA, AIV, October 17, 1967, DY 30/IV A 2/20/963, SAPMO-BArch, p. 399.

71. Vladimir Iordanskii, Review of *Protivorechiia nekapitalistichesogo razvitiia v Afrike* [Contradictions of noncapitalist development in Africa], *Narodi Azii i Afriki* 3 (1968): 49.

72. Eberhard Kunz to GDR MFA, AIV, October 17, 1967, p. 400; Gottfried Lessing to Georg Stibi, September 25, 1967, DY 30/IV A 2/20/963, SAPMO-BArch, pp. 363–364, 381.

73. "Aktenvermerk über ein Gespräch des Gen. Dr. Lessing mit Minister Oscar Kambona anlässlich eines Essens in der Residenz am 21.7.66" [Memorandum on a conversation between Comrade Dr. Lessing and Minister Oscar Kambona on the occasion of a meal in the residence, July 21, 1966], July 21, 1966, DY 30/IV A 2/20/963, SAPMO-BArch, p. 211.

74. See Toussaint, "Tanzania's New Revolution," *African Communist* 39, fourth quarter (1969): 31; and B. Ngotyana, "The Strategy of Rural Development: Tanzania's Second Five-Year Plan," *African Communist* 39, fourth quarter (1969): 37.

75. Iordanskii, review of *Protivorechiia Nekapitalistichesogo Razvitiia v Afrike*, 50.

76. C. F. MacLaren to D. M. Biggin, March 3, 1967, FCO 95/231, UKNA. There was no British high commissioner in Dar es Salaam at the time because Tanzania had broken relations with the UK over its response to Rhodesia's unilateral declaration of independence in November 1965 and would not reestablish relations until July 1968.

77. Wilson, "Tanzania after Arusha"; Australian high commissioner to UK FCO, "The Arusha Declaration: A Novel Approach to African Problems."

78. Telegram, US Embassy Dar es Salaam to US Department of State, "This Week in Tanzania, September 8–14, 1967," September 15, 1967, RG 59, box 2513, folder Pol 2 Tanzan 6/1/67, NARA.

79. "Vermerk über ein Gespräch mit Denis Phombea, Mitglied der Delegation der Regierung Tansania zur Leipziger Frühjahrsmesse 1967 a.m. 4 März im Gästhaus der Partei" [Memorandum of a conversation with Denis Phombea, member of the Tanzanian government delegation to the Leipzig Spring Fair of 1967 on March 4, 1967 in the guest house of the party"), DY 30/IV A 2/20/963, SAPMO-BArch, pp. 333–337.

80. Canadian high commissioner Allen S. McGill to UK undersecretary of state for external affairs, "Tanzanian Socialism," March 1, 1967, FCO 31/156 UKNA; report on conversation of Paul Bomani with Aleksader Bachurin, deputy chairman of Gosplan, sent to D. Degtiar', deputy chairman of GKES, November 17, 1967, F.365 O.2 D.2977, RGAE, pp. 66–68.

81. I. Arkhipov, GKES, to V. N. Novikov, deputy chairman of the Council of Ministers, February 1968, F.365 O.2 D.701, RGAE, p. 118.

82. Gottfried Lessing to Wolfgang Kiesewetter, October 19, 1966, DY 30/IV A 2/20/963, SAPMO-BArch, p. 233.

83. Report on conversation of Bomani and Bachurin, November 17, 1967, p. 68.

84. See, for example, the report of A. Glukhov, advisor Soviet embassy in Dar es Salaam, July 13, 1968, F.5 O.60 D.458, RGANI, p. 69; US Embassy Tanzania to US Department of State,

"Reports of Popular Discontent," February 5, 1966, RG 59, box 2688, folder Pol 2 Tanzan 1/1/64, NARA.

85. "Einschätzung der innenpolitischen Entwicklung im Festlanteil der VRT" [Evaluation of the domestic political situation in the URT (United Republic of Tanzania)], January 5, 1968, DY 30/IV A 2/20/964, SAPMO-BArch, pp. 25–28.

86. Breetzman, "Zur Entwicklung in Tansania," p. 347.

87. Arkhipov to Novikov, February 1968, pp. 116–119.

88. For the comment about competing with the Chinese, see the conversation of G. Samsonov, advisor Soviet embassy in Dar es Salaam, with Piliso, October 7, 1966, F.365 O.2 D.1070, RGAE, p. 58. For the report of the Soviet geologists on their mission to Tanzania from December 21, 1967, to January 15, 1968, see F.365 O.2 D.3012, RGAE, p. 3.

89. Conversation of D. Degtiar' with Daniel Mfinanga, May 17, 1967, F.365 O.2 D.663, RGAE, p. 22; conversation of I. P. Shatokhin with S. D. Msuya, head secretary of the ministry of finance, November 3, 1970, F.365 O.9 D.598, RGAE, p. 81.

90. Conversation of G. Samsonov with J. Viriu, advisor Czechoslovak embassy in Dar es Salaam, December 12, 1967, F.365 O.2 D.2977, RGAE, p. 96.

91. Nikulin, head of Soviet economic mission in Tanzania, to D. Degtiar', August 1968, F.365 O.2 D.719, RGAE, pp. 171–172.

92. Gottfried Lessing to Wolfgang Kiesewetter, April 9, 1968, DY 30/IV A 2/20/964, SAPMO-BArch, p. 109.

93. Lawi Sijaona, "Smash Enemies of Socialism," *Nationalist* (Dar es Salaam, Tanzania), September 5, 1968.

94. Nyerere, "Socialism and Rural Development," 349; TANU Central Committee meeting, quoted in Schneider, *Government of Development,* 47.

95. For more on the Ruvuma Development Association, see Schneider, *Government of Development,* 19–68.

96. Telegram, US Embassy Dar es Salaam to US Department of State, "This Week in Tanzania, March 7–13, 1969," March 14, 1969, RG 59, box 2513, folder Pol 2 Tanzan 1/1/69, NARA; telegram, US Embassy Dar es Salaam to US Department of State, "This Week in Tanzania, February 28–March 6, 1969," March 7, 1969, RG 59, box 2513, folder Pol 2 Tanzan 1/1/69, NARA.

97. For the notice of the TANU Central Committee decision, see telegram, US Embassy Dar es Salaam to US Department of State, "This Week in Tanzania, July 25–31, 1969," August 1, 1969, RG 59, box 2514, folder Pol 2 Tanzan 7/1/69, NARA. For Bryceson's conversation with Shatokhin, see F.369 O.5, D.285, RGAE, p. 10.

98. Telegram, US Embassy Dar es Salaam to US Department of State, "This Week in Tanzania, May 30–June 5, 1969," June 6, 1969, RG 59, box 2513, folder Pol 2 Tanzan 1/1/69, NARA.

99. Gottfried Lessing to Wolfgang Kiesewetter, September 24, 1968, DY 30/IV A 2/20/964, SAPMO-BArch, pp. 205–208.

100. Report from GDR General Consulate Dar es Salaam, "Jahresanalyse über die Entwicklung der Republik Tansania im Jahre 1968" [Annual analysis on the development of the Republic of Tanzania in 1968], n.d. [early 1969], DY 30/IV A 2/20/964, SAPMO-BArch, pp. 270–271.

101. Lessing to Kiesewetter, September 24, 1968, p. 207.

102. Andrei Timoshchenko to D. F. Safonov, head of third Africa division Soviet MFA, sending report of Soviet specialist economist V. N. Dem'ianenko working in Tanzania, "Sotsialisticheskie derevni—Udzhamaa" [Socialist Villages—Ujamaa], F.653 O.12 P.10 D.6, 50, AVPRF, pp. 57, 65, 68.

103. V. V. Pavlov, "Sotsial'no-ekonomicheskoe preobrazovanie v Tanzanii posle Arushskoi Deklaratsii" [Socio-economic transformation in Tanzania after the Arusha Declaration], F.365 O.12 P.10 D.6, AVPRF, p. 104.

104. "To Live in Villages Is an Order—Mwalimu," *Daily News* (Dar es Salaam), November 7, 1973.

105. Andrew Coulson, *Tanzania: A Political Economy,* 2nd ed. (Oxford: Oxford University Press, 2013), 295.

106. F. A. Byabato to A. Mushi, "Ujamaa Village Plans," copied to principal secretaries at State House; Second Vice President's Office; DevPlan, Kilimo (State agency for agriculture); and the Ministries of Communications, Education, and Landsurvey, July 20, 1970, PMO, box 323, file RARD/U/U/C/13, item 38, TNA-DRRC.

107. "No Ujamaa Villages by Force—TYL," *Daily News* (Dar es Salaam), August 9, 1973.

108. C. M. Mnyaonga, "A Report of Observation and Experience While Working and Learning in an Ujamaa Village with Peasants Attempt to Implement Socialist Principles in Their Own Way," Department of Economics, University College Dar es Salaam, 1970, PMO, box 323, file RARD/U/U/C/13, item 22, TNA-DRRC, p. 7.

109. "Draft E.C.C. Paper: Report of Ujamaa Village Planning Team—Sumbawanga," 1970, Acc. No. 4/1/04, box 286, file Ref CCU/S/100/3 Ujamaa Villages General 1969–1971, item 147, TNA-DRRC, p. 3.

110. "Report of Stay in Some Ujamaa Villages in Sumbawanga District 22.10.70 to 6.11.70," Ministry of Agriculture and Cooperatives, Z.J. Twaha, Cooperative Inspector, to Commissioner for Cooperative Development, Dar es Salaam, November 27, 1970, Acc. No. 4/1/04, box 286, file Ref CCU/S/100/3 Ujamaa Villages General 1969–1971, item 140, TNA-DRRC, p. 8.

111. "Economic Paper of the Cabinet, Paper No. 59 of 1970: Ujamaa Village Plans for Rufiji District: Memorandum by the Minister of State, President's Office, Regional Administration and Rural Development," August 13, 1970, PMO, box 323, file RARD/U/U/C/13 Ujamaa Villages Pwani 1969–1972, item 45, TNA-DRRC, p. 9.

112. Mnyaonga, "A Report of Observation and Experience," p. 12.

113. US Embassy Dar es Salaam to US Department of State, "Social-Economic-Political Observations on a Trip through Central Tanzania," September 25, 1971, RG 59, box 2616, folder Pol 2 Tanzan 1/1/71, NARA.

114. I. P. Shatokhin to GKES, October 22, 1970, F.365 O.9 D.614, RGAE, pp. 72–74.

115. V. Samoshin, vice consul of the USSR in Zanzibar, report on Tanzania, October 1, 1970, F.653 O.13 P.12 D.5, AVPRF, pp. 13–14.

116. I. P. Shatokhin to GKES, October 22, 1970, p. 73.

117. Vyacheslav Ustinov to D. F. Safonov, forwarding report of F. Kurnikov, "Dvizhenie Udzhamaa I ego znachenie dlia razvitiia Tanzaniia po nekapitalisticheskomu puti" [The Ujamaa Movement and its significance for the development of Tanzania on the non-capitalist path], June 25, 1971, F.365 O.14 P.13 D.5, AVPRF, pp. 116–121.

118. See, for example, I. L. Andreev, "Tendentsii i formy kooperirovaniia krest'ianstva v usloviiakh nekapitalisticheskogo razvitiia" [Tendencies and forms of cooperativization of peasantry in conditions of noncapitalist development], *Narody Azii i Afriki* 6 (1972): 20–33.

119. A. Glukhov, advisor Soviet embassy in Dar es Salaam, "O nekotorykh napravleniiakh deiatel'nosti partii TANU na sovremennom etape" [On certain directions of the activities of the TANU party in the contemporary stage], F.5 O.63 D.592, RGANI, p. 17.

120. See Issa Shivji, John Saul, Walter Rodney, and Thomas Szentes, *Tanzania: The Silent Class Struggle* (Lund, Sweden: Zenit, 1970); Leon Trotsky, *The Revolution Betrayed: What Is the Soviet Union and Where Is It Going?,* trans. Max Eastman (New York: Pathfinder, 1973); and Milovan Djilas, *The New Class: An Analysis of the Communist System* (London: Mariner Books, 1982).

121. Shivji et al., *Tanzania: Silent Class Struggle,* 43–44.

122. "Ujamaa: A Not So Silent Class Struggle," *Daily News* (Dar es Salaam), November 26, 1972.

123. On the increasing numbers of experts from socialist countries relative to those from the West during the Second Five-Year Plan as opposed to the First Five-Year Plan, see the report of I. P. Shatokhin to V. G. Morozov, head of the GKES department of cadres, and V. N. Gaidukov, head of

the GKES department of Africa and Latin America, August 27, 1970, F.365 O.9 D.614, RGAE, p. 15. On the desire to have Soviet experts act as agents of ideological struggle, see the report of D. Khairullin to V. N. Gaidukov, March 23, 1973, F.365 O.9 D.1423, RGAE, p. 92.

124. Dean McHenry Jr., *Limited Choices: The Political Struggle for Socialism in Tanzania* (Boulder, CO: Lynne Rienner, 1994), 17–19.

125. Kingunge Ngombale-Mwiru, interview with the author, Dar es Salaam, Tanzania, July 19, 2016.

126. Kingunge Ngombale-Mwiru, "TANU: A Mass Party with a Vanguard," interview with Philip Ochieng, *Daily News* (Dar es Salaam), December 31, 1972.

127. Kingunge Ngombale-Mwiru interview.

128. "Mr. Phillips' Despatch: Tanzania in Travail," June 25, 1971, FCO 31/968, UKNA.

129. "We Cannot Tolerate More Bombing—Mwalimu," *Daily News* (Dar es Salaam), September 21, 1971.

130. For more on the origin of Mwongozo within the party, see McHenry, *Limited Choices,* 19–21.

131. "Are Workers Going Too Far?," *Daily News* (Dar es Salaam), June 1, 1973.

132. See Brennan, *Taifa,* 159–195.

133. Annual report for 1972 of M. K. Ewans, FCO 31/1556, UKNA.

134. Report of James Ayres, January 5, 1972, FCO 31/1285, UKNA. For more on the assassination of Kleruu, see Coulson, *Tanzania,* 294.

135. "Mr. Phillips' Despatch: Tanzania in Travail," n.d. [likely May 1971], FCO 31/968, UKNA.

136. Julius K. Nyerere, "The Rational Choice," in *Freedom and Development*, 379–390.

137. Vyacheslav Ustinov to S. P. Kozyrev, February 5, 1973, F.653 O.16 P.15 D.2, AVPRF, p. 1.

138. "Opening Speech to E.A. [East African] Staff College Seminar by the Hon Peter Kisumo, Minister for Regional Administration and Rural Development 'Why Tanzania Must be Based on Cooperative Farming,'" Acc. No 523 C 50/12/Vol I Seminars-General, item 81, TNA, p. 7.

139. See J. Ann Zammit, ed., *The Chilean Road to Socialism: Proceedings of an ODEPLAN-IDS Roundtable, March 1972* (Austin: University of Texas Press, 1973). The book was reviewed in Tanzania; see Karim Essack, "The Chilean Road to Socialism," *Daily News* (Dar es Salaam), June 5, 1973.

140. R. Baguma, "Tanzania and Socialism: Are We Deviating or Setting a Precedent?," *Daily News* (Dar es Salaam), January 5, 1972.

141. See, for example, "Algerians Get Nationalized Land," *Daily News* (Dar es Salaam), July 10, 1973; and "Somalia's Own Road to Scientific Socialism," *Daily News* (Dar es Salaam), November 4, 1973.

142. "Our Ujamaa in Chile," *Daily News* (Dar es Salaam), February 8, 1972.

143. "What We Can Learn from Hungarian Agriculture," *Daily News* (Dar es Salaam), August 9, 1972.

144. "TANU Outlines Policy for Better Farming," *Daily News* (Dar es Salaam), May 14, 1972. See also Coulson, *Tanzania,* 295.

145. "Giving Regions More Power," *Daily News* (Dar es Salaam), January 28, 1972.

146. Issa Shivji, interview with the author, Dar es Salaam, Tanzania, July 19, 2016.

147. Conversation of Vyacheslav Ustinov with Julius Nyerere, February 23, 1972, F.5 O.64 D.545, RGANI, p. 11.

148. Government of Tanzania, *Draft Planning and Control Guide,* p. 3.

149. D. Khairullin to P. Ia. Koshelev, July 19, 1973, F.365 O.9 D.1423, RGAE, pp. 170–184.

150. For more on the Tanzanian state's difficulty fulfilling its promises on social services, see Coulson, *Tanzania,* 298–309.

151. H. I. Vima, "Allende's Failure a Lesson to Us," *Daily News* (Dar es Salaam), September 18, 1973.

152. Nyerere, *The Arusha Declaration Ten Years After,* 11–12.

153. Coulson, *Tanzania,* 308.

154. McHenry, *Limited Choices,* 172.

155. Conversation of Sergey Slipchenko with Julius Nyerere, February 16, 1974, F.5 O.67 D.793, RGANI, pp. 31–33.

156. McHenry, *Limited Choices,* 171.

157. Speech of Julius Nyerere, broadcast to the country on August 15, 1974, FCO 31/1766, UKNA.

158. World Bank, quoted in Arthur Kellas, "Agricultural Production in Tanzania," November 18, 1974, FCO 31/1767, UKNA.

159. Edward Lidderdale, "Visit of World Bank Team," October 2, 1974, FCO 31/1767, UKNA.

160. Helen Kimble, "The Tanzanian Economy," October 1, 1974, FCO 31/1767, UKNA.

161. Arthur Kellas to East Africa Department, UK FCO, "The USSR and Tanzania," April 22, 1974, FCO 31/1761, UKNA.

162. A. V. Kiva, "Tropicheskaia Afrika: Nekotorye problemy revoliutsionno-demokraticheskikh preobrazovanii v derevne ('udzhamaa' v Tanzanii)" [Tropical Africa: Some problems of revolutionary-democratic transformation in the village ("ujamaa" in Tanzania], *Narody Azii i Afriki* 5 (1974): 23.

163. Sergey Slipchenko to Vyacheslav Ustinov, head third Africa division Soviet MFA, July 3, 1975, F.653 O.18 P.16 D.3, AVPRF, pp. 70, 84, 90.

164. V. Lipniakov, second secretary Soviet embassy in Dar es Salaam, to Soviet MFA, report on visit of Nyerere to Yugoslavia, Romania, Mexico, and Jamaica, June 5, 1975, F.653 O.17 P. 16 D.3, AVPRF, p. 20.

165. Pierre Razoux, *The Iran-Iraq War,* trans. Nicolas Elliott (Cambridge, MA: Harvard University Press, 2015), 465.

166. Lusinde interview.

167. British high commissioner Dar es Salaam Horace Phillips to East Africa Department, UK FCO, January 4, 1971, passing on US embassy report, "Mainland Tanzania's Relations with Communist Countries," FCO 31/976, UKNA.

168. Butiku interview; and George Kahama, interview with the author, Dar es Salaam, Tanzania, August 8, 2016.

169. Report of Sergey Slipchenko, December 5, 1974, RGANI F.5 O.67 D.793, pp. 241–242.

170. Sergey Slipchenko, "O nekapitalisticheskogo puti razvitiia Tanzanii" [On the noncapitalist path of development of Tanzania], July 30, 1975, F.5 O.69 D.2570, RGANI, p. 79.

171. "Reise einer Lektorengruppe in die VR Angola zur Durchführung eines Lehrganges zur Qualifizierung von Leitern für die Wirtschaft" [Trip of a group of lecturers in the People's Republic of Angola to conduct a course for the qualification of leaders for the economy], March 17, 1977, DY 30/J IV 2/3J 2182, SAPMO-BArch, p. 3. Despite the fact that the seminar itself was actually conducted by East Germans, the content was closely coordinated with the Soviets, as the report itself attests: "The group of lecturers coordinated its approach with the Soviet advisory group on planning and economy then in Luanda and maintained consistent contact with them" (p. 7).

4. Lenin without Marx

Epigraphs: Soviet Embassy Luanda to Soviet Ministry of Foreign Affairs (MFA), report on the press, F.658 O.75 P.4 D.6, Arkhiv Venshneĭ Politikoĭ Rossisskoĭ Federatsii (Foreign Policy Archive of the Russian Federation; hereafter AVPRF), p. 20; Agostino Neto, *Quem é o inimigo? Qual é o nosso objectivo?* [Who is our enemy? What is our objective?], 2nd ed. (Lisbon: Edições Maria da Fonte, 1977), 12.

1. Arbeitsprotokoll, Politburo, Report on visit to Angola, July 6, 1976, DY 30/J IV 2/2A/1992 Stiftung Archiv der Parteien und Massenorganisationen der DDR—Bundesarchiv (Archive of the Parties and Mass Organizations of the German Democratic Republic—Federal Archives; hereafter SAPMO-BArch), p. 82.

2. See the information on the African Socialism Conference in Tunis, July 1975, F.5 O.68 D.1940, Rossisskiĭ Gosudarstvennyĭ Arkhiv Noveisheĭ Istorii (Russian State Archive of Contemporary History; hereafter RGANI).

3. Soviet Foreign Ministry report on Angola, January 7, 1963, F.658 O.3 P.1 D.1, AVPRF, pp. 31–32.

4. *O Mundo Portugês* [The Portuguese world] (a journal published in conjunction with the General Agency for Colonies and the Secretariat of National Progaganda in Portugal), 2 (1935): 218, quoted in Fernando Andresen Guimarães, *The Origins of the Angolan Civil War: Foreign Intervention and Domestic Political Conflict* (New York: St. Martin's, 2001), 10. For more information on *O Mundo Portugês,* see James Duffy, *Portuguese Africa* (Cambridge, MA: Harvard University Press, 1959), 273.

5. Guimarães, *Origins of the Angolan Civil War,* 23–25.

6. John Marcum, *The Angolan Revolution,* vol. 1, *The Anatomy of an Explosion (1950–1962)* (Baltimore: Port City, 1969), 191, 50.

7. Marcum, *The Angolan Revolution,* 1:27–28; "Aktenvermerk über die Aussprache mit Herrn da Cruz, Führer der nationalen Angolas Volksbefreiungsbewegung am 1.10.1960" [Record of the conversation with Mr. da Cruz, leader of the national People's Liberation Movement of Angola on 1.10.1960], DY 30/IV 2/20/416, SAPMO-BArch, p. 3.

8. Jean-Michel Mabeko-Tali, *Dissidências e poder de estado: O MPLA perante si próprio* [Dissidences and state power: The MPLA before itself] *(1962–1977),* vol. 1, *1962–1974* (Luanda, Angola: Editorial Nzila, 2001), 63.

9. Mabeko-Tali, *Dissidências e poder de estado,* 1:66–67.

10. Marcum, *The Angolan Revolution,* 1:42.

11. Soviet Foreign Ministry Report on Angola, January 7, 1963, F.658 O.3 P.1 D, AVPRF, p. 38; "Aktenvermerk über die Aussprache mit Herrn da Cruz, Führer der nationalen Angolas Volksbefreiungsbewegung am 1.10.1960" [Record of the conversation with Mr. da Cruz, leader of the national People's Liberation Movement of Angola on 1.10.1960], p. 3.

12. See PRC Foreign Ministry documents on MPLA delegation visit in 1960, Docs 108-00098-01, 108-00098-02, and 108-00098-06, 中国外交部开放档案 (Zhongguo Waijiaobu kaifang dang'an—Declassified Chinese Foreign Ministry Archives; hereafter CFMA).

13. See, for example, Marcum, *The Angolan Revolution,* 1:129–30. For Cruz's conversation with the East Germans, see "Zur Lage in Angola" [On the situation in Angola], April 17, 1961, DY 30/IV 2/20/416, SAPMO-BArch, p. 7.

14. Report of Second African Division, Soviet MFA, May 24, 1961, F.658 O.1 P.1 D.1, AVPRF, pp. 34–35, 36.

15. PRC Embassy in Guinea to PRC MFA, June 2, 1961, Doc 108-00264-01, CFMA, p. 2.

16. Draft resolution from International Department to Central Committee on parties and amounts to be funded by International Aid Fund to Left Workers' Organizations in 1962, n.d., F.89 Per. 38 No. 4, RGANI, p. 1. By comparison, the PCP was given fifty thousand dollars that same year. The total budget of the fund for 1962 was $10.64 million, over half of which went to the French and Italian Communist Parties.

17. "Zur Lage in Angola," p. 7.

18. "Beziehungsbericht 1961: Angola" [Report on relations 1961: Angola], n.d., DY 30/IV 2/20/416, SAPMO-BArch, p. 17.

19. PRC MFA correspondence on Cruz's request for aid, May 10–July 8, 1961, Doc 108-00273-01 CFMA, pp. 1, 4, 6.

20. Marcum, *The Angolan Revolution,* 1:254–255.

21. Mabeko-Tali, *Dissidências e poder de estado,* 1:83. Mabeko-Tali, a Congolese scholar educated in France, had become a sort of adopted son of Lucio Lara, a leading figure in the MPLA, in the 1960s in Brazzaville and continued to live with the Laras when they moved to Luanda in the 1970s. See Piero Gleijeses, *Conflicting Missions: Havana, Washington, and Africa, 1959–1976* (Chapel Hill: University of North Carolina Press, 2003), 235.

22. Mabeko-Tali, *Dissidências e poder de estado,* 1:82–84.

23. "Bericht über den Besuch des Präsidenten der MPLA, Dr. Agostinho Neto, in der DDR vom 20 bis 23 Mai 1963" [Report on the visit of the president of the MPLA Dr. Agostinho Neto to the GDR from 20 to 23 May 1963], June 13, 1963, DY/30/IV A 2/20 948, SAPMO-BArch, p. 3.

24. First African Division Soviet MFA, background report on Agostinho Neto, December 24, 1963, F.658 O.3 P.1 D.1, AVPRF, p. 70; Marcum, *The Angolan Revolution,* vol. 2, *Exile Politics and Guerilla Warfare (1962–1976)* (Cambridge, MA: MIT Press, 1978), 81–85; MPLA to Soviet Committee for Solidarity with the Countries of Asia and Africa, July 22, 1963, F.9540 O.1 D.137, Gosudarstvennyï Arkhiv Rossisskoï Federatsii (State Archive of the Russian Federation; hereafter GARF), p. 20.

25. First African Division, Soviet MFA, background report on Holden Roberto, December 24, 1963, F.658 O.3 P.1 D.1, AVPRF, p. 73.

26. PRC Embassy Ghana to PRC MFA, May 3, 1963, Doc 108-00938-02, CFMA, p. 1.

27. SCSCAA presidium discussion of Khartoum Conference, February 18, 1969, F.9540 O.1 D.255, GARF, pp. 56–96, 92.

28. Bulletin, "Vitoria ou Morte" [Victory or Death], January 8, 1967, DEFINT Group 15, box 213 FRef VS 20 Vol 5A, South African National Defence Force Archive (hereafter SANDFA), p. 1.

29. First African Department, Soviet MFA, background report on Roberto, p. 74; "Aktenvermerk über ein Gespräch von Botschafter Dr. Scholz mit dem Minister für Auswärtige Angelegenheiten der angolesischen Exilregierung, Herrn Jonas Malheiro Savimbi, am 20.1.1964 im BdB" [Record of a conversation with Ambassador Dr. Scholz with the Minister for Foreign Affairs of the Angola government in exile, Mr. Jonas Malheiro Savimbi, on 20.1.1964 in the embassy], January 20, 1964, DY/30/IV A 2/20 948, SAPMO-BArch, p. 2.

30. "Information über den Besuch des Aussenministers der angolesischen Exilregierung, Dr. Jonas Savimbi und seines Begleiters Florentino Duarte in der DDR vom 19–21.4.1964" [Information on a visit of the foreign minister of the Angolan government in exile Dr. Jonas Savimbi and his companion Florentino Duarte in the GDR from 19–21.1964], April 22, 1964, DY/30/IV A 2/20 948, SAPMO-BArch, p. 3.

31. First African Division, Soviet MFA, background report on Roberto, p. 74.

32. PRC MFA conference on possible FNLA delegation visit, Docs 108-01384-01, 108-01384-02, and 108-01384-03, CFMA.

33. PRC Peace Committee to PRC MFA, February 21, 1964, Doc 108-00573-05, CFMA, pp. 6–7.

34. PRC MFA to PRC Embassy Guinea, February 28, 1964 Doc 108-00573-05, CFMA, p. 8.

35. PRC Embassy United Arab Republic to PRC Peace Committee, April 19, 1964, Doc 108-00573-05, CFMA, p. 20.

36. PRC Peace Committee, first report, June 20, 1964, Doc 108-00573-05, CFMA, pp. 37–38.

37. PRC Peace Committee, sixth report, June 29, 1964, Doc 108-00573-05, CFMA, p. 55.

38. PRC Peace Committee, ninth report, July 1, 1964, Doc 108-00573-05, CFMA, p. 64.

39. PRC Foreign Affairs Institute report, July 13, 1964, Doc 108-00575-01, CFMA.

40. Draft resolution from International Department to Central Committee on parties and amounts to be funded by International Aid Fund to Left Workers' Organizations in 1967, December 26, 1966, F.89 Per. 38 No. 9, RGANI, p. 4.

41. For the MPLA, see "Ofício No 4194-Cl(2)-04Dez67-PIDE Lisboa-Rel.anexo," December 10, 1967, PIDE/DGS Del. A. S. S. Fundo L Serie Gab No de Proc 537 No das unidades 8046–8048, "Daniel Julio Chipenda 'Sango,' vol. 1, 1963–1967," Instituto dos Arquivos Nacionais da Torre do Tombo (Institute of National Archives of the Torre do Tombo; hereafter IAN-TT), p. 4. For the FNLA, see Portuguese MFA to Portuguese Polícia Internacional e de Defesa do Estado (International State and Defense Police), October 7, 1966, PT/TT AC, PIDE/DGS SC Serie SR No de Proc 882/61 No das unidades 3079 "FNLA," IAN-TT, p. 29; for Cruz's faction, see "Informação No 32-SC/Cl(2) assunto: Actividades terroristas em Angola" [Information No 32-SC/CL(2) subject: terrorist activites in Angola], January 16, 1965, PIDE/DGS SC Serie SR No de Proc 1153/51 No das Unidades 2691 "Viriato da Cruz," IAN-TT, p. 136; for UNITA, see "Informação No 512-SC/Cl(2) 5/28/1968 assunto: Apoio da China Comunista a UNITA" [Information No 512-SC/CL92] 5/28/1968 subject: Support of Communist China to UNITA], PIDE/DGS SC Serie Cl(2) No de Proc 19603 No das unidades 7842, "Jonas Sidonia Malheiro Savimbi," IAN-TT, p. 282.

42. For more on Cuban military aid to Angola in 1965–1967, see Gleijeses, *Conflicting Missions,* 174–184; Marcum, *The Angolan Revolution,* 2:174–178; and Mabeko-Tali, *Dissidências e poder de estado,* 1:109–110.

43. South African consul general in Luanda to South African secretary of foreign affairs Hilgard Muller, "Portugal in Africa," May 19, 1967, FRef 1/22/1 Vol.1 Angola: Political Situation and Developments 19/5/67–23/5/83, South African Department of Foreign Affairs Archive (hereafter SADFAA), p. 1.

44. KGB report on MPLA, June 4, 1970, F.5 O.62 D.536, RGANI, pp. 73–76.

45. Vyacheslav Ustinov, "O natsion'no-osvobidtel'noi bor'be na Iuge Afriki" [On the national liberation struggle in Southern Africa], April 27, 1972, F.5 O.64 D.549, RGANI, pp. 93–107.

46. Evgeni Afansenko, "O polozhenii v Narodnom Dvizhenii za Osvobozhdenie Angoly" [On the situation in the MPLA], March 30, 1974, F.5 O.67 D.758, RGANI, pp. 37–45.

47. Petr Ivashutin to CPSU Central Committee, July 24, 1969, F.5 O.61 D.542, RGANI, pp. 74–77.

48. KGB Report on MPLA, June 4, 1970, pp. 73–76.

49. Yuri Andropov to CPSU Central Committee, October 8, 1970, F.5 O.62 D.536, RGANI, pp. 212; Report on conversation of Dmitri Belokolos with Agostino Neto and Iko Carreira on September 25, 1970, Dmitri Belokolos to CPSU International Department, October 5, 1970, F.5 O.62 D.536, RGANI, pp. 215–218.

50. "Actividades e situacao do MPLA, relatadas pelo detido Armindo Augusto Fortes 'O Mongol,' euro-africano, que fez parte dos efectivos da base de Banga" [Activities and situation of the MPLA related by the detainee Armindo August Fortes "The Mongol," Euro-African, who was one of the fighters of the base in Banga], November 27, 1967, PIDE/DGS Del.A. S.S.Fundo L Serie Gab No de Proc 537 No das unidades 8046–8048, "Daniel Julio Chipenda 'Sango,' vol 1, 1963–1967," IAN-TT, p. 9.

51. "PIDE Angola Assunto: Actividades do MPLA" [PIDE Angola subject: Activities of MPLA], October 19, 1967, PIDE/DGS Del.A. Serie P Inf No de Proc 110.00.30 No das unidades 2545–2562 "MPLA," vol. 13, IAN-TT, p. 161.

52. "PIDE Luanda Assunto: Amilcar Cabral" [PIDE Luanda subject: Amilcar Cabral], July 8, 1968, IAN-TT, PIDE/DGS Del.A. Serie P Inf No de Proc 110.00.30 No das unidades 2545–2562 "MPLA," vol. 15, IAN-TT, p. 251.

53. Portuguese Information Bulletin No 488, August 14–21, 1971, DEFINT Group 15, box 219 VS 21 Vol 2A, Port. Info Bulletin No 488 14–21/8/71, SANDFA.

54. For South Africa, see "Die Oorlog in Angola 1971" [The war in Angola 1971], DEFINT Group 15, box 187 FRef VS 17 Vol 4B, SANDFA, p. 9. For the Soviet side, see the conversation of A. V. Budakov with Agostinho Neto, December 12, 1971, F.5 O.64 D.549, RGANI, pp. 2–4.

55. "Carta datada de 29Set71, dirigida por 'Kwanza Sul' a 'Viet Cong,' do seguinte teor: Lusaka/Zambia" [Letter dated 29 September 1971, sent by "Kwanza Sul" to "Viet Cong" with the following content: Lusaka, Zambia], September 29, 1971, PIDE/DGS Del.A. Serie P Inf No de Proc 110.00.30 No das unidades 2545–2562 Vol 21 "MPLA," IAN-TT, p. 291.

56. "Assunto: Joao Arnaldo Saraiva de Carvalho, o 'Tetembwa'" [Subject: Joao Arnaldo Saraiva de Carvalho, the 'Tetembwa'"], PIDE/DGS Del A SS Fundo L Serie Gab No de Proc 537 No das unidades 8046–8048 "Daniel Julio Chipenda 'Sango,'" DGS Angola March 23, 1972, IAN-TT, pp. 426–453.

57. DInf-2a Confidencial "MPLA-Organizaçao politico-military e administrativo" [MPLA—political-military and administrative organization], PIDE/DGS Del. A SS Fundo L No das unidades: 9089 MPLA: Relatorios Imediates 4/2/1967–12/18/1972, DGS Luanda No 243/72 IAN-TT, pp. 55–57.

58. Mabeko-Tali, *Dissidências e poder de estado,* 1:146.

59. (DGS—general director of security) Luanda to DGS Lisbon, "Movimento de Reajustamento do MPLA" [Movement of readjustment of MPLA], May 14, 1973, PIDE/DGS Del. SC Serie Cl(2) No de Proc. 404/73 No das unidades 7858, IAN-TT, pp. 5–34.

60. DGS Angola "Assunto: Joao Arnaldo Saraiva de Carvalho, o 'Tetembwa'" [Subject: Joao Arnaldo Saraiva de Carvalho, the 'Tetembwa'], March 23, 1972, PIDE/DGS Del A SSFundo L Serie Gab No de Proc 537 No das unidades 8046–8048 "Daniel Julio Chipenda 'Sango,'" DGS Angola 3/23/1972 "Assunto: Joao Arnaldo Saraiva de Carvalho, o 'Tetembwa,'" IAN-TT, p. 453.

61. Abteilung Internationale Verbindungen (AIV; International Relations Department), Sozialistische Einheitspartei Deutschlands (SED; Socialist Unity Party Germany), to GDR Politburo, No 155/71, December 30, 1971, DY 30/J IV 2/2J 3880, SAPMO-BArch, p. 5.

62. Mabeko-Tali, *Dissidências e poder de estado,* 1:126–128, 135.

63. Conversation of Dmitri Belokolos with Daniel Chipenda, December 14, 1972, F. 5 O.66 D.844, RGANI, pp. 9–11.

64. Conversation of Dmitri Belokolos with Daniel Chipenda, December 14, 1972, F. 5 O.66 D.844, RGANI, pp. 9–11; conversation of Dmitri Belokolos with Agostinho Neto, January 15, 1973, F. 5 O.66 D.844, RGANI, pp. 12–16.

65. Conversation of Dmitri Belokolos with A. G. Zulu, May 28, 1973, F.5 O.66 D.844, RGANI, pp. 71–74.

66. Viktor Kulikov to Soviet Central Committee, December 21, 1973, F.89 Per 46 No 104, RGANI, p. 4. Vladimir Shubin, who was involved in supporting the liberation movements in Africa through both the SCSCAA and the International Department, writes that if there was any interruption in Soviet aid to the MPLA it could only have taken place for a few months in 1974. See Vladimir Shubin, *The Hot "Cold War": The USSR in Southern Africa* (London: Pluto, 2008), 27–31.

67. Telegram, Soviet Central Committee to Soviet Embassy Zambia, F.89 Per 46 No 104, RGANI, p. 2.

68. Odd Arne Westad, "Moscow and the Angolan Crisis, 1974–1976: A New Pattern of Intervention," *Cold War International History Project Bulletin* 8–9 (1996–1997): 23.

69. Kulikov to Central Committee, December 21, 1973, p. 6.

70. E. Afanasenko, political letter, March 30, 1974, F. 5 O.67 D.758, RGANI, pp. 37–45.

71. Agostinho Neto, quoted in report from Sergey Slipchenko, February 21, 1974, F. 5 O.67 D.758, RGANI, pp. 27–29.

72. Conversation of Iu. A. Iukalov, chargé d'affaires of USSR in Tanzania, with Julius Nyerere, April 18, 1974, F.5 O.67 D.793, RGANI, pp. 78–81.

73. Conversation of Iu. A. Iukalov with Julius Nyerere, April 23, 1974, F.5 O.67 D.793, RGANI, p. 83.

74. Marcum, *The Angolan Revolution,* 2:245, 230.

75. Gleijeses, *Conflicting Missions,* 239–242.

76. Portuguese support would lead to tension with the PRC, including a delay in the establishment of relations, as Beijing sought to pressure Lisbon to give up its support for the pro-Soviet MPLA. See Telegram no. 044754, Lisbon (M. Iliescu) to Romanian MFA, Dosar 1439 220/1975, Arhive Diplomatice ale Ministerul Afacerilor Externe, p. 9. For more on MPLA talks and coordination with Portuguese authorities in Angola in 1974, see the conversation of B. G. Putilin, with Agostinho Neto, November 25, 1974, F.5 O.67 D.758, RGANI, pp. 140–141; and the conversation of Sergey Slipchenko with Agostinho Neto, December 1, 1974, F.5 O.67 D.758, RGANI, pp. 142–150.

77. Conversation of Slipchenko with Neto, December 1, 1974, p. 144.

78. Conversation of G. P. Predvechnyi with Domingos da Silva, MPLA vice president, June 14, 1974, F.5 O.67 D.758, RGANI, pp. 72–73; conversation of B. G. Putilin with Jantel Viana and Fernando Paiva, June 18, 1974, F.5 O.67 D.758, RGANI, pp. 74–75.

79. Soviet Solidary Committee conversation with ZAPU delegation, May 27, 1974, F.9540 O.1 D.371a, GARF, p. 60.

80. Telegram, Report to DGS Luanda, July 3, 1974, PIDE/DGS Del.A Serie P Info No de Proc 110.00.30 No das unidades 2545–2562 "MPLA," vol. 27, Perintrep No 930 QG/RMA-2a, IAN-TT, p. 357. The telegram was read to Neto by Soviet ambassador Evgeni Afanasenko in Brazzaville, June 8, 1974; see F.5 O.67 D.758, RGANI, pp. 78–81.

81. Aleksader Dzasokhov, report to CPSU Central Committee based on conversation with MPLA congress delegates José Nelumba de Karlmo and Sebastian Coreia, September 17, 1974, F.5 O.67 D.759, RGANI, pp. 101–110. See also Mabeko-Tali, *Dissidências e poder de estado*, 1:196–204.

82. Commander in Chief of armed forces of Angola quarter-general, "Assunto: Actividades do MPLA" [Subject: Activities of MPLA], September 27, 1974, PIDE/DGS Del A Serie P Info No de Proc 110.00.30 No das unidades 2545–2562 "MPLA," vol. 28, IAN-TT, p. 225; Commander in Chief of armed forces of Angola quarter-general, "Assunto: MPLA/Movimento de reponsaveis e situacao psicologico dos militantes" [Subject: MPLA/movement of people in charge and psychological situation of militants], August 21, 1974, PIDE/DGS Del.A Serie P Info No de Proc 110.00.30 No das unidades 2545–2562 "MPLA," vol. 27, IAN-TT, p. 30; conversation of Evgeni Afanasenko with José Eduardo dos Santos, October 10, 1974, F.5 O.67 D.758, RGANI, pp. 121–122. See also Odd Arne Westad, *Global Cold War: Third World Interventions and the Making of Our Times* (Cambridge: Cambridge University Press, 2005), 224.

83. "Der Gespräch zwischen den Delegationen der Sozialistischen Einheitspartei Deutschlands unter Leitung des Genossen Hermann Axen und der Volksbefreiungsfront von Angola unter Leitung von Dr. Agostinho Neto im Hause des Zentralkomitees der SED am 7 und 8 Mai 1974" [The conversation between delegations of the Socialist Unity Party of Germany under the leadership of comrade Hermann Axen and the People's Liberation Front of Angola under the leadership of Dr. Agostino Neto in the building of the Central Committee of the SED on 7 and 8 May 1974], DY/30 11387, SAPMO-BArch; "Weitere Unterstützung der Volksbefreiungsbewegung von Angola (MPLA)" [Further support for the People's Liberation Movement of Angola (MPLA)], November 26, 1974, DY 30/J IV 2/3A 2606 Sek Protokoll No. 128 SAPMO-BArch, p. 128.

84. GS/RMA -2a Report for DGS Luanda, October 8, 1974, PIDE/DGS Del.A Serie P Info No de Proc 110.00.30 No das unidades 2545–2562 "MPLA," vol. 27, IAN-TT, p. 126.

85. Iko Carreira of the MPLA referred to this agreement during his visit to the GDR in August 1975; see "8. Unterstützung der Volksbefreiungsbewegung Angolas (MPLA) in Vorbereitung der Unabhängigkeit Angolas am 11 November 1975" [8. Support for the People's Liberation Movement of Angola (MPLA) in preparation for the independence of Angola on 11 November 1975], DY 30/J IV 2/2A 1911 Politburo Protocol No 38/75 9/9/75, SAPMO-BArch, 71. See also Westad, *Global Cold War,* 224.

86. Westad, *Global Cold War,* 225.

87. GAP DINF (Department of Information) daily report, February 21, 1975, IAN-TT PIDE/DGS Del.A Serie P Inf No de Proc 110.00.30 No das unidades 2545–2562 "MPLA," vol. 31, p. 21; GAP DINF daily report, February 24, 1975, IAN-TT PIDE/DGS Del.A Serie P Inf No de Proc 110.00.30 No das unidades 2545–2562 "MPLA," vol. 31, p. 14.

88. Gleijeses, *Conflicting Missions*, 247–255.

89. Westad, *Global Cold War*, 226–227; Marcum, *The Angolan Revolution*, 2:245–246.

90. Marcum, *The Angolan Revolution*, 2:246–248.

91. Mabeko-Tali, *Dissidências e poder de estado*, 1:224–225.

92. Vice consul Luanda to chief of staff of intelligence, "The Situation in Angola," February 5, 1975, DEFINT Group 1, box 51 AMI/SK/1/8/3 Vol 2 EIE MA: Angola: Algemene Inligting Ex Angola 21/10/74–17/5/75, SANDFA, p. 92.

93. Shubin, *The Hot "Cold War,"* 38, 39.

94. See Gleijeses, *Conflicting Missions*, 268; and Shubin, *The Hot "Cold War,"* 40.

95. Consul general Luanda to chief of staff of intelligence, "The Week in Angola," June 26, 1975, DEFINT Group 3, vol. 2, box 601 MI/INT/1/5 Vol.I Aktiwiteite in Angola 6/3/75–27/10/75, SANDFA, p. 50.

96. Shubin, *The Hot "Cold War,"* 43.

97. SCSCAA presidium session, June 5, 1975, F.9540 O.1 D.387, GARF, pp. 108–109.

98. SED Politburo Protocol No 38/75, September 9, 1975, DY 30/J IV 2/2A 1911, SAPMO-BArch, pp. 66–77; Horst Dohlus to Erich Honecker, August 25, 1975, DY 30/IV B 2/12/55, SAPMO-BArch, p. 141; Westad, *Global Cold War*, 231–236.

99. See Gleijeses, *Conflicting Missions*, 254–257. The issue of whether or not Cuba acted on its own or as a Soviet proxy has long been a subject of debate regarding events in Angola, but Gleijeses, who has had unprecedented access to Cuban documents, convincingly makes the case that Cuba acted initially on its own without Soviet direction or support.

100. Weekly Report No 16/75, November 28, 1975, DEFINT Group 3, vol. 2, box 602 FRef MI/INT/1/5 Vol III 28/11/75–1/3/76, SANDFA, p. 15. The report mentions the end of Chinese aid to the FNLA as a blow to the movement, and says a "top UNITA leader" confirmed that Chinese aid to UNITA had been ended, but no specific dates are given. See also Marcum, *The Angolan Revolution*, 2:265.

101. Colin Legum and Tony Hodges, *After Angola: The War over Southern Africa* (New York: Africana, 1976); Angola Weekly Report No 8/75, "Summary of the Situation," October 3, 1975, DEFINT Group 3, vol. 2, box 601 MI/INT/1/5 Vol. I Aktiwiteite in Angola 6/3/75–27/10/75, SANDFA, pp. 96–100; Weekly Report No 3/76, "Summary of the Situation," January 23, 1976, Archive Group MinDef (PW Botha) Group 4, box 171 FRef MV/56/6/1 Vol III 1/12/75–12/2/76, SANDFA.

102. Marcum, *The Angolan Revolution*, 2:265, Steven F. Jackson, "China's Third World Foreign Policy: The Case of Angola and Mozambique, 1961–93," *China Quarterly* 142 (1995): 407.

103. For more information on PRC-US exchanges regarding Angola in 1975, and particularly Chinese attempts to encourage the United States to do more to confront the Soviet Union, see Henry Kissinger, *The Kissinger Transcripts: The Top-Secret Talks with Beijing and Moscow*, ed. William Burr (New York: New Press, 1998), 382, 400–403; and Jackson, "China's Third World Foreign Policy," 409–410. For the best narrative of the American involvement in Angola at the time, see John Stockwell, *In Search of Enemies: A CIA Story* (New York: W. W. Norton, 1978).

104. Deng Xiaoping, speech at a special session of the United Nations General Assembly, April 10, 1974, in Barbara Barnouin and Yu Changgen, *Chinese Foreign Policy during the Cultural Revolution* (London: Routledge, 1998), 214–226.

105. Westad, "Moscow and the Angolan Crisis," 25.

106. Rector of the Moscow State Institute of International Relations Nikolai Lebedev to L. F. Il'ichev, "Sootnoshenie sil i interesov v Angole" [Correlation of forces and interests in Angola], Feb-

ruary 12, 1976, F. 658 O.75 P.4 D.6, AVPRF, pp. 108–126. Though the report was delivered in February, it specifies that the analysis was conducted in January.

107. For more on the Cuba-South Africa debates, see Gleijeses, *Conflicting Missions,* 300–327; Westad, *Global Cold War,* 230–235; Shubin, *The Hot "Cold War,"* 50–56; and Marcum, *The Angolan Revolution,* 2:266–275.

108. "Mitteilung des Ausserordentlichen und Bevollmächtigen Botschafters der UdSSR in der DDR, Genossen P.A. Abrassimow vom 2 November 1975, 19:00 Uhr, an Genossen Axen" [Message from the Ambassador extraordinare and plenipotentiary of the USSR in the GDR comrade P.A. Abrasimov from 2 November 1975, 19:00 hours to comrade Axen], November 2, 1975, DY 30/13914, SAPMO-BArch, p. 1; Shubin, *The Hot "Cold War,"* 65.

109. For more on these committees and the political situation in Angola after the coup, see Jean-Michel Mabeko-Tali, *Dissidências e poder de estado: O MPLA perante si próprio* [Dissidences and the power of the state: The MPLA before itself] *(1962–1977),* vol. 2, *1974–1977* (Luanda, Angola: Editorial Nzila, 2001), 45–75.

110. Paul Fauvet, "Angola: The Rise and Fall of Nito Alves," *Review of African Political Economy* 9 (1977): 93, 91.

111. B. G. Putilin, "O polozhenii v MPLA" [On the situation in the MPLA], March 27, 1976, F.5 O.69 D.2513, RGANI, p. 34.

112. Fauvet, "Angola: The Rise and Fall of Nito Alves," 84–88.

113. Soviet Embassy Luanda to Soviet MFA, on creation of organs of people's power in Angola, June 16, 1976, F.658 O.75 P.4 D.6, AVPRF, p. 202.

114. Shubin, *The Hot "Cold War,"* 63; Soviet Embassy Luanda to Soviet MFA, June 16, 1976, p. 202.

115. Soviet Embassy Luanda to Soviet MFA, June 16, 1976, p. 202.

116. Soviet Embassy Luanda to Soviet MFA, June 16, 1976, p. 203.

117. Daily Report 27/76, March 30, 1976, DEFINT Group 3, vol. 2, box 602 FRef MI/INT/1/5 29/3/76–20/7/76, SANDFA, p. 72.

118. Conversation of Slipchenko with Neto, December 1, 1974, p. 147.

119. V. Muzalev, second secretary Soviet embassy Luanda, "Polozhenie v Angol'skikh profsoiuzakh" [Situation in the Angolan trade unions], August 14, 1976, F.5 O.69 D.2513, RGANI, pp. 89–95.

120. Conversation of Sergey Slipchenko with Agostinho Neto, September 30, 1974, F.5 O.67 D.758, RGANI, p. 119.

121. B. G. Putilin, 1st secretary embassy Brazzaville, "Nekotorye sotsial'no-ekonomicheskie aspekty polozheniia v Angole na sovremennom etape" [Some socioeconomic aspects of the situation in Angola at the current stage], December 25, 1974, F.5 O.68 D.1941, RGANI, p. 17.

122. Soviet Embassy Luanda to Soviet MFA, information on MPLA, May 24, 1976, F.658 O.75 P.4 D.6, AVPRF, p. 221.

123. Soviet Embassy Luanda to Soviet MFA, report on the press, F.658 O.75 P.4 D.6, AVPRF, p. 20.

124. "Informationen über den Aufenthalt der Genossen Siegfried Büttner und Hans Schaul in der Volksrepublik Angola vom 25. Febr. Bis 1 März 1976" [Information about the stay of comrades Siegfried Büttner and Hans Schaul in the People's Republic of Angola from 25 February to 1 March 1976], DY 30/J IV 2/2.035/128, SAPMO-BArch, pp. 114–115.

125. Franzisco Garcia Valls to Gerhard Weiss, March 10, 1976, DY 30/J IV 2/2.035/128, SAPMO-BArch, pp. 127–129.

126. Mabeko-Tali, *Dissidências e poder de estado,* 2:173–174.

127. Arbeitsprotokoll, Politburo, report on visit to Angola, July 6, 1976, DY 30/J IV 2/2A/1992, SAPMO-BArch, p. 82.

128. Boris Ponamarev and Leonid Brezhnev, quoted in Shubin, *The Hot "Cold War,"* 67.

129. Soviet Embassy Luanda to Soviet MFA, report on arrival of trade union delegation in Angola, April 19, 1976, F.658 O.75 P.4 D.6, AVPRF, pp. 256–257; Soviet Embassy Luanda to Soviet MFA, report on MPLA youth organization, July 16, 1976, F.658 O.75 P.4 D.6, AVPRF, p. 262.

130. Soviet Embassy Luanda to Soviet MFA, report on arrival of group of Bulgarian agricultural and food experts, July 10, 1976, F.658 O.15 P.8 D.7, AVPRF, p. 54.

131. Plan of cooperation between the Cuban Communist Party and the MPLA, July 29, 1976, F.658 O.15 P.8 D.7, AVPRF, pp. 120–122. For a list of tasks divided up among members of the embassy, see the control plan for fulfillment of Soviet-Angola agreements, August 14, 1976, F.658 O.75 P.4 D.6, AVPRF, pp. 173–179.

132. Daily Report 67/76, June 24, 1976, DEFINT Group 3, vol. 2, box 602 FRef MI/INT/1/5 29/3/76–20/7/76, SANDFA, p. 205.

133. For a specific narrative of one particular paper factory during and after the war, see Soviet Embassy Luanda to Soviet MFA, August 14, 1976, F.658 O.15 P.8 D.7, AVPRF, pp. 144–145.

134. Daily Report No 22/76, March 23, 1976, DEFINT Group 3, vol. 2, box 602 FRef MI/INT/1/5 29/3/76–20/7/76, SANDFA, p. 49.

135. "Informationen über den Aufenthalt der Genossen Siegfried Büttner und Hans Schaul in der Volksrepublik Angola vom 25. Febr. Bis 1 März 1976" [Information about the stay of comrades Siegfried Büttner and Hans Schaul in the People's Republic of Angola from 25 February to 1 March 1976], DY 30/J IV 2/2.035/128, SAPMO-BArch, pp. 97, 98.

136. Conversation of Vladimir Shubin and other SCSCAA members with Rozheio Rodriguez de Carvalho, April 1, 1976, F.9540 O.1 D.405b, GARF, p. 27.

137. Arbeitsprotokoll, Politburo, report on visit to Angola, July 6, 1976, DY 30/J IV 2/2A/1992, SAPMO-BArch, p. 75.

138. Daily Report 39/76, April 29, 1976, DEFINT Group 3, vol. 2, box 602 FRef MI/INT/1/5 29/3/76–20/7/76, SANDFA, p. 100.

139. Agostinho Neto, speech of June 20, 1976, translated by V. Muzalev, second secretary of Soviet embassy Luanda, F.658 O.75 P.4 D.6, AVPRF, pp. 36–40.

140. Daily Report 126/76, September 27, 1976, DEFINT Group 3, vol. 2, box 602 MI/INT/1/5 Vol V 4/8/76–7/12/76, SANDFA, p. 80.

141. Soviet Embassy Luanda to Soviet MFA, information on the situation in Angolan trade unions, August 14, 1976, F.658 O.75 P.4 D.6, AVPRF, pp. 267–273.

142. Soviet Embassy Luanda to Soviet MFA, information on second national conference of workers of Angola, October 30, 1976, F.658 O.75 P.4 D.6, AVPRF, pp. 187–190.

143. "Bericht über den Besuch des Premierministers der Volksrepublik Angola, Lopo do Nascimento, Mitglied des Politbüros des ZK der MPLA, am 8 und 9 November 1977 in der DDR" [Report on the visit of the prime minister of the PRA, Lopo do Nascimento, member of the Politburo of the CC of the MPLA, on November 8–9, 1977, in the GDR], November 15, 1977, DY 30/J IV 2/2A 2117, SAPMO-BArch, p. 108.

144. A. Smirnov, third secretary Soviet embassy Mozambique, "Sotsial'no-politicheskie aspekty prevrashcheniia FRELIMO v partiiu" [Sociopolitical aspects of the transformation of FRELIMO into a party], December 21, 1976, F.5 O.69 D.2556, RGANI, p. 82.

145. Conversation of Dmitrije Babic with Maria Eugenia Neto, April 8, 1976, 1306/87 No. 264/1, Arhiv Jugoslavije (Archive of Yugoslavia; hereafter AJ).

146. Report on the visit of a League of Communists of Yugoslavia delegation to Angola for the celebration of the twentieth anniversary of the MPLA, 1406/87 No. 26/1, AJ.

147. For more on the oil industry in this period, see Ricardo Soares de Oliveira, "Business Success, Angola-Style: Postcolonial Politics and the Rise of Sonangol," *Journal of Modern African Studies* 45, no. 4 (2007): 595–619.

148. Yugoslav Federal Secretariat for Foreign Affairs, Department for Sub-Saharan Africa, report on official visit of Agostinho Neto to Yugoslavia, April 22–25, 1977, May 12, 1977, Fond No. 837. KPR, Folder No. I-3-a/3-6, AJ, p. 142.

149. Agostinho Neto, quoted in report on visit of MPLA party delegation to USSR, October 25, 1976, DY 30/13914, SAPMO-BArch, p. 9.

150. Shubin, *The Hot "Cold War,"* 66.

151. Report on MPLA party government delegation, October 25, 1976, DY 30/13914, SAPMO-BArch, pp. 8–11.

152. Daily Report 150/76, November 1, 1976, DEFINT Group 3, vol. 2, box 602 MI/INT/1/5 Vol V 4/8/76–7/12/76, SANDFA, pp. 147–148.

153. "Reise einer Lektorengruppe in die VR Angola zur Durchführung eines Lehrganges zur Qualifizierung von Leitern für die Wirtschaft" [Trip of a group of lecturers to the PR Angola for the conduct of seminars for the qualification of leaders for the economy], March 17, 1977, DY 30/J IV 2/3J 2182, SAPMO-BArch, p. 3.

154. Despite the fact that the seminar itself was actually conducted by East Germans, the content was closely coordinated with the Soviets, as the report itself attests: "The group of lecturers coordinated its approach with the Soviet advisory group on planning and economy then in Luanda and maintained consistent contact with them." "Reise einer Lektorengruppe in die VR Angola," 7.

155. "Reise einer Lektorengruppe in die VR Angola," 5.

156. Mabeko-Tali, *Dissidências e poder de estado,* 2:188.

157. G. Zverev, "Informatsiia o vstreche s chlenom Politburo votorym sekretarem TsK Kompartii Kuby ministrom oborony tovarischem Raulem Kastro, 15 maia 1976g. v Luande" [Information on a meeting with Politburo member, second secretary of the CC CP Cuba, minister of defense Raul Castro, 15 May 1976 in Luanda], F.5 O.69 D.2513, RGANI, p. 47.

158. Conversation of Günther Kleiber with Boris Vorob'ev, June 23, 1976, DY 30/J IV 2/2A/1992, SAPMO-BArch.

159. "Informacije o novim zbivanjima u sovjetsko-angolskim odnosima i predlozi za našu reakciju" [Information about new developments in Soviet-Angolan relations and suggestions for our reaction], March 15, 1977, 1406/87 No. 213/1, AJ.

160. Report on Neto's visit to Moscow, October 4, 1977, DY 30/13914, p. 12.

161. AJ 1406/87 No. 26/1, SAPMO-BArch, p. 7.

162. Mabeko-Tali, *Dissidências e poder de estado,* 2:219, 181, 185.

163. SED Politburo Protocol No 49/77, "3. Bericht über die Teilnahme einer Delegation des ZK der SED am I. Parteitag der Volksbefreiungsbewegung von Angola (MPLA) vom 4 bis 10 Dezember 1977 und Bericht über den offiziellen Besuch einer Delegations der DDR unter Leitung des Mitglieds des Politbüros des ZK der SED und Stellvertreter des Vositzenden des Staatsrates der DDR, Genossen H. Sindermann, in der demokratischen Republik Sao Tome und Prinzipe (DRSTP) vom 1 bis 14 Dezember 1977" [Report on the participation of a delegation of the CC SED to the first party congress of the People's Liberation Movement of Angola (MPLA) from 4 until 10 December 1977 and report on the official visit of a delegation of the HDR under the leadership of member of the politburo of the CC SED and deputy chairman of the state council of the GDR comrade H. Sindermann in the democratic republic of Sao Toe and Principe from 1 to 14 December 1977], December 20, 1977, DY 30/J 2/2A 2125, SAPMO-BArch, pp. 140–150.

164. For the 1978 figure, see Embassy of Yugoslavia in Angola, report for 1978, January 1979, 2106/86, No. 294/1, attachment 4, AJ. For the 1981 figure, see State Council of the People's Republic of Bulgaria, "Obsht doklad za Narodnata republika Angola" [General report on the People's Republic of Angola], 1981, F. 630 O. 12c D. 11, Tsentralen D'rzhaven Arkhiv (Central State Archives of Bulgaria; hereafter CStAB), p. 3.

165. Tom Young, "The Politics of Development in Angola and Mozambique," *African Affairs* 87, no. 347 (1988): 173.

166. Manuel Ennes Ferreira, *A indústria em tempo de guerra (Angola, 1975–91)* [Industry in time of war (Angola, 1975–91)] (Lisbon: Instituto da Defesa Nacional, 1999), 16.

167. State Council of the People's Republic of Bulgaria, "Obsht doklad za Narodnata republika Angola" [General report on the People's Republic of Angola], p. 12.

168. Conversation of Todor Zhivkov with José Eduardo dos Santos, October 3, 1981, F.16 O.60 D.283, CStAB, p. 10.

169. Report on visit of the secretary of organization of the Central Committee, MPLA-PT, Lucio Lara, May 14–May 31, 1981, August 11, 1981, 2408/87 Doc. 363/1, AJ.

170. M. R. Bhagavan, "Angola: Prospects for Socialist Industrialisation" (Uppsala, Sweden: Scandinavian Institute of African Studies, 1980), 22, 19, 21.

171. Young, "The Politics of Development," 184.

172. Quoted in Ricardo Soares de Oliveira, *Magnificent and Beggar Land: Angola since the Civil War* (Oxford: Oxford University Press, 2015), 141.

5. Opiate of the Masses, or Stimulant?

Epigraph: Dialogue between Mehdi Bazargan and Vladimir Vinogradov, quoted in Vladimir M. Vinogradov, *Diplomatiia: Liudi i sobytiia* [Diplomacy: People and events] (Moscow: ROSSPEN, 1998), 423.

1. Stephanie Cronin, introduction to *Reformers and Revolutionaries in Modern Iran: New Perspectives on the Iranian Left*, ed. Stephanie Cronin (London: RoutledgeCurzon, 2004), 5.

2. UK Middle Eastern Department, "Render Therefore unto Caesar," August 2, 1979, FCO 8/33/56 no. 1, UK National Archives (hereafter UKNA).

3. Report to GDR Politburo, "Die innenpolitische Lage in Iran nach der Proklamierung der Islamischen Republik" [The internal political situation in Iran after the proclamation of the Islamic Republic], April 1, 1980, DY 30/IV B 2/20/370, Stiftung Archiv der Parteien und Massenorganisationen der DDR—Bundesarchiv (Archive of the Parties and Mass Organizations of the German Democratic Republic—Federal Archives; hereafter SAPMO-BArch), p. 15.

4. Report from UK ambassador in Tehran to UK Foreign Office (FO), September 27, 1979, FCO 8/3358, UKNA.

5. See, for example, Albert Hourani, *Arabic Thought in the Liberal Age, 1798–1939* (Cambridge: Cambridge University Press, 1983); and Cemil Aydin, *The Politics of Anti-Westernism in Asia: Visions of World Order in Pan-Islamic and Pan-Asian Thought* (New York: Columbia University Press, 2007).

6. For more on the connection between nationalism, anti-imperialism, and the success of the Chinese Communist Party, see Chalmers Johnson, *Peasant Nationalism and Communist Power: The Emergence of Revolutionary China, 1937–1945* (Stanford, CA: Stanford University Press, 1962).

7. For more on the rise of the Iranian working class, see Mansoor Moaddel, *Class, Politics, and Ideology in the Iranian Revolution* (New York: Columbia University Press, 1993), 122–129.

8. See Cosroe Chaqueri, *The Soviet Socialist Republic of Iran: Birth of the Trauma* (Pittsburgh: University of Pittsburgh Press, 1995); Cosroe Chaqueri, "The Left in Iran, 1905–1940," *Revolutionary History* 10, no. 2 (2010): 34–47 and Jamil Hasanli, *At the Dawn of the Cold War: The Soviet-American Crisis Over Iranian Azerbaijan, 1941–1946* (New York: Rowan and Littlefield, 2006).

9. Fred Halliday, "The Iranian Left in International Perspective," in Cronin, ed., *Reformers and Revolutionaries in Modern Iran*, 30.

10. See, for example, "Baku Congress of the Peoples of the East: Fourth Session," September 4, 1920, https://www.marxists.org/history/international/comintern/baku/ch04.htm.

11. Rostislav Ul'ianovskii, "Nekotorye voprosy nekapitalisticheskogo razvitiia osvobodivshi-khsia stran" [Certain questions on the noncapitalist development of liberated countries], *Kommunist* 1 (1968): 117–118.

12. See, for example, Artemy Kalinovsky, *Laboratory of Socialist Development: Cold War Politics and Decolonization in Soviet Tajikistan* (Ithaca, NY: Cornell University Press, 2018); Timothy Nunan, *Humanitarian Intervention: Global Development in Cold War Afghanistan* (Cambridge: Cambridge University Press, 2016); Gregory Massell, *The Surrogate Proletariat: Muslim Women and Revolutionary Strategies in Soviet Central Asia, 1919–1929* (Princeton, NJ: Princeton University Press, 2015); and Eren Tasar, *Soviet and Muslim: The Institutionalization of Islam in Central Asia* (Oxford: Oxford University Press, 2017).

13. L. P. Polonskaia and A. D. Litman, "Vliianie religii na obshestvennuiu mysl' narodov Vostoka" [The influence of religion on the social thought of the peoples of the East], *Narody Azii i Afriki* 4 (1966): 9, 14, 15.

14. Alla Ionova, "Religiia i sovremennaia obshestvennaia mysl' narodov zarubezhnogo Vostoka" [Religion and contemporary social thought of the peoples of the foreign East], *Narody Azii i Afriki* 4 (1966): 264–270. See also Elena Alekseevna Doroshenko, *Shi'itskoe dukhovenstvo v sovremennom Irane* [Shi'ite clergy in contemporary Iran] (Moscow: Nauka, 1975).

15. M. Andreev, "Katolitsizm v bor'be za vliianie na rabochii klass" [Catholicism in the struggle for influence over the working class], *Mirovaia ekonomika i mezhdunarodnye otnosheniia* 1 (1966): 51–59.

16. Irina Grigulevich, "Tserkov' i revoliutsiia v Latinskoi Amerike" [The church and revolution in Latin America], *Mirovaia ekonomika i mezhdunarodnye otnosheniia* 2 (1973): 78–79.

17. Irina Grigulevich, *Miatezhnaia tserkov' v Latinskoi Amerike* [The rebellious church in Latin America] (Moscow: Nauka, 1972. For an article based on this book that Grigulevich subsequently published, see *Mirovaia ekonomika i mezhdunarodnye otnosheniia* 2 (1973): 68–79.

18. Irina Zorina, "Katoliki i revoliutsiia" [Catholics and revolution], *Mirovaia ekonomika i mezhdunarodnye otnosheniia* 8 (1973): 157.

19. For more on the Soviet relationship with Somalia in this period, see Radoslav A. Yordanov, *The Soviet Union and the Horn of Africa during the Cold War: Between Ideology and Pragmatism* (London: Lexington Books, 2016), 85–118.

20. Alexei Pasiutin to Council of Affairs of Religious Cults, Soviet Council of Ministers, February 2, 1971, F.5 O.63 D.590, Rossisskiĭ Gosudarstvennyĭ Arkhiv Noveisheĭ Istorii (Russian State Archive of Contemporary History; hereafter RGANI), pp. 16–22.

21. Rostislav Ul'ianovskii to Vladimir Solodovnikov, director of the Institute of Africa, August 31, 1972, F.5 O.63 D.590, RGANI, pp. 75–133.

22. Mohamed Siad Barre, quoted in Ul'ianovskii to Solodovnikov, August 31, 1972, 128.

23. Liudmila Polonskaia, "Religii sovremennogo Vostoka" [Religion of the contemporary East], *Mirovaia ekonomika i mezhdunarodnye otnosheniia* 1 (1973): 68, 76, 77–79, 80, 82.

24. See, for example, Doroshenko, *Shi'itskoe dukhovenstvo v sovremennom Irane*; Alla I. Ionova, *Musulmanskii natsionalizm v sovremennoi Indonezii* [Muslim nationalism in contemporary Indonesia] (Moscow: Nauka, 1972); and Liudmila R. Polonskaia, *Musulmanskie techeniia v obshchestvennoi mysli Indii i Pakistana: Kritika 'musulmanskogo natsionalizma'* [Muslim tendencies in the social thought of India and Pakistan: Critique of "muslim nationalism"] (Moscow: Izdatel-stvo Vostochnoi Literatury, 1963).

25. See *Narody Azii i Afriki* 3 (1979): 165–166.

26. A. G. Belskii, "Kontseptsii 'kul'turnoi samobytnosti' v ideologii razvivaiuschikhsia stran" [The conception of "cultural authenticity" in the ideology of developing countries], *Narody Azii i Afriki* 6 (1972): 222–224.

27. Ervand Abrahamian, *Iran between Two Revolutions* (Princeton, NJ: Princeton University Press, 1982), 81.

28. Pezhmann Dilami, "The First Congress of the Peoples of the East and the Iranian Soviet Republic of Gilan 1920–21," in Cronin, ed. *Reformers and Revolutionaries in Modern Iran,* 86, 88.

29. See Cosroe Chaqueri, "The Left in Iran, 1905–1940."

30. Yakov Blumkin, quoted in Halliday, "The Iranian Left in International Perspective," 23.

31. For a detailed account of the Fifty-Three and the opposition under Reza Shah, see Abrahamian, *Iran between Two Revolutions,* 154–165.

32. See Cosroe Chaqueri, "Iradj Eskandary and the Tudeh Party of Iran," *Central Asian Survey* 7, no. 4 (1988): 103–104.

33. Assef Bayat, *Making Islam Democratic: Social Movements and the Post-Islamist Turn* (Stanford, CA: Stanford University Press, 2007), 26.

34. For more on the USSR and the Azerbaijan crisis, see Hasanli, *At the Dawn of the Cold War;* Louise Fawcett, *Iran and the Cold War: The Azerbaijan Crisis of 1946* (Cambridge: Cambridge University Press, 2009); and Homa Katouzian, *Mussadiq and the Struggle for Power in Iran* (New York: St. Martin's, 1990), 57–59.

35. Mohammad Mossadeq, quoted in Vladislav Zubok and Constantine Pleshakov, *Inside the Kremlin's Cold War: From Stalin to Khrushchev* (Cambridge, MA: Harvard University Press, 1996), 29.

36. See Vladislav M. Zubok, "Stalin, Soviet Intelligence, and the Struggle for Iran, 1945–53," *Diplomatic History* 44, no. 1 (2020): 24; and Katouzian, *Mussadiq and the Struggle for Power in Iran,* 115. For more on the Tudeh Party's policy during the Mossadeq era, see Katouzian, *Mussadiq and the Struggle for Power in Iran,* 57–59; and Ervand Abrahamian, *The Coup: The CIA, and the Roots of Modern U.S.-Iranian Relations* (New York: The New Press, 2013), 59. For the ideological divergences between Mossadeq and the Tudeh Party, see Farkheddin Azimi, "The Overthrow of the Government of Mossadeq Reconsidered," *Iranian Studies* 45, no. 5 (2012): 701–703. On the Soviet side, Artemy Kalinovsky describes Soviet suspicion of Mosaddeq and the skepticism with which Stalin viewed the policy of oil nationalization, though documents directly linking Soviet and Tudeh Party policy are still unavailable in Moscow. See Artemy Kalinovsky, "The Soviet Union and Mosaddeq: A Research Note," *Iranian Studies* 47, no. 3 (2014): 401–418.

37. V. Grigor'ian to Vyacheslav Molotov, report on Tudeh activity, March 18, 1952, f.82 o.2 d.1221, Rossisskiĭ Gosudarstvennyĭ Arkhiv Sotsial'no-Politicheskoĭ Istorii (Russian State Archive of Sociopolitical History), p. 150.

38. Vladimir Kuzichkin, *Inside the KGB: Myth and Reality* (London: Andre Deutsche, 1990), 216–218.

39. For more reasons for the Soviet shift in approach toward Iran, see V. Ivanenko and Michel Vale, "Twenty Years of Soviet-Iranian Economic and Technical Cooperation," *Soviet and Eastern European Foreign Trade* 21, nos. 1–3 (1985): 135–143; Roham Alvandi, "Flirting with Neutrality: The Shah, Khrushchev, and the Failed 1959 Soviet-Iranian Negotiations," *Iranian Studies* 47, no. 3 (2014): 419–440; and Roham Alvandi, "The Shah's Détente with Khrushchev: Iran's 1962 Missile Base Pledge to the Soviet Union," *Cold War History* 14, no. 3 (2014): 423–444.

40. Horst Bittner to Gerhard Weiss, ZR 1614/81, Politisches Archiv des Auswärtigen Amts (Political Archive of the Federal Foreign Office; hereafter PAAA).

41. For more on Soviet-Iranian economic cooperation in third period, see Ivanenko and Vale, "Twenty Years of Soviet-Iranian Economic and Technical Cooperation," 135–143.

42. For an extensive treatment of the splintering of the communist world in the 1960s and 1970s, see Jeremy Friedman, *Shadow Cold War* (Chapel Hill: University of North Carolina Press, 2015).

43. Maziar Behrooz, "The Iranian Revolution and Legacy of the Guerrilla Movement," in Cronin, ed., *Reformers and Revolutionaries in Modern Iran,* 191.

44. See Bizhan Jazani, *Capitalism and Revolution in Iran* (London: Zed, 1980).

45. Peyman Vahabzadeh, *A Guerrilla Odyssey: Modernization, Secularism, Democracy, and the Fadai Period of National Liberation in Iran, 1971–1979* (Syracuse, NY: Syracuse University Press, 2010), 133–134, 49–59.

46. Ervand Abrahamian, *The Iranian Mojahedin* (New Haven, CT: Yale University Press, 1989), 81–104. See also Behrooz, "The Revolution and the Guerrilla Movement."

47. Abrahamian, *Iranian Mojahedin*, 85–92.

48. Iraj Eskandari to Leonid Brezhnev, November 26, 1976, F.89 per.27 d.26, RGANI.

49. Hamid Dabashi, *Theology of Discontent* (New York: New York University Press, 1993), 222.

50. Katouzian, *Mussadiq and the Struggle for Power in Iran*, 97, 111, 100.

51. Jalal Al-e-Ahmad, *Gharbzadegi* [Plagued by the West] (Delmar, NY: Caravan Books, 1982).

52. Jalal Al-e-Ahmad, quoted in Dabashi, *Theology of Discontent*, 68.

53. Kingshuk Chatterjee, *'Ali Shari'ati and the Shaping of Political Islam in Iran* (New York: Palgrave Macmillan, 2011), 2.

54. Dabashi, *Theology of Discontent*, 137.

55. For an extensive treatment of Shariat's conceptions of Alid and Savafid Shi'ism, see Nikki R. Keddie, *Modern Iran: Roots and Results of Revolution* (New Haven, CT: Yale University Press, 2006), 203–204.

56. Ali Shari'ati, *On the Sociology of Islam*, trans. Hamid Algar (Berkeley: Mizan, 1978), 67. See also Chatterjee, *'Ali Shari'ati*, 160.

57. Dabashi, *Theology of Discontent*, 222.

58. Seyyed Mahmood Taleqani, *Islam and Ownership*, trans. Ahmad Jabbari and Farhang Rajaee (Lexington, KY: Mazda, 1983), 132, 74, 148.

59. Dabashi, *Theology of Discontent*, 385.

60. Conversation of Hermann Axen with Nuredin Kianouri, February 11, 1980, DY/IV B 2/20/370, SAPMO-BArch, p. 40.

61. Dabashi, *Theology of Discontent*, 386.

62. GDR Embassy in Tehran, "Information zum Wirtschaftsseminar der Regierung" [Information on the economics seminar of the government], ZR 1628/81, PAAA.

63. Doroshenko, *Shi'itskoe dukhovenstvo v sovremennom Irane*, 158–161, 149.

64. Abrahamian, *Iranian Mojahedin*, 123.

65. Negin Nabavi, *Intellectuals and the State in Iran: Politics, Discourse, and the Dilemma of Authenticity* (Gainesville: University of Florida Press, 2003), 149.

66. For the full story of the February 1979 revolution in Iran, see Abrahamian, *Iran between Two Revolutions*; Ali M. Ansari, *Modern Iran: The Pahlavis and After* (Essex, UK: Pearson Education, 2007); Keddie, *Modern Iran*; and Charles Kurzman, *The Unthinkable Revolution in Iran* (Cambridge, MA: Harvard University Press, 2005).

67. Asef Bayat, quoted in Maziar Behrooz, *Rebels with a Cause: The Failure of the Left in Iran* (London: I. B. Tauris, 1999), 148; Moaddel, *Class, Politics, and Ideology*, 122–129.

68. Abrahamian, *Iran between Two Revolutions*, 518.

69. Moaddel, *Class, Politics, and Ideology*, 155.

70. Halliday, "The Iranian Left in International Perspective," 27.

71. "Vermerk über ein Gespräch mit dem Journalisten Fariborz Atapor [*sic*] am 12.3.1979" [Note on a conversation with the journalist Fariborz Atapour on March 12, 1979], ZR 1611/81, PAAA. On the lack of an Islamic social movement before the revolution, see Bayat, *Making Islam Democratic*, 21–24.

72. Vinogradov, *Diplomatiia*, 418–419.

73. Keddie, *Modern Iran*, 233–234.

74. For more on Bazargan's background, see Dabashi, *Theology of Discontent*, 325–337.

75. Vinogradov, *Diplomatiia*, 410. See also Nuredin Kianouri, "Narodnaia revoliutsiia v Irane" [The popular revolution in Iran], *Kommunist* 5 (1979): 84. Kianouri also talks about "dual power."

76. Klaus Wolff to Hans-Joachim Willerding, October 18, 1978, ZR 1603/81, PAAA.

77. Report of November 13, 1978 sent by USSR (likely CPSU International Department) to SED, DY 30/13940, SAPMO-BArch, pp. 12–13.

78. For the description of Kianouri, see Abteilung Internationale Verbindungen (AIV; International Relations Department) to GDR Ministry of Foreign Affairs (MFA), "Lage in der Parteiführung der Volkspartei (Tudehpartei) Irans" [Situation in the party leadership of the People's Party (Tudeh Party) of Iran], January 31, 1979, DY 30/IV B 2/20/369, SAPMO-BArch, p. 10. For Kianouri's position against the shah in internal Tudeh debates, see Chaqueri, "Iradj Eskandary and the Tudeh Party of Iran," 111. For more on the attempted assassination of the shah, see Katouzian, *Mussadiq and the Struggle for Power in Iran*, 60–61.

79. Mohsen M. Milani, "Harvest of Shame: Tudeh and the Bazargan Government," *Middle Eastern Studies* 29, no. 2 (1993): 309.

80. Iraj Eskandari, "Krizis rezhima v Irane" [Crisis of the regime in Iran], *Problemy mira i sotsializma* 11 (1978): 46. In another study, Kianouri talks about Eskandari's dissent from the Tudeh Party's pro-Khomeini policy; see Nuredin Kianouri, *Khaterat-e Nuredin Kianuri* [Memoirs of Nuredin Kianouri] (Tehran: Information, 1993), 513–515.

81. Eskandari, "Krizis rezhima v Irane," 3. Eskandari himself blamed the Azerbaijan Communist Party rather than the Irani International Department or Foreign Ministry. See Chaqueri, "Iradj Eskandary and the Tudeh Party of Iran," 114.

82. "Vermerk über ein Gespräch zwischen dem Ersten Sekretär des ZK der Tudeh-Partei des Iran, Genossen Kianouri, und Genossen Guttman am 3.August 197c" [Note on a conversation between the first secretary of the Tudeh Party of Iran, Comrade Kianouri, and Comrade Guttman on August 3, 1979], DY 30/IV B 2/20/369, SAPMO-BArch, p. 93.

83. AIV, "Disposition für die Konsultations mit Genossen Ponomarjow" [Disposition for consultation with Comrade Ponomarev], January 24, 1979, DY 30/IV B 2/20/154, SAPMO-BArch, p. 11.

84. Conversation of Boris Ponomarev with Hermann Axen, January 25–26, 1979, DY 30/IV B 2/20/154, SAPMO-BArch, p. 56.

85. Kuzichkin, *Inside the KGB,* 285, 261.

86. AIV to GDR MFA, "Zu den Auseinandersetzungen im Iran" [On the confrontations in Iran], January 26, 1979, DY 30/IV B 2/20/369, SAPMO-BArch, p. 5.

87. See Friedman, *Shadow Cold War,* 57–58.

88. AIV to GDR MFA, "Zu den Auseinandersetzungen im Iran," p. 4.

89. Near and Middle East Sector, GDR Ministry of Foreign Affairs (NMS), "Zur Rolle des Schiismus und der schiitischen Geistlichkeit im Iran" [On the role of Shi'ism and the Shi'ite clergy in Iran], February 1, 1979, DY 30/IV B 2/20/369, SAPMO-BArch, p. 15.

90. AIV to GDR MFA, "Lage in der Parteiführung der Volkspartei (Tudehpartei) Irans," p. 11.

91. AIV to GDR Politburo based on conversation with Jila Siassi, Tudeh representative for international relations, DY 30/IV B 2/20/369, SAPMO-BArch, p. 102.

92. NMS, "Innenpolitische Lage Irans" [The domestic political situation in Iran], September 18, 1979, DY 30/IV B 2/20/369, SAPMO-BArch, p. 138.

93. "Vermerk über das Gespräch mit dem Botschafter der UdSSR im Iran, Gen. W.M. Winogradow am 22.10.1979" [Note on a conversation with the ambassador of the USSR in Iran, Comrade V. M. Vinogradov on October 22, 1979], October 22, 1979, DY 30/IV B 2/20/369, SAPMO-BArch, p. 145.

94. Telegram, Hucke, to NMS and AIV, July 19, 1979, DY 30/IV B 2/20/369, SAPMO-BArch, p. 70.

95. Open letter of Tudeh Party, *Mardom,* July 24, 1979, ZR 3512/82, p. 15, PAAA.

96. "Information über die Gespräche zwischen Genossen B. N. Ponomarjow, Kandidat des Politburos und Sekretär des ZK der KPdSU, und Genossen Hermann Axen, Mitglied des Politburos und Sekretär des ZK der SED, am 25. und 26. Januar 1979" [Information on a conversation between Comrade B. N. Ponomarev, candidate member of the Politburo and secretary of the Central Committee of the Communist Party of the Soviet Union and Comrade Hermann Axen, member of the Politburo and secretary of the Central Committee of the SED, on January 25 and 26, 1979], January 26, 1979, DY 30/IV B 2/20/154, SAPMO-BArch, pp. 43–66.

97. For more on the relationship between the United States and Bakhtiar's government, and in particular the Iranian military leadership, see Robert Huyser, *Mission to Tehran* (New York: Harper and Row, 1986). Huyser was the deputy commander of US forces in Europe and sent to Tehran in January 1979 to coordinate the Iranian military's strategy during the revolution. While he seemed in favor of a coup, it seems that Washington was hesitant to order one and that he and the US ambassador in Iran, William Sullivan, were working at cross purposes, since Sullivan was trying to make contact with Khomeini and the opposition. See also William H. Sullivan, *Mission to Iran* (New York: W. W. Norton, 1981). Zbigniew Brzezinski, President Jimmy Carter's national security adviser, claims that the White House considered but rejected the idea of a coup. See Zbigniew Brzezinski, *Power and Principle: Memoirs of the National Security Advisor, 1977–1981* (New York: Farrar, Straus and Giroux, 1983).

98. Central Committee (CC), CPSU International Department, to AIV, SED, February 5, 1979, DY 30/13940, SAPMO-BArch, pp. 16–17.

99. Vinogradov, *Diplomatiia,* 444.

100. Politburo Information "Die Bedeutung und die Lehren des revolutionären Prozesses in Chile: Die nachfolgende Material ist eine erste Analyse sowjetischer Wissenschaftler, die keinen offiziellen Charakter trägt, sondern als vorläufiges Arbeitsmaterial zu betrachten ist" [The meaning and lessons of the revolutionary process in Chile: The following material is a first analysis of Soviet scholars that has no official character, but is to be viewed as provisional working material], DY 30/J IV 2/2J 4974, SAPMO-BArch, p. 15.

101. See Olga Ulianova, "Soviet Perceptions and Analyses of the Unidad Popular Government and the Military Coup in Chile," *Estudios publicos* 79 (2000), 34; and Victor Figueroa Clark, "Nicaragua, Chile, and the End of the Cold War in Latin America," in *The End of the Cold War and the Third World: New Perspectives on Regional Conflict,* ed. Artemy M. Kalinovsky and Sergey Radchenko (London: Routledge, 2011), 192–207.

102. AIV, "16. Plenum des ZK der Volkspartei (Tudehpartei) Irans" [Sixteenth Plenum of the CC of the People's Party (Tudeh Party) of Iran], March 15, 1979, DY 30/11537, SAPMO-BArch, p. 15.

103. NMS, "Zur Entwicklung der Lage im Iran" [On the development of the situation in Iran], March 13, 1979, DY 30/IV B 2/20/369, SAPMO-BArch, p. 17.

104. Deputy head of the AIV to Hermann Axen, report on the situation in Iran, May 2, 1979, DY 30/IV B 2/20/369, SAPMO-BArch, p. 44.

105. Report of NMS, "Zur innenpolitischen Entwicklung in Iran" [On domestic political development in Iran], May 18, 1979, DY 30/IV B 2/20/369, SAPMO-BArch, p. 51.

106. Telegram, Klaus Wolff to CC SED and NMS, June 12, 1979, DY 30/IV B 2/20/369, SAPMO BArch, p. 61

107. Siavush Randjbar-Daemi, "Building the Islamic State: The Draft Constitution of 1979 Reconsidered," *Iranian Studies* 46, no. 4 (2013): 657.

108. Open letter of Tudeh Party, July 24, 1979, pp. 11, 15.

109. Mikhail Krutikhin, "Iran: Transition," *New Times* 29 (1979): 10–11.

110. See, for example, Kianouri, "Narodnaia revoliutsiia v Irane."

111. UK Embassy Tehran, "Brief for the Commonwealth Heads of Government Meeting in Lusaka, Zambia," July 9, 1979, FCO 8/3381, no. 68, UKNA, 3.

112. R. S. Gorham, "Iran: Outlook for the Future," November 15, 1979, FCO 8/3382, no. 99, UKNA.

113. The available evidence suggests that the United States was not actively supporting any groups opposing the IRI or looking to overthrow the new government during this period. See Mark Gasirowski, "US Covert Operations toward Iran, February–November 1979: Was the CIA Trying to Overthrow the Islamic Regime?" *Middle Eastern Studies* 51, no. 1 (2015): 115–135. Gasirowski writes elsewhere that the United States was not involved in the Nuzhih Plot of July 1980, though Shahpur Bakhtiar gave others the impression that he had American support. See Mark Gasirowski, "The Nuzhih Plot and Iranian Politics," *International Journal of Middle East Studies* 34, no. 4 (2002): 652. The Tudeh Party and IRI sources have often credited the party with helping the regime stop the coup attempt; see Gasirowski, "The Nuzhih Plot and Iranian Politics," 656; and Farhang Jahanpour, "Iran: The Rise and Fall of the Tudeh Party," *The World Today* 40, no. 4 (1984): 158.

114. "Einige Gedanken aus den Unterhaltungen während des Buffet dinners beim 1.Sekretär der Botschaft der CSSR in Tehran am 17.5.79" [Several thoughts from the encounters during the buffet dinner at the first secretary of the Embassy of Czechoslovakia in Tehran on May 17, 1979], ZR 1611/81, PAAA, p. 59.

115. Telegram, GDR ambassador in Tehran Klaus Wolff to CC SED and NMS, May 28, 1979, DY 30/IV B 2/20/369, SAPMO-BArch, pp. 59, 58.

116. Telegram, GDR ambassador in Tehran Klaus Wolff to Hans-Joachim Willerding, Hermann Axen, Egon Winkelmann, and Rainer Neumann, May 7, 1979, DY 30/IV B 2/20/369, SAPMO-BArch, p. 49.

117. Telegram, Klaus Wolff to CC SED, AIV, and NMS, August 22, 1979, DY 30/IV B 2/20/369, SAPMO-BArch, p. 98.

118. AIV to GDR Politburo, "Information über die Lage in Iran und in der Tudeh-Partei Irans" [Information on the situation in Iran and in the Tudeh Party of Iran], September 14, 1979, DY 30/IV B 2/20/369, SAPMO-BArch, p. 103.

119. NMS, "Zur den Auseinandersetzungen in Iranisch-Kurdistan" [On the confrontations in Iranian Kurdistan], September 4, 1979, DY 30/IV B 2/20/369, SAPMO-BArch, p. 100.

120. "Vermerk über das Gespräch mit dem Botschafter der UdSSR im Iran, Gen. W.M. Winogradow am 22.10.1979" [Note on a conversation with the ambassador of the USSR in Iran, Comrade V. M. Vinogradov on October 22, 1979], October 22, 1979, DY 30/IV B 2/20/369, SAPMO-BArch, p. 147. For more on Soviet reaction to the Kurdish uprising, see Aryeh Y. Yodfat, *The Soviet Union and Revolutionary Iran* (New York: St. Martin's, 1984).

121. On Afghanistan, see "Vermerk über ein Gespräch des Genossen Hermann Axen, Mitglied des Politburos und Sekretär des ZK der SED, mit Genossen Nureddin Kianouri, Erster Sekretär des ZK der Tudeh-Partei Irans, am 11.2.1980" [Note on a conversation of Comrade Hermann Axen, member of the Politburo and secretary of the CC SED, with Comrade Nureddin Kianouri, first secretary of the CC of the Tudeh Party of Iran, on February 11, 1980], February 11, 1980, DY 30/IV B 2/20/370, SAPMO-BArch, p. 42. Khomeini even asked the Tudeh Party to intercede with the Soviets on Afghanistan; see "Vermerk über 2 Gespräche des Genossen Hermann Axen, Mitglied des Politburos und Sekretär des ZK der SED, mit Genossen Nureddin Kianouri, 1 Sekretär des ZK der Tudeh-Partei Irans, am 16.6 und 17.6.1980" [Note on two conversations of Comrade Hermann Axen, member of the Politburo and secretary of the CC SED, with Comrade Nureddin Kianouri, first secretary of the Tudeh Party of Iran, on June 16 and June 17, 1980], June 17, 1980, DY 30/IV B 2/20/370, SAPMO-BArch, p. 54.

122. Telegram, Kluas Wolff to Hans-Joachim Willerding, and Egon Winkelmann, CC SED, and NMS, June 12, 1979, DY 30/IV B 2/20/369, SAPMO-BArch, p. 62.

123. NMS, "Zum Verfassungsentwurf der Islamischen Republik Iran" [On the draft constitution of the Islamic Republic of Iran], July 2, 1979, DY 30/IV B 2/20/369, SAPMO-BArch, p. 68.

124. Telegram, GDR Embassy Tehran to Hans-Joachim Willerding, Wolfgang Konschel, Hermann Axen, and Egon Winkelmann, July 19, 1979, DY 30/IV B 2/20/369, SAPMO-BArch, p. 71.

125. "Vermerk über ein Gespräch zwischen dem Ersten Sekretär des ZK der Tudeh-Partei des Iran, Genossen Kianouri, und Genossen Guttman am 3.August 1979" [Note on a conversation between the first secretary of the Tudeh Party of Iran, Comrade Kianouri and Comrade Guttman on August 3, 1979], August 3, 1979, DY 30/IV B 2/20/369, SAPMO-BArch, p. 95. Kianouri informed Guttman about his recent conversation with Ponomarev and Ul'ianovskii.

126. Leonid Medvedko, "Islam and Liberation Movements," *New Times* 43 (1979): 19–21.

127. A. I. Ionova, "Sovremennaia ideinaia evoliutsiia Islama" [The contemporary evolution of Islamic ideas], *Narody Azii i Afriki* 6 (1979): 27–29.

128. Report from ambassador in Tehran John Graham to UK FO, September 27, 1979, FCO 8/3358, UKNA.

129. Report from ambassador in Tehran John Graham, "Iran: Annual Review," December 31, 1979, FCO 8/3358, UKNA.

130. West German Embassy Tehran to MFA, Bonn, "Akzentverschiebungen in der künftigen iranischen Wirtschaftspolitik" [Shifts in emphasis in future Iranian economic policy], February 18, 1979, Wi400.00 IRN Iranische Wirtschaftspolitik 1979–1987 D 14570, PAAA.

131. GDR Embassy Tehran, "Information zum Wirtschaftsseminar der Regierung" [Information on the economic seminar of the government], PAAA-GDR MFA ZR 1627/81, PAAA.

132. Iranian minister of foreign affairs Ibrahim Yazdi, quoted in telegram, UK FO to UK Embassy Tehran, October 5, 1979, FCO 8/3358, UKNA.

133. See Moaddel, *Class, Politics, and Ideology,* 249–251.

134. Asef Bayat, *Street Politics: Poor People's Movements in Iran* (New York: Columbia University Press, 1997), 129.

135. "Vermerk über 2 Gespräche des Genossen Hermann Axen, Mitglied des Politbüros und Sekretär des ZK der SED, mit Genossen Nureddin Kianouri, 1 Sekretär des ZK der Tudeh-Partei Irans, am 16.6 und 17.6.1980" [Note on 2 conversations of comrade Hermann Axen, member of the politbüro and secretary of the CC SED with comrade Nuredin Kianouri, first secretary of the CC of the Tudeh Party of Iran on 16.6 and 17.6.1980], June 17, 1980, DY 30/IV B 2/20/370, SAPMO-BArch, p. 60.

136. Bayat, *Street Politics,* 127. For an excellent treatment of the successes and failures of the economic reform program, see Moaddel, *Class, Politics, and Ideology,* 224–255. See also Kevan Harris, *A Social Revolution: Politics and the Welfare State in Iran* (Berkeley: University of California Press, 2017), 100–115.

137. For more on the social justice rhetoric of the regime, see Mohammad Ayatollahi Tabaar, *Religious Statecraft: The Politics of Islam in Iran* (New York: Columbia University Press, 2018).

138. For Ponomarev and Ul'ianovskii, see "Vermerk über ein Gespräch zwischen dem Ersten Sekretär des ZK der Tudeh-Partei des Iran, Genossen Kianouri, und Genossen Guttman am 3.August 1979" [Note on a conversation between the first secretary of the Tudeh Party of Iran, Comrade Kianouri and Comrade Guttman on August 3, 1979], August 3, 1979, DY 30/IV B 2/20/369, SAPMO-BArch, pp. 92–95.

139. "Stenografische Niederschrift der Zusammenkunft des Generalsekretärs des ZK der SED und Vositzenden des Staatsrates der DDR, Gen. Erich Honecker, sowie der weiteren Mitglieder und Kandidaten des Politbüros des ZK der SED mit der Generalsekretär des ZK der KPdSU und Vorsitzenden des Präsidiums des Obersten Sowjets der UdSSR, Genossen Leonid Iljitsch Breschnew sowie den anderen Mitgliedern der sowjetischen Partei und Regierungsdelegation, am Donnerstag, dem

4.Oktober 1979, im Amtsitz des Staatsrates der DDR" [Stenographic account of the meeting between the general secretary of the CC SED and chairman of the State Council of the GDR, Comrade Erich Honecker, as well as other members and candidates of the Politburo of the CC SED with the general secretary of the CC CPSU, Comrade Leonid Brezhnev, as well as other members of the Soviet Party and government delegation, on Thursday, October 4, 1979], October 4, 1979, DY 30/2378, SAPMO-BArch, p. 79.

140. AIV to GDR Politburo, "Information über die Lage in Iran und in der Tudeh-Partei Irans" [Information on the situation in Iran and in the Tudeh Party of Iran], September 14, 1979, DY 30/IV B 2/20/369, SAPMO-BArch, p. 104, 105.

141. Arthur Koestler, *The God That Failed* (New York: Harper and Brothers, 1949), 54.

142. Behrooz, *Rebels with a Cause,* 106. While most historians do not think that Khomeini knew about the embassy seizure in advance, Tabaar writes that Ahmad Khomeini, Ruhollah Khomeini's son, indicated that the seizure had been coordinated with the imam's office in advance. See Tabaar, *Religious Statecraft,* 132–133.

143. Kuzichkin, *Inside the KGB,* 299–300. See also Vinogradov, *Diplomatiia,* 466–467. The East German embassy reached the same conclusion as well; see telegram, Wolfgang Konschel to Hermann Axen, November 22, 1979, DY 30/IV B 2/20/369, SAPMO-BArch, p. 181. The British embassy, at a minimum, quickly perceived that Khomeini wanted to use the US embassy seizure as an excuse to "reintensify" the revolution; see telegram, John Graham to UK FO, "Situation in Iran," November 13, 1979, TNA FCO 8/3358, no.527.

144. "Information über ein Gespräch des Hermann Axen, Mitglied des Politburos und Sekretär des ZK, mit Genossen Nureddin Kianouri, 1. Sekretär des ZK der Tudeh-Partei Irans, am 8.11.1979" [Information on a conversation of Hermann Axen, member of the Politburo and secretary of CC, with Comrade Nureddin Kianouri, first secretary of the CC of the Tudeh Party of Iran, on November 8, 1979], November 8, 1979, DY 30/IV B 2/20/369, SAPMO-BArch, p. 164.

145. GDR Embassy Moscow to Hermann Axen, November 16, 1979, DY 30/IV B 2/20/369, SAPMO-BArch, pp. 178, 179.

146. Conversation of Hermann Axen with Nuredin Kianouri, November 8, 1979, DY 30/IV B 2/20/369, SAPMO-BArch, p. 158.

147. GDR MFA, "Innenpolitische Auseinandersetzungen in Iran" [Domestic political confrontations in Iran], December 21, 1979, DY 30/IV B 2/20/369, SAPMO-BArch, p. 226.

148. ‏است رد‟ نظام توحیدی "نقض آشکار میثاق خون شهدای انقلاب: ایدئولوژی حاکم بر مجلس خبرگان مدافع استثمار و نظام " طبقاتی‎ [Rejection of the monotheist system, an explicit break of the bloody covenant with the martyrs of the revolution: The dominant ideology in the Assembly of Experts defends exploitation and class system], *Mujahid,* October 29, 1979, https://www.iran-archive.com/sites/default/files/sanad/mojahedine-khalgh-mojahed.

149. Conversation of Axen with Kianouri, November 8, 1979, p. 160, 167.

150. Report from British Embassy Tehran, March 10, 1981, FCO 8/4005, no. 34, UKNA.

151. Conversation of Axen with Kianouri, November 8, 1979, p. 168.

152. Report of GDR Embassy Moscow to Herrman Axen, Herbert Krolikowski, Egon Winkelmann, Hans-Joachim Willerding, and Helmut Ziebart, "Information über einige Fragen der Lage im Iran und der sowjetisch-iranischen Beziehungen" [Information on certain questions of the situation in Iran and Soviet-Iranian relations], May 21, 1980, DY 30/IV B 2/20/370, SAPMO-BArch, p. 36.

153. Report, Wolfgang Grabowski to Egon Winkelmann, September 16, 1980, DY 30/IV B 2/20/370, SAPMO-BArch, p. 201.

154. E. A. Doroshenko, "Politicheskie traditsii Shi'izma i antimonarkhicheskoe dvizhenie v Irane (1978–1979)" [Political traditions of Shi'ism and the antimonarchical movement in Iran (1978–1979)], *Narody Azii i Afriki* 6 (1980): 64. For more on the state of Iran scholarship in the USSR in this period, see Muriel Atkin, "Soviet and Russian Scholarship on Iran," *Iranian Studies* 20, nos. 2–4 (1987): 223–271.

155. Yevgeny Primakov, "Islam i protsessy obschestvennogo razvitiia stran zarubezhnogo Vostoka" [Islam and the processes of social development of the countries of the foreign east], *Voprosy filosofii* 8 (1980): 60–71.

156. Report of Wolfgang Konschel to Hans-Joachim Willerding on conversations with socialist ambassadors, May 21, 1980, DY 30/IV B 2/20/370, SAPMO-BArch, pp. 48–53; Wolfgang Konschel, "Zum iranisch-amerikanischen Konflikt" [On the Iranian-American conflict], DY 30/IV B 2/20/370, SAPMO-BArch, p. 177.

157. "Vermerk über ein Gespräch des Genossen Hermann Axen, Mitglied des Politburos und Sekretär des ZK der SED, mit Genossen Nureddin Kianouri, Erster Sekretär des ZK der Tudeh-Partei Irans, am 11.2.1980" [Note on a conversation of Comrade Hermann Axen, member of the Politburo and secretary of the CC SED with Comrade Nureddin Kianouri, first secretary of the CC of the Tudeh Party of Iran, on February 11, 1980], February 11, 1980, DY 30/IV B 2/20/370, SAPMO-BArch, p. 42.

158. "Vermerk über 2 Gespräche des Genossen Hermann Axen, Mitglied des Politburos und Sekretär des ZK der SED, mit Genossen Nureddin Kianouri, 1 Sekretär des ZK der Tudeh-Partei Irans, am 16.6 und 17.6.1980" [Note on two conversations of Comrade Hermann Axen, member of the Politburo and secretary of the CC SED, with Comrade Nureddin Kianouri, first secretary of the Tudeh Party of Iran, on June 16 and June 17, 1980], June 17, 1980, DY 30/IV B 2/20/370, SAPMO-BArch, pp. 59, 60, 61–62.

159. "Vermerk über ein Gespräch des Genossen Hermann Axen, Mitglied des Politburos und Sekretär des ZK der SED, mit Genossen Nureddin Kianouri, Erster Sekretär des ZK der Tudeh-Partei Irans, am 11.2.1980" [Note on a conversation of Comrade Hermann Axen, member of the Politburo and secretary of the CC SED with Comrade Nureddin Kianouri, first secretary of the CC of the Tudeh Party of Iran, on February 11, 1980], February 11, 1980, DY 30/IV B 2/20/370, SAPMO-BArch, p. 42.

160. Report of East German Embassy Moscow, "Information über einige Fragen der Lage im Iran und der sowjetisch-iranischen Beziehungen," p. 38. On State Committee for Foreign Economic Relations chairman Skachkov's visit, see M. J. Williams, to Robin Gorham, "Visit of Mr. Skachkov," June 3, 1979, FCO 8/3371, UKNA, pp. 41–42.

161. For more on the confrontation between President Bani-Sadr and the IRP, see Keddie, *Modern Iran*, 249–253; Shaul Bakhash, *The Reign of the Ayatollahs: Iran and the Islamic Revolution* (New York: Basic Books, 1984), 92–165; Mohsen M. Milani, "Power Shifts in Revolutionary Iran," *Iranian Studies* 26, nos. 3–4 (1993): 359–374; Mohsen M. Milani, "The Evolution of the Iranian Presidency from Bani Sadr to Rafsanjani," *British Journal of Middle Eastern Studies* 20, no. 1 (1993), 83–97; and Eric Rouleau, "The War and the Struggle for the State," *MERIP Reports* 98 (1981), 3–8.

162. "Zur Lage in Iran (erarbeitet auf der Grundlage eines Gesprächs mit Genossen A. Baranow, Mitarbeiter in der Int. Abteilung des ZK der KPdSU, am 1.2.1980)" [On the situation in Iran (produced on the basis of a conversation with Comrade A. Baranov, worker in the International Department of the CC CPSU, on February 1, 1980)], February 1, 1980, DY 30/IV B 2/20/370, SAPMO-BArch, pp. 2, 5.

163. "Vermerk über ein Gespräch des Genossen Hermann Axen, Mitglied des Politburos und Sekretär des ZK der SED, mit Genossen Nureddin Kianouri, Erster Sekretär des ZK der Tudeh-Partei Irans, am 11.2.1980" [Note on a conversation of Comrade Hermann Axen, member of the Politburo and secretary of the CC SED with Comrade Nureddin Kianouri, first secretary of the CC of the Tudeh Party of Iran, on February 11, 1980], February 11, 1980, DY 30/IV B 2/20/370, SAPMO-BArch, pp. 45, 41.

164. Report of Konschel to Willerding on conversations with socialist ambassadors, May 21, 1980, p. 53.

165. Behrooz, *Rebels with a Cause*, 110.

166. "On the Issue of the Divide in the Communist Movement and Our Responsibility," *Kar,* February 2, 1981.

167. Behrooz, *Rebels with a Cause,* 112–113.

168. Mikhail Krutichin, "Die linken Kräfte in Iran" [The left forces in Iran], June 24, 1980, DY 30/IV B 2/20/370, SAPMO-BArch, p. 125.

169. "Die Innenpolitische Lage in Iran nach der Proklamierung der Islamischen Republik" [The domestic political situation in Iran after the proclamation of the Islamic Republic], April 1, 1980, DY 30/IV B 2/20/370, SAPMO-BArch, p. 15.

170. On the initial response of the Iranian regime to the war, and particularly the organization of resistance to the Iraqi invasion in the context of the domestic battle for power, see Pierre Razoux, *The Iran-Iraq War* (Cambridge, MA: Harvard University Press, 2015), 121–134.

171. Telegram, Wolfgang Konschel to Hans-Joachim Willerding, Egon Winkelmann, Schüssel, and NMS , "Hintergründe Zuspitzung Situation Iran/Irak (auf Grundlage Consultation mit Bruderbotschaften)" [Background on the deteriorating situation Iran/Iraq (on the basis of consultation with brother embassies], September 17, 1980, DY 30/IV B 2/20/370, SAPMO-BArch, p. 209; telegram, Wolfgang Konschel to Hans-Joachim Willerding, Egon Winkelmann, Schüssel, CC, and NMS based on conversation with Vladimir Vinogradov, September 25, 1980, DY 30/IV B 2/20/370, SAPMO-BArch, p. 213.

172. Telegram, Wolfgang Konschel to Hans-Joachim Willerding, Egon Winkelmann, Schüssel, and NMS, October 1, 1980, DY 30/IV B 2/20/370, SAPMO-BArch, pp. 215–216.

173. CIA, "Special National Intelligence Estimate: Soviet Interests, Policies, and Prospects with Respect to the Iran-Iraq War," December 24, 1980, https://www.cia.gov/library/readingroom/docs /DOC_0000273317, p. 6. For more on the Soviet attitude toward the Iran-Iraq war, see Yodfat, *Soviet Union and Revolutionary Iran,* 106–110. Razoux, *The Iran-Iraq War,* 82–86, tells of specific divisions within the Soviet leadership on the decision about whether to support Iraq or Iran, but the providence of his information is unclear.

174. See Yodfat, *Soviet Union and Revolutionary Iran,* 94–97.

175. Telegram, Wolfgang Konschel to Hans-Joachim Willerding, Egon Winkelmann, Schüssel, and NMS, November 11, 1980, DY 30/IV B 2/20/370, SAPMO-BArch, p. 219.

176. Tabaar, *Religious Statecraft,* 157.

177. Report from Middle East Department of UK FO, October 13, 1980, FCO 8/3572, no. 251, UKNA.

178. For more on domestic and international developments in the IRI in this period, see Keddie, *Modern Iran,* 250–253.

179. Wolfgang Konschel, "Zum iranisch-amerikanischen Konflikt" [On the Iranian-American conflict], n.d. [likely October 1980], DY 30/IV B 2/20/370, SAPMO-BArch, p. 77, 178–180, 181.

180. "Auszüge aus einer Antwort des Genossen Nureddin Kianouri, 1st Sekretär des ZK der Tudeh, auf Fragen eines Moslems (Aus einer Frage-und-Antwort Veranstaltung vom November 1980)" [Excerpts from answers of Comrade Nureddin Kianouri, first secretary of the CC of the Tudeh, to questions of Muslims (from a question-and-answer session from November 1980)], January 27, 1981, DY 30/11537, SAPMO-BArch, pp. 40–45.

181. "Die Errungenschaften der iranischen Revolution (Auszüge aus einem Artikel des Zentralorgans der Tudeh-Partei, Nameh Mardom, 1981" [The achievements of the Iranian Revolution (excerpts from the central organ of the Tudeh Party, Nameh Mardom, 1981], May 26, 1981, DY 30/ 11537, SAPMO-BArch, pp. 46–63.

182. Conversation of Fred Halliday with John Graham, January 6, 1981, FCO 8/4005, no. 1, UKNA.

183. "Erklärung des ZK der Tudeh-Partei Irans aus Anlass der Wahl des zweiten Staatspräsidenten der IRI (Juli 1981)" [Statement of the CC of the Tudeh Party of Iran on the occasion of the

election of the second state president of the IRI (July 1981)], August 13, 1981, DY 30/11537, SAPMO-BArch, pp. 71–72, 73.

184. "Auszüge aus einer Erklärung der Tudeh-Partei Irans 'Zur Herstellung einer auf dem Gesetz und auf sozialer Gerechtigkeit beruhenden Ordnung'" [Excerpts from a statement of the Tudeh Party of Iran "On the establishment of an order based on law and social justice"], October 5, 1981, DY 30/11537, SAPMO-BArch, p. 80.

185. Kuzichkin, *Inside the KGB*, 291. See also Behrooz, *Rebels with a Cause*, 126.

186. On the situation in July 1982, see "Über die gegenwärtige Lage der Tudeh-Partei Irans" [On the present situation of the Tudeh Party of Iran], July 20, 1982, DY 30/11537, SAPMO-BArch, p. 87. On the reaction of the Tudeh Party to the arrests, see "Zur Lage in der Tudeh-Partei Irans (TPI)" [On the situation in the Tudeh Party of Iran (TPI)], January 9, 1984, DY 30/11537, SAPMO-BArch, p. 88.

187. See Ervand Abrahamian, *Tortured Confessions: Prisons and Public Recantations in Modern Iran* (Berkeley: University of California Press, 1999).

188. "Zur Lage in der Tudeh-Partei Irans (TPI)," p. 90.

189. "Information über ein Gespräch mit dem Genossen Khavari, Mitglied des Politburos der Tudeh-Partei Irans, am 12.2.1983" [Information on a conversation with Comrade Khavari, member of the Politburo of the Tudeh Party of Iran, on February 12, 1983], February 12, 1983, DY 30/IV 2/2.035/142, SAPMO-BArch, pp. 55–7.

190. For more on the land reform issue, see Khadija V. Frings-Hessami, "The Islamic Debate about Land Reform in the Iranian Parliament, 1981–1986," *Middle Eastern Studies* 37, no. 4 (2001): 136–181.

191. Bahman Baktiari, *Parliamentary Politics in Revolutionary Iran: The Institutionalization of Factional Politics* (Gainesville: University Press of Florida, 1996), 80–81.

192. Baktiari, *Parliamentary Politics in Revolutionary Iran*, 87–88.

193. British Interests Section Tehran to UK Middle Eastern Department, "The Land Reform Bill," January 26, 1983, FCO 8/5131, no. 25, UKNA.

194. Telegram, Nicholas Barrington to UK FO, "Iran Internal," January 27, 1983, TNA FCO 8/5131, no.5.

195. British Interests Section to UK Middle Eastern Department, "Iran: Internal Stresses," March 23, 1983, FCO 8/5131, no. 32, UKNA.

196. Leonid Brezhnev, quoted in I. Timofeev, "Rol' Islama v obshchestvenno-politicheskoi zhizni stran zarubezhnogo Vostoka" [The role of Islam in the sociopolitical life of the countries of the foreign East], *Mirovaia ekonomika i mezhdunarodnye otnosheniia* 5 (1982): 51.

197. Rostislav Ul'ianovskii, quoted in Behrooz, *Rebels with a Cause*, 127.

198. Rostislav Ul'ianovskii, "Iranskaia Revoliutsiia i ee Osobennosti" [The Iranian Revolution and its particularities], *Kommunist* 10 (1982): 115, 116.

199. UK Embassy Moscow to UK FO, "Kommunist Article on Iran," August 12, 1982, FCO 8/4574, no. 49, UKNA.

200. UK Embassy Moscow to UK FO, "Soviet Attitude to Internal Developments in Iran," September 16, 1982, FCO 8/4574, no. 53, UKNA. For more on the Soviet attitude toward the Mujahideen, see Timofeev, "Rol' Islama v obschestvenno-politicheskoi zhizni stran zarubezhnogo Vostoka," 55; and Doroshenko, "Politicheskie traditsii Shi'izma i antimonarkhicheskoe dvizhenie v Irane," 63.

201. D. E. Fremeev, "Otrazhenie patriarkhal'nykh i rodo-plemennykh traditsii v shariate" [Reflection of patriarchal and tribal traditions in shari'a], *Narody Azii i Afriki* 1 (1983): 46–56.

202. Eremeev, "Otrazhenie patriarkhal'nykh i rodo-plemennykh traditsii v shariate" [Reflection of patriarchal and tribal traditions in shari'a], 13.

203. Dmitry Volsky, "The Revolution at a Crossroads," *New Times* 2 (1983): 15, 13.

204. UK Embassy Moscow to East European and Soviet Department, UK FO, "Soviet Comment on Iran," June 30, 1983, FCO 8/5135, no. 40, UKNA.

205. "Zur politik der Tudeh-Partei Irans" [On the policy of the Tudeh Party of Iran], July 24, 1985, DY 30/11537, SAPMO-BArch, p. 95.

206. "Zur Lage in der Volkspartei Irans (Tudeh)" [On the situation in the People's Party of Iran (Tudeh)], March 30, 1987, DY 30/11537, SAPMO-BArch, p. 101.

207. Hermann Axen to Erich Honecker on the conversation between Axen and Ali Khavari, February 2, 1984, DY 30/IV 2/2.035/142, SAPMO-BArch, p. 64.

208. Vijay Prashad, *The Darker Nations: A People's History of the Third World* (New York: The New Press, 2007), xviii.

209. See, for example, Khadija V. Frings-Hessami, "The Islamic Debate about Land Reform in the Iranian Parliament, 1981–1986," *Middle Eastern Studies* 37, no. 4 (2001): 136–181; and Eva-leila Pesaran, "Towards an Anti-Western Stance: The Economic Discourse of Iran's 1979 Revolution," *Iranian Studies* 41, no. 5 (2008): 693–718.

210. Milani, "Harvest of Shame," 308.

Conclusion

1. Fred Halliday, *Revolution and World Politics: The Rise and Fall of the Sixth Great Power* (Durham, NC: Duke University Press, 1999), 91.

2. Kathleen Knight, "Transformations of the Concept of Ideology in the Twentieth Century," *American Political Science Review* 100, no. 4 (2006): 624–625. I thank Scott Boorman for bringing this article to my attention.

3. See, for example, Julius K. Nyerere, *The Arusha Declaration Ten Years After* (Dar es Salaam: Government Printer, 1977); and Julius K. Nyerere, "The Inherited Cross of Independent Africa," in *Freedom and Liberation: A Selection from Speeches, 1974–1999* (Dar es Salaam: Oxford University Press, 2011), 136–145.

4. Johanna Bockmann, *Markets in the Name of Socialism: The Left-Wing Origins of Neoliberalism* (Stanford, CA: Stanford University Press, 2011).

5. Yakov Feygin, "Reforming the Cold War State: Economic Thought, Internationalization, and the Politics of Soviet Reform" (PhD diss., University of Pennsylvania, 2017).

6. Julian Gewirtz, *Unlikely Partners: Chinese Reformers, Western Economists, and the Making of Global China* (Cambridge, MA: Harvard University Press, 2017).

7. See Evan Osnos, "Crossing the Water," *New Yorker,* October 1, 2010, https://www.newyorker.com/news/evan-osnos/crossing-the-water.

8. See, for example, Chen Jian, "China's Changing Policies toward the Third World and the End of the Global Cold War," in *The End of the Cold War and the Third World,* ed. Artemy Kalinovsky and Sergey Radchenko (London: Routledge, 2011),119.

9. Richard Fagen, Carmen Diana Deere, and José Luis Coraggio, introduction to *Transition and Development: Problems of Third World Socialism,* ed. Richard Fagen, Carmen Diana Deere, and José Luis Coraggio (Berkeley: Monthly Review Press, 1986), 9.

10. Edmund V. K. Fitzgerald and Marc Wuyts, *Markets within Planning: Socialist Economic Management in the Third World,* (London: Frank Cass, 1988), 2.

11. See Allen Isaacman and Barbara Isaacman, *Mozambique: From Colonialism to Revolution, 1980–1982* (Boulder, CO: Westview Press, 1983); James H. Mittelman, *Underdevelopment and the Transition to Socialism: Mozambique and Tanzania* (London: Academic Press, 1981); and M. Anne Pitcher, *Transforming Mozambique: The Politics of Privatization, 1975–2000* (Cambridge: Cambridge University Press, 2002).

12. See, for example, "Mozambik: Nekotorye aspekty vnutripoliticheskogo polozheniia" [Mozambique: Certain aspects of the domestic political situation], April 19, 1976, F.5 O.69 D.2556, Rossisskiĭ Gosudarstvennyĭ Arkhiv Noveisheĭ Istorii (Russian State Archive of Contemporary History; hereafter RGANI), pp. 35–46; and Maputo S. Bedrinskii, "Nekotorye problemy

vnutripoliticheskogo polozheniia NRM za pervyi god nezavisimogo razvitiia strany" [Certain problems of the domestic political situation in the People's Republic of Mozambique during the first year of independent development of the country], August 7, 1976, F.5 O.69 D.2556, RGANI, pp. 55–65.

13. Pitcher, *Transforming Mozambique*, 101–178.

14. Teodoro Petkoff, quoted in Barry Carr and Steve Ellner, introduction to *The Latin American Left: From the Fall of Allende to Perestroika,* ed. Barry Carr and Steve Ellner (Boulder, CO: Westview, 1993), 5.

15. Gordon White, "Revolutionary Socialist Development in the Third World: An Overview," in *Revolutionary Socialist Development in the Third World,* ed. Gordon White, Robin Murray, and Christine White (Brighton, UK: Wheatsheaf Books, 1983), 1.

16. Fagen, Deere, and Coraggio, "Introduction," 10.

17. Yasheng Huang, "China Has a Big Economic Problem, and It Isn't the Trade War," *New York Times,* January 17, 2020, https://www.nytimes.com/2020/01/17/opinion/china-economy.html.

18. Ayatollah Ali Khamene'i, quoted in Suzanne Maloney, *Iran's Political Economy since the Revolution* (New York: Cambridge University Press, 2015), 500.

19. Richard Lowenthal, "The Model of the Totalitarian State," in *Model or Ally: The Communist Powers and the Developing Countries* (New York: Oxford University Press, 1977), 47–172.

20. White, "Revolutionary Socialist Development in the Third World," 17.

21. Melanie O'Gorman, "Why the CCM Won't Lose: The Roots of Single-Party Dominance in Tanzania," *Journal of Contemporary African Studies* 30, no. 2 (2012): 313.

22. John Ishiyama, "The Former Marxist Leninist Parties in Africa after the end of the Cold War," *Acta Politica* 40 (2005): 477. See also See O'Gorman, "Why the CCM Won't Lose," 314.

23. Angola Press News Agency, "Angola: ANC, FRELIMO, and SWAPO Secretaries Jet In," *Mozambique Tribune,* May 17, 2017, https://mozambiquetribune.com/angola-anc-frelimo-and-swapo-secretaries-general-jet-in/; "Cuban Delegation Attends Seventh MPLA Congress in Angola," *Granma,* August 22, 2016, http://en.granma.cu/mundo/2016-08-22/cuban-delegation-attends-seventh-mpla-congress-in-angola; Abdulrahman Kinana, conversation with the author, Dar es Salaam, August 22, 2016.

24. Maximilian Mmuya, *Political Parties and Democracy in Tanzania* (Bonn: Friedrich Ebert Stiftung, 1994).

25. Anthony Butler, "How Democratic Is the African National Congress?," *Journal of Southern African Studies* 31, no. 4 (2005): 732. See also Thokozani Chilenga Butao, "ANC Should Stop Recycling Old Ideas," *Mail and Guardian* (Johannesburg), June 14, 2019, https://mg.co.za/article/2019-06-14-00-anc-should-stop-recycling-old-ideas/.

26. See Kanan Makiya, *Republic of Fear: The Politics of Modern Iraq* (Berkeley: University of California Press, 1998); and Vijay Sanghvi, *The Congress: Indira to Sonia Gandhi* (Delhi: Kalpaz, 2006), 128–129.

27. Lowenthal, "The Model of the Totalitarian State," 171.

28. O'Gorman, "Why the CCM Won't Lose," 327.

29. See, for example, Sabelo J. Ndlovu-Gatsheni, "Making Sense of Mugabeism in Local and Global Politics: 'So Blair, Keep Your England and Let Me Keep My Zimbabwe,'" *Third World Quarterly* 30, no. 6 (2009): 1139–1158.

30. John S. Saul and Richard Saunders, "Mugabe, Gramsci, and Zimbabwe at 25," *International Journal* 60, no. 4 (2005): 957.

31. Benjamin Mkapa, quoted in Ian Phimister and Brian Raftopoulos, "Mugabe, Mbeki, and the Politics of Anti-imperialism," *Review of African Political Economy* 31, no. 101 (2004): 398.

32. Thabo Mbeki, quoted in Phimister and Raftopoulos, "Mugabe, Mbeki, and the Politics of Anti-imperialism," 390.

ACKNOWLEDGMENTS

This book has been a long time coming, and it is the product of interactions with many generous and talented individuals at the institutions that have been kind enough to be my professional homes along the way. Parts of the book go back to my time as a graduate student at Princeton University, and were aided by Stephen Kotkin, Daniel Rodgers, and Gilbert Rozman. Much of the work also took place during my time at Yale University as a postdoctoral fellow with International Security Studies and as the associate director of the Brady-Johnson Program in Grand Strategy. During my time at Yale and since, my work benefited from the support of Amanda Behm, Jadwiga Biskupska, Scott Boorman, John Lewis Gaddis, Ryan Irwin, Paul Kennedy, Paul Solman, Adam Tooze, and Anand Toprani, among others. Since coming to Harvard Business School, I have had many intellectually fruitful interactions with my multidisciplinary colleagues within the Business, Government, and International Economy unit. I would especially like to thank Mattias Fibiger, Meg Rithmire, and Sophus Reinert, who have always been available to read drafts and discuss ideas.

Odd Arne Westad has been an invaluable mentor, colleague, and sounding board. Chen Jian, Li Danhui, Shen Zhihua, and Xia Yafeng have provided help with Chinese sources, especially as research in China has become more difficult over the past decade. Paul Bjerk and James Brennan were instrumental in helping me secure interviews in Tanzania and accessing local archives. Pippa Armerding and Ricardo Soares de Oliveira helped me make connections in Angola. Many others have helped with research advice, reading drafts, or discussing my work, including Yakov Feygin, Kevin Fogg, Kate Geoghegan, Artemy Kalinovsky, Lorenz Lüthi, Timothy Noonan, Michelle Paranzino, Sergey Radchenko, and Siavush Randjbar-Daemi. I was helped on this project by a number of research assistants who gathered and helped me translate certain materials—namely Janko Jankovic and Andrijana Misovic, who helped with Yugoslav documents; Yuliya Gevrenova and Sibel Hasan, who helped with Bulgarian documents; and Masoud Ariankhoo and Homa Taheri, who helped with Iranian materials. I thank my faculty support specialist Jefferson Zhu for help with finding and securing copyrights for the images in this book.

During the course of my research and writing, I have received support from the Brady-Johnson Program in Grand Strategy at Yale University, Harvard Business School, Princeton University, and the Social Science Research Council. Portions of Chapter 5 were first published as "The Enemy of My Enemy: The Soviet Union, East Germany, and the Iranian Tudeh Party's Support for Ayatollah Khomeini," *Journal of Cold War Studies* 20, no. 2 (2018): 3–37. I am grateful to Kathleen Mc-Dermott, my editor at Harvard University Press, for all of her hard work during trying pandemic times to make this book a reality, and to the anonymous peer reviewers who went over the entire manuscript with a fine-toothed comb.

Finally, I want to thank my talented wife, Ingrid Burke. We met back in 2013 in a prerevolutionary apartment in Moscow, where I was conducting research for this book, and ever since she has been more excited than anyone about my research—at times even including myself. I could not have finished this without her support.

INDEX

Abdulgani, Ruslan, 54–55
Abrahamian, Ervand, 230
Abteilung Internationale Verbindungen (AIV; Department of International Ties), 131
Acheson, Dean, 58
Adalat Party, 221
al-Afghani, Jamal ad-Din, 212
Afghanistan, 242
Africa: adapting socialism to, 141; bourgeoisie in, 138; building socialism in, 125, 131, 165 (*See also* Angola; Tanzania); class in, 138–139, 140, 148, 149; decolonization in, 181; leadership quality in, 164; legacy of Leninist model in, 270–271; liberation struggles in, 270–272, 273; Marxism-Leninism and, 168–169, 208–209 (*See also* Angola; MPLA); nationalism in, 130; postcolonial, 125; race in, 16 (*See also* Angola; MPLA); revolutionary prospects in, 1, 126; socialism in, 125, 131, 143, 153; Soviets and, 15, 125, 165, 201; Zhou on, 1, 126, 136. *See also* developing countries; Third World; *individual countries*
African Communist (journal), 141, 144
Africanization, 138
African National Congress (ANC), 209, 270, 272
agricultural economies, 9–10, 71
agriculture: in Angola, 171, 204; building socialism and, 15; in Tanzania, 124, 137, 138, 140, 147–148, 158 (See also *ujamaa*; *ujamaa* villages)
agriculture, collective, 10, 17, 147. *See also* land / land reform; *ujamaa* villages
Al-e-Ahmad, Jalal, 226, 227, 229
Ahmadzadeh, Masoud, 224
aid, 4, 5. *See also individual countries*
Aidit, Dipa Nusantara, 34, 37, 39, 57; China and, 48; coup attempt and, 67; death of, 70; defense of parliamentary democracy, 43–44; on Guided Democracy, 52, 56; on independence of PKI, 73; on industry, 59; land reform and, 64; leadership of PKI, 71; on Murba Party, 67; response to Economic Declaration, 59; Soviets and, 62, 63; Stalin and, 39–40, 48; on taking power, 68, 69; on ties to foreign communists, 43; views of Sukarno, 53, 60
AIV (Abteilung Internationale Verbindungen; Department of International Ties), 131
aksi sepihak, 64, 65
Algeria, 223, 243
Alikhanov, A. I., 132, 133
Alimin, 29, 53
Ali Sastroamidjojo, 42, 69
Allende, Beatriz "Tati," 86
Allende, Salvador, 8, 14, 75, 78; anti-imperialism of, 81; attempts to avoid coup, 115–116; China and, 91–93; Congress and, 80; constraints on, 88; coup attempt and,

on, 228; Tanzania and, 143, 148, 149–150, 153–155. *See also* armed struggle; Cuba; guerrilla warfare; power, taking

clergy, in Iran: expectations for, 234, 236; as progressive, 234 (*See also* ulama)

Cold War, 5; Angolan liberation movements and, 173; in Asia, 65 (*See also* Indonesia); end of, 273–274; latter stages of, 208; legacies of, 7. *See also* Soviet Union; United States

Cold War, The (Westad), 6

collectivization: in China, 160; in Soviet Union, 160; in Tanzania, 147–148, 149, 150–153, 159–162

colonialism, 178; religion and, 214, 217; Soviets and, 226. *See also* anti-imperialism; decolonization; imperialism; national liberation movements

Comintern, 2, 6, 26, 27–28, 29, 214–215

Committees of Amilcar Cabral, 195

communism: in Indonesia, 26, 48; religion and, 71–72, 214; in Western Europe, 11, 14, 76, 94, 118, 120, 247

communist movement, international, 4, 5, 25–26, 56, 121–122. *See also* communist parties; Sino-Soviet split; socialist transition/revolution, global

Communist Organization of Angola, 195, 196

communist parties: coalitions with other parties, 118; in Europe, 11, 14, 76, 94, 118, 120, 247; independence of, 37, 56, 57; lack of, 8; relations between, 25, 63, 73–74 (*See also* international communist movement; Sino-Soviet split); relationship with socialist parties, 85; in Third World, 2. *See also individual parties*

communist states, existing, 4–5. *See also* China; Germany, East; Soviet Union

Congo, 179–180, 185, 189

cooperatives. See *ujamaa* villages

copper, 93, 94, 98, 105, 106–107, 109, 122

Coraggio, José Luis, 267, 269

Corbalán González, Salomón, 84

Cornell University, 22

Corvalán, Luis, 83, 85, 88, 94, 96, 103, 106, 110, 112; on Allende, 97; on mistakes, 117; on Pinochet, 116; on Sino-Soviet split, 78; Soviets and, 122; on Soviet weapons, 114, 115

Coulson, Andrew, 161

countryside. *See* agriculture; land/land reform; peasantry

Coutinho, Rosa, 189

CPSU (Communist Party of the Soviet Union), 220; Chilean Left and, 85; in international communist movement, 57; as model for Angola, 168; MPLA and, 203; on Somalia, 218; TANU and, 153; Twentieth Congress, 75, 78; Twenty-Fourth Congress, 78; Twenty-Fifth Congress, 198. *See also* Soviet Union; Ul'ianovskii, Rostislav

Cronin, Stephanie, 211

Cruz, Viriato da, 173, 174, 176–177, 179, 180

Cruz Aguayo, Luciano, 85

Cuba, 6, 10, 64, 265; Angola and, 193, 207; Chile and, 82, 89, 115, 116, 265; Chile as alternative model to, 90; influence of, 83, 84; MIR and, 86–87, 104; as model for Iran, 223; MPLA and, 180, 192, 194, 199; Neto and, 199; promotion of armed struggle by, 77; recognition of, 91; Soviets and, 77, 86, 91, 108

Cuban Revolution, 84

cultural authenticity, 214, 220, 230

cultural identity, 226–227

cultural self-assertion, 227

Czechoslovakia, 6, 86

Dabashi, Hamid, 225–226, 227

Debray, Régis, 86

decentralization, in Tanzania, 158, 160

decolonization, 2, 168; in Africa, 181; international politics after, 6; religion and, 215–216. *See also* Africa; colonialism; nationalism; national liberation struggles

Deere, Carmen Diana, 267, 268–269

De Groot, Paul, 32

del Canto, Hernán, 113

Indian National Congress, 271–272

Indische Sociaal-Democratische Vereeniging (ISDV; Indies Social Democratic Association), 26–27

Indonesia, 8, 13, 14; anti-imperialism in, 22, 24, 36, 39, 46, 60–61; China and, 24–25, 56–57, 66, 69, 81; communism in, 26, 48; constitution, 51–52; coup attempt in, 67–68, 81; coup in, 69–70; democracy and, 11, 21, 42–44, 45, 47–48, 73; described, 19–20; diversity in, 12, 20–21; DPR, 41, 42; economy of, 24, 42, 46–47, 48, 49–50, 53–54, 57, 58–60, 66; elections (1955), 42–44; ethnic Chinese in, 24, 34, 56–57, 70; events of 1965, 65–70; FDR, 31, 32; fear of class struggle in, 46; *gotong royong* government, 44, 49, 52, 56; Guided Democracy, 19, 22, 45, 51–53, 56, 64, 73, 123; importance of in Cold War, 22; independence struggle in, 14, 19, 26–27, 34; instability in, 65; ISDV, 26–27; Islam in, 12–13, 14, 20, 21, 26, 27, 28, 43, 44; KNIP, 29; Labor Party, 29; land/land reform in, 10, 38, 39–40, 55, 64–65; lessons learned from, 71–74, 244, 259; living conditions in, 58; Madiun Affair, 32–33, 34, 40, 41; Marxist-Leninist literature in, 39; massacres in, 70; Murba Party, 66–67, 69, 74; national cohesion/ identity in, 21; nationalism in, 26, 30, 58, 214 (*See also* SI; Sukarno); Netherlands and, 30, 31, 58; New Order, 71; NU, 44, 50, 71, 216; Pan-Islamism in, 27–28; peasantry in, 37, 38, 40, 41, 55, 58, 64–65; PNI, 36, 42, 46, 48, 50; political parties in, 21, 50–51; PSI, 29, 50–51; Sajap Kiri, 29, 30, 31; SI, 27, 28, 214; Soviets and, 24, 25, 30–31, 53–59, 63–64, 66–67, 68–70, 81, 265; United States and, 19, 22, 24, 25, 34, 37–38, 42, 70; uprising in, 29; West Irian campaign, 58–59, 61. *See also* PKI; Sukarno

Indonesian Communist Party. *See* PKI

industrial capitalism, 6. *See also* capitalism

industrial development, 10, 15, 47

industrialization, aid-based, 15

industrialization, state-led, 266

Intermediate Zone, 226

international communist movement, 4, 5, 25–26, 56, 121–122. *See also* communist parties; Sino-Soviet split; socialist transition/revolution, global

internationalism, 263

International Monetary Fund, 59, 163

Ionova, Alla, 72, 216, 243–244

Iordanskii, Vladimir, 144

Iran, 13, 16–17; anti-imperialism in, 226, 230, 248; Assembly of Experts, 248; bourgeoisie in, 232, 237–238, 243, 248, 250; Britain and, 211, 213, 240, 244; capitalism in, 269; China's similarities to, 212; class in, 248; constitution of, 248; Cuba as model for, 223; cultural revolution in, 252, 254, 255, 273; democracy and, 11; economy of, 229, 240, 242–243, 244–246, 249–250, 257–258 (*See also* Islamic economy); February Revolution, 230–240; East Germany and, 223, 233, 234, 236, 238, 239, 242, 249, 253, 254–255; West Germany and, 244; Guardian Council, 258, 260; influences on, 212; Iraqi invasion of, 253–254; Islam's progressive role in, 216; Kurdish situation in, 242; land/land reform in, 10, 246, 250, 257–258, 260; Marxism's popularity in, 214; military clashes in, 231; mixed regime in, 17; models for, 212, 223, 224; National Democratic Front, 239; National Front, 232, 239; nationalism in, 222, 230; nationalizations in, 222, 242, 250, 251, 260; noncapitalist path of development and, 249, 250; November Revolution, 247–253; oil in, 213, 222, 231; opposition to shah in, 223, 225; oppression by West, 227; peasantry in, 232, 234, 236, 246, 250, 251, 253; polarization in, 248; power in, 9, 232; private property in, 248; religion in, 12–13 (*See also* Islam); Revolutionary Council, 232, 258; SAVAK, 216, 222, 225, 228; Soviets and, 17, 212, 223, 232, 233, 234, 236–237, 239, 242, 249, 251, 253; strategic location of, 213; strikes in, 231;

INDEX

Soviet Union (*continued*)
Khrushchev, Nikita); Maleki's criticism
of, 226; Mozambique and, 169, 268, 270;
MPLA and, 166, 173, 174, 175–176, 179,
180, 181–183, 184, 185, 186, 187–188,
189, 190, 191, 192, 194; Neto and, 180,
187–188, 189, 203, 206; PC and, 83, 117,
120; peaceful coexistence and, 174, 264;
peaceful path and, 76, 77, 117, 118–119;
persecution of religion, 214, 215; PKI and,
37–41, 50, 55–56, 57, 61–62, 63, 66–67,
71–74, 123; promotion of socialism in
developing world, 142, 143, 261; PS and,
90, 98, 117, 120; race and, 176, 177–178;
Roberto and, 178; Somalia and, 220;
state-led industrialization by, 266; status
of, 4; Suharto and, 25; Sukarno and, 30,
45–48, 49, 61, 64; Tanganyika and,
132–133; Tanzania and, 15, 141–142,
146, 149, 152–153, 159, 162–163, 165;
Tudeh Party and, 237, 259, 261; UP and,
80, 87, 88–89, 113–114, 116, 119–120.
See also Cold War; CPSU; GKES; KGB
Sozialistische Einheits Partei (SED; Socialist
Unity Party), 85, 229, 247
Spindler, Harry, 113
Spínola, António de, 188
Stalin, Joseph, 48, 265; denunciation of, 57,
75; Maleki's criticism of, 226; PKI and,
28–29, 38, 39–40, 43
State and Revolution (Lenin), 8
state planning, 7
states of national democracy, 233–234
strikes: in Angola, 197, 200; in Chile, 105;
in Iran, 231
Subandrio, 55, 63, 66
Subekti, Iskandar, 39
Sudisman, 36, 40, 62
Suharto, 24, 25, 67, 71, 81, 244
Sukarno, 8, 14, 22, 29, 32; anti-imperialism
and, 22, 24, 36, 39, 46, 60–61; attempt to
restore political stability, 65; background
of, 18–19; China and, 45, 57, 60, 64, 67;
communism and, 48; Economic Declaration, 59–60; economics and, 54; Guided
Democracy, 19, 22, 45, 51–53, 56, 64,

73, 123; in independence struggle, 19;
Indonesian economy and, 59–60; Japanese
and, 42; *Konfrontasi*, 60–61, 63–64;
konsepsi, 48–49, 51; lessons learned
from, 259; limitations of, 44, 72–73;
Nasakom, 52, 64; opposition to Western
democracy, 44–45; PKI and, 24, 48, 49,
52–53, 54, 64, 73; in PNI, 36; Political
Manifesto, 52; Soviets and, 30, 45–48,
49, 61, 64; US policy and, 22, 24; views
of, 19. *See also* Indonesia
Sukiman, 42
Sumatra, 20. *See also* Indonesia
Supreme Council for the Liberation of
Angola, 184
Suslov, Mikhail, 33, 46
Sutan Sjahrir, 29
Swai, Nzilo, 145
SWAPO (South West Africa People's
Organization), 270, 271
Syria, 271

Tabaar, Mohammad Ayatollahi, 254
Tabari, Ehsan, 233
Taleqani, Sayyid Mohammed, 224, 228–229
Tanganyika, 130, 131, 132–133. *See also*
Nyerere, Julius; TANU; Tanzania
Tan Ling Jie, 34, 36
Tan Malaka, 27–28, 29, 66–67
TANU, 137, 139; CPSU and, 153; forma-
tion of, 130; guarded from foreign
ideology, 165; before independence, 131;
membership, 140, 143, 144; political
education teams, 151–152; "Siasa ni
Kilimo" policy, 158. *See also* Nyerere,
Julius; Tanganyika; Tanzania
Tanzania, 8, 13, 15, 168, 266, 268; agricul-
ture in, 134, 137, 138, 140, 147–148, 158
(See also *ujamaa*; *ujamaa* villages); Asian
community in, 156; Britain and, 133;
CCM in, 271, 272; China and, 126–128,
134–137, 141–142, 146–147, 157, 164–165;
class in, 138–139, 143, 148, 149; class
struggle and, 143, 148, 149–150, 153–155;
collectivization in, 10 (See also *ujamaa*
villages); conditions in after independence,

Yugoslavia, 190, 198, 202, 207, 265, 266

Zaire, 185, 186, 189, 190
Zambia, 181, 184, 185, 189
ZANU-PF (Zimbabwe African National Union—Patriotic Front), 271, 272
Zanzibar, 133. *See also* Tanzania
ZAPU (Zimbabwean African People's Union), 181, 189
Zhdanov, Andrei, 30

Zhou Enlai, 1, 40, 107–108, 110, 126–127, 136, 183
Zhou Taomo, 70
Zhukov, E. M., 31
Zimbabwe, 209, 272
Zimbabwe African National Union—Patriotic Front (ZANU-PF), 271, 272
Zimbabwean African People's Union (ZAPU), 181, 189
Zorina, Irina, 217–218
Zorina, N. I., 89, 90